MEDIA, FEMINISM, CULTURAL STUDIES

Stepping Forward: Essays, Lectures and Interviews
by Wolfgang Iser

Wild Zones: Pornography, Art and Feminism
by Kelly Ives

Global Media Warning: Explorations of Radio, Television and the Press
by Oliver Whitehorne

'Cosmo Woman': The World of Women's Magazines
by Oliver Whitehorne

Andrea Dworkin
by Jeremy Mark Robinson

Cixous, Irigaray, Kristeva: The Jouissance of French Feminism
by Kelly Ives

Sex in Art: Pornography and Pleasure in Painting and Sculpture
by Cassidy Hughes

The Erotic Object: Sexuality in Sculpture From Prehistory to the Present Day
by Susan Quinnell

Women in Pop Music
by Helen Challis

Detonation Britain: Nuclear War In the UK
by Jeremy Mark Robinson

Julia Kristeva: Art, Love, Melancholy, Philosophy, Semiotics
by Kelly Ives

Luce Irigaray: Lips, Kissing, and the Politics of Sexual Difference
by Kelly Ives

Helene Cixous I Love You: The Jouissance of Writing
by Kelly Ives

The Poetry of Cinema
by John Madden

The Sacred Cinema of Andrei Tarkovsky
by Jeremy Mark Robinson

Feminism and Shakespeare
by B.D. Barnacle

The Cinema of Richard Linklater
by Thomas A. Christie

Walerian Borowczyk
by Jeremy Mark Robinson

The Cinema of Hayao Miyazaki
Jeremy Mark Robinson

Liv Tyler
by Thomas A. Christie

EROTIC ART
In the 18th Century

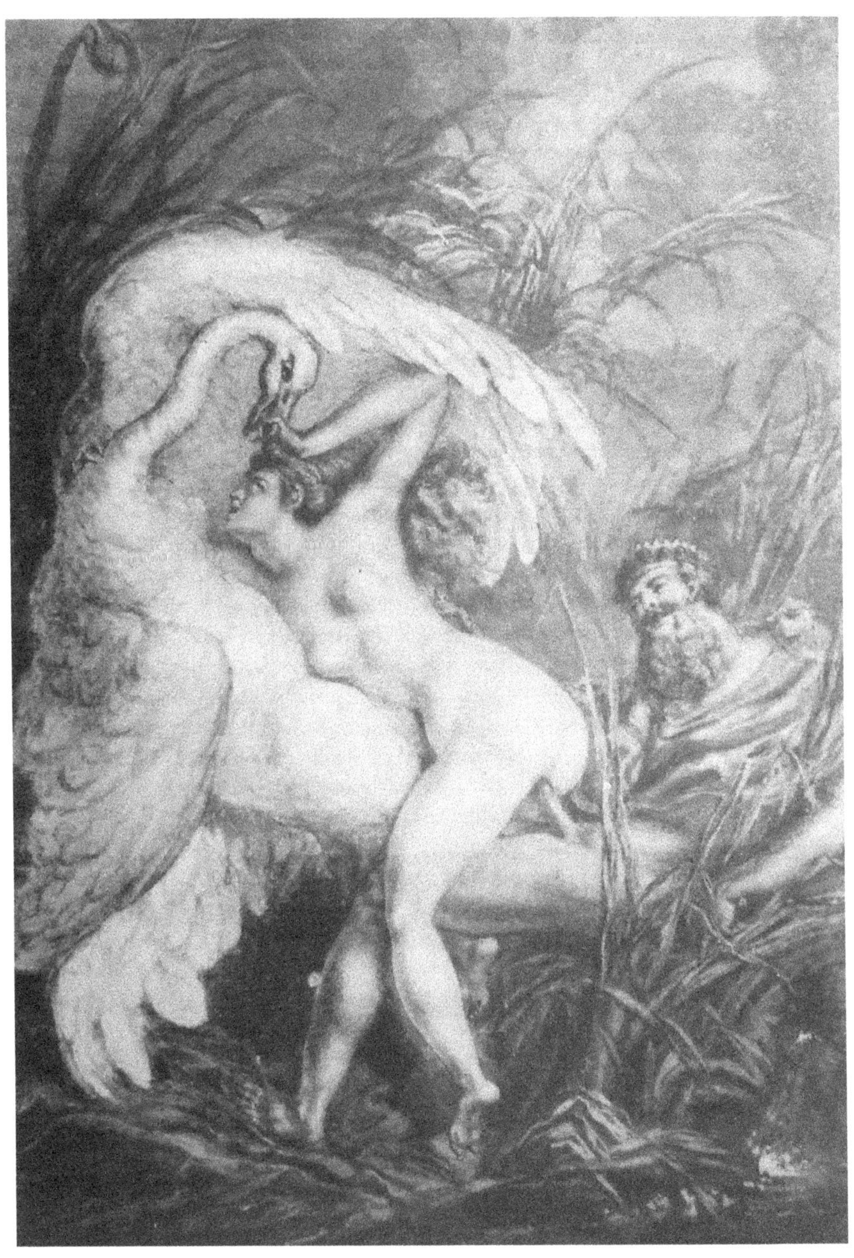

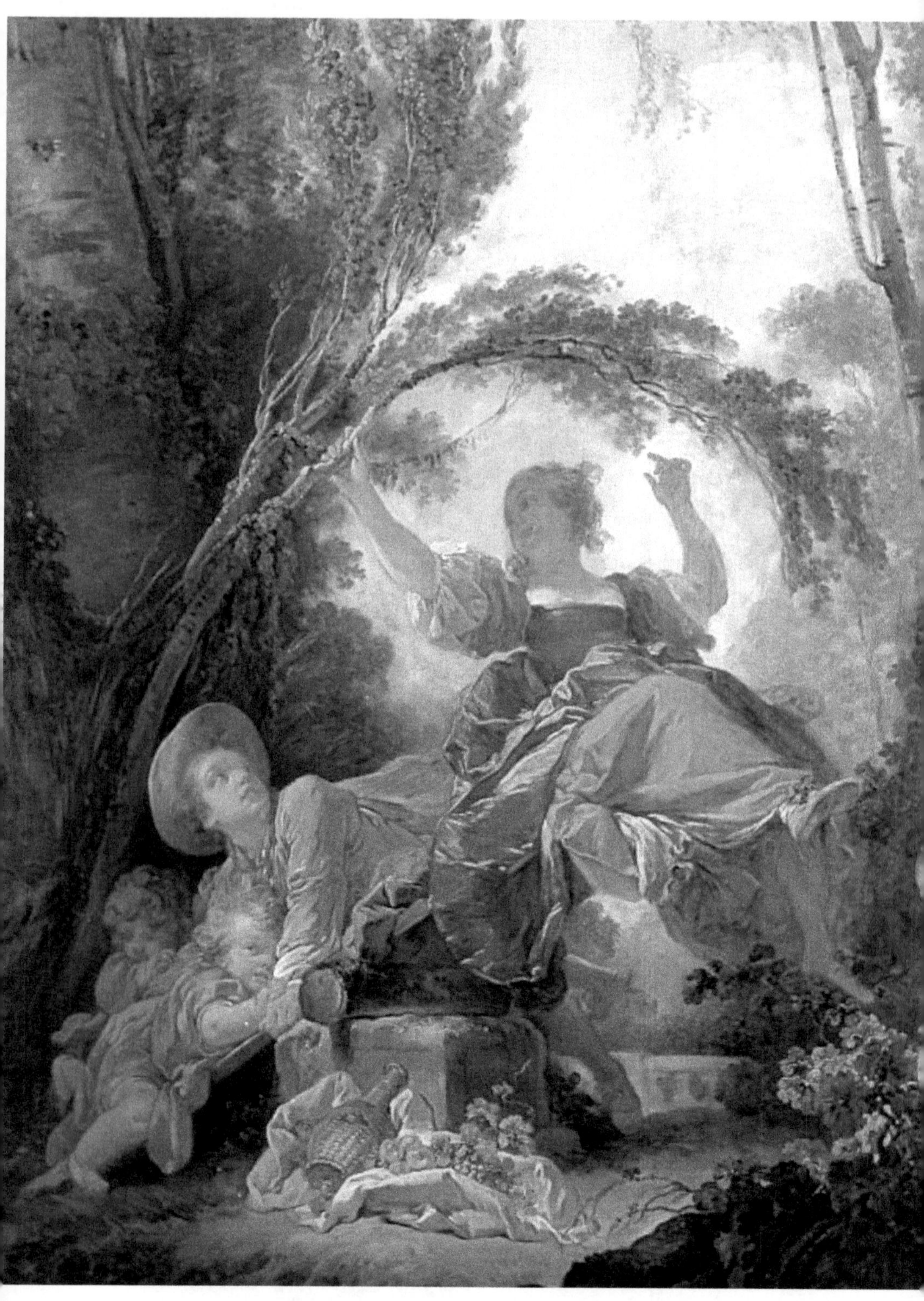

Jean Honoré Fragonard, The See Saw, 1750-75

EROTIC ART

In the 18th Century

Cassidy Hughes

Crescent Moon

First published 2023.

Set in Book Antiqua 10 on 14pt.
Designed by Radiance Graphics.

Thanks to the authors and publishers quoted.

British Library Cataloguing in Publication data

Hughes, Cassidy
Erotic Art In the 18th Century
I. Title
704.9

ISBN-13 9781861710758

CRESCENT MOON PUBLISHING
P.O. Box 1312, Maidstone, Kent, ME14 5XU
Great Britain, www.crmoon.com

CONTENTS

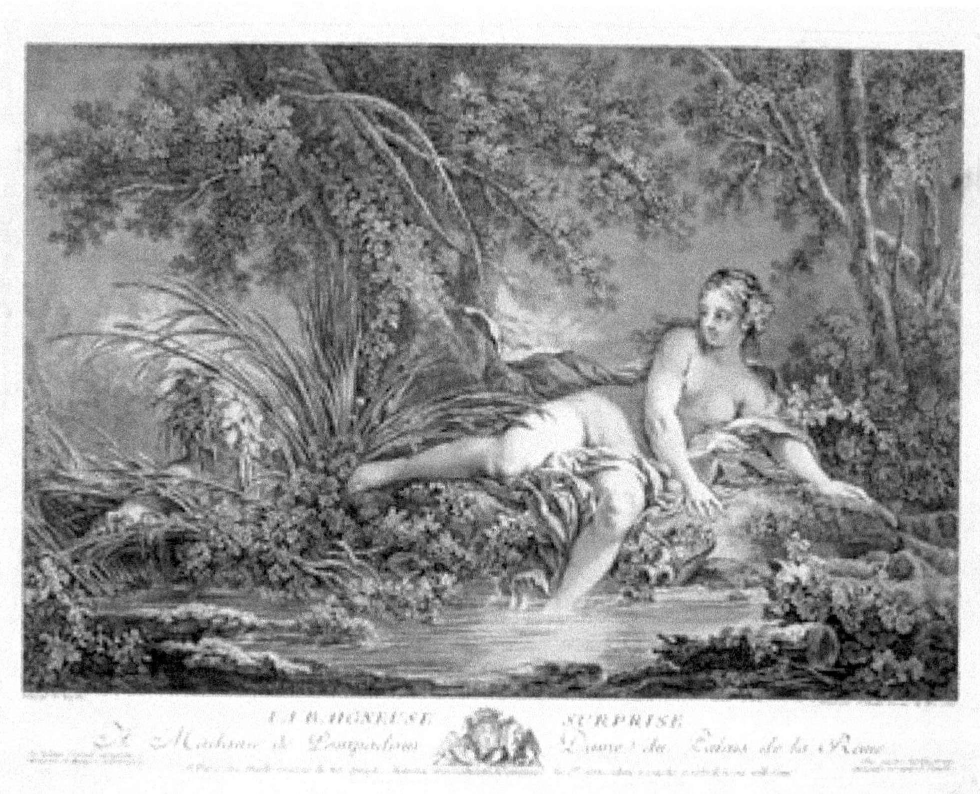

François Boucher, La Baigneuse Surprise

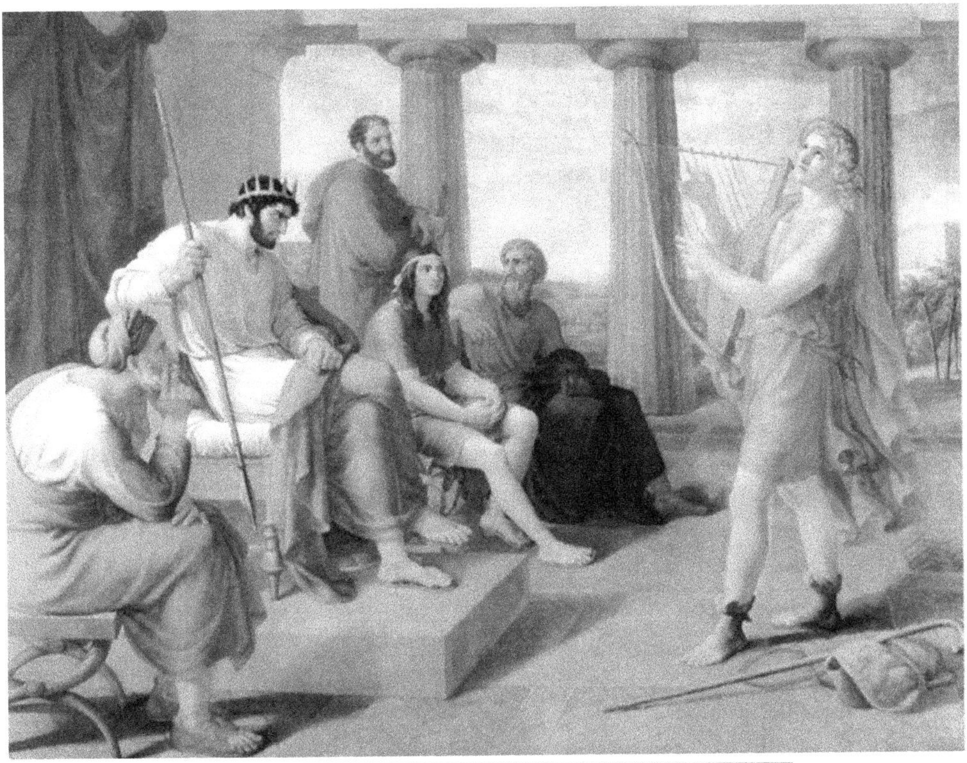

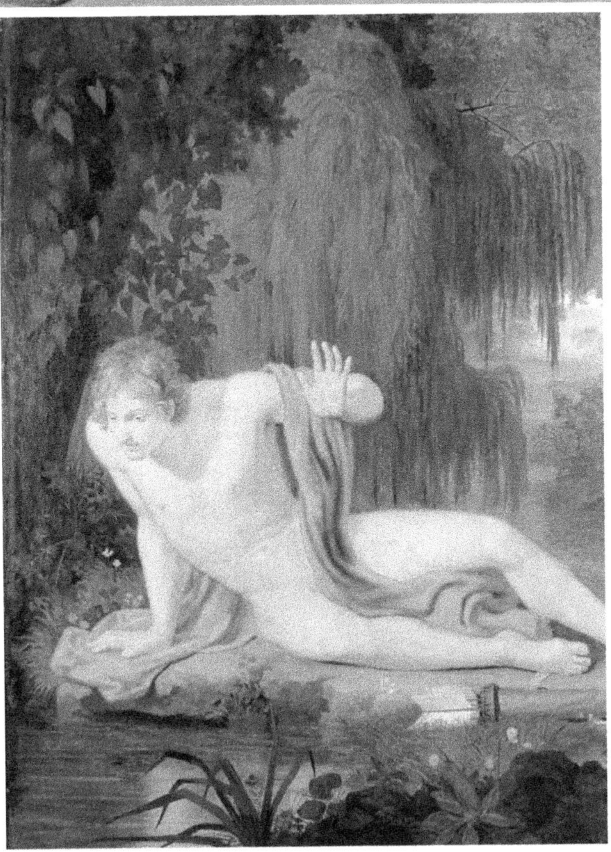

Philipp Otto Runge, David Plays For Saul,
Stuttgart (top). Narcissus (above).

François-Marie-Isidore-Queverdo, from Monrose, ou suite de Felicia, 1795 (right).

François Rolland Elluin, Thérèse Philosophe, 1785, a famous erotic text (below).

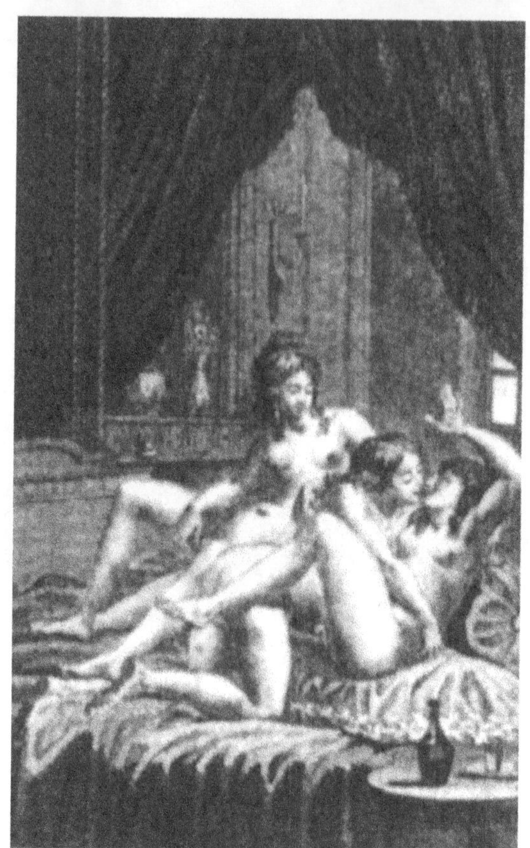

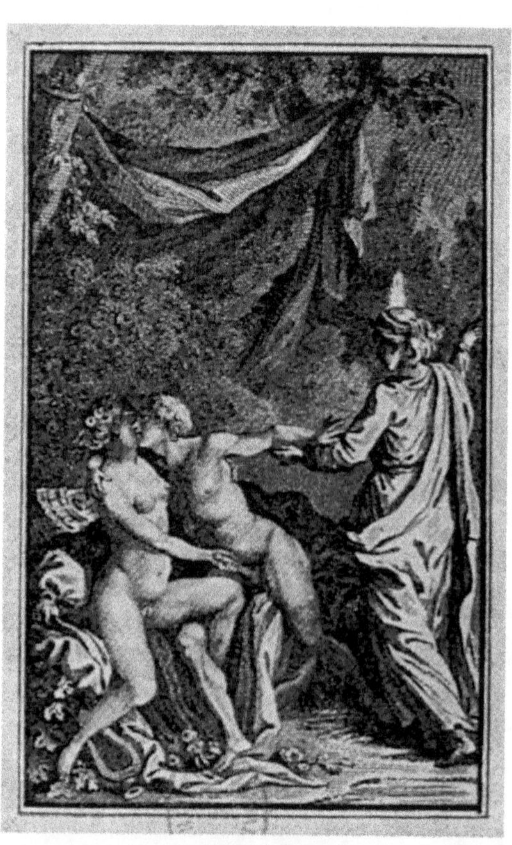

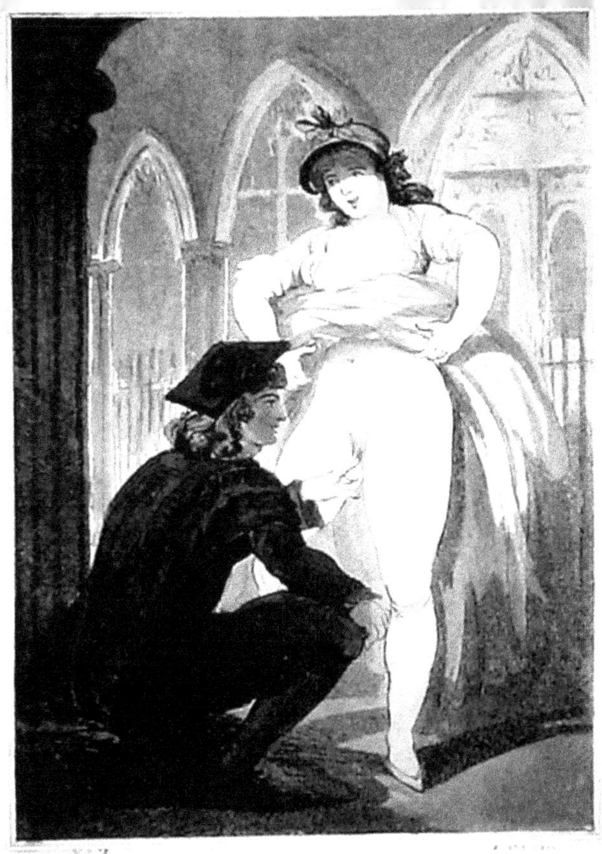

Thomas Rowlandson

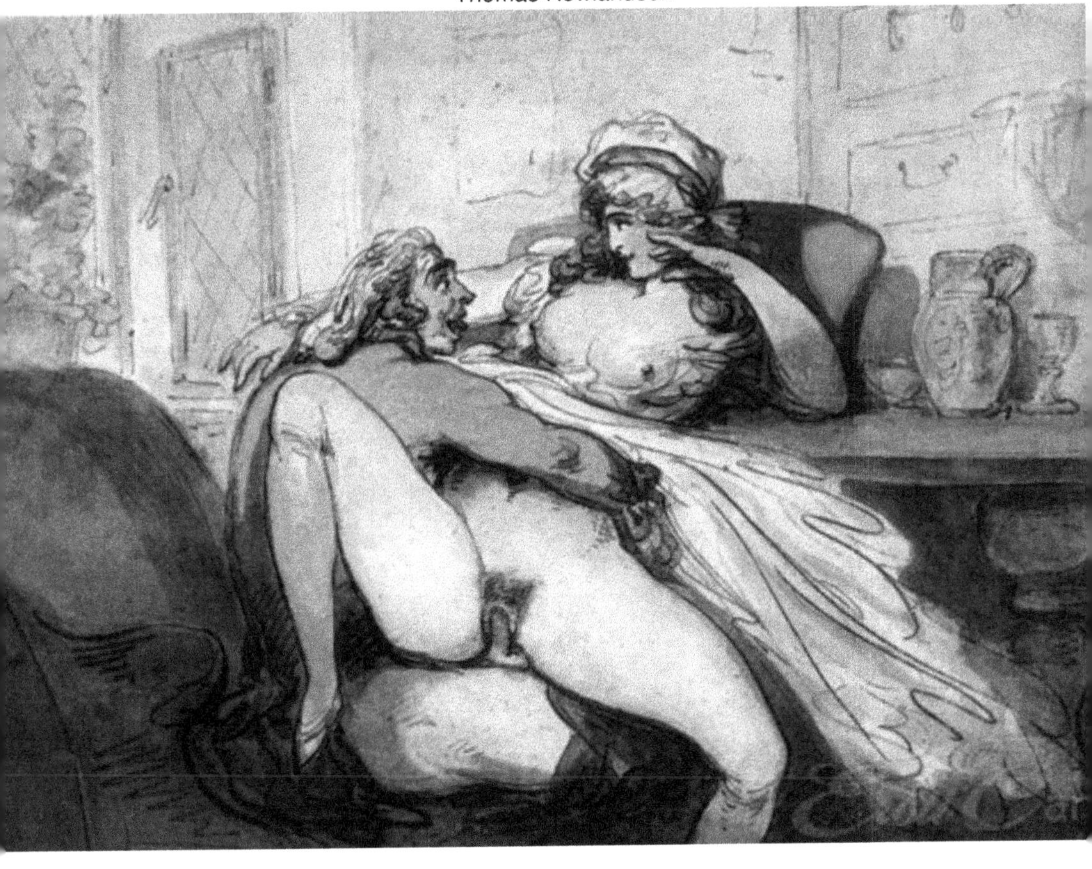

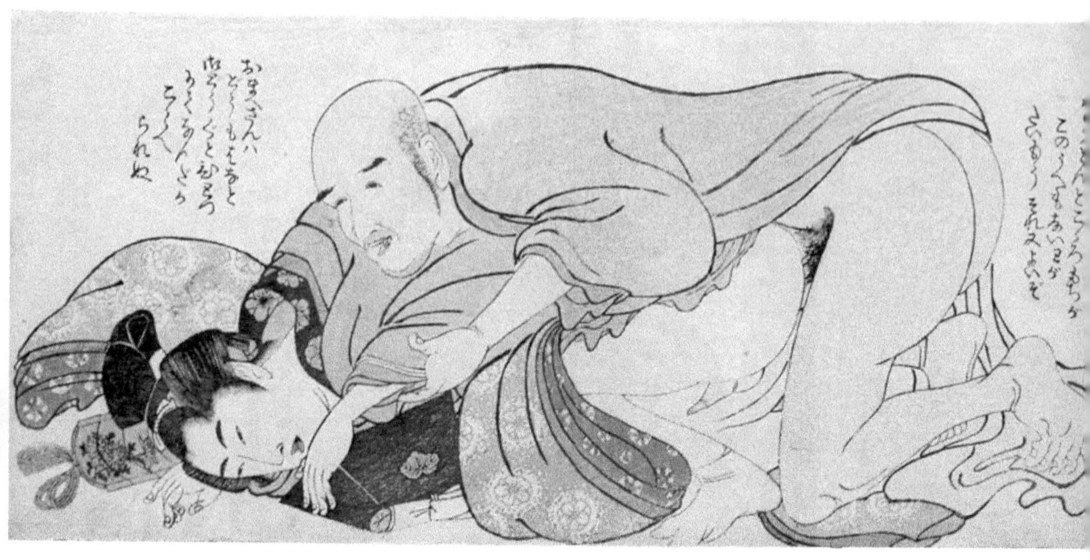

Two homoerotic images by Kitagawa Utamaro

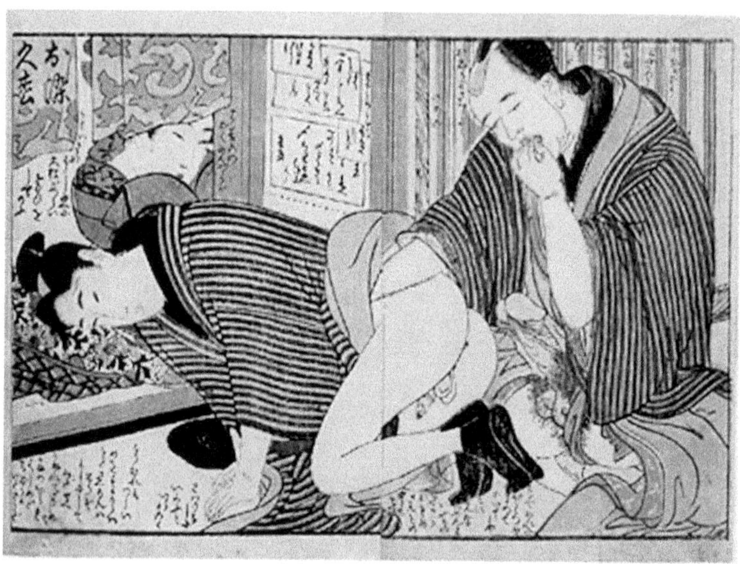

The first part of this book on 18th century erotic art uses short entries about aspects of erotic art (with examples from the whole history of erotic art).

The bulk of the second part of the book focusses on the celebrated artists of the 18th century whose work is considered erotic, as well as many anonymous works.

Part One

Issues In Erotic Art

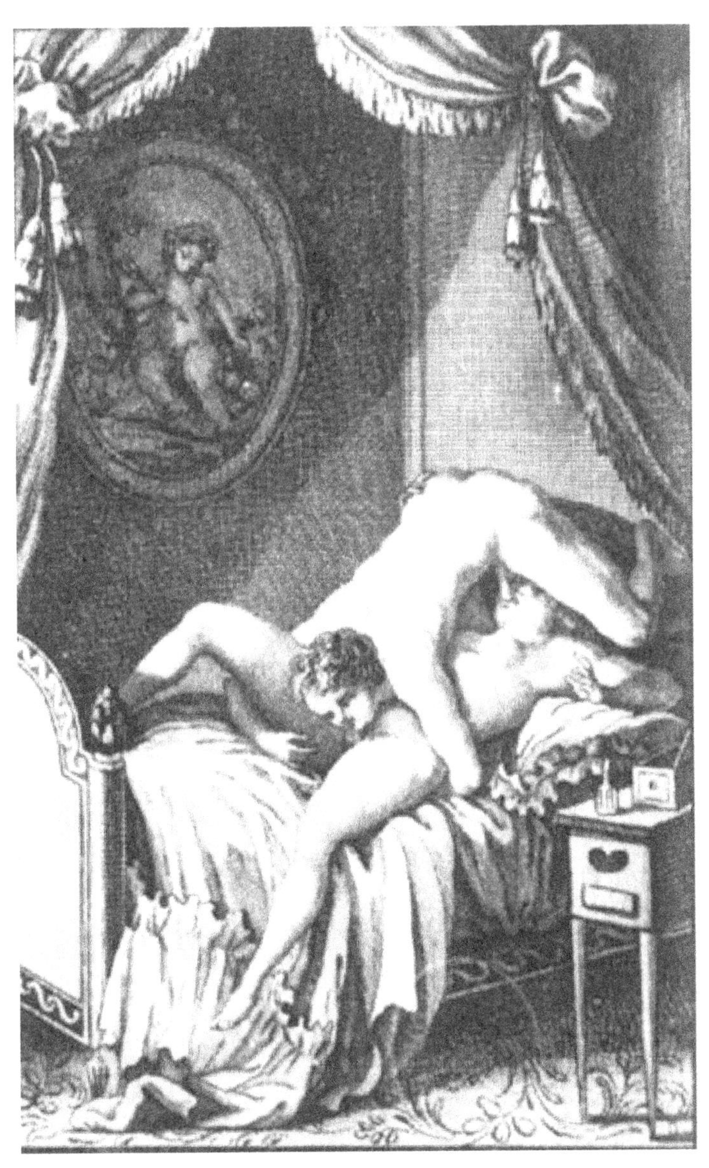

EROTIC ART AND PORNOGRAPHY

The establishment art historical view of erotic art and pornography is that true erotic or high art engenders quiet contemplation, a detached ravishing of the senses, a meditation on Platonic, Aristotlean and Kantian ideas of 'beauty' and æsthetics. 'High art', which is legitimate art, art which justifies itself by its 'genius' or obvious 'greatness', is about distance and disinterested pleasure. The high art nude, in painting or sculpture, in the patriarchal view, justifies its existence by the brilliance of its production, the sumptuousness of its colour and form, the marvel of its human touches, the grandeur of its design, the loftiness of its ambition, the dynamism of its structures, and so on. As that producer of exquisite bodies, French Neo-Classical artist J.A.D. Ingres, wrote:

> There are not two arts, there is only one: it is the one which has as its foundation the beautiful, which is eternal and natural.[1]

1 J.A.D. Ingres, quoted in R. Goldwater, 216

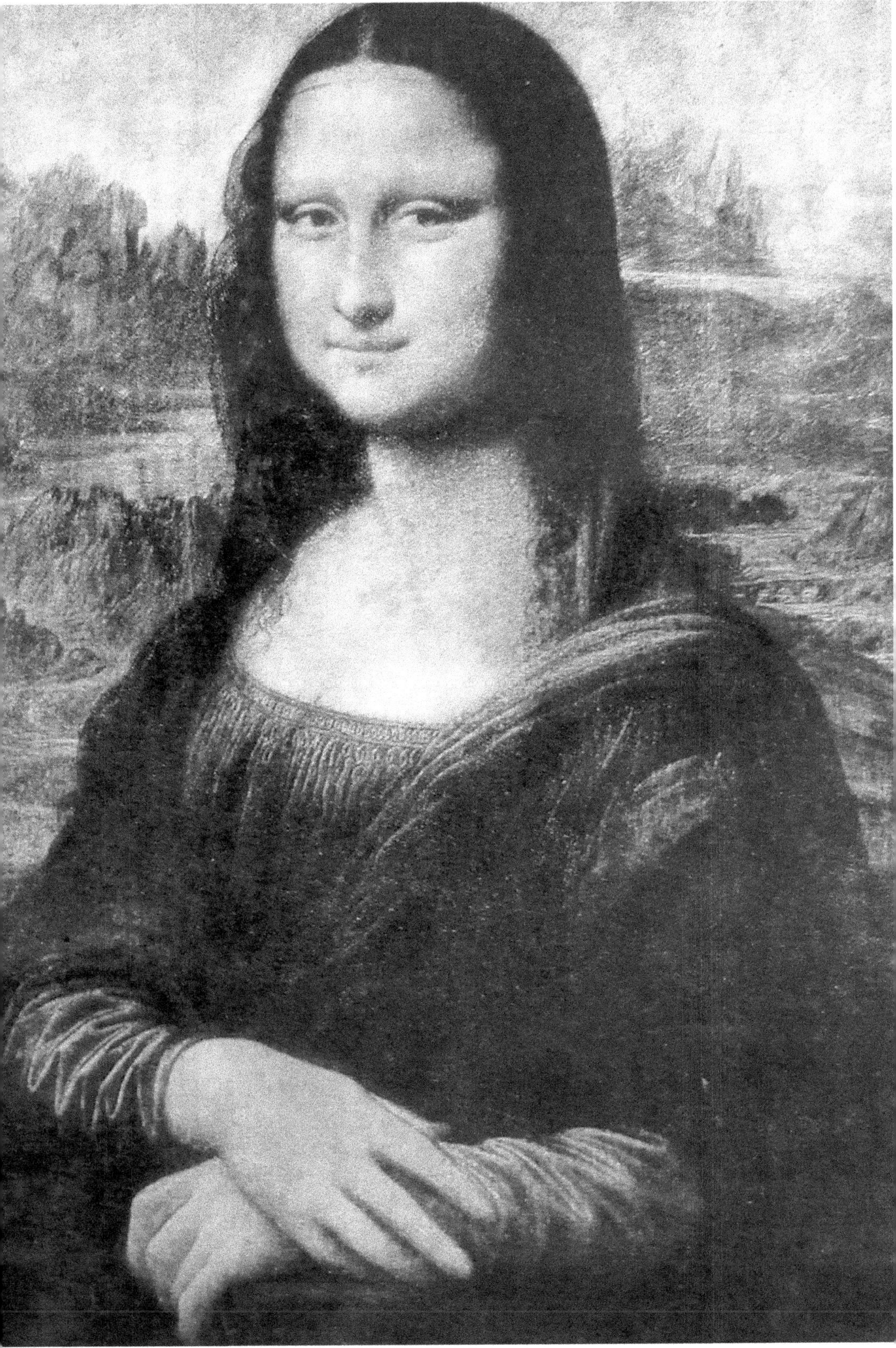

EROTIC ART VERSUS PORNOGRAPHY

We know the male/ patriarchal view of the art versus pornography debate. Eroticism is justified and good because it is 'high art', it is superbly crafted, it is a 'work of art'. Thus the Kronhausens, the organizers of a major exhibition of 'erotic art' (of 1968),[1] write:

> one can perhaps distinguish between pornography and art. The criterion would be that the more a picture contains evidence of interpretative, creative elaboration, the closer it is to art.[2]

For the Kronhausens, as for so many artists and philosophers and intellectuals, erotic art is art because it is done well. Pornography is simply bad art.

Many guardians of æsthetics, many professors of art history and dons of 'the beautiful' go along with this view. Kenneth Clark is a typical establishment critic who puts forward the patriarchal view: nudes are OK provided they are æsthetically pleasing, provided they remain 'in the realm of contemplation' as he put it.[3]

---

1 The 'first international exhibition of erotic art' was at the Museum of Art, Lund, Sweden, and Aarhus, Denmark, in 1968

2 Phyllis & Eberhard Kronhausen: *Erotic Art: A survey of erotic fact and fancy in the fine arts*, W.H. Allen, 1971, 3

3 Quoted in Lord Longford: *Pornography: The Longford Report*, Coronet, 1972, 99f

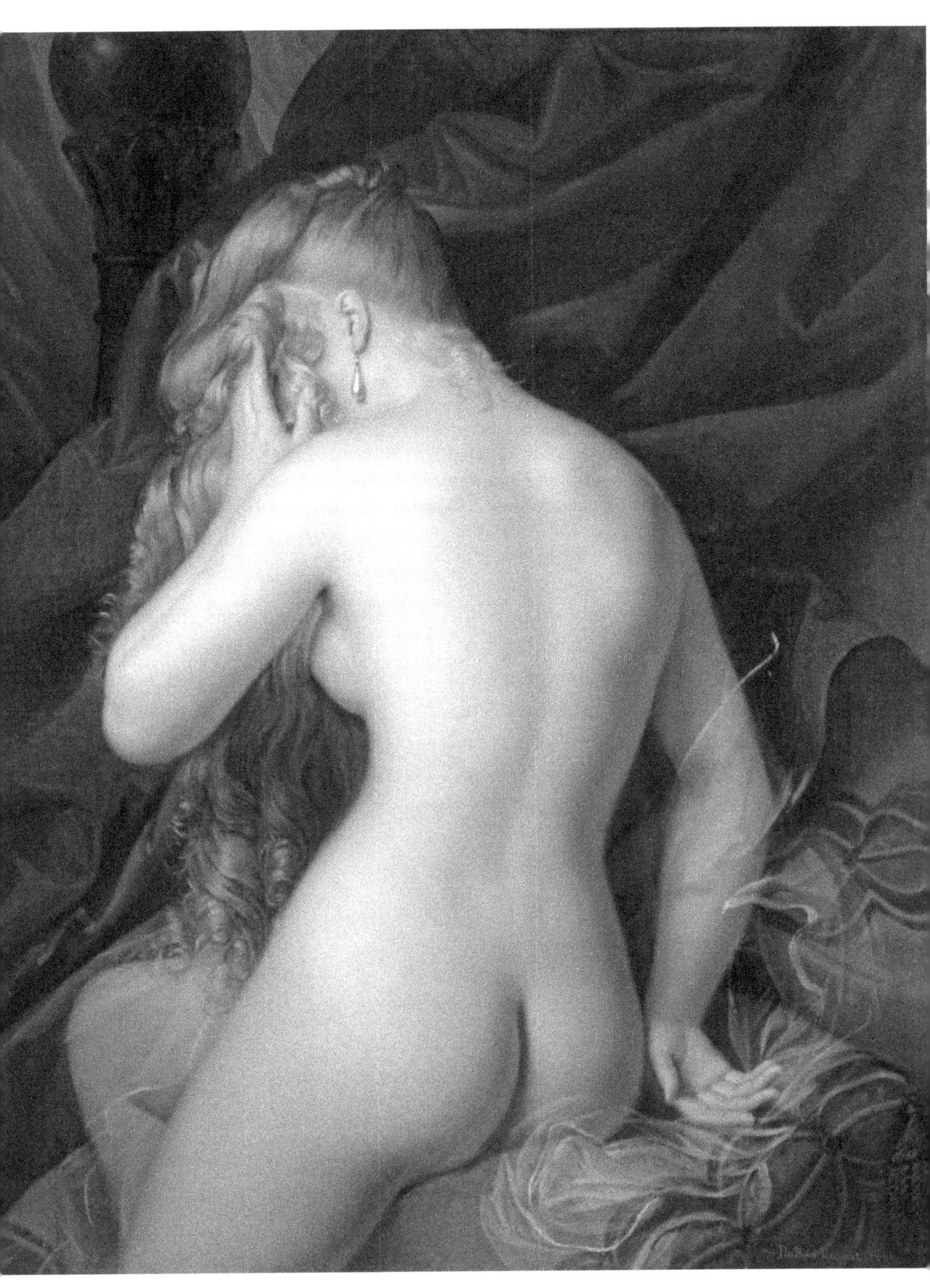

Alexandre-Jean Dubois-Drahonet,
Female Nude, 19th century

THE FEMALE NUDE

The 'sublime' qualities of high art, to use one popular adjective of art criticism, are crucial to its success, as Carol M. Armstrong notes in her essay on Edgar Degas:

> One of the things any painted object does is to resist signification at some level because of its very objecthood. And the female nude - because of *its* objecthood may be seen as almost emblematic of that level of resistance. In fact, the female nude has been linked to that stratum of painting most in tension with the work of signification - the stratum we connect to what we call, inadequately, "abstraction"; facture, the handling of paint per se, foregrounded as an obvious fact of the painting. Femaleness and facture, facture and the female nude, they go together somehow. One need only think of Titian, the first great painter of the female nude in the Western tradition.[1]

Much as worshippers properly gaze at an icon or an image of a deity with wonder, the art critic and historian kneels before 'great art' and worships it.[2] The female nude is the highest form of non-religious art, and it confers a religious awe in its æsthete consumers. The emphasis is on Neoplatonic terms such as 'purity', 'beauty', 'form' and 'symmetry'. As Aristotle puts it: '[t]he chief forms of beauty are order and symmetry and definiteness.'[3]

---

1 Carol M. Armstrong; "Edgar Degas and the Representation of the Female Body", in S. Suleiman, 223

2 See Pierre Bourdieu: *Distinction: A Social Critique of the Judgment of Taste*, tr Richard Nice, Routledge & Kegan Paul, New York 1984

3 Aristotle: *Metaphysics*, book XIII, in Albert Hofstadter & Richard Kuhns, eds: *Philosophies of Art and Beauty: Selected Readings in Aesthetics From Plato to Heidegger*, Random House, New York 1964, 96

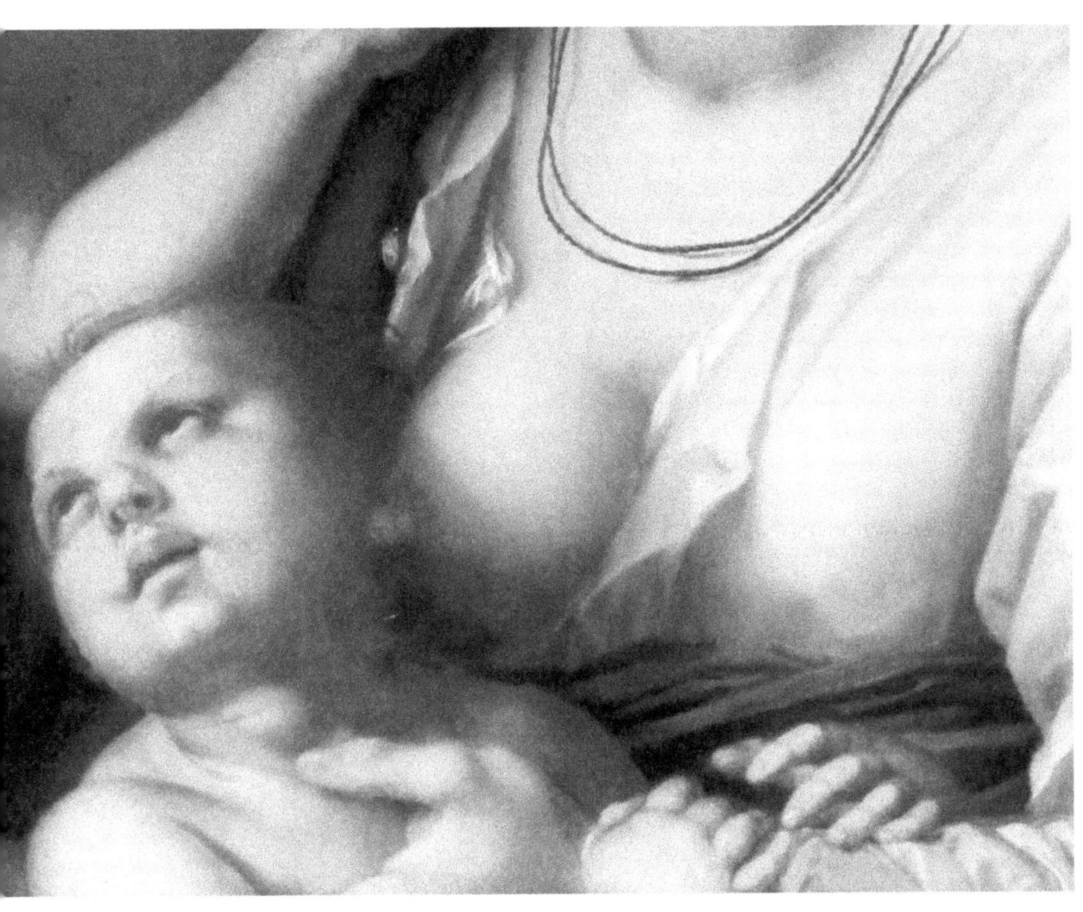

Andrea del Sarto, Madonna and Child, detail

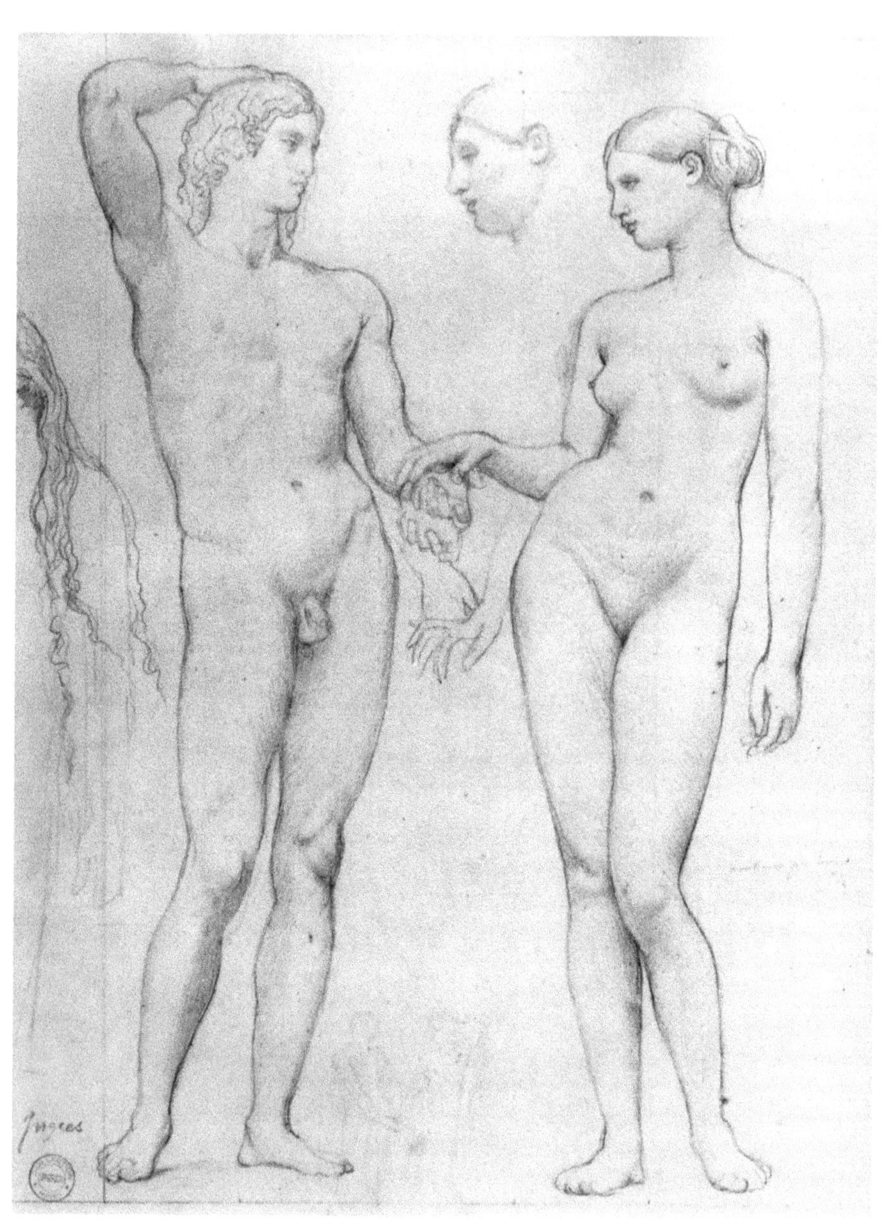

J.A.D. Ingres, Study For L'Age d'Or, 1862

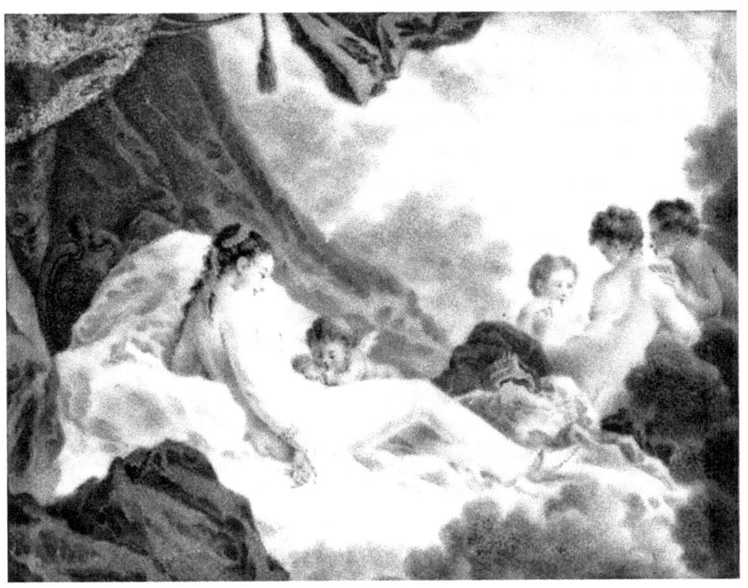

Daniel Chodowiecki, Venus and Cupid, 1750

THE FEMALE NUDE

Depictions of the female nude and of erotic gestures or acts can be problematic. The female body, for instance, is already 'objectified' even before it is painted or represented. Once painted, it becomes a cultural artifact, a mass of codes, meanings, signs and values, none of them fixed, all of them dependent on the context of consumption, dependent on the socio-political make-up of the viewer, and so on. None of this, however, has prevented erotic nudes and female nudes from being produced.

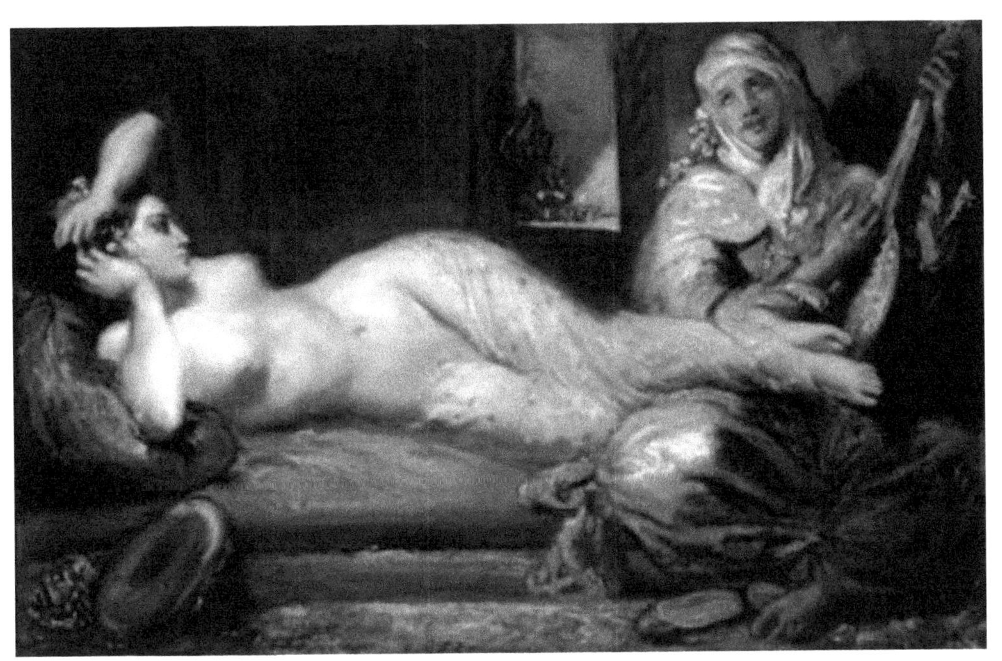

Théodore Chasséreau (1819-56)

William Bouguereau,
The Birth of Venus,
above

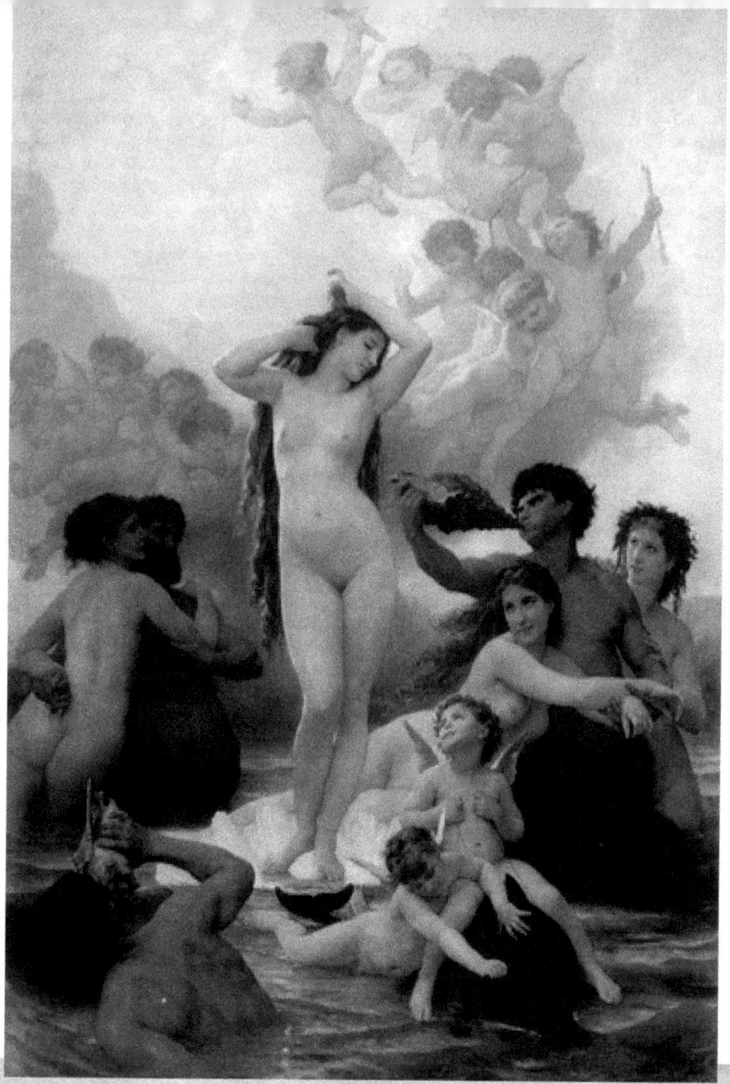

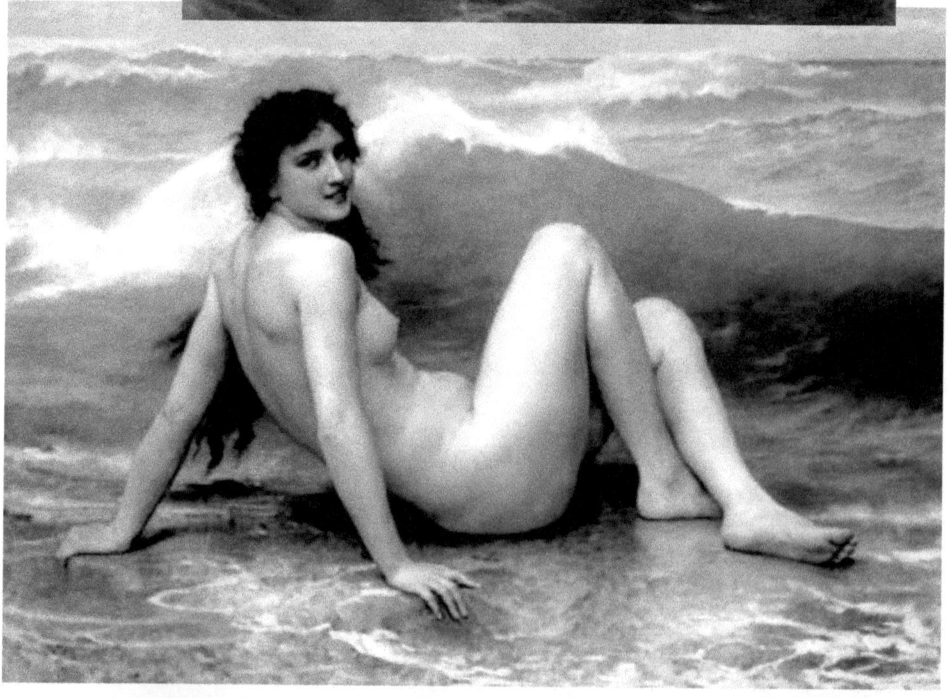

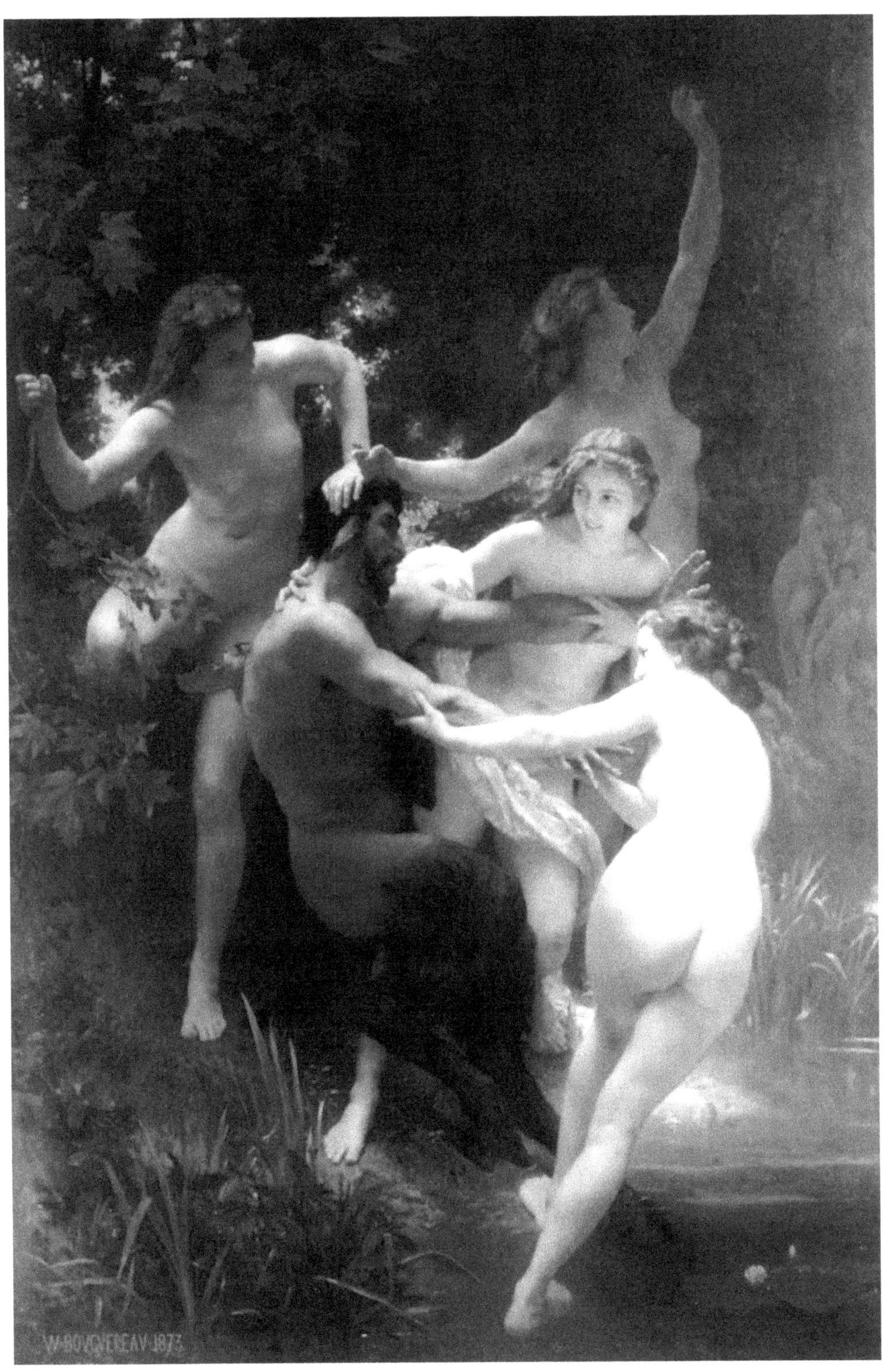

William Bouguereau, Nymphs and Satyr

THE FEMALE NUDE

Context is crucial in matters of eroticism. An image that is seen as 'erotic' in one context can easily be seen as 'pornographic' in another context. Take an image out of context, and soon a new, often ironic set of meanings are set in motion. Jacques Derrida has shown that a text may have many contexts, and is not fixed in one context forever.[1] Feminist artists have explored meanings and contexts, by placing traditional images in new contexts. Meanings are constantly in a state of flux. Nothing is fixed anymore. As Catherine Belsey writes: 'meanings circulate between text, ideology and reader' (144). Roland Barthes wrote that '[a]ll images are polysemous...they imply, underlying their signifiers, a floating chain of signifieds'. The consumer has the ability to 'choose some and ignore others'.[2] The cultural environment, socialization, economy, power relations, education, any number of factors can influence the meanings drawn from an image. With the female nude, in painting or erotica, the meanings are contextualized as erotic. As Anne Hollander notes, the nude always has a sexual dimension to it.

For instance, men can 'possess' and yet never 'possess' a female nude painting. It remains an image. The 'possession' or consumption is of a cerebral order, which is why critics and professors such as Kenneth Clark, Bernard Berenson, Jacob Burckhardt, Walter Pater, John Ruskin, Aby Warburg, Roger Fry, Ernst Gombrich and other art critics emphasize the *intellectual* nature of enjoying art. Art for the head, not the body, art for the eyes, not the full five senses.

---

1 Jacques Derrida: *Eperons. Les styles de Nietzsche*, Flammarion, Paris 1978, 103f
2 Roland Barthes: *Image-Music-Text*, Hill & Wang, New York 1977, 39

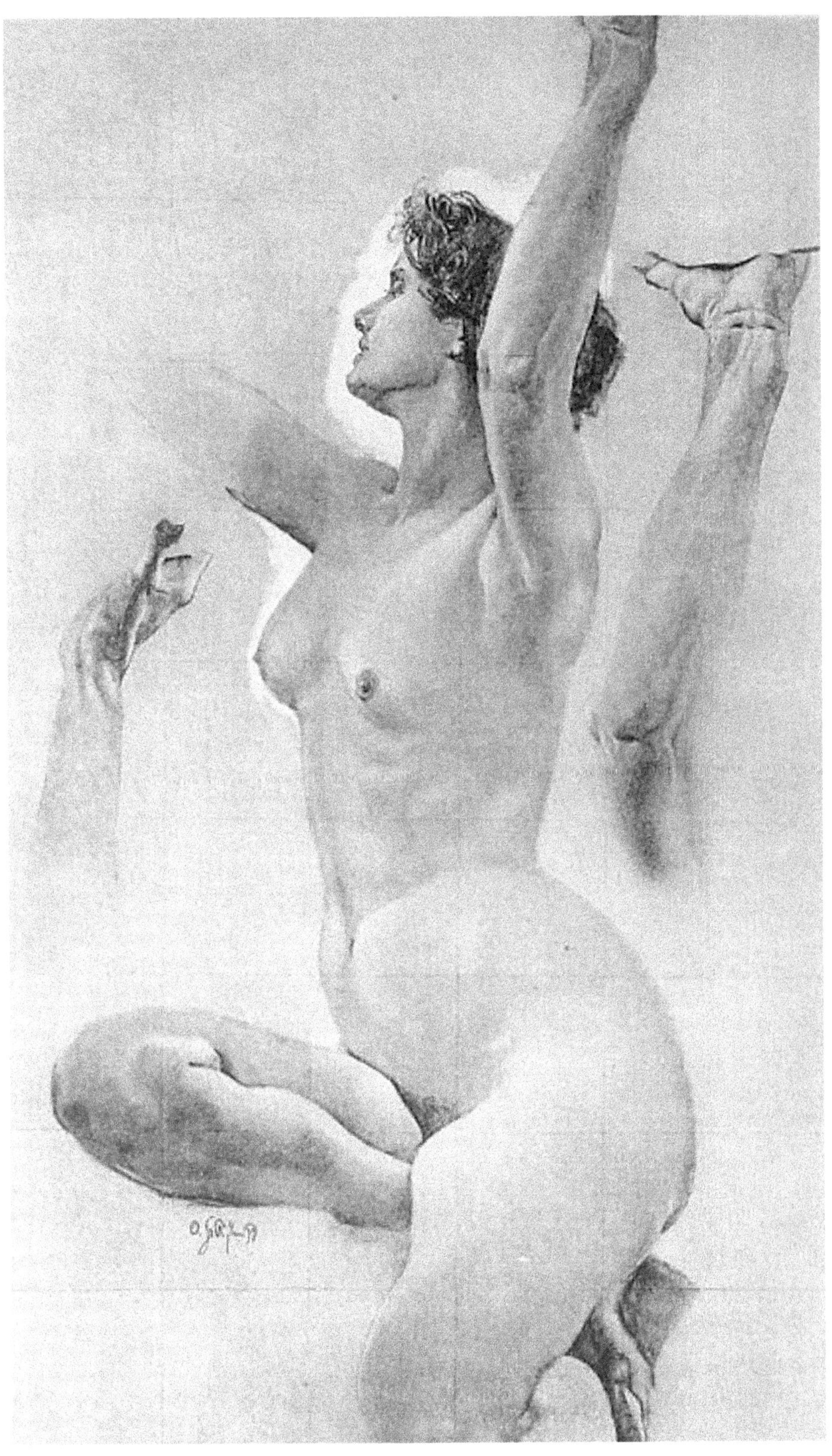

Otto Grenier, Study For Odysseus, 1912-33

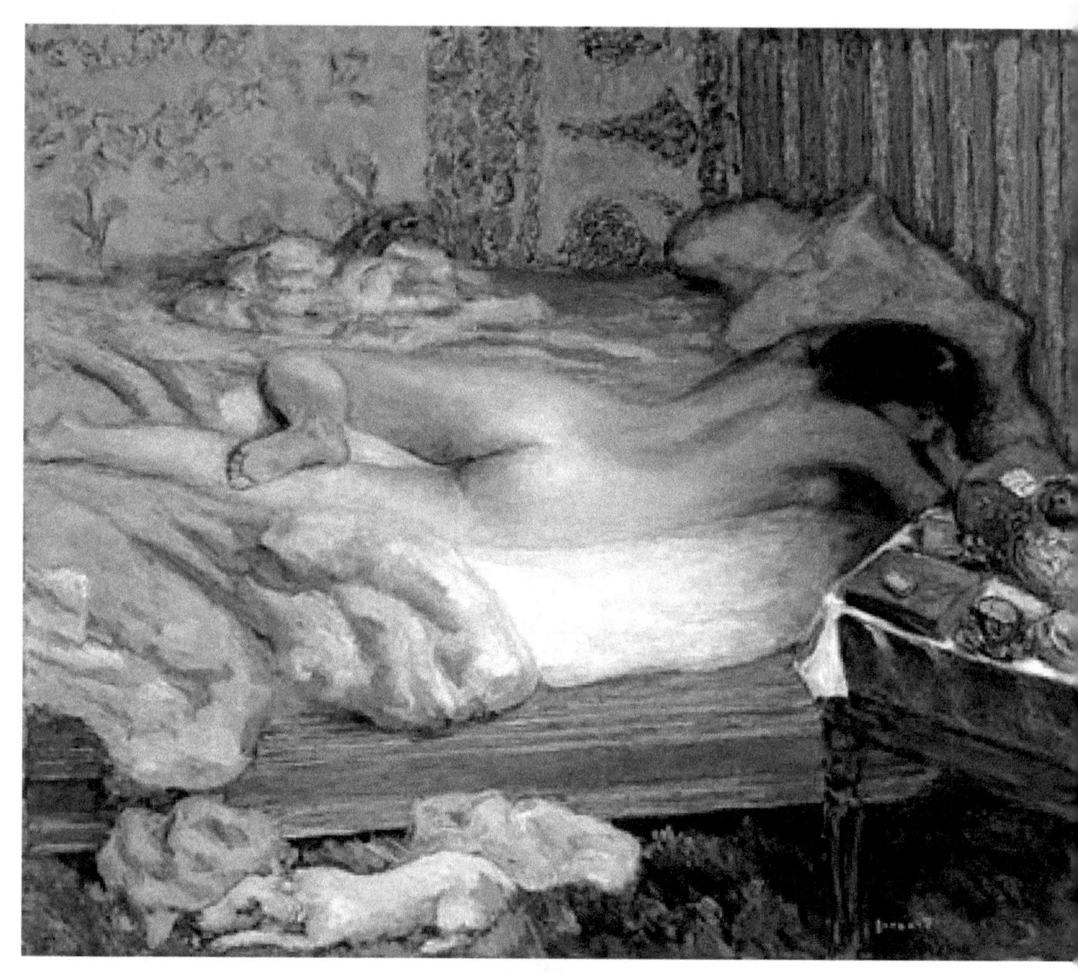

Pierre Bonnard

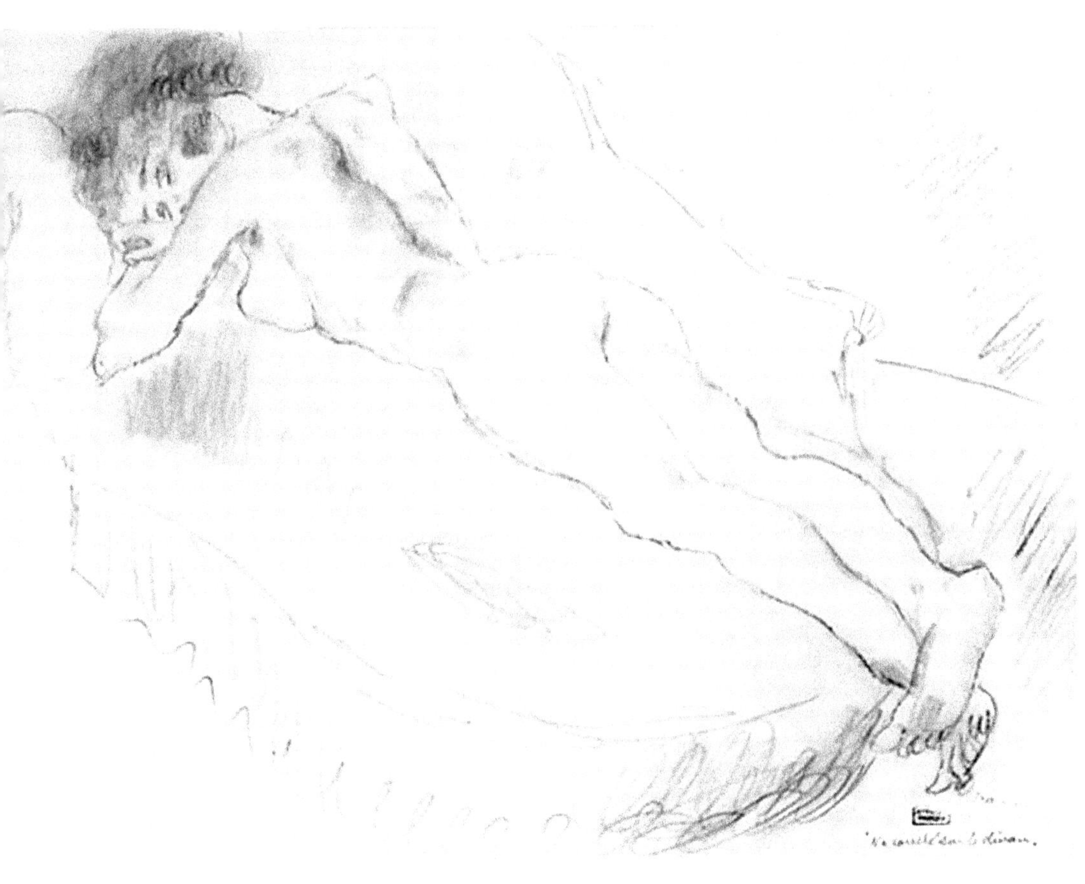

Jules Pascin

THE FEMALE NUDE

The high art nude, then, is a site of political and economic manipulation, an expression of the power relations between patron and painter, between connoisseur, artist and model. In the trinity of people linked by the painting - patron, painter and model - the model is clearly at the bottom of the pile. She is dependent on both painter and patron. She has to please both of them to be successful. The relation of artist to model thus is another manifestation, like that of husband and wife, of male power, of patriarchal culture in action, of the sexual economics which are at work everywhere in the world, and everywhere in history.

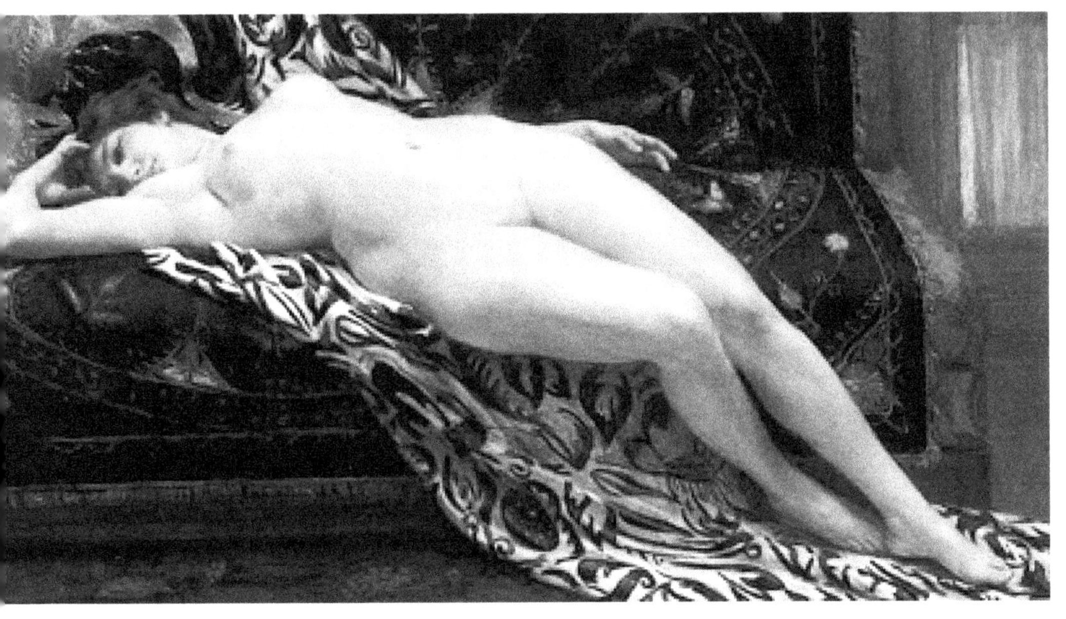

Guillaume Seignac, L'Abandon (above).
The Wave (below).

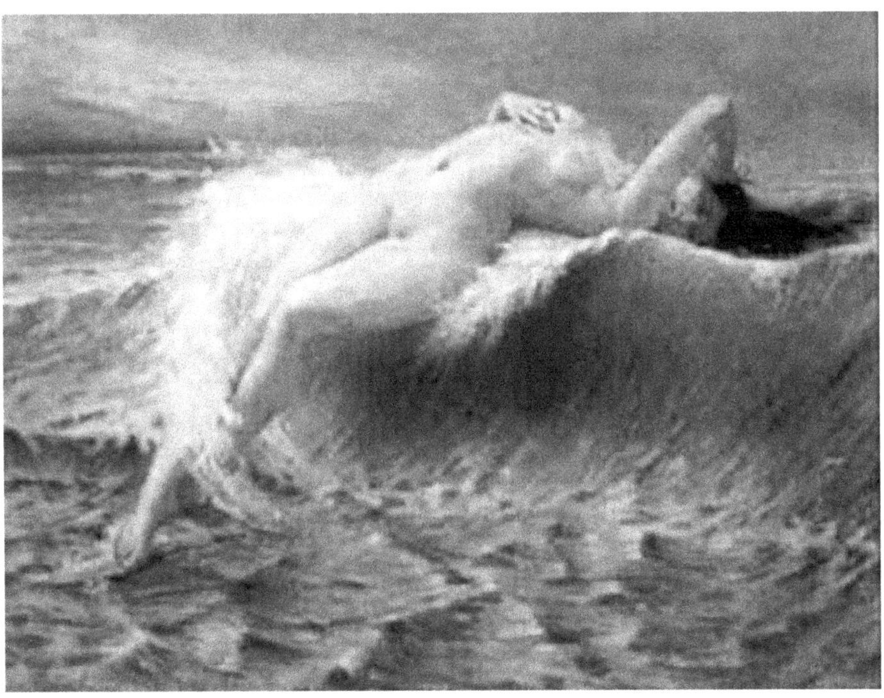

MALE NUDES

The male nude can be seen as a phallus, as Gill Saunders pointed out:

> The male body, while not constructed as the site of sexual pleasure, is often symbolic of phallic power. The whole body, muscular, potent, active, may come to represent the phallus.[1]

The penis isn't a phallus, so, to make up for the disappointing insufficiency of the penis, macho masculinity is demonstrated by bulging muscles, clenched fists, sturdy poses. The male nude poses with a body of 'rippling muscles', bizarrely exaggerated, or gripping a gun, or standing next to a motorcycle, a car, a machine, something that can connote phallic power.

1 G. Saunders: *The Nude*, 26.

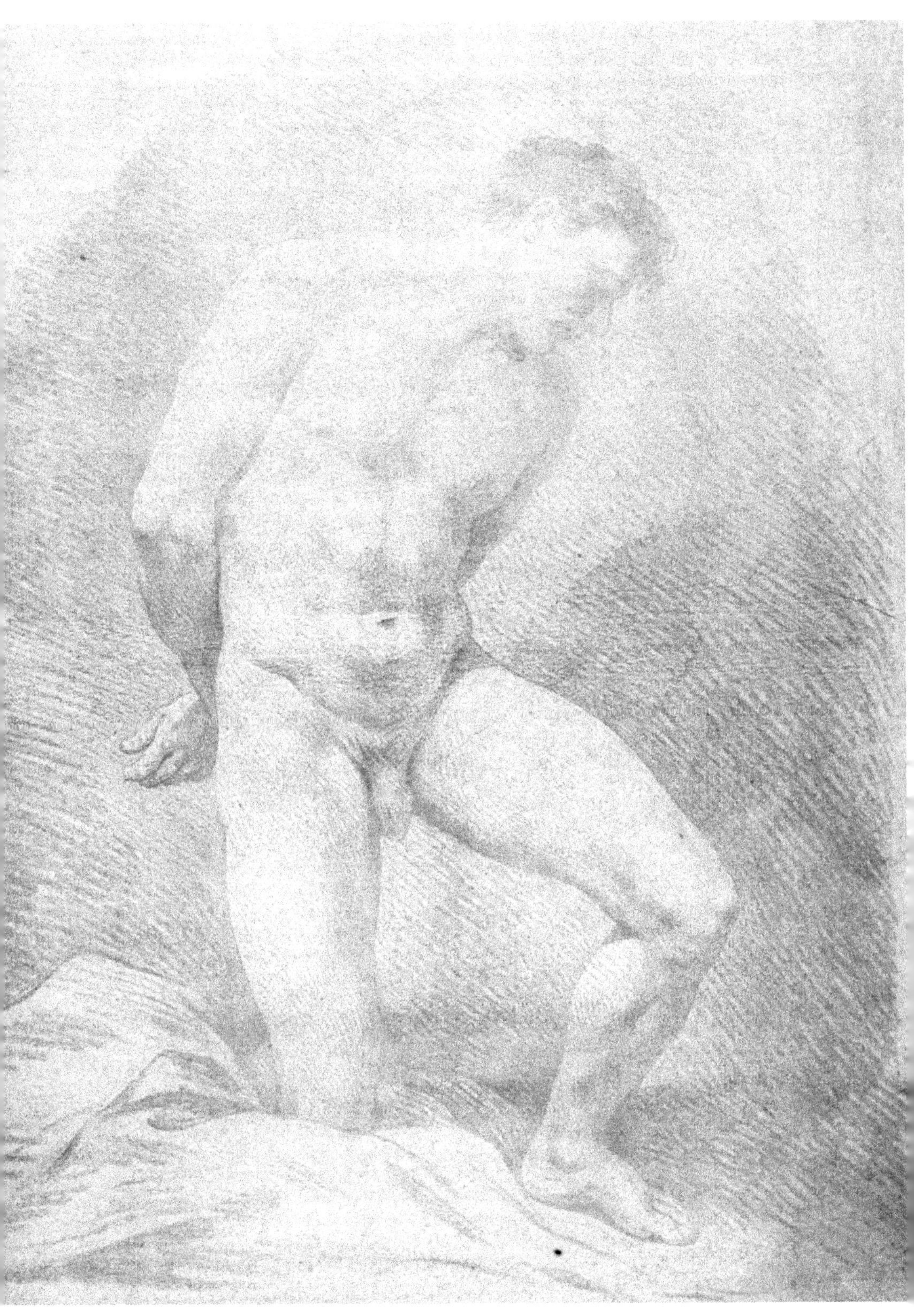

Male Nude, 19th century

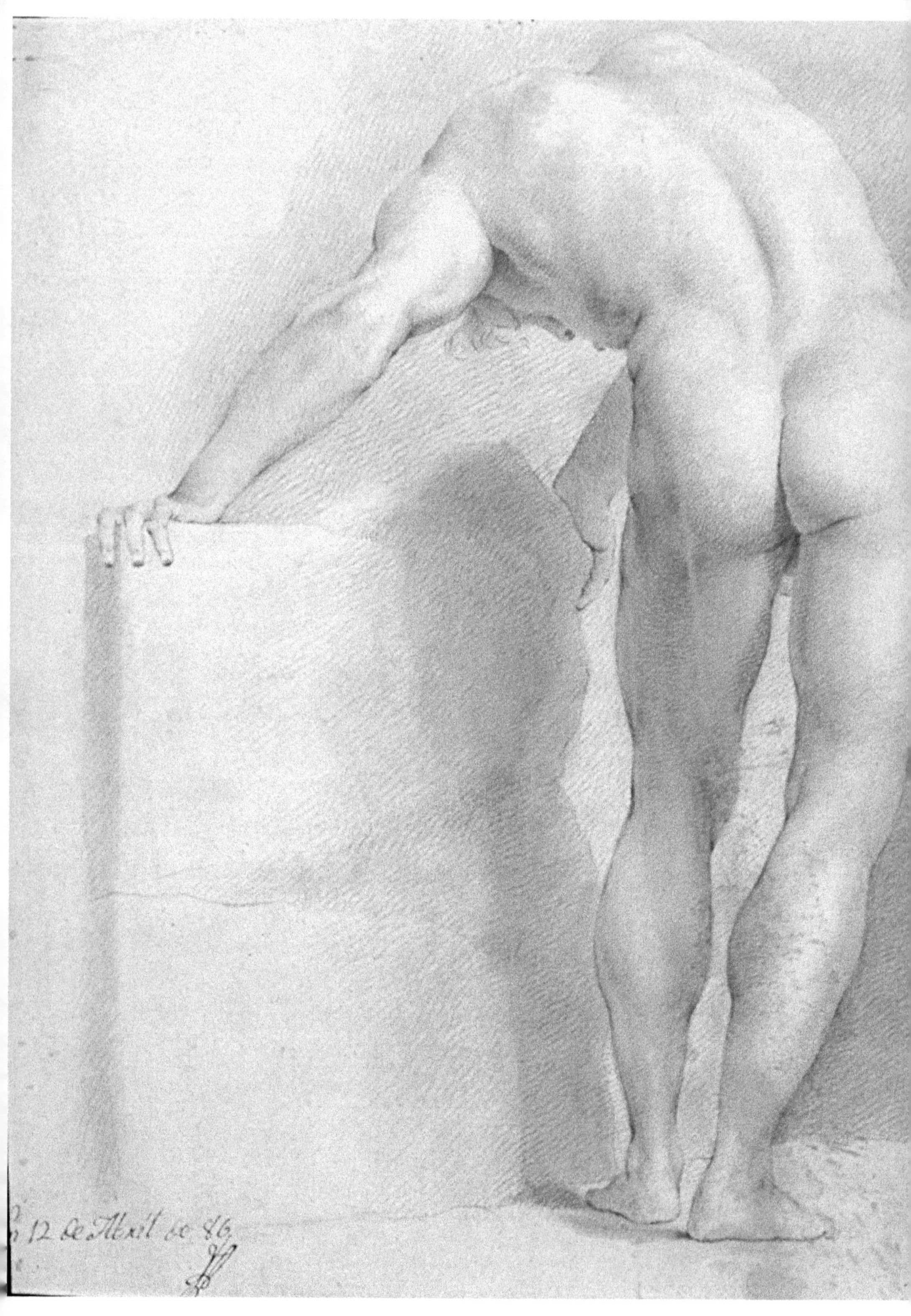

Mariano Amare, Male Nude, 1786.

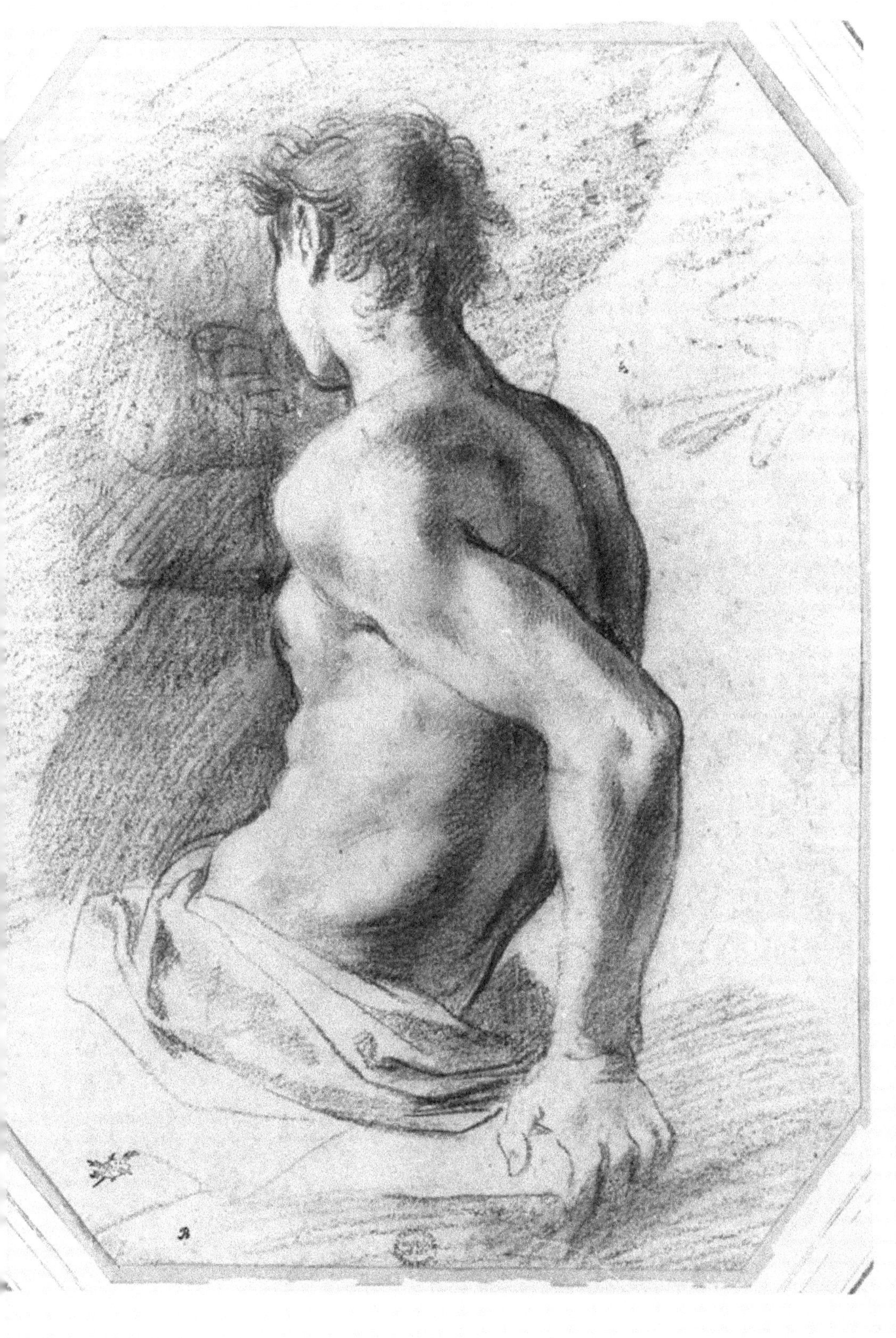

Annibale Carracci, Male Nude, Half-Figure, 16th century

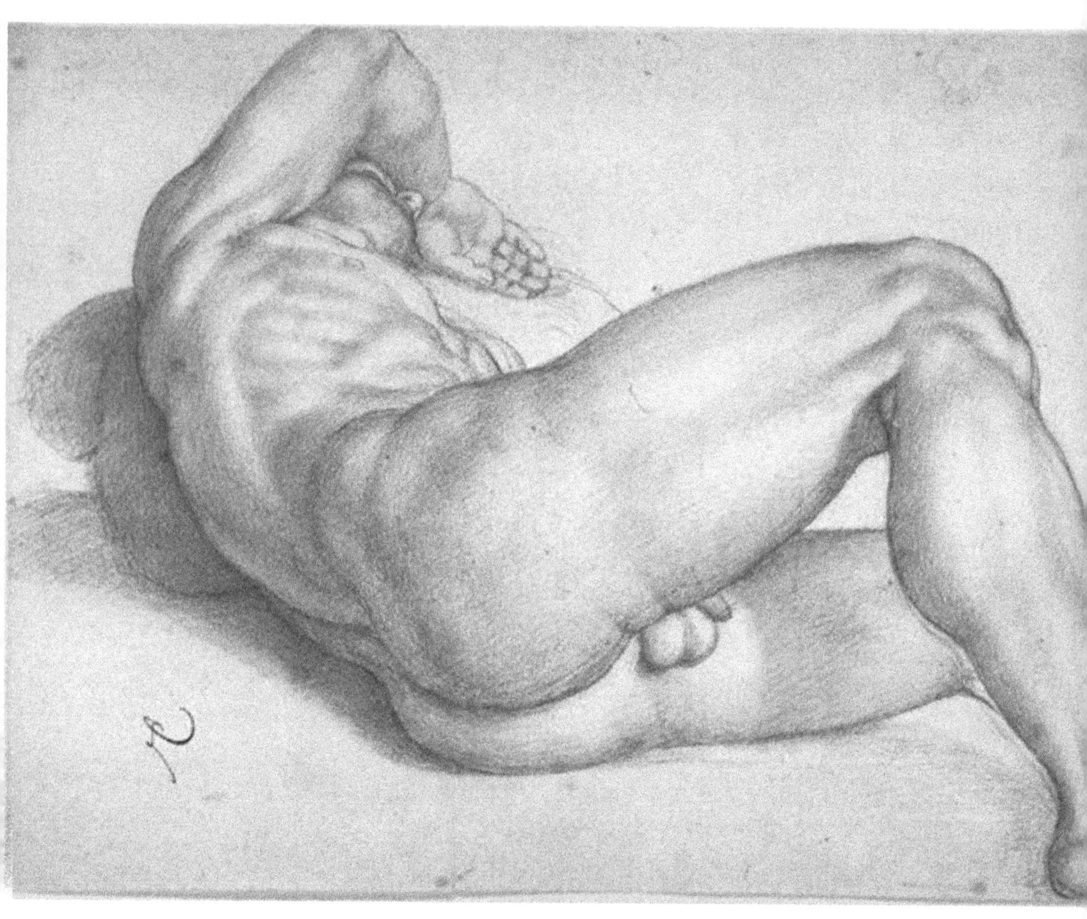

Agnolo di Cosimo (Il Bronzino),
Naked Man Lying On His Back, 16th century

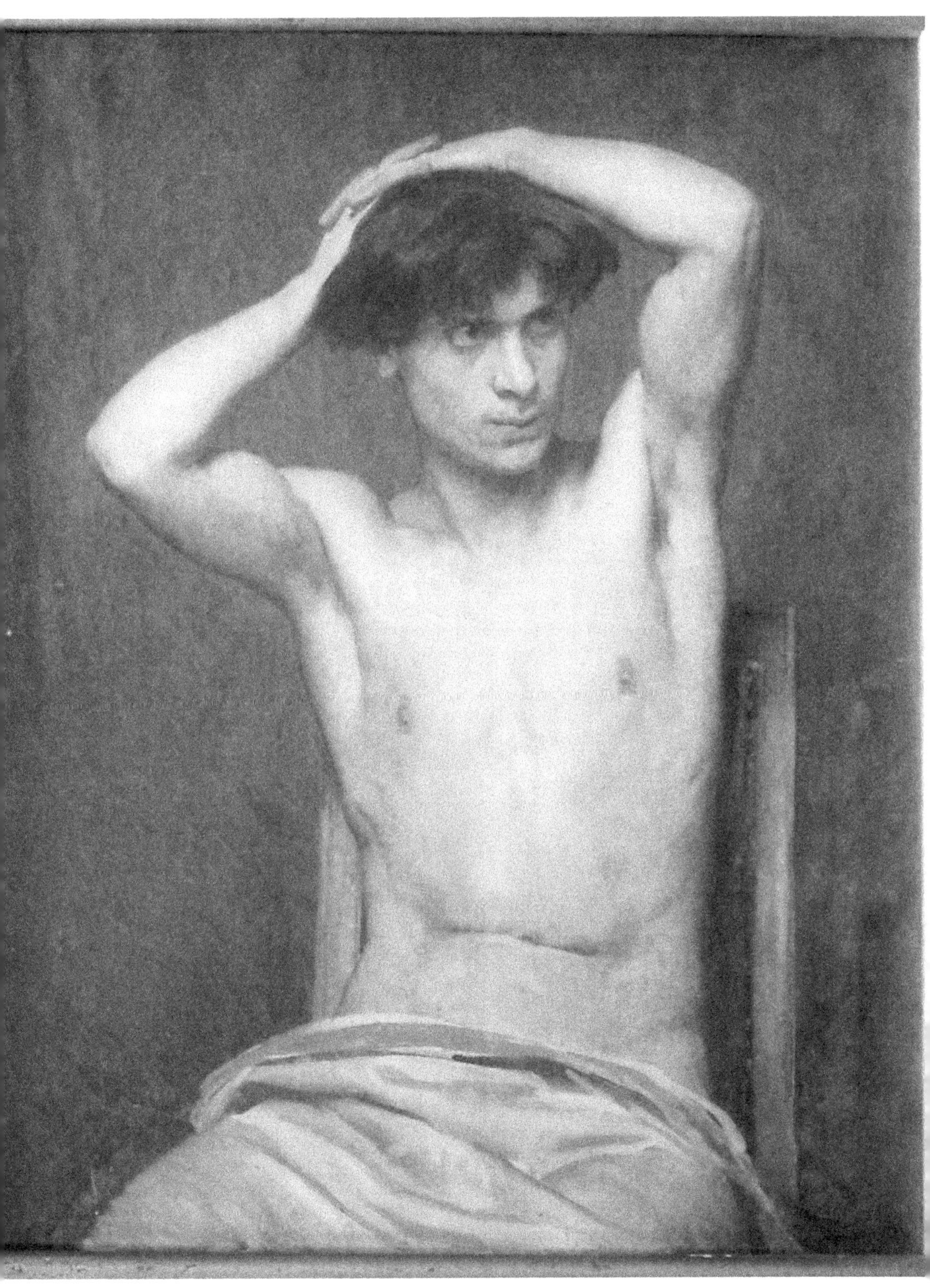

Henri-Lucien Doucet, Half-Nude Figure, 1879

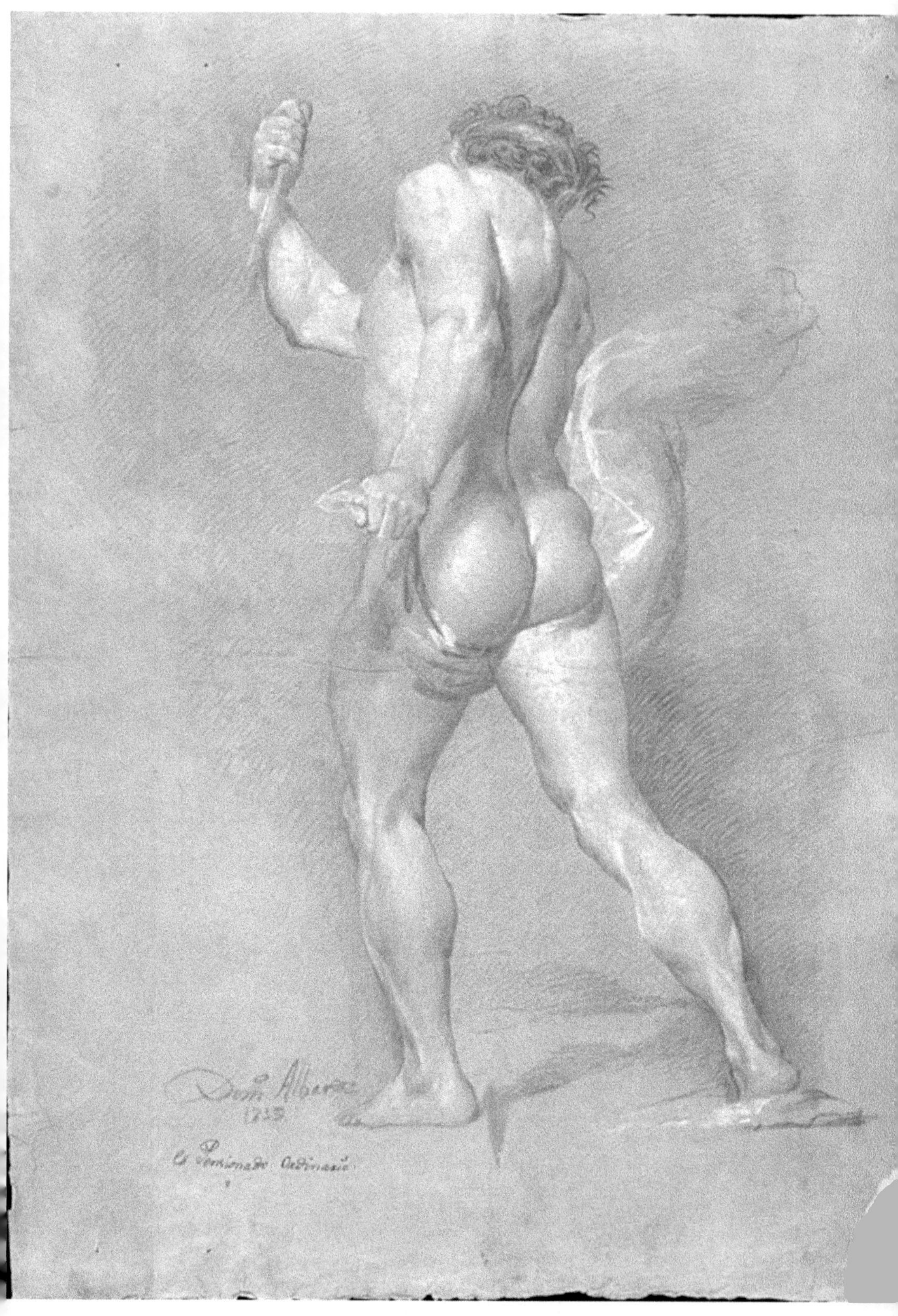

Domingo Alvarez Enciso, Male Nude, 1759

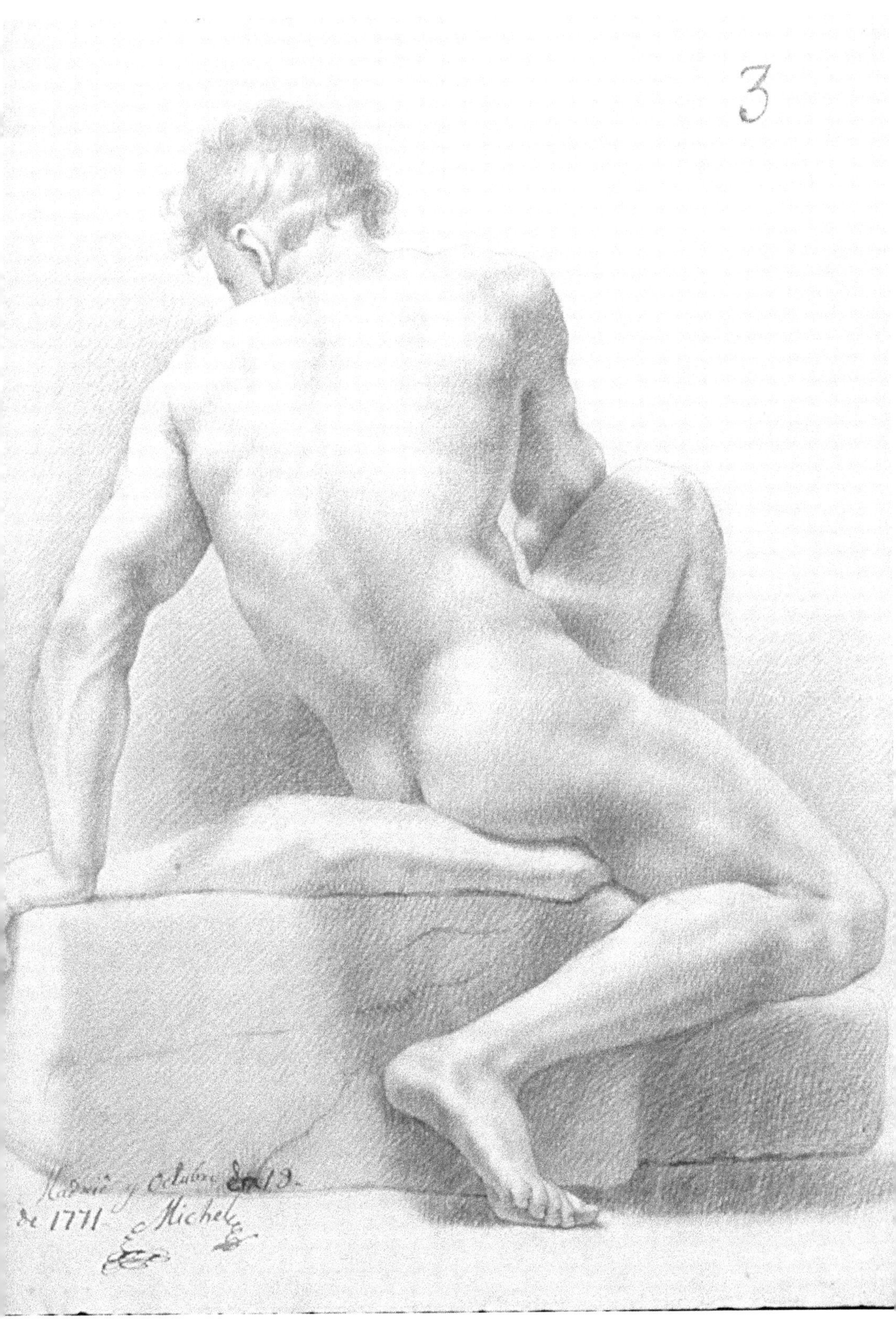

Pedro Pascual Munoz, Seated Male Nude, 1771

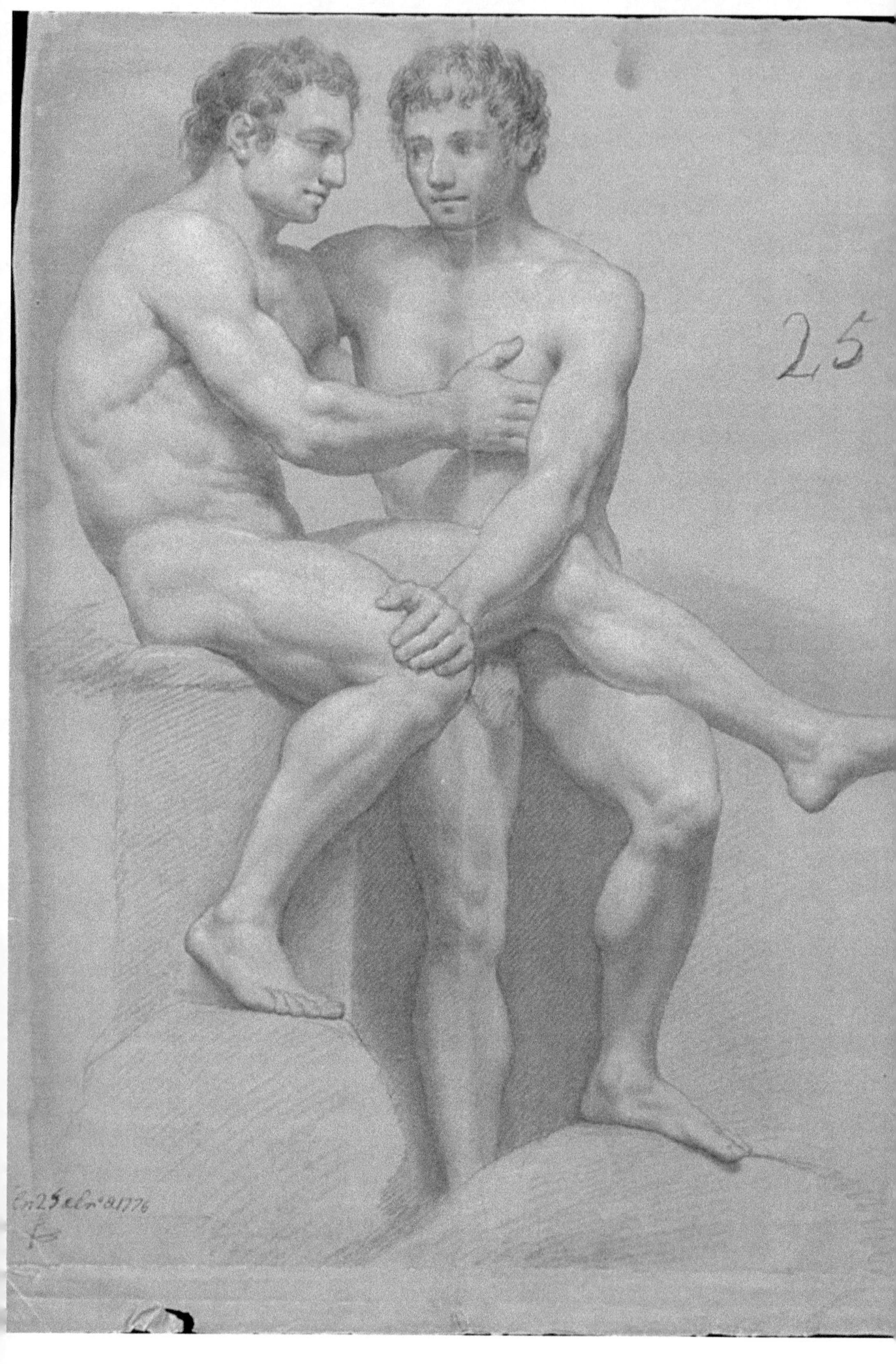

Gustin Esteve Marques, Two Male Nudes, 1776

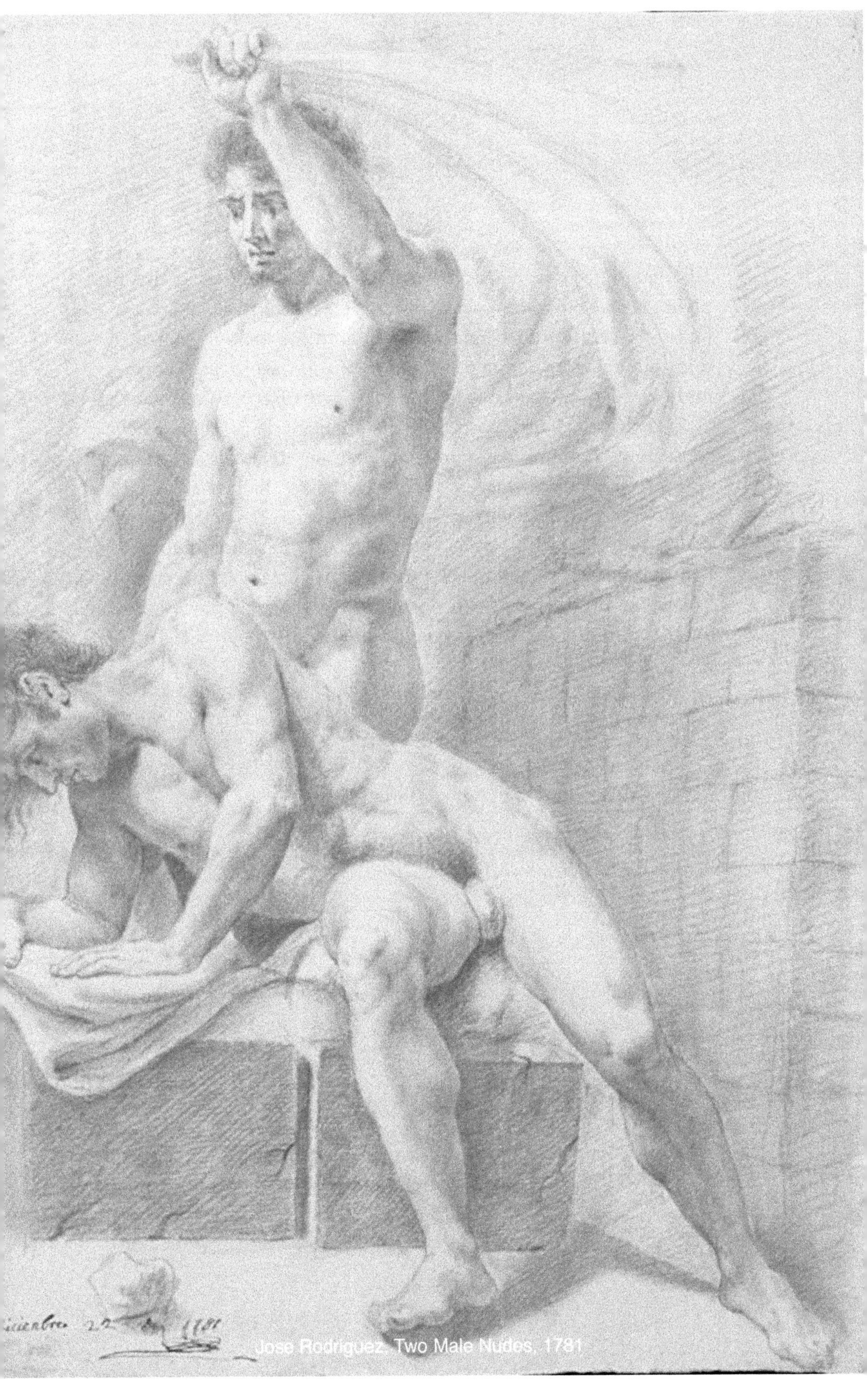

Jose Rodriguez. Two Male Nudes, 1781

MALE NUDES

The male nude can be appear uncomfortable. He doesn't like his photograph or painting or sculpture to be looked at like female nudes. He is used to being the one doing the looking. When the roles are reversed, ambiguity and confusion seeps in. The male nude is set up as spectacle, and as a passive object. To counter the awkwardness of this passivity, the male nude is shown *doing* something. Running, throwing a spear, fighting, etc. It tries to engage a position of activity, because to be the 'looked-at' one, the passive sex object, is very disquieting. Further, the activity of the male nude, which's seen everywhere - in photographs by Eadweard Muybridge,[1] in sculptures by Michelangelo Buonarroti, in movies, in gay porn - aims at portraying phallic power. 'Even in an apparently relaxed, supine pose,' Richard Dyer in 1983,

> the model tightens and tautens his body so that the muscles are emphasized, hence drawing attention to the body's potential for action. More often, the male pin-up is not supine anyhow, but standing taut ready for action.[2]

1 See L. Williams: "Film Body, an implantation of perversions", *Cinétracts*, vol. 3, no.4, Winter 1981, 19-25.

2 Richard Dyer: 'Don't Look Now", *Screen*, vol. 23, 3/ 4, 1983, 20, and in Angela McRobbie, 206

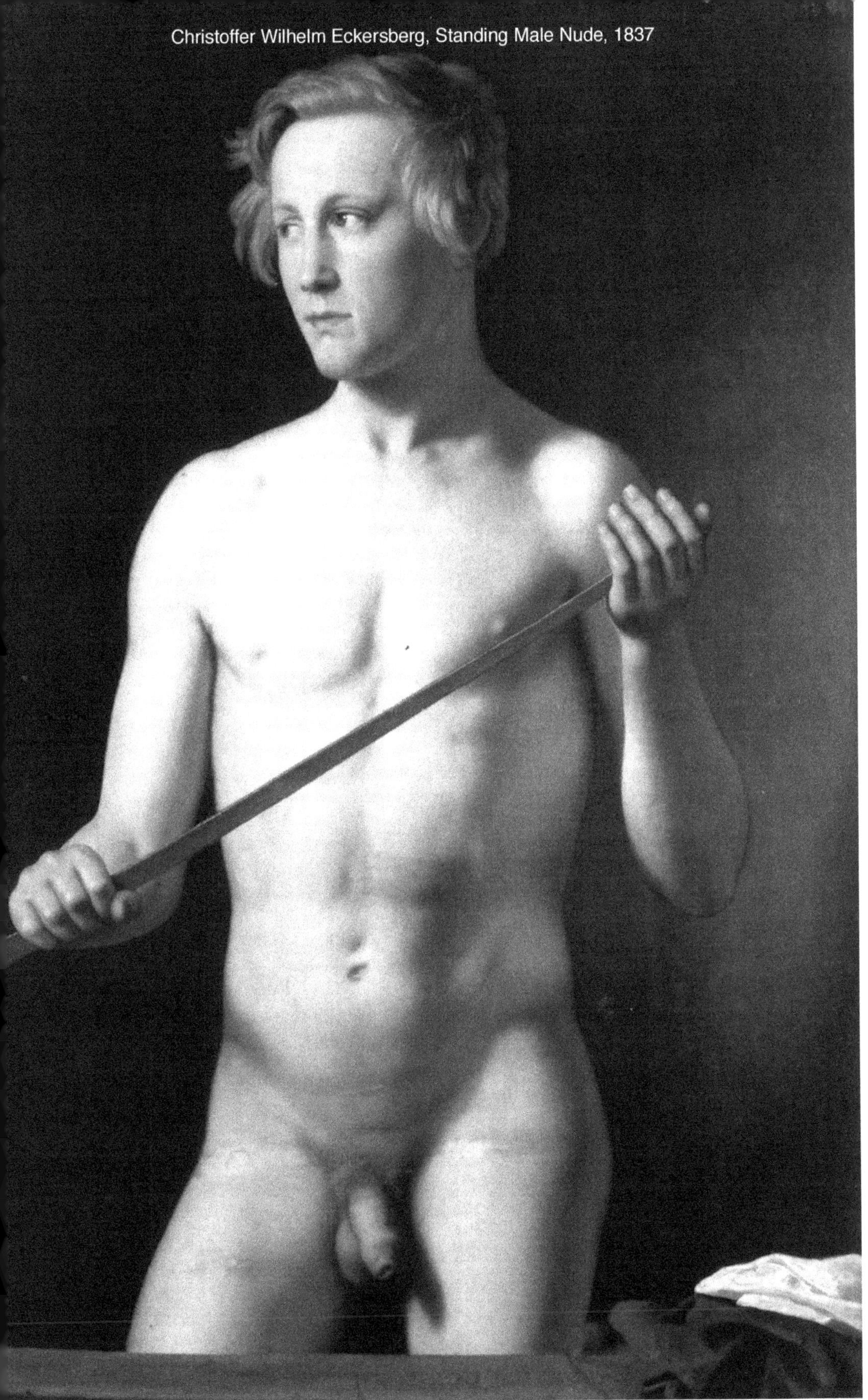

Christoffer Wilhelm Eckersberg, Standing Male Nude, 1837

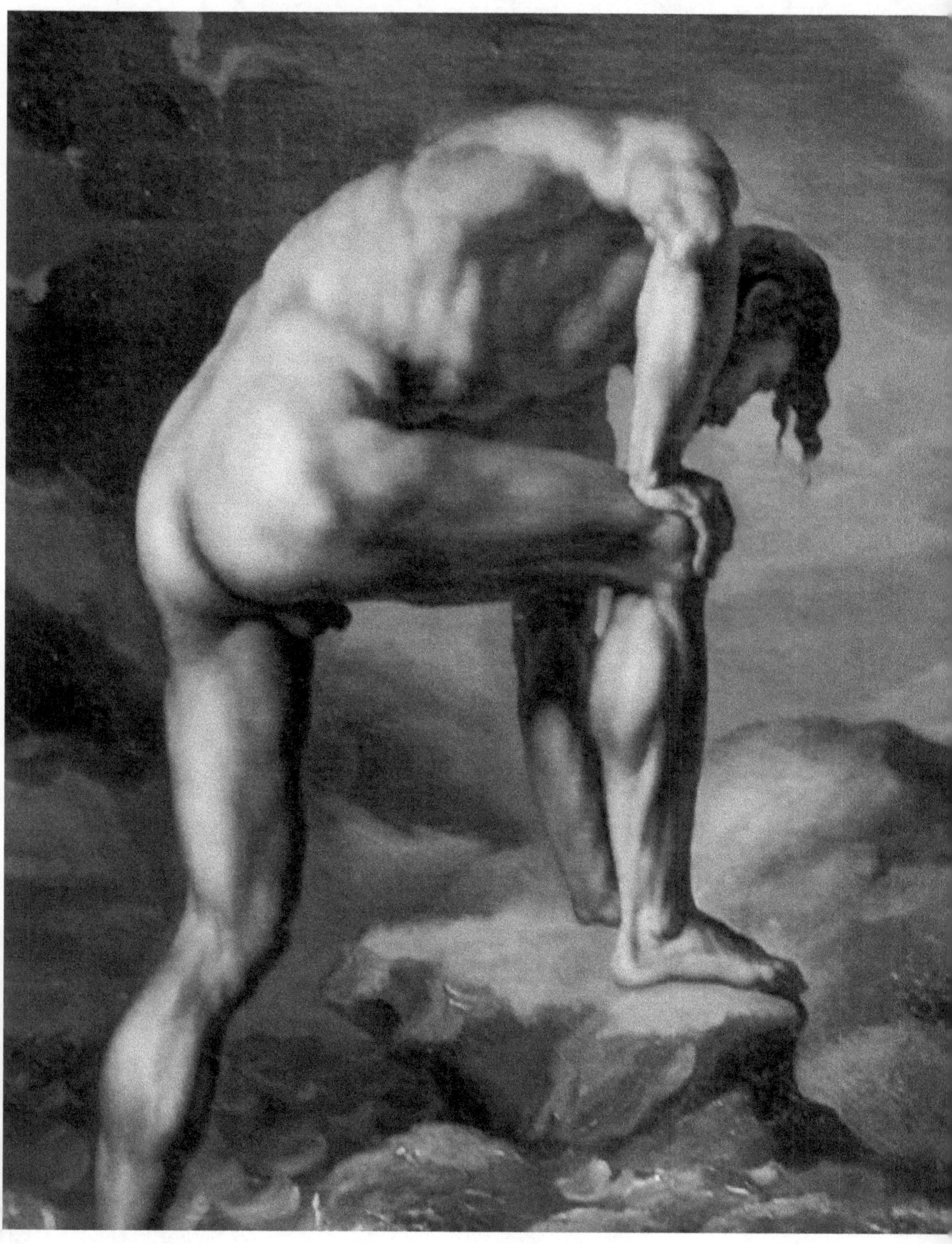

Jean-Louis Andre Theodore Géricault, A Shipwreck, c. 1819

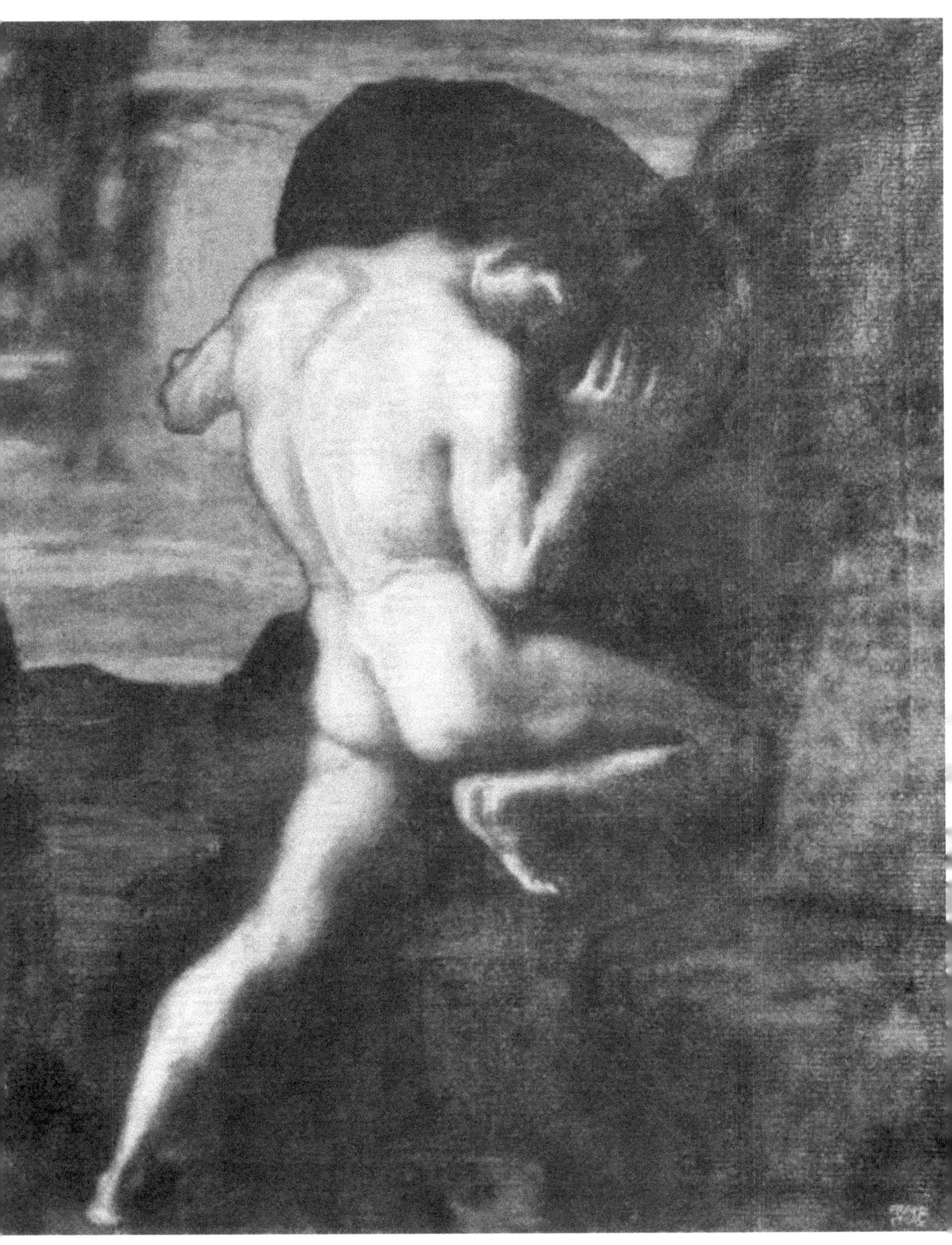

Franz von Stuck, Sisyphus

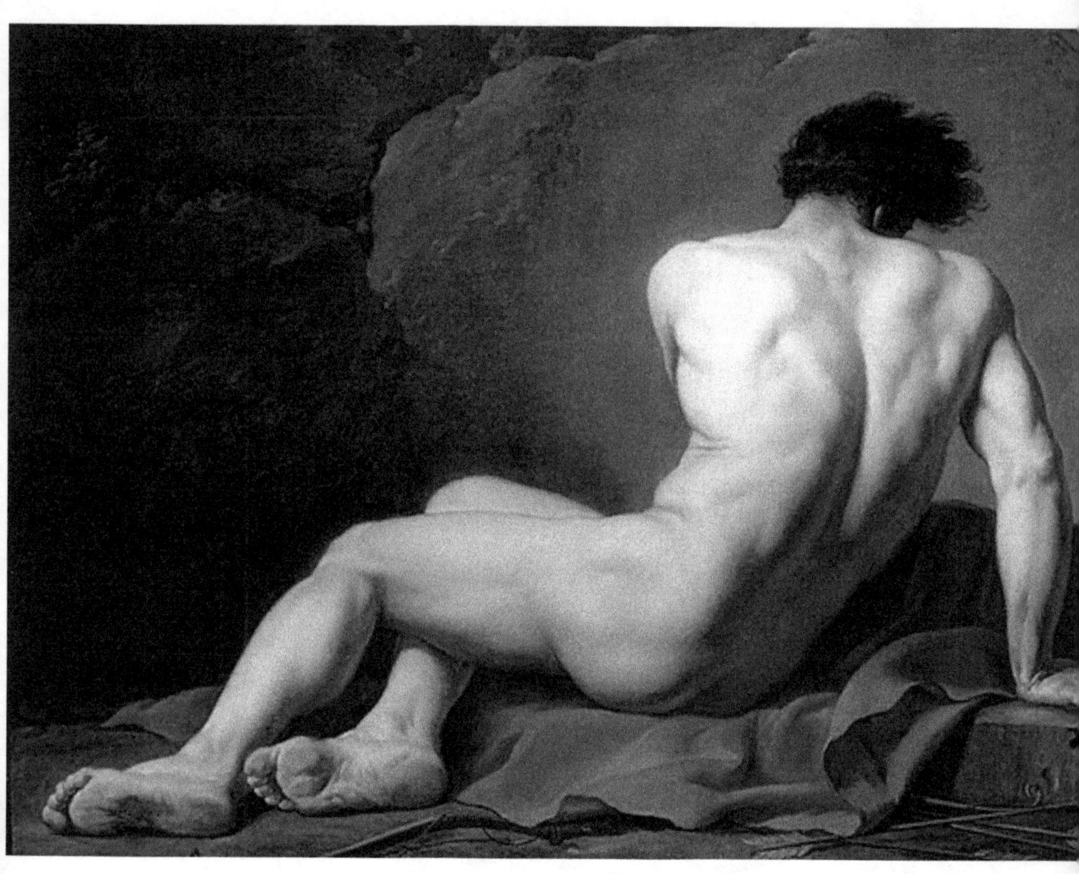

A classical French male nude painting
by Jacques-Louis David (known as Patrocles)

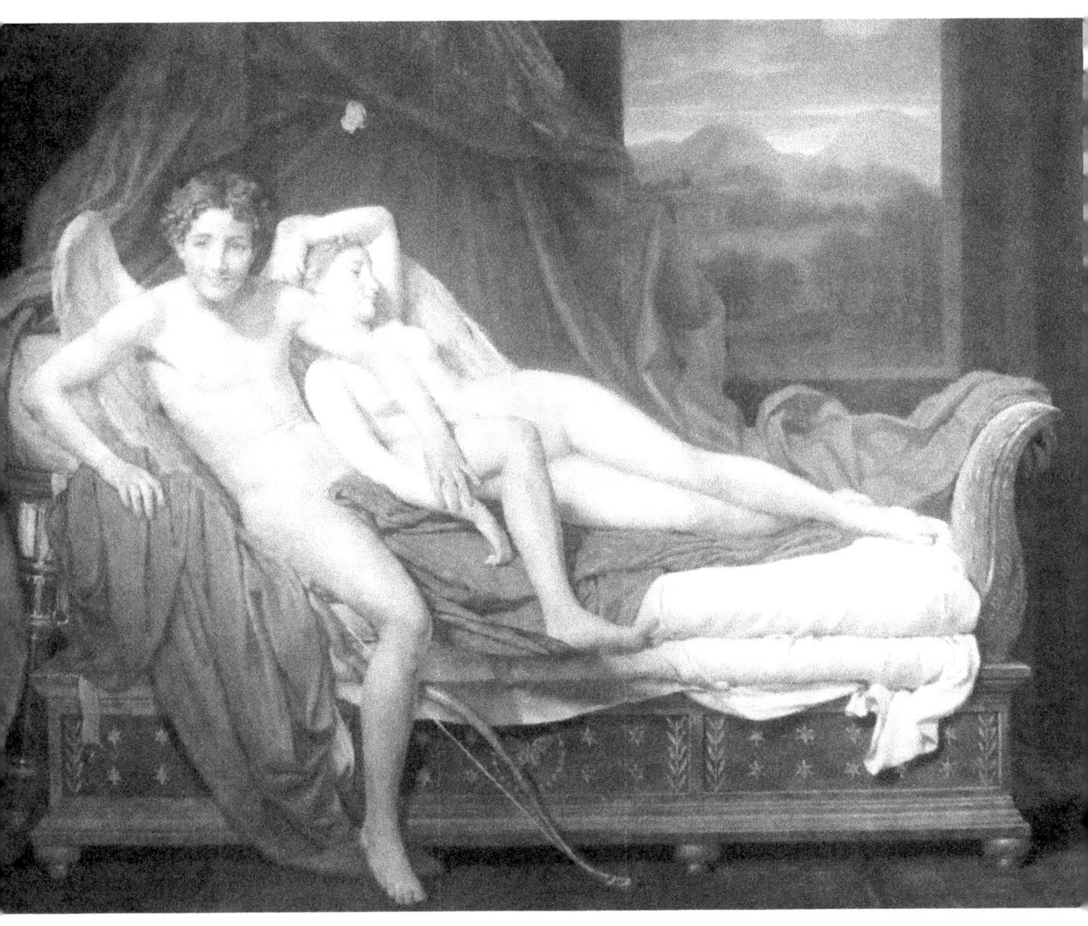

Jacques-Louis David, Cupid and Psyche, 1817,
Cleveland Museum of Art

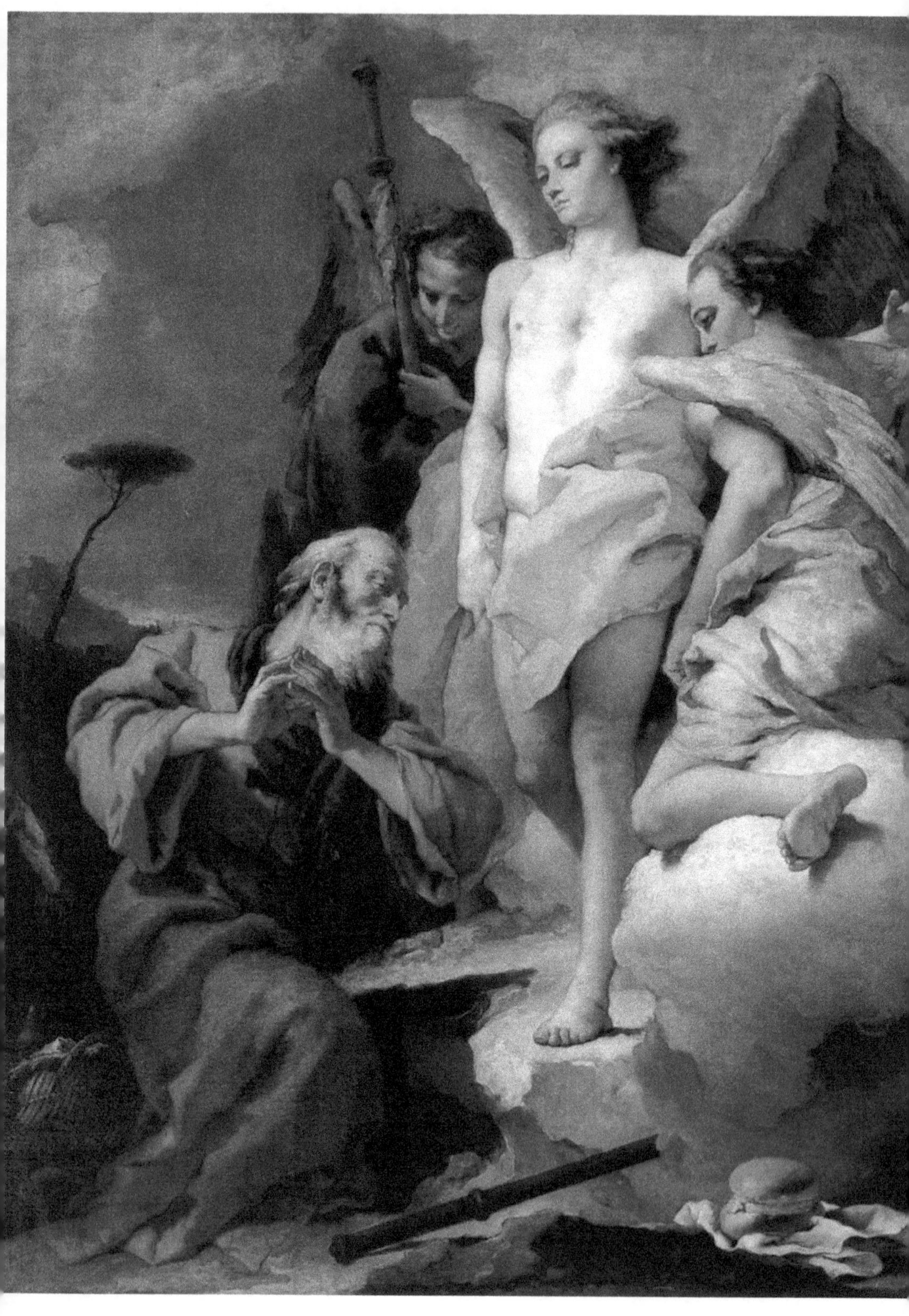

Giovanni Battista Tiepolo, Abraham and Three Angels, c. 1770

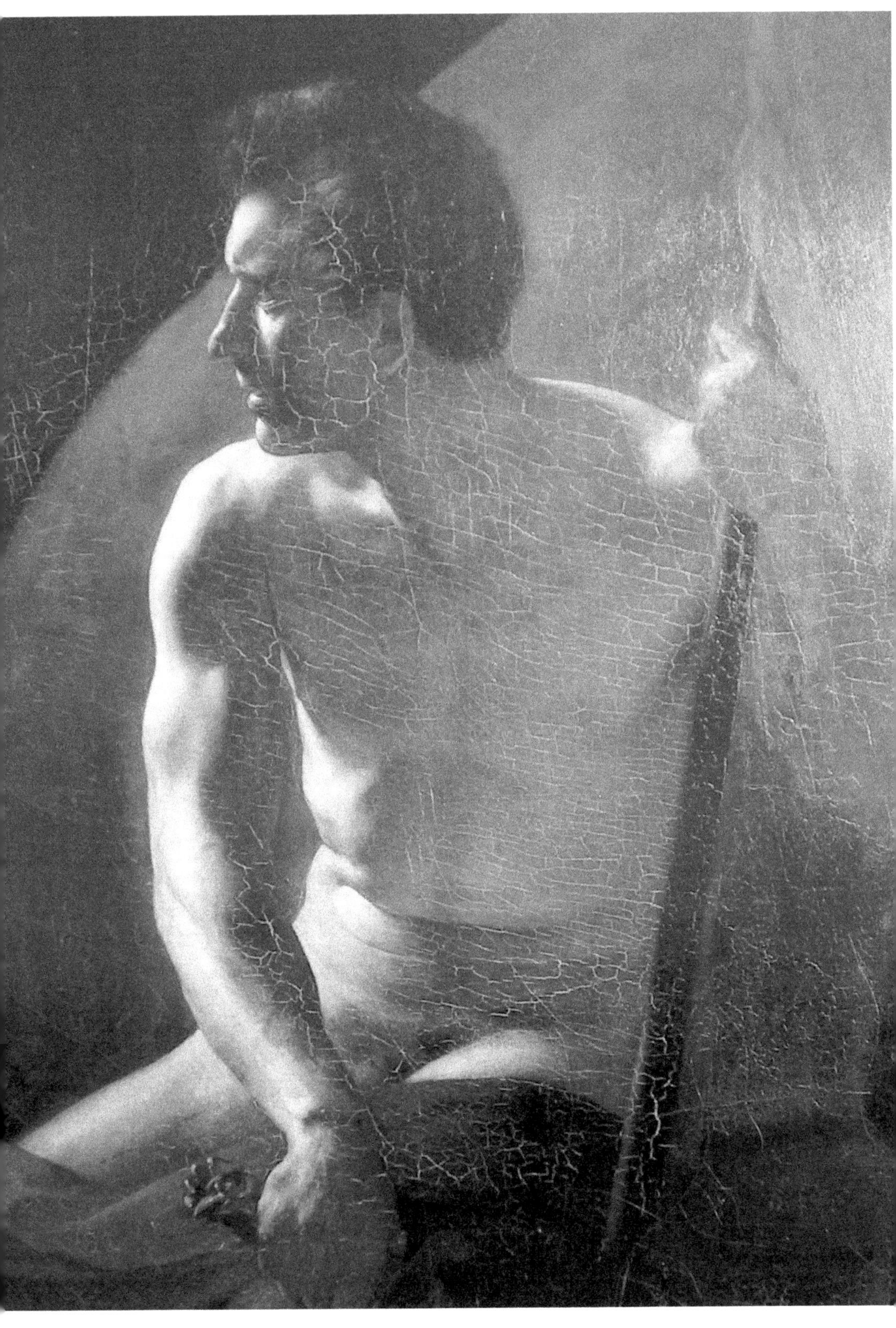

Hippolyte Dominique Holfeld, Half-Nude Figure, 1831

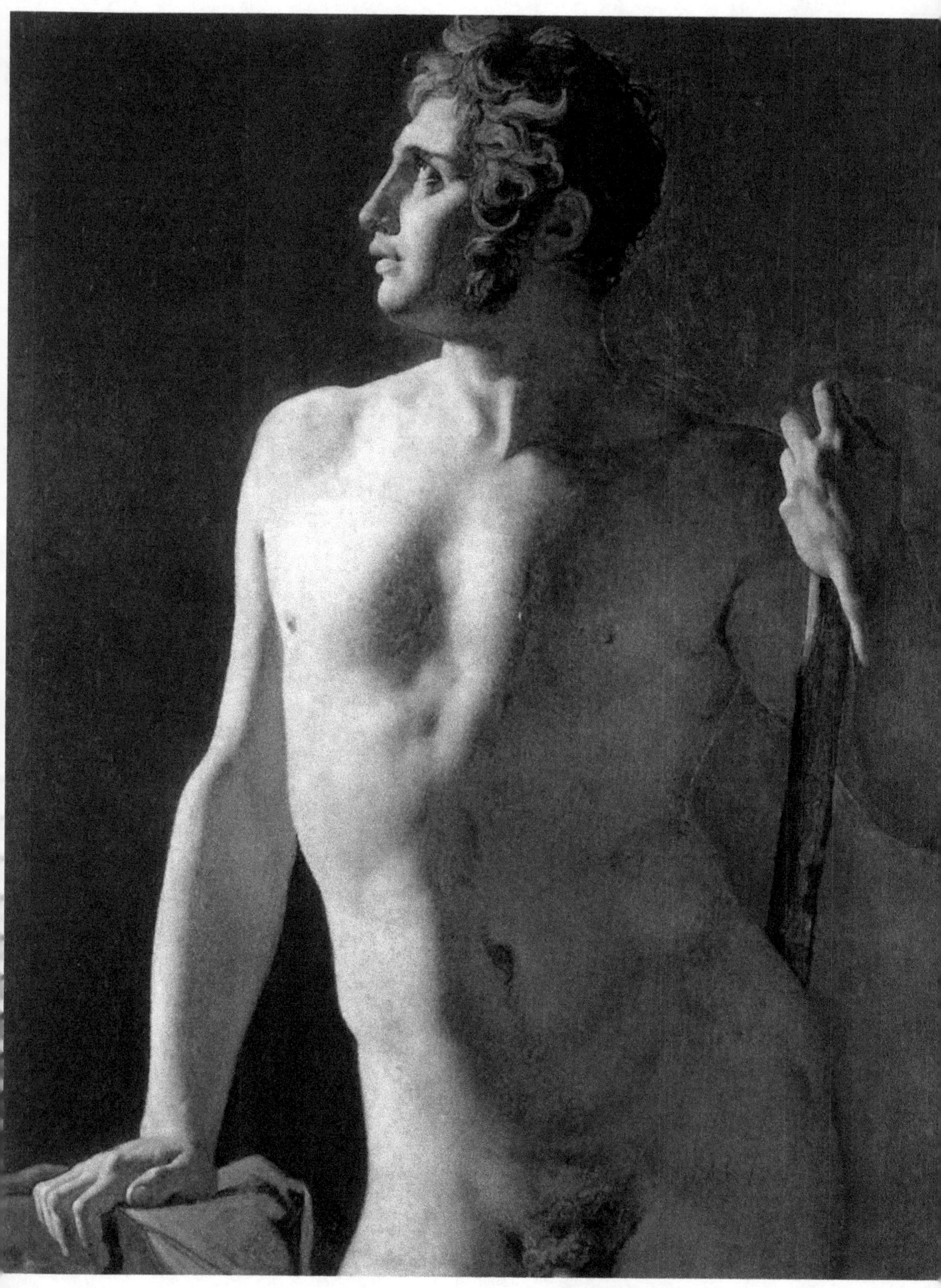

J.A.D. Ingres, Study of a Male Nude, 1801

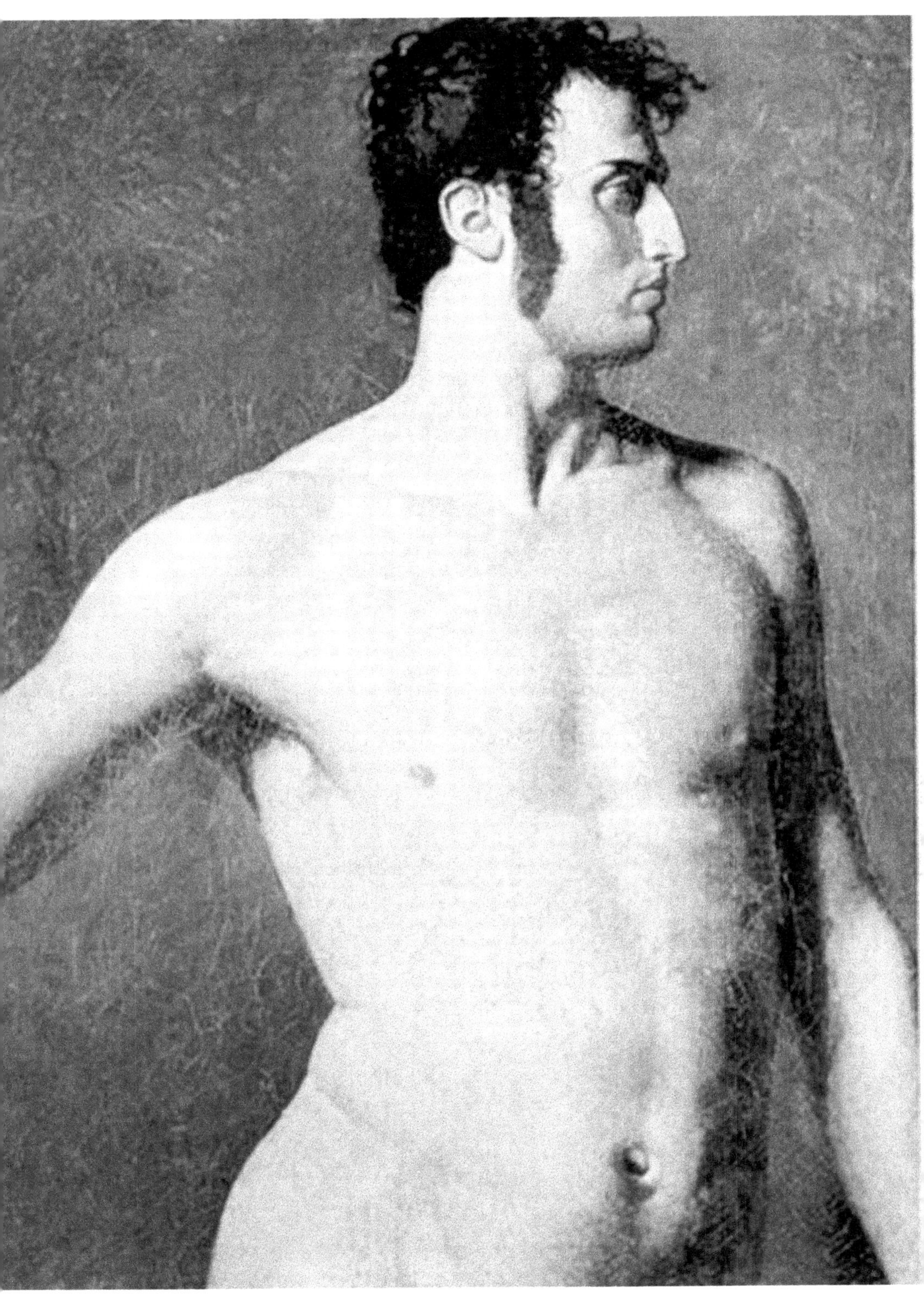

J.A.D. Ingres, Male Torso, 1801, Musée Ingres

MALE NUDES

The male nude image is subject to the same changes in culture as anything else: if you look at the nudes included here, you'll see the changes in fashion and style, at the superficial level, as well as the developments in the politics and society of the time, reflected in the nude images. Even though the body is nude, there are still numerous marks of culture upon it.

In the advanced capitalist, technological world, the body is not a 'natural' form any more, as Elizabeth Grosz explains in *Volatile Bodies*: clothing, exercise, jewellery, lifestyle, habits, negotiations of the cultural and social as well as the physical environment, and all sorts of activities alter it, inscribe it, turn it into something definitely not 'natural':

> Makeup, stilettos, bras, hair sprays, clothing, underclothing mark women's bodies, whether black or white, in ways in which hair styles, professional training, personal grooming, gait, posture, body building, and sports may mark men's. There is nothing natural or ahistorical about these modes of corporeal inscriptions. Through then, bodies are made amenable to the prevailing exigencies of power. They make the flesh into a particular type of body – pagan, primitive, medieval, capitalist, Italian, American, Australian. (142)

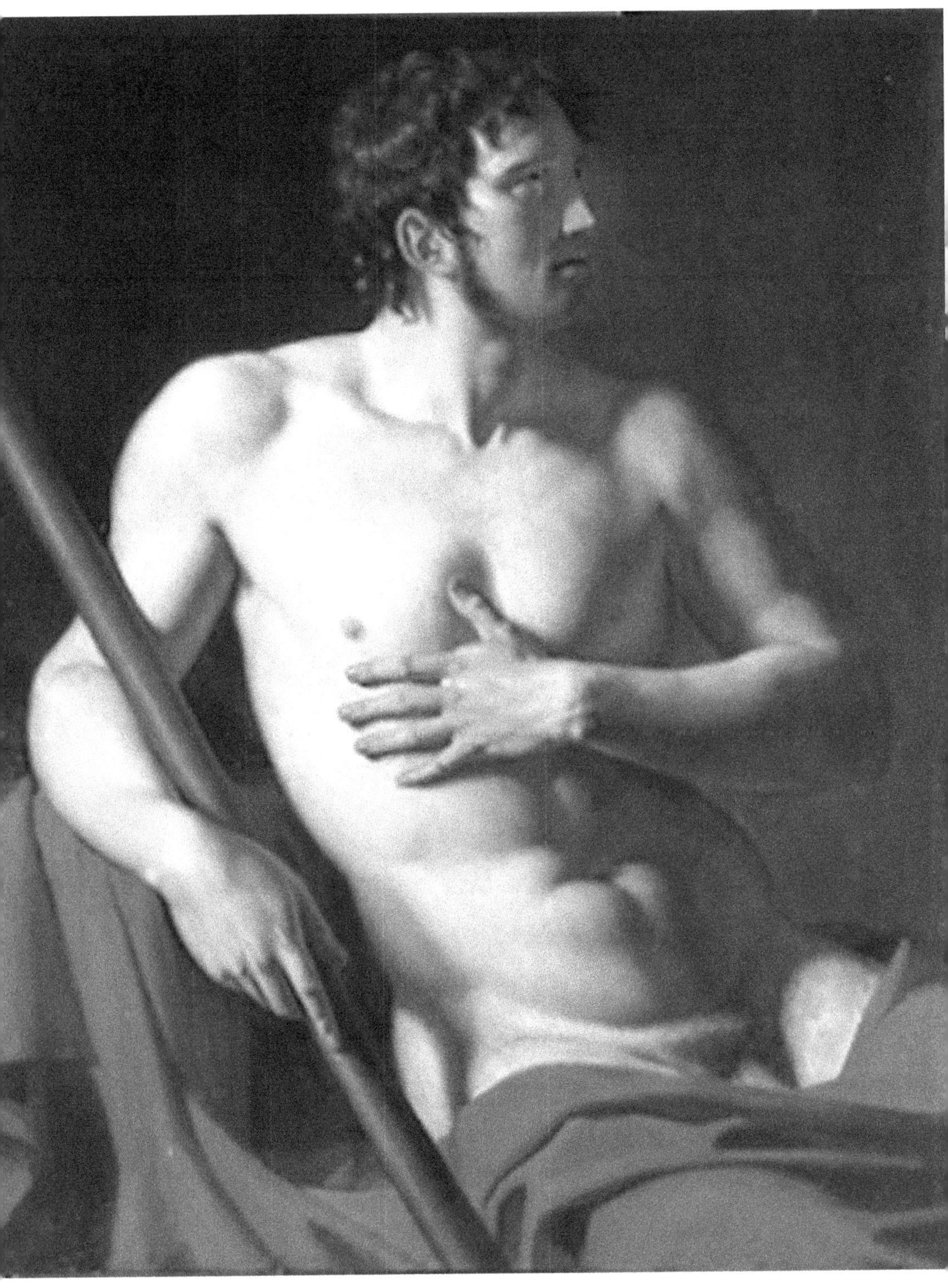

Auguste-Alphonse Gaudar de la Verdine, Male Nude, 1799

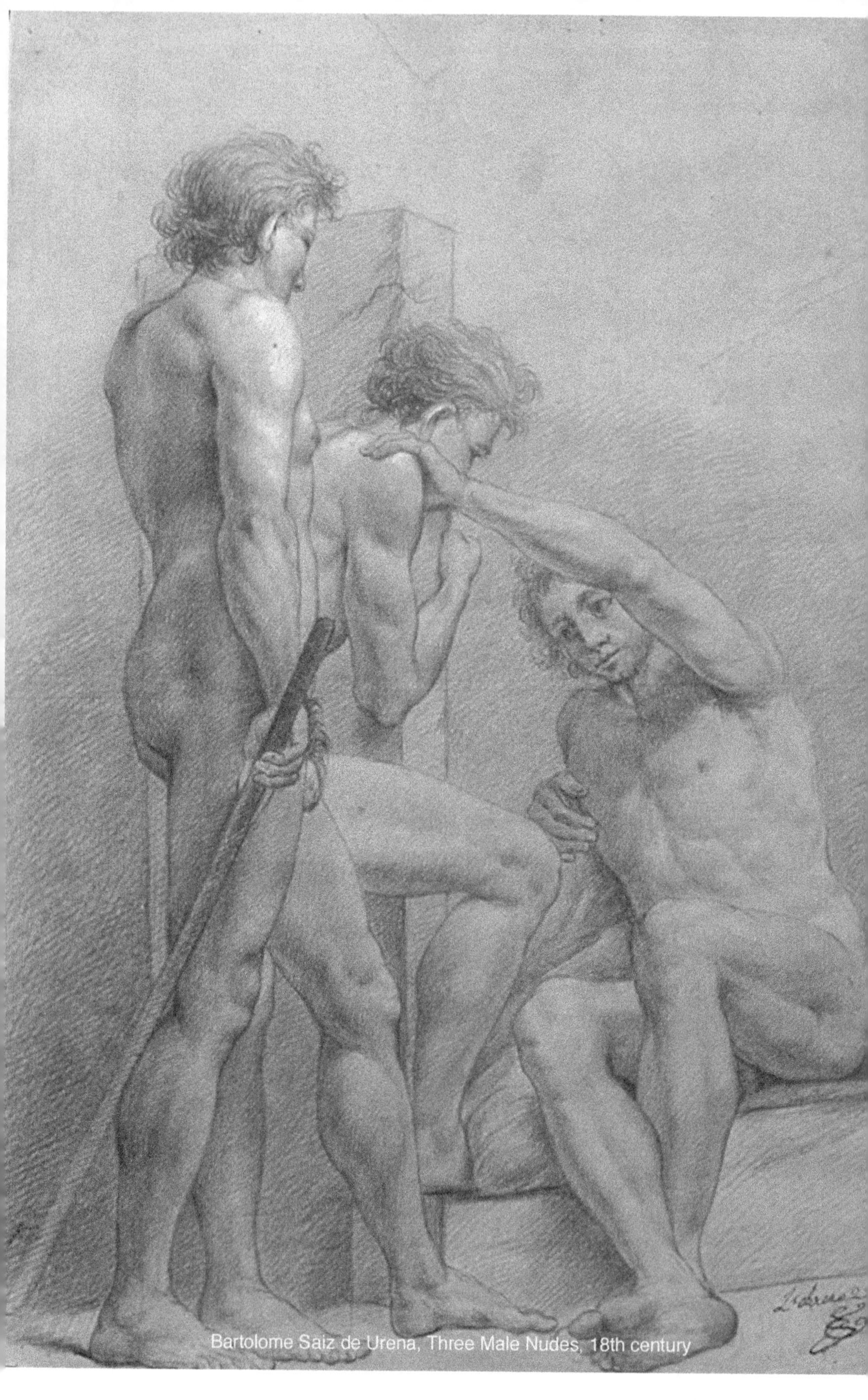

Bartolome Saiz de Urena, Three Male Nudes, 18th century

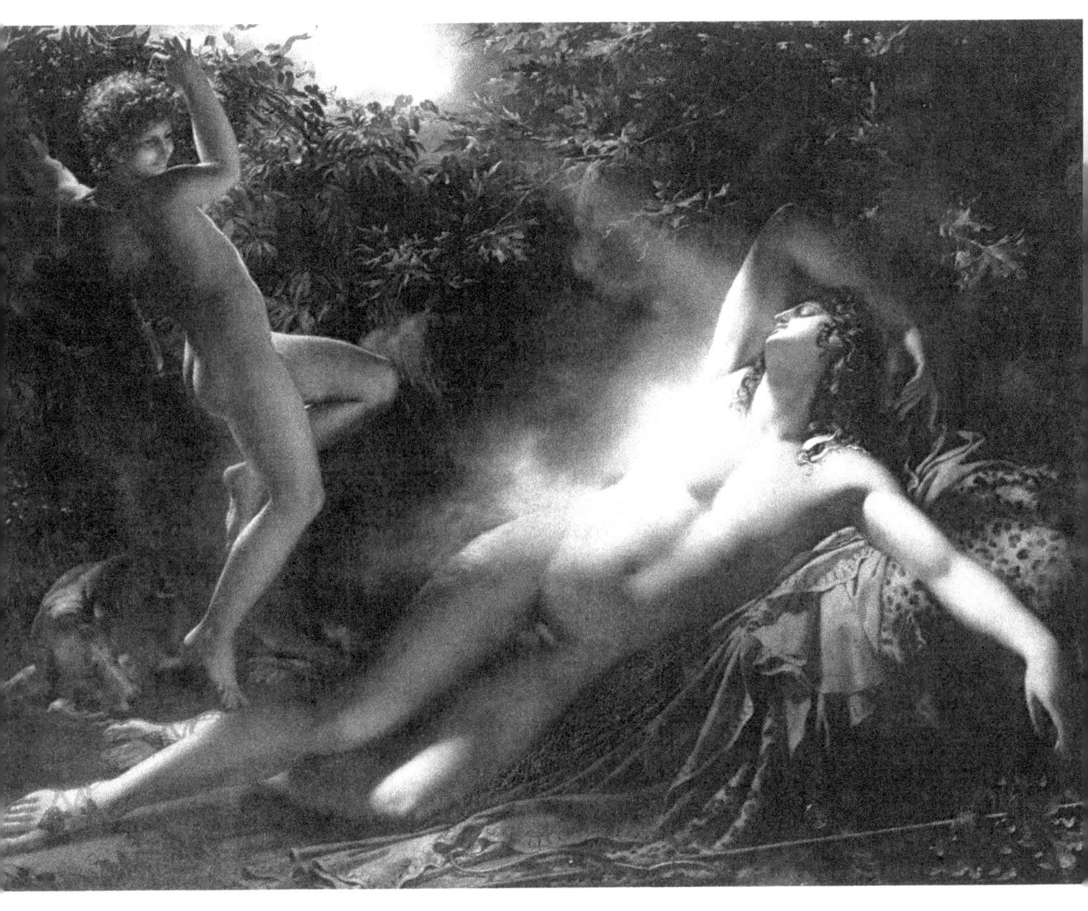

Anne-Louis Girodet-Trioson, Endymion, 1793

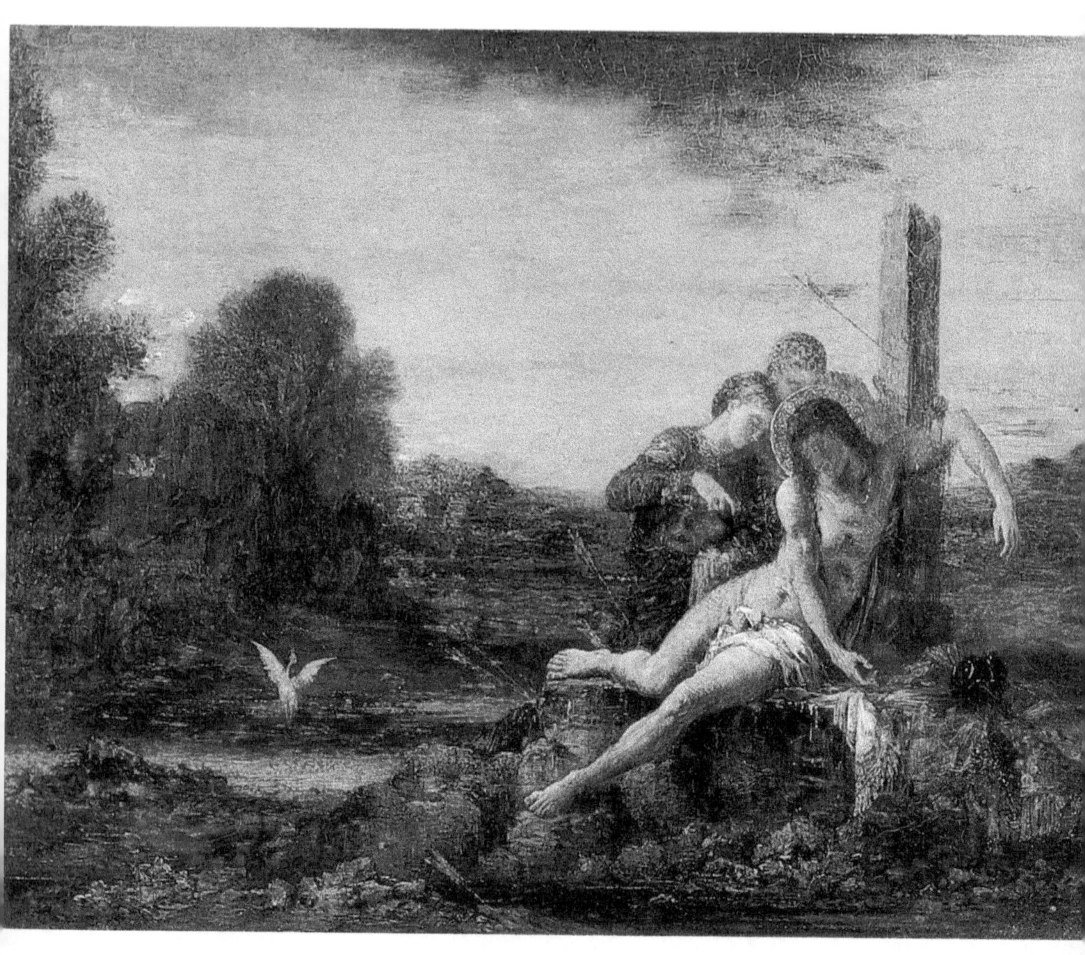

Gustave Moreau, St Sebastian, 1869

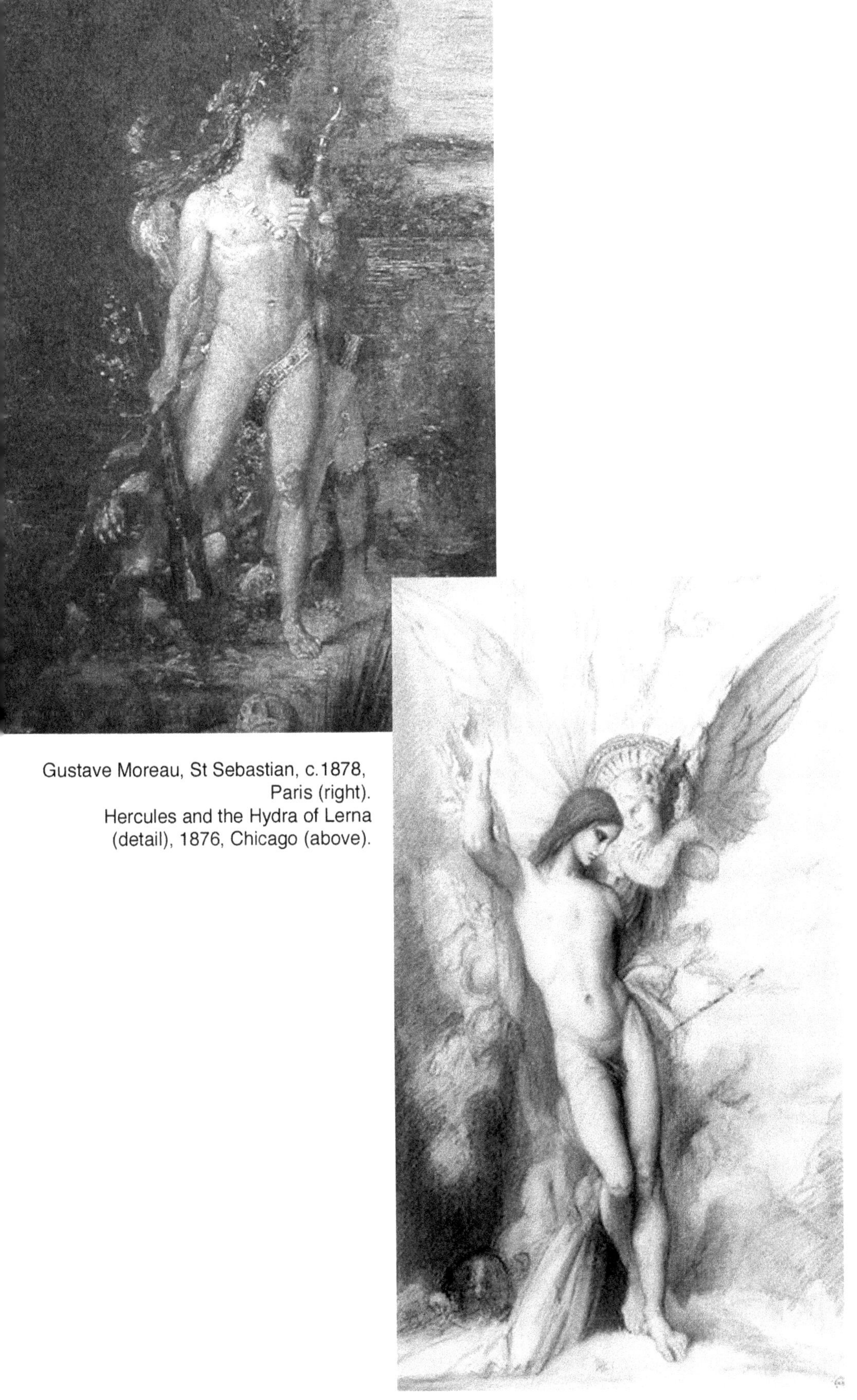

Gustave Moreau, St Sebastian, c.1878, Paris (right).
Hercules and the Hydra of Lerna (detail), 1876, Chicago (above).

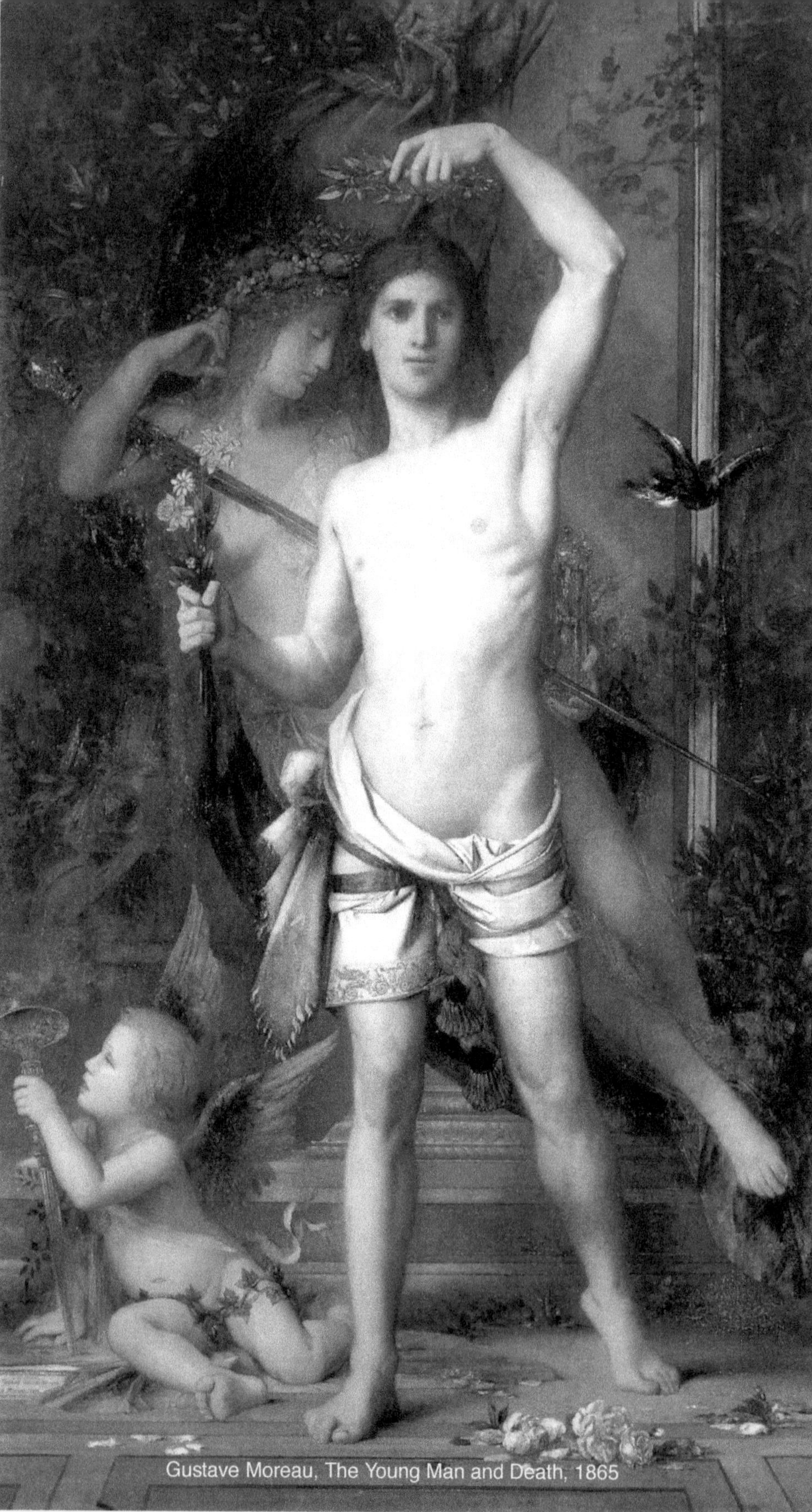
Gustave Moreau, The Young Man and Death, 1865

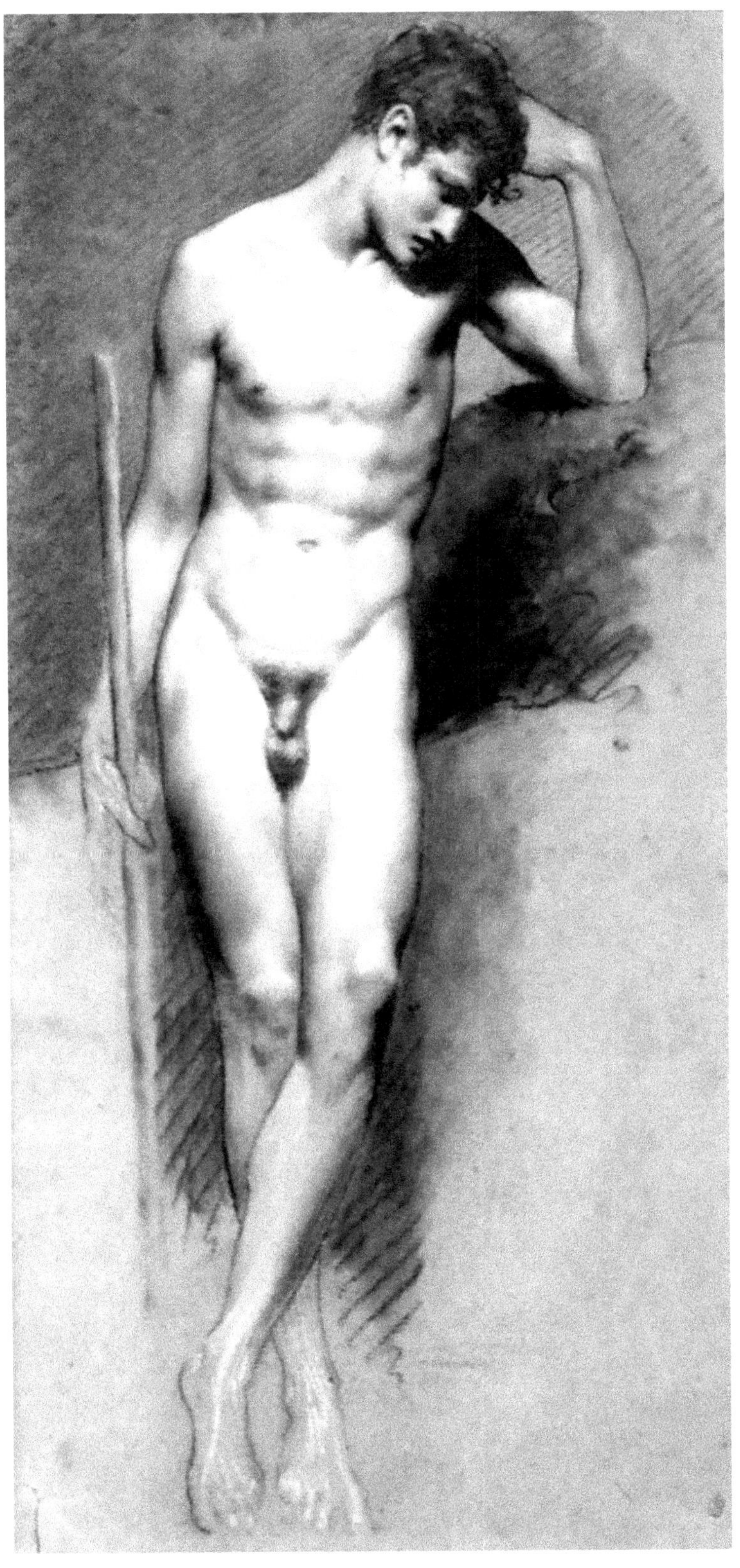

Pierre-Paul Prud'hon (1758-1823), Male Nude Standing

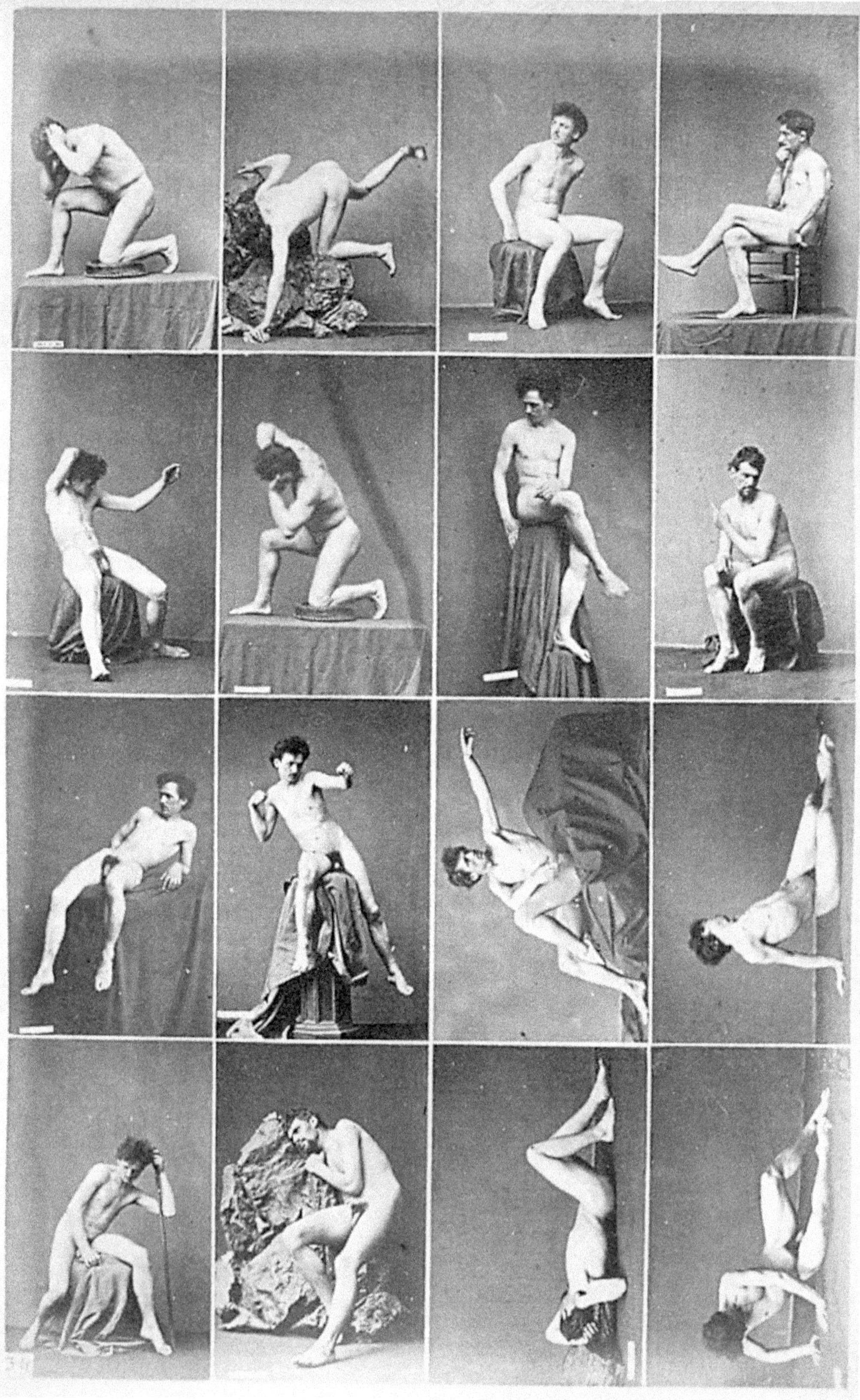

Ignout, Male Nude Studies, 1875

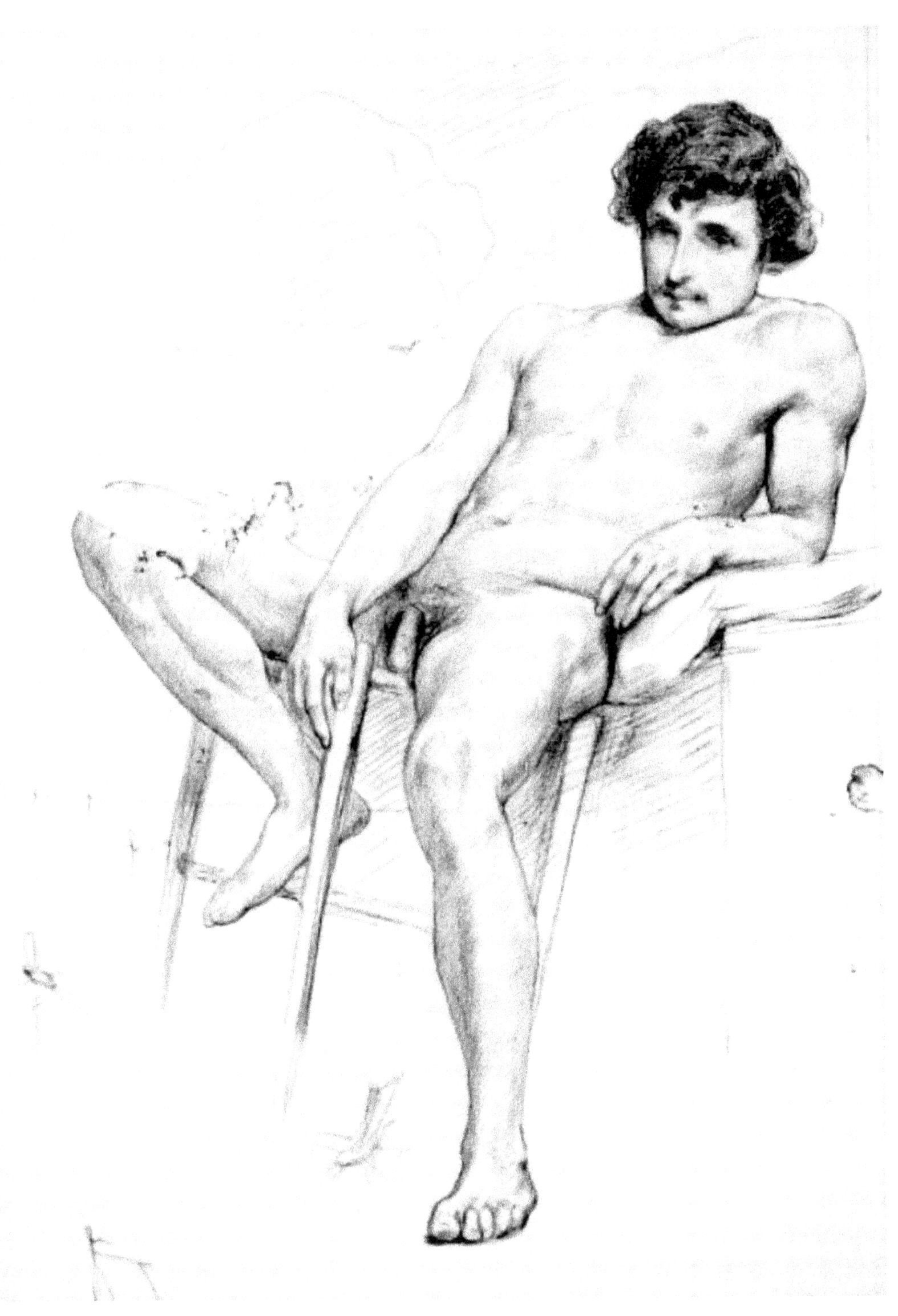

Lord Leighton, life drawing

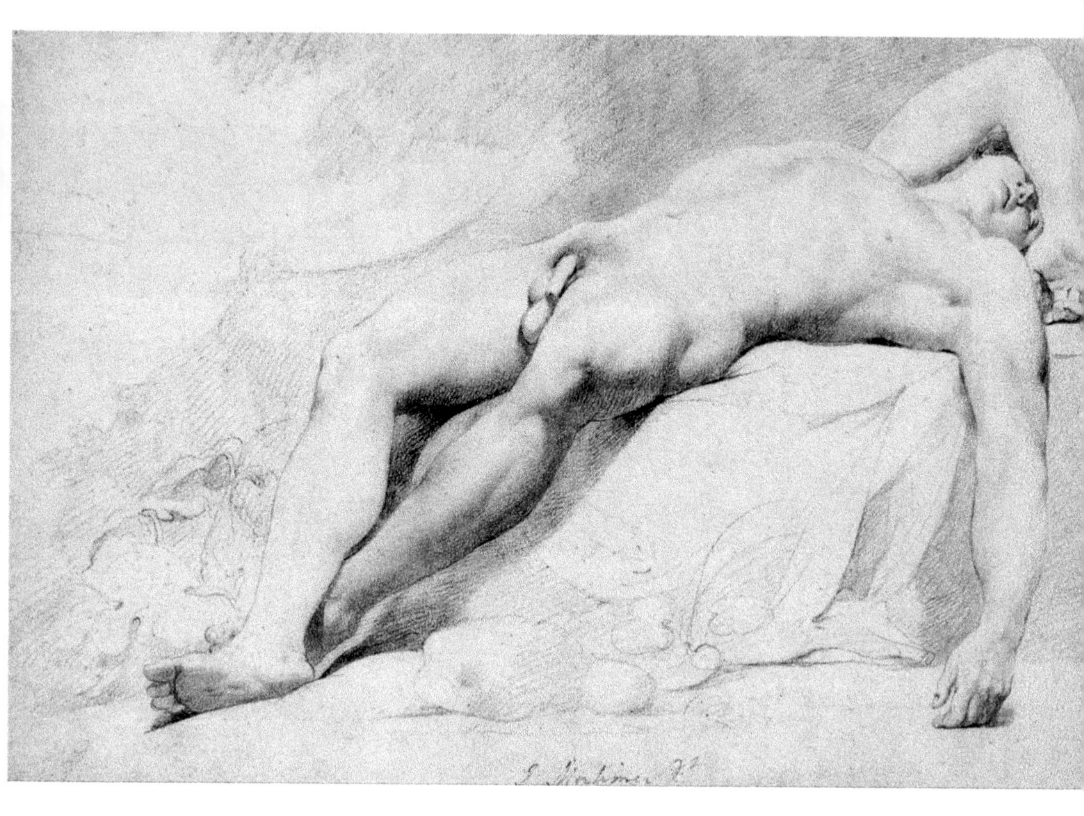

John Hamilton Mortimer, Recumbent Male Nude, c. 1773

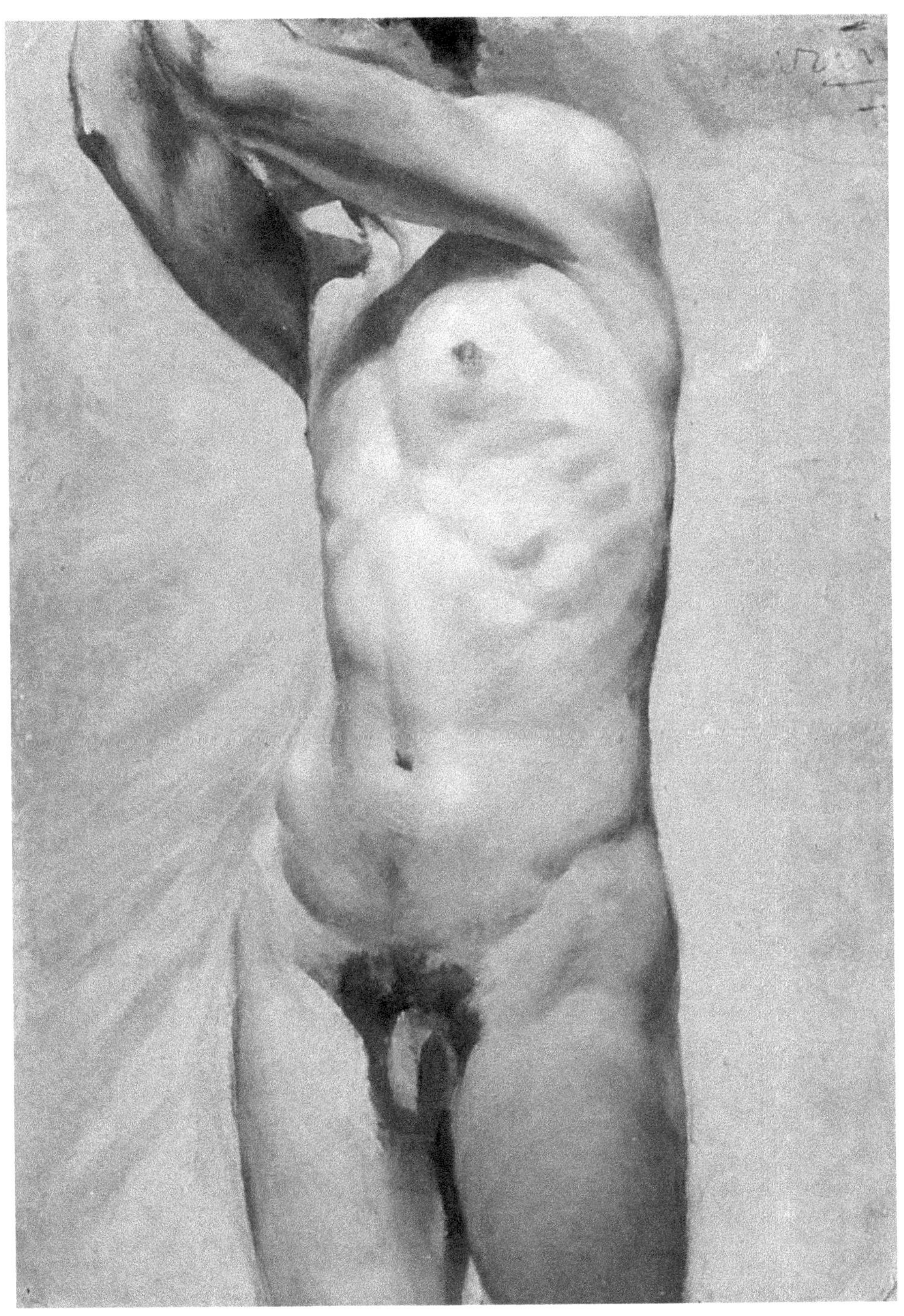

French school, c. 1890

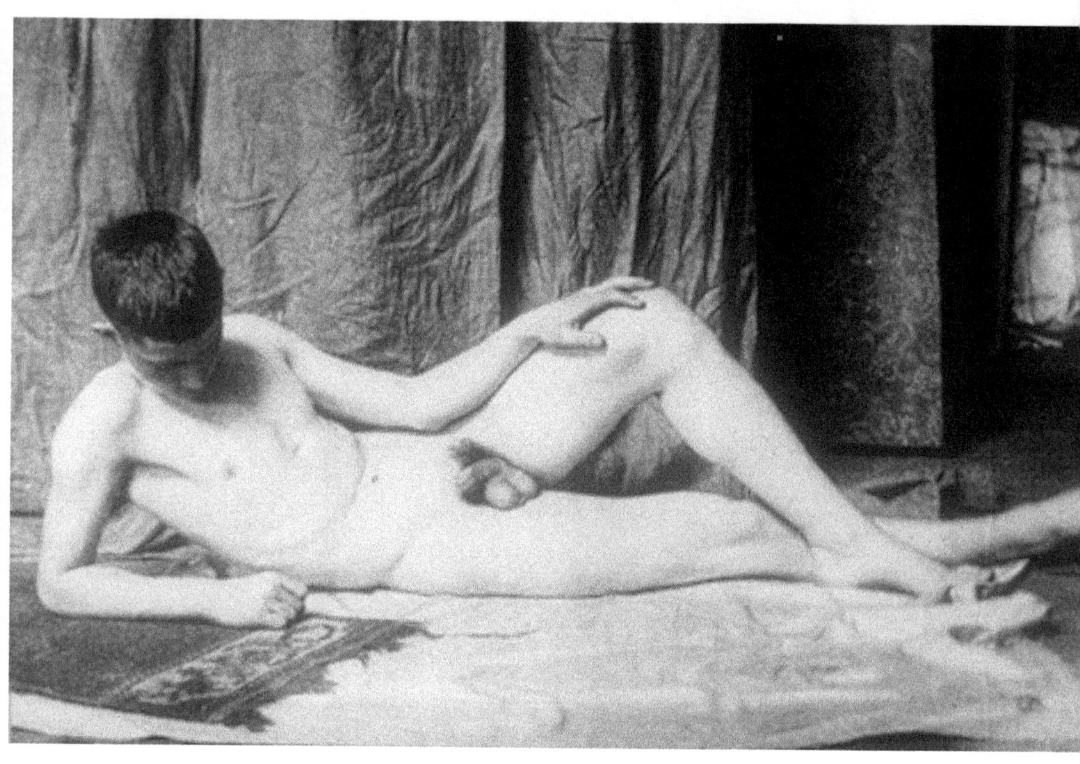

Reclining Male Nude, 1887–92,
Thomas Eakins, platinum print

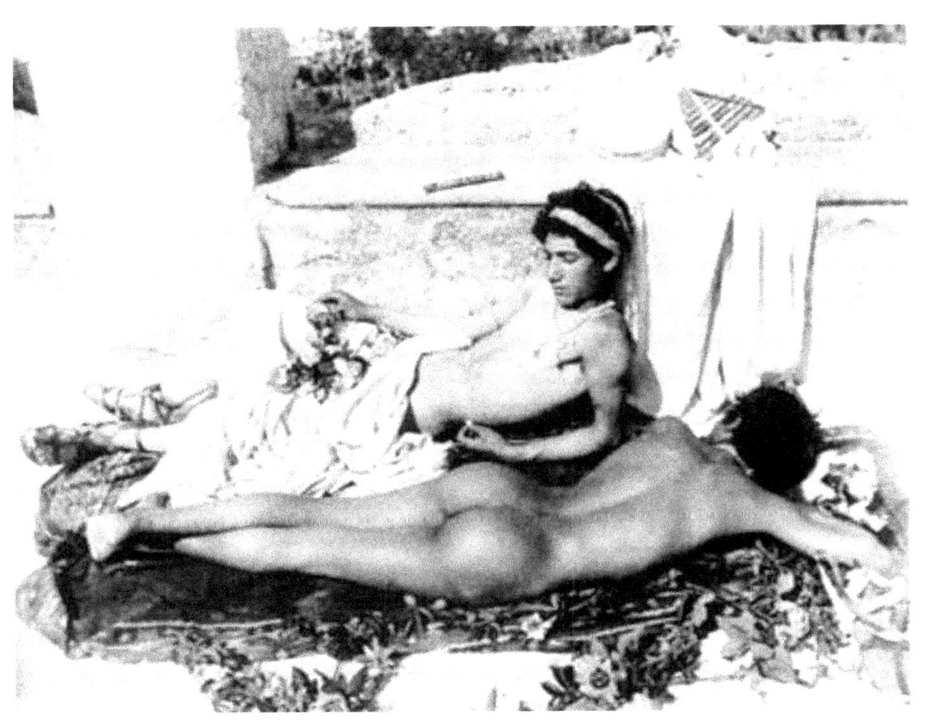

Wilhelm von Gloeden, c. 1900

PORNOGRAPHY

There are many different kinds of pornography, as there are many different kinds of art or feminism. Seen through cultural or postmodern or deconstructionist or semiological theory, pornography can be viewed as a realm of codes, meanings, contexts, signifiers, values, experiences and attitudes, which are politically controlled, manufactured by social, economic and political needs and demands. Pornography is thus the *representation* of... something; maybe certain kinds of sexuality, maybe somebody's thoughts on certain kinds of sexuality. Pornography is not *sexuality in itself,* it is mediation, representation, communication, a relic, a trace.

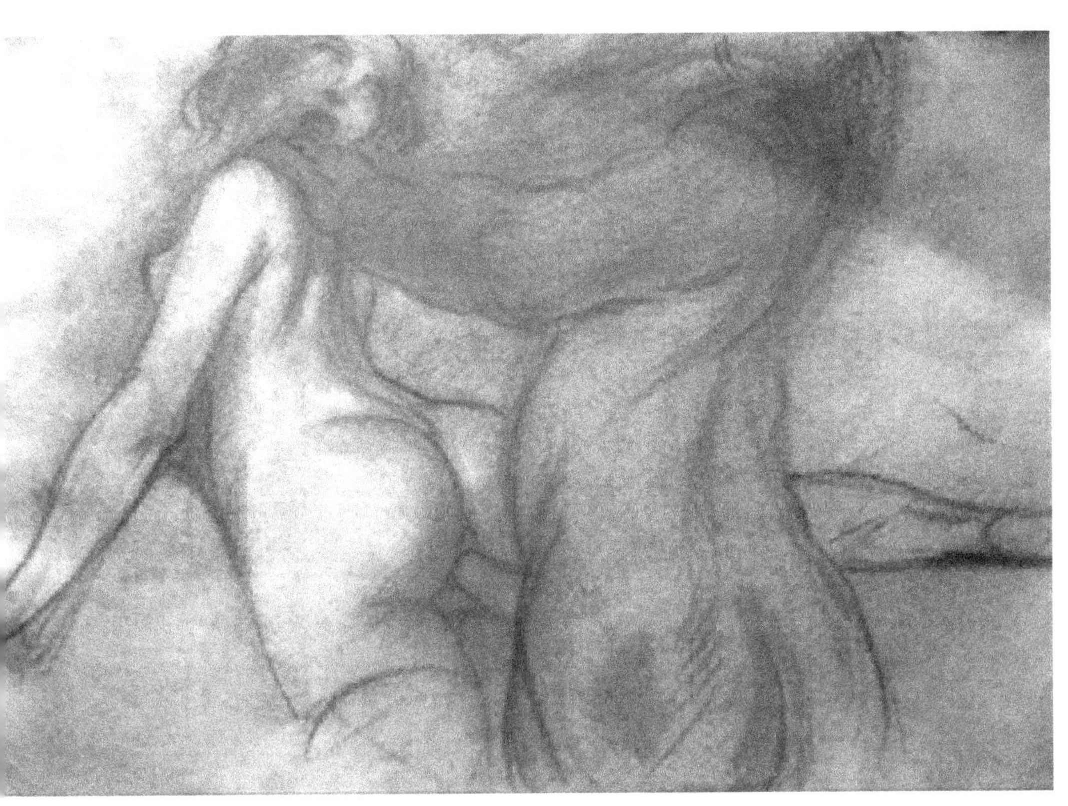

Aroldo Bonzagni

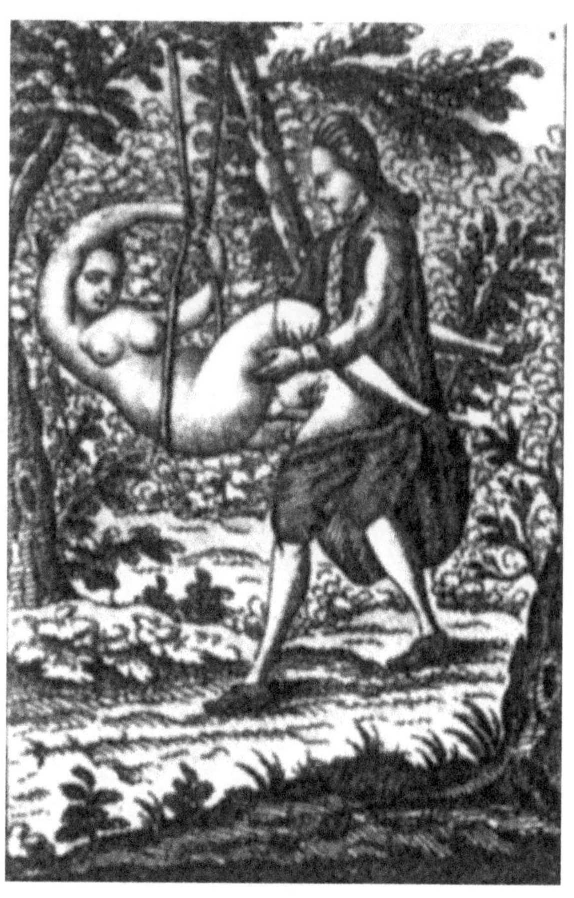

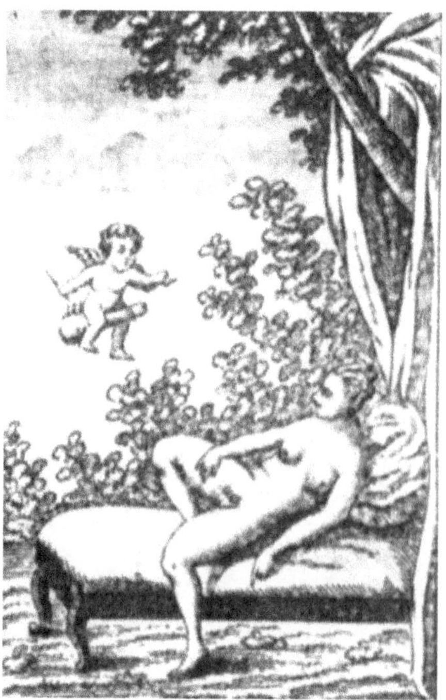

Anonymous,
Memoires du Suzon

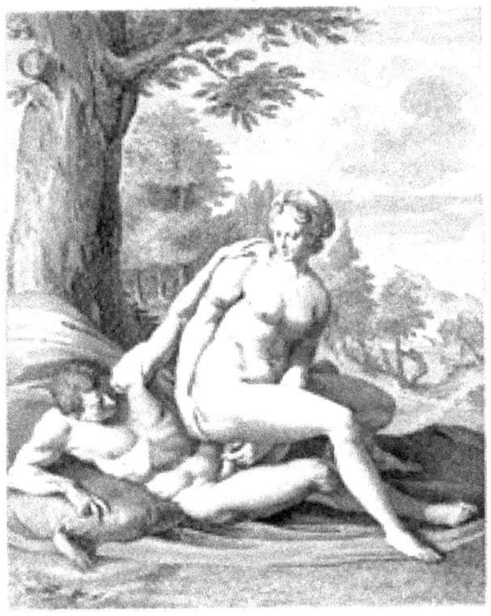

ANGELIQUE ET MEDOR

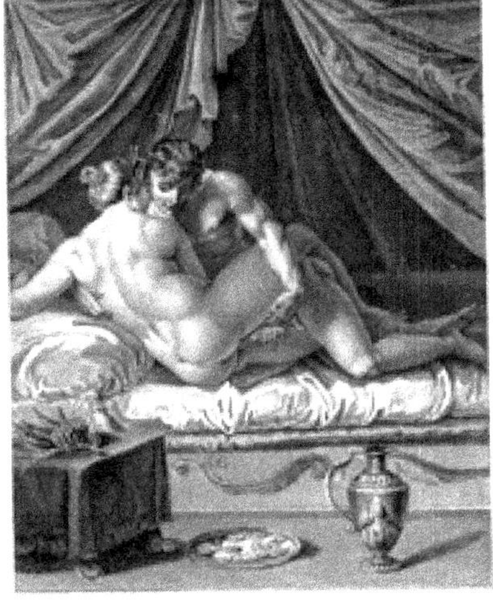

ANTOINE ET CLEOPATRE

Jacques Joseph Coiny, after Agostino Caracci,
I Modi, 1524, and Pietro Aretino

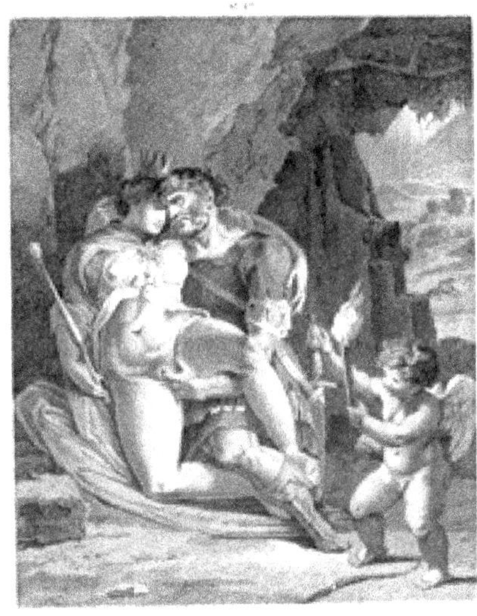

ENEE ET DIDON

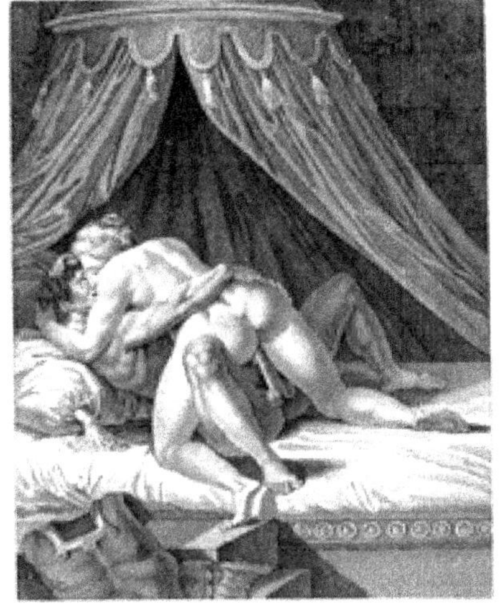

MARS ET VENUS

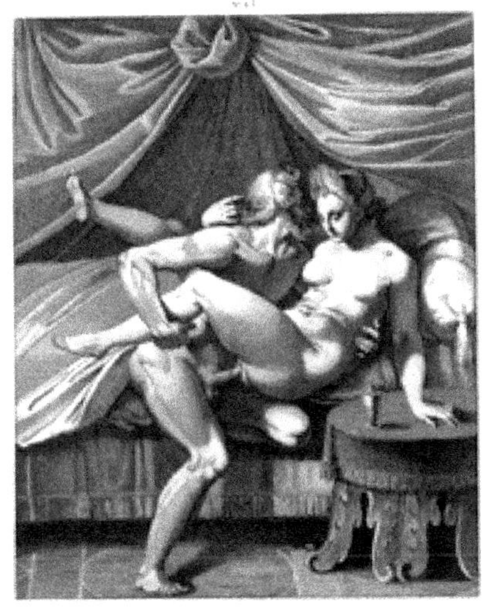

JUPITER ET JUNON

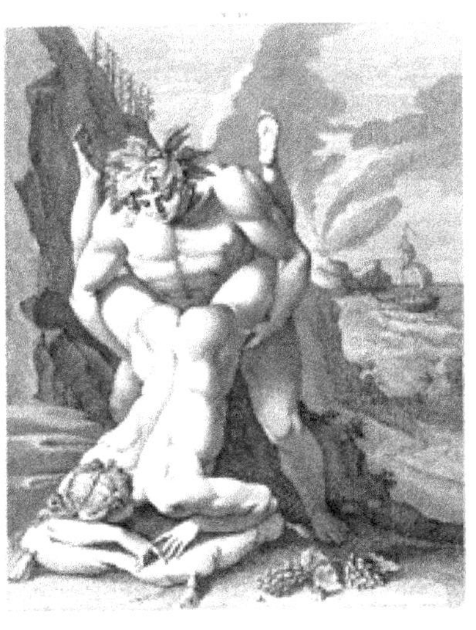

BACHUS ET ARIANE

Pornography has its own 'genres' of sub-categories: there is S/M, hardcore, lesbian, gay porn, soft core, and pornography geared to any number of fetishes; rubber, leather, boots, large breasts, bondage, etc.[1] What's your fetish? Porn will have something for you!

The history of art too has its categories and forms of erotic art, with the reclining (female) nude as perhaps the most well-known, and the most celebrated in art criticism. Other forms include humans and deities, humans and animals (often gods in beast-form), sexual positions, religious subjects, mythological subjects, Venus and Cupid, etc.

1 These sub-genres are institutions in themselves, with their own codes and structures, but their institutionalized sexual images do not express the real eroticism that people experience (they suggest it, perhaps, or reflect parts of it).

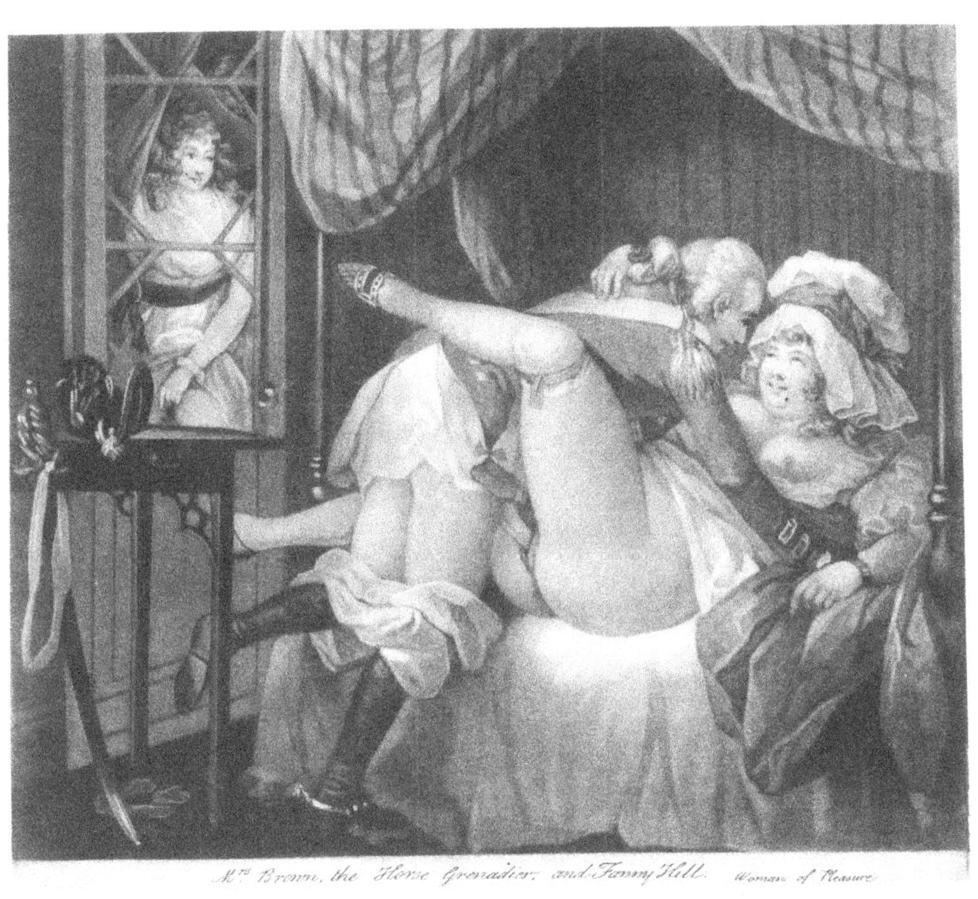

Mrs Brown, the Horse Grenadier, and Fanny Hill, 1750-1800.

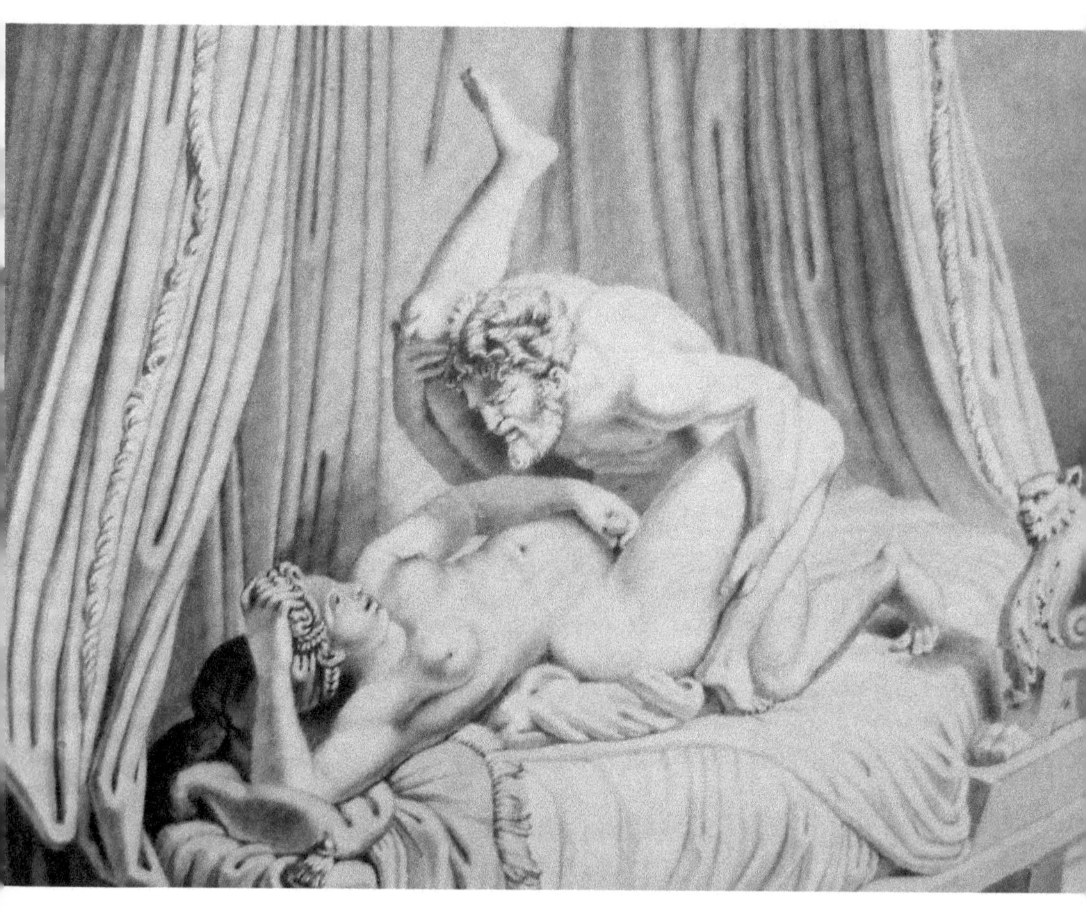

Friedrich von Waldeck, from Postures, c. 1858
(This page and following pages)

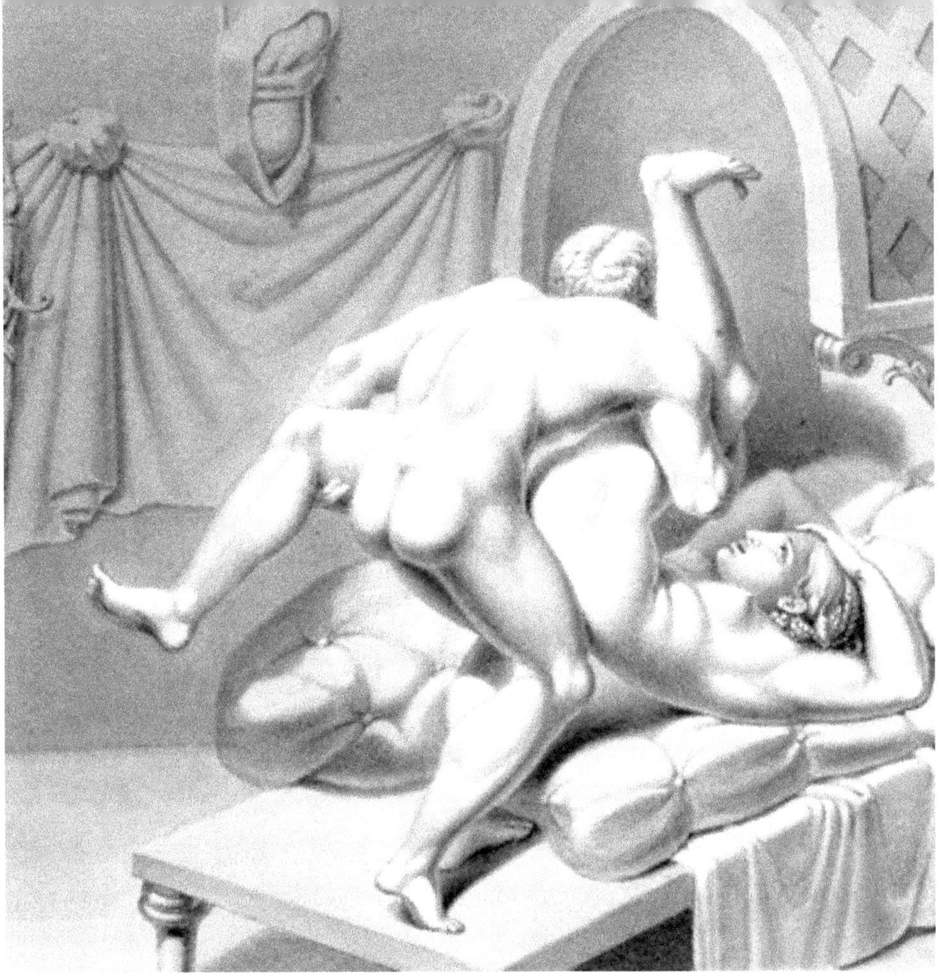

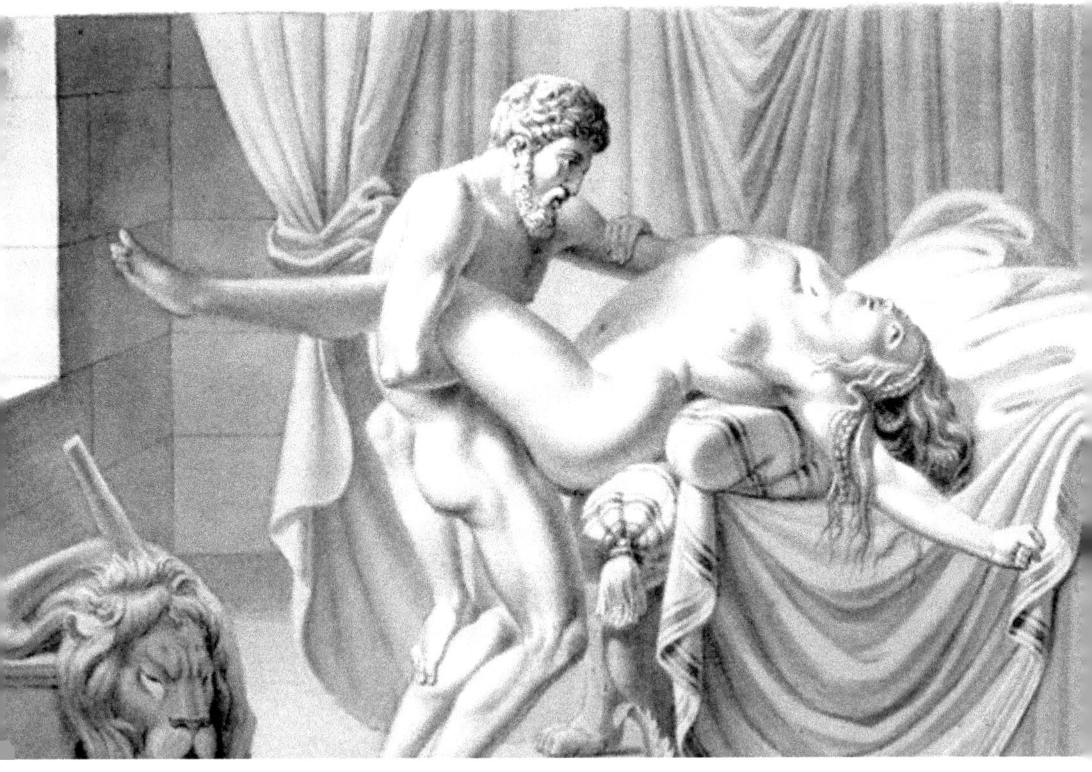

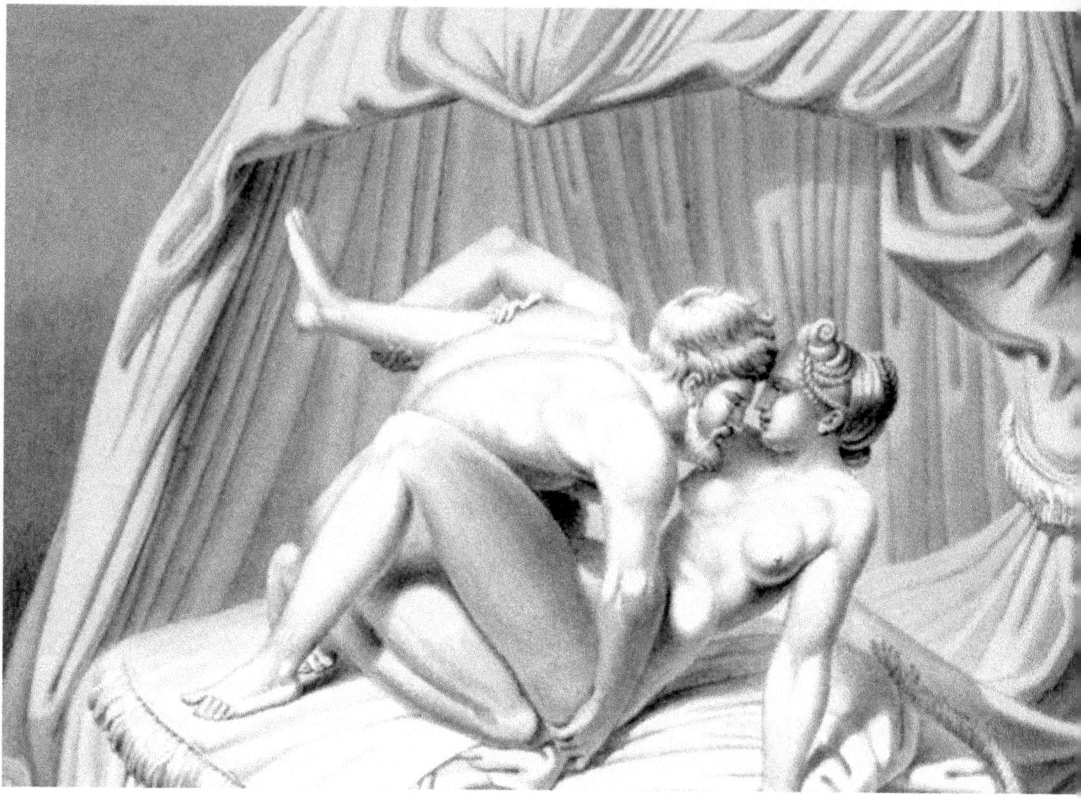

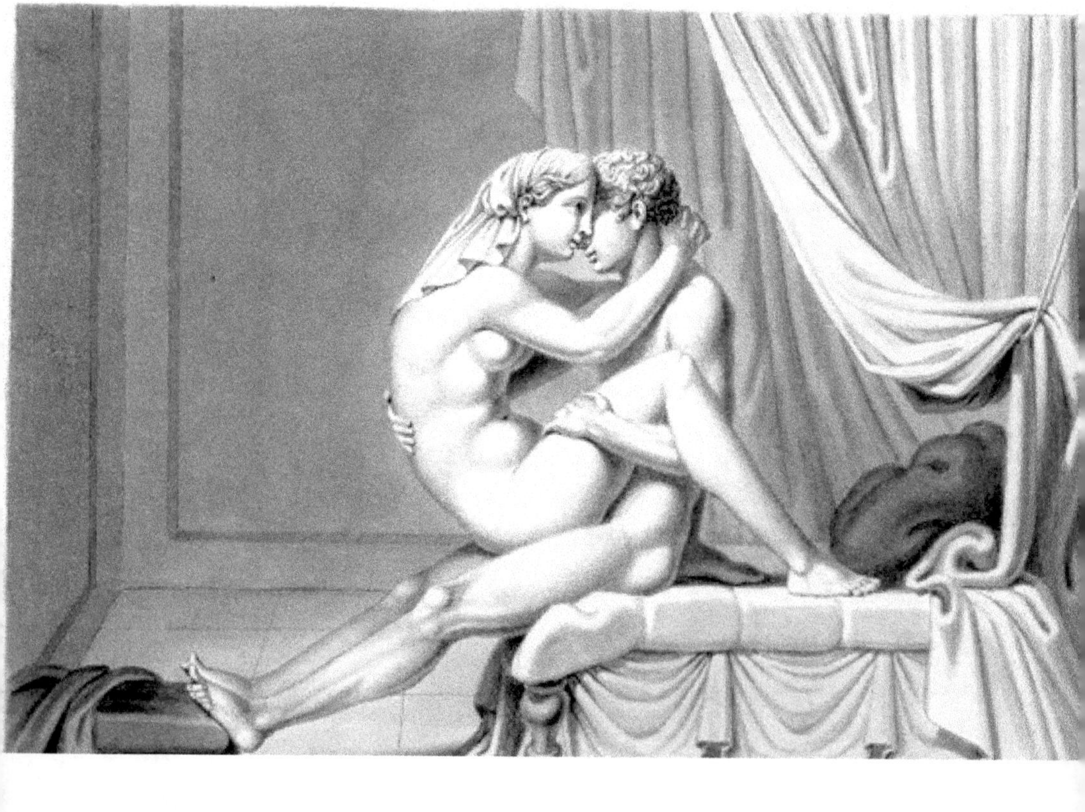

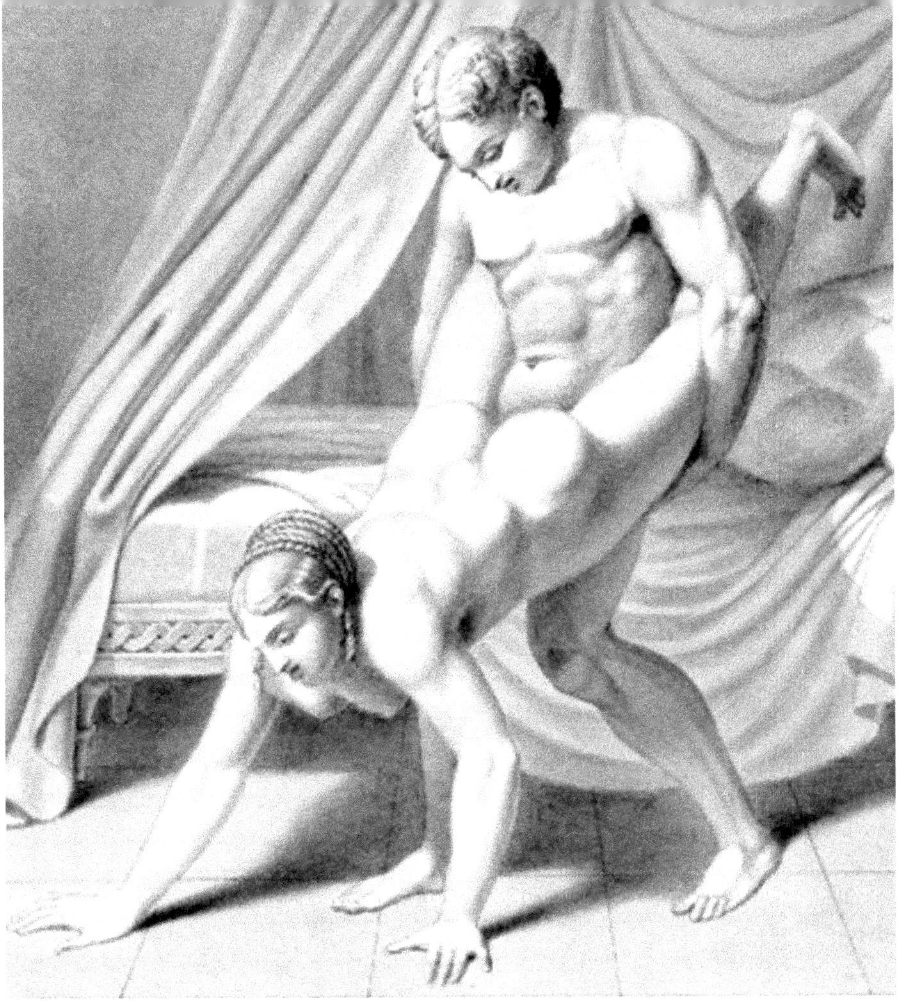

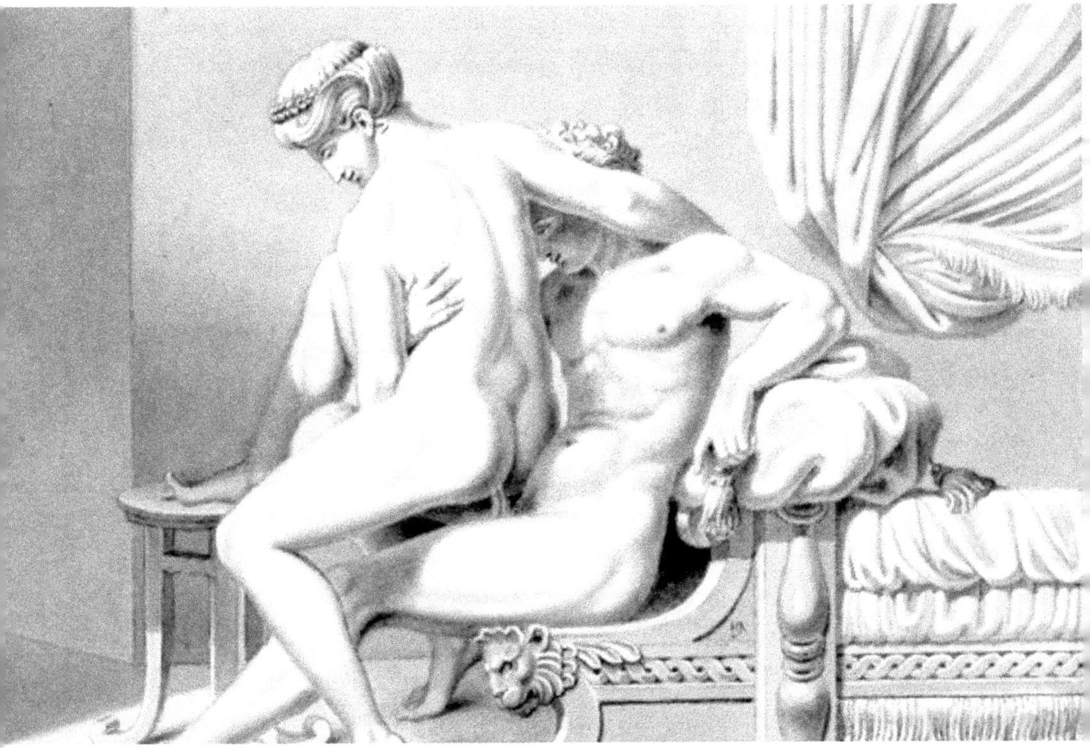

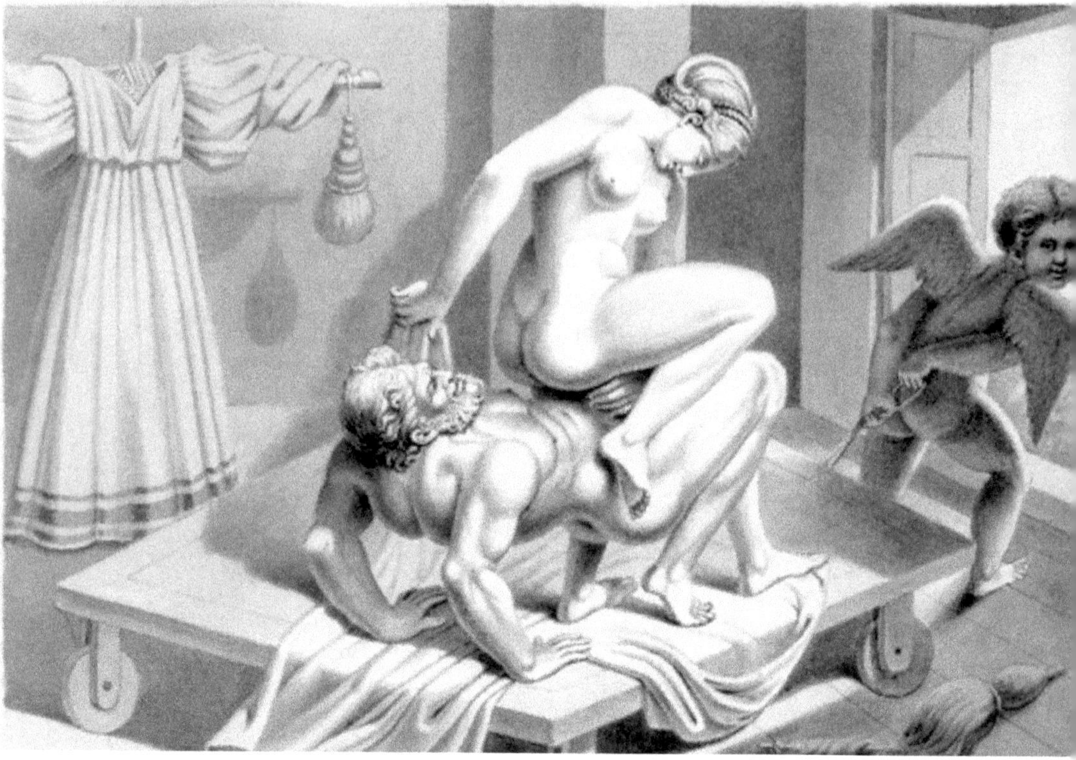

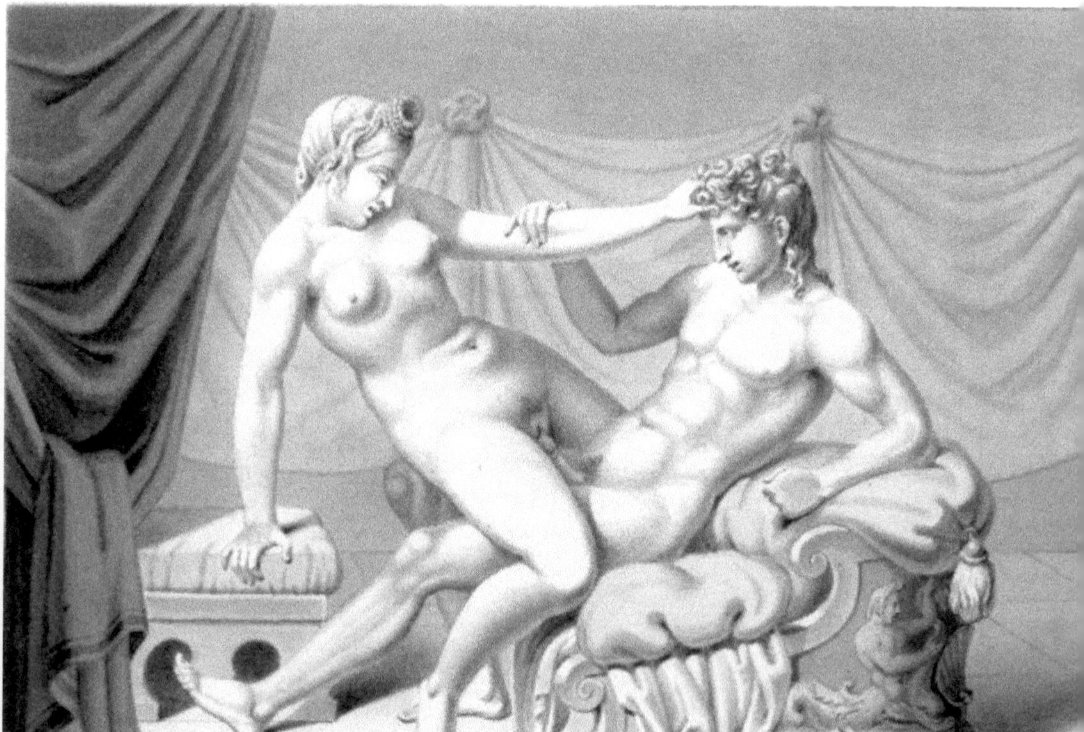

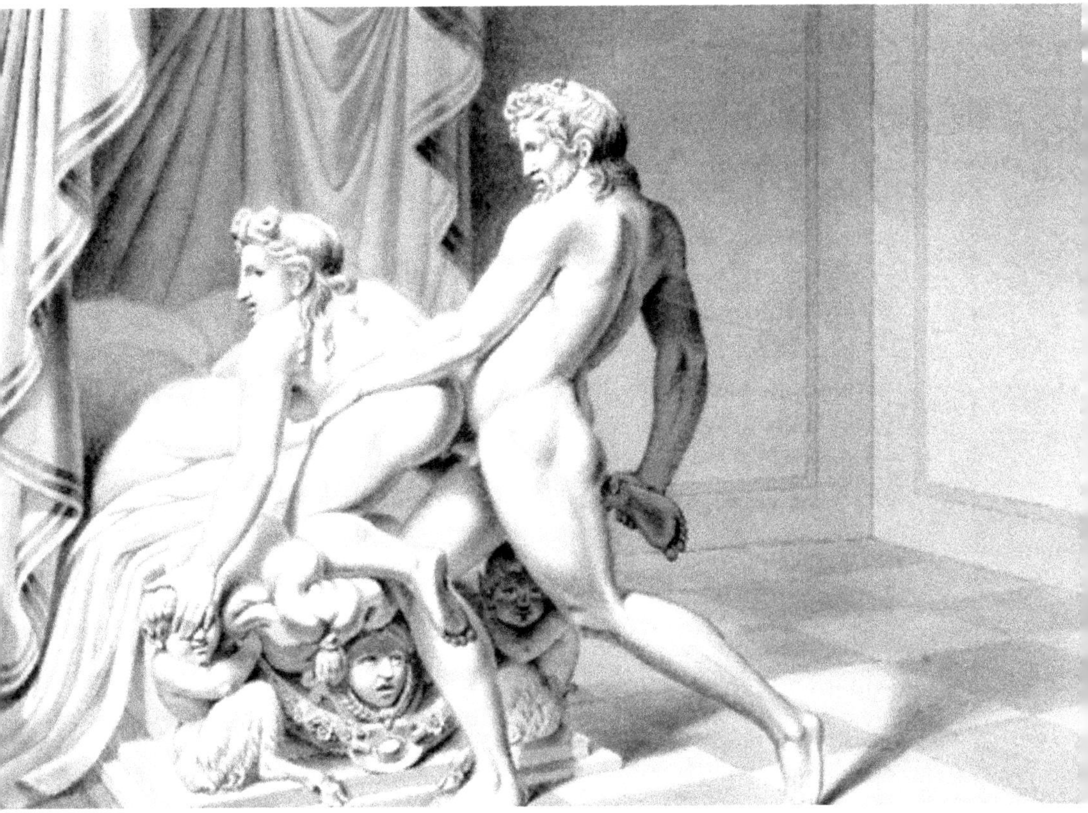

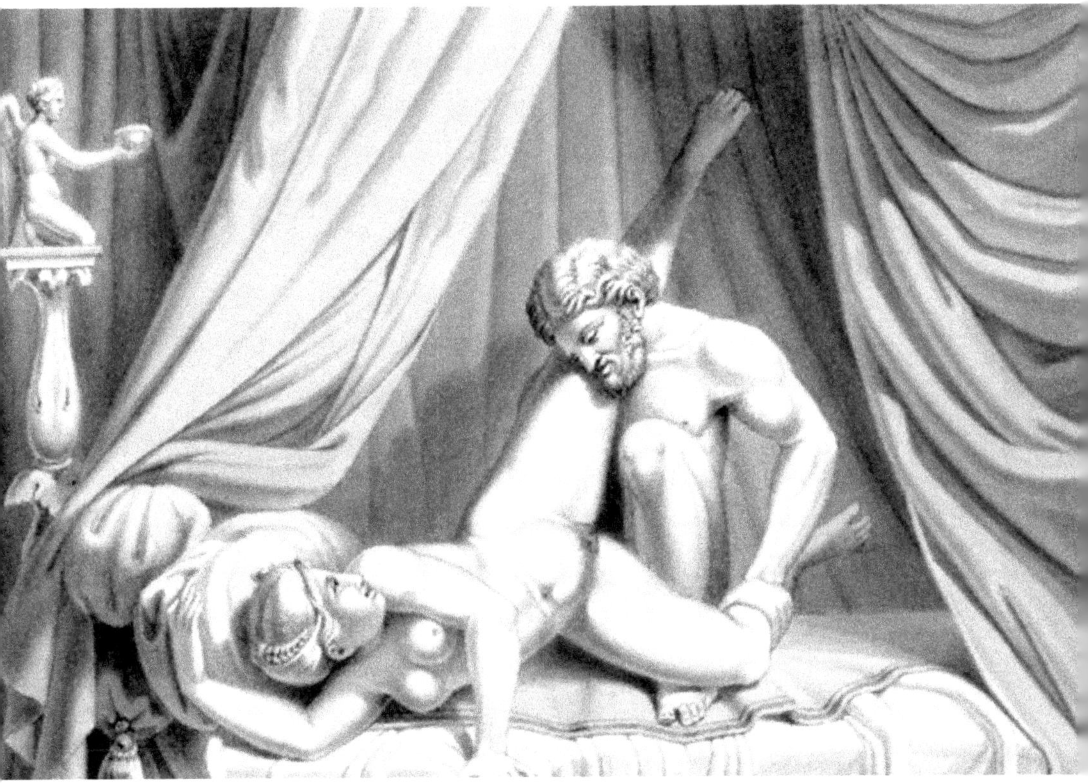

What occurs in most Western art, from Greek and Roman sculpture through the glories of the Renaissance to the latest pornography are male representations of female eroticism. Feminists say that there are no real depictions of female *jouissance* in art or literature. 'In my opinion,' wrote Marguerite Duras, 'women have never expressed themselves.'[1] What she means, perhaps, is that women have expressed themselves thus far in the terms and means and social structures defined by men. There is no 'feminine' or 'women's' writing, according to some feminists. Hélène Cixous reckons she's found only three 'inscriptions of femininity' this century: Colette, Marguerite Duras and Jean Genet.[2] In art, there are many women artists who have tackled erotic issues, but in the history of art, going back to, say, the Renaissance, the number of women artists who have survived are far fewer.

1 Duras, interview in *Signs*, Winter 1975, in E. Marks, 175.
2 H. Cixous: "The Laugh of the Medusa", *Signs*, summer 1976, in E. E. Marks, 249.

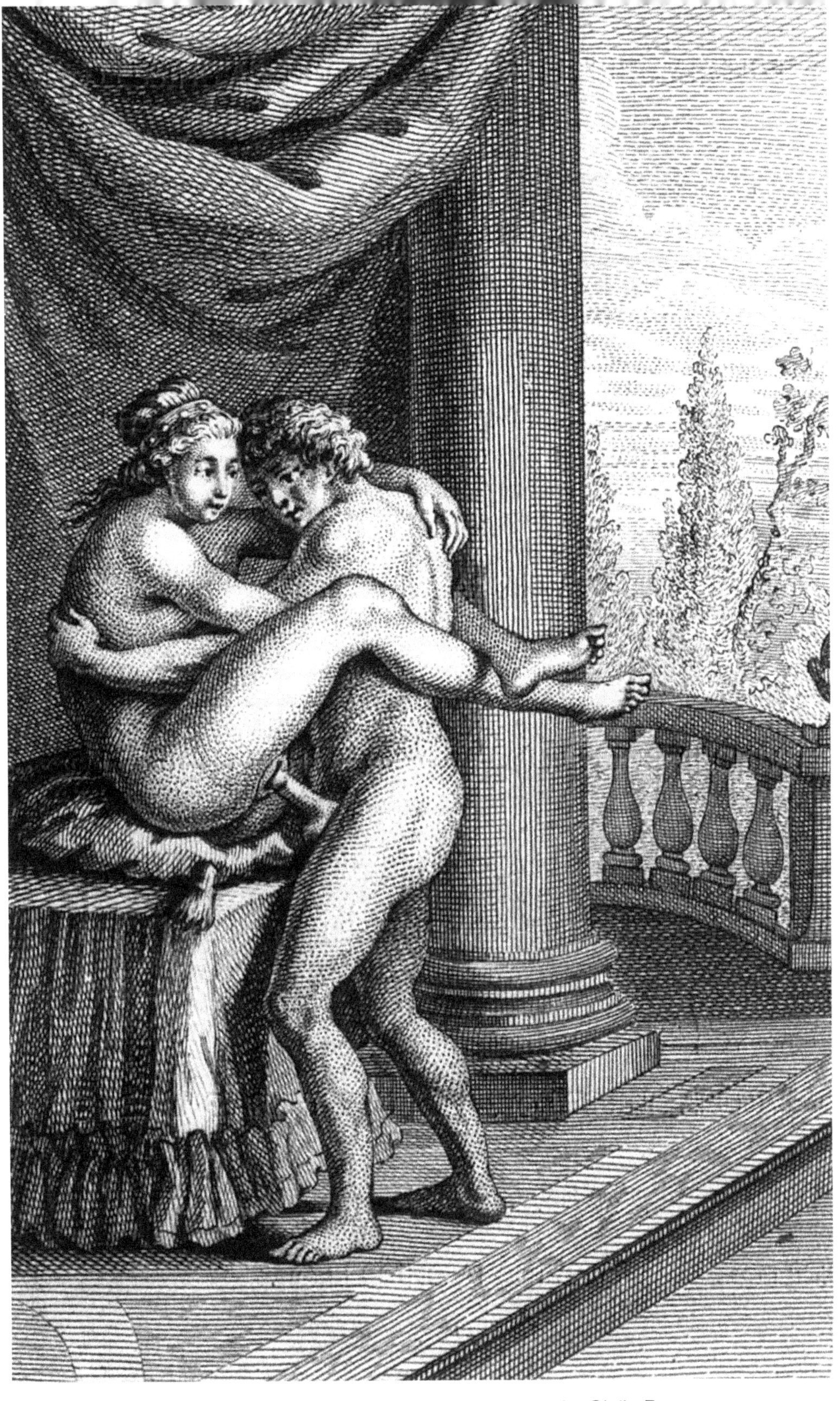

From L'Aretin Francais, engravings after paintings by Giulio Romano, illustrating the Sonnets of Pietro Aretino (this page and following pages)

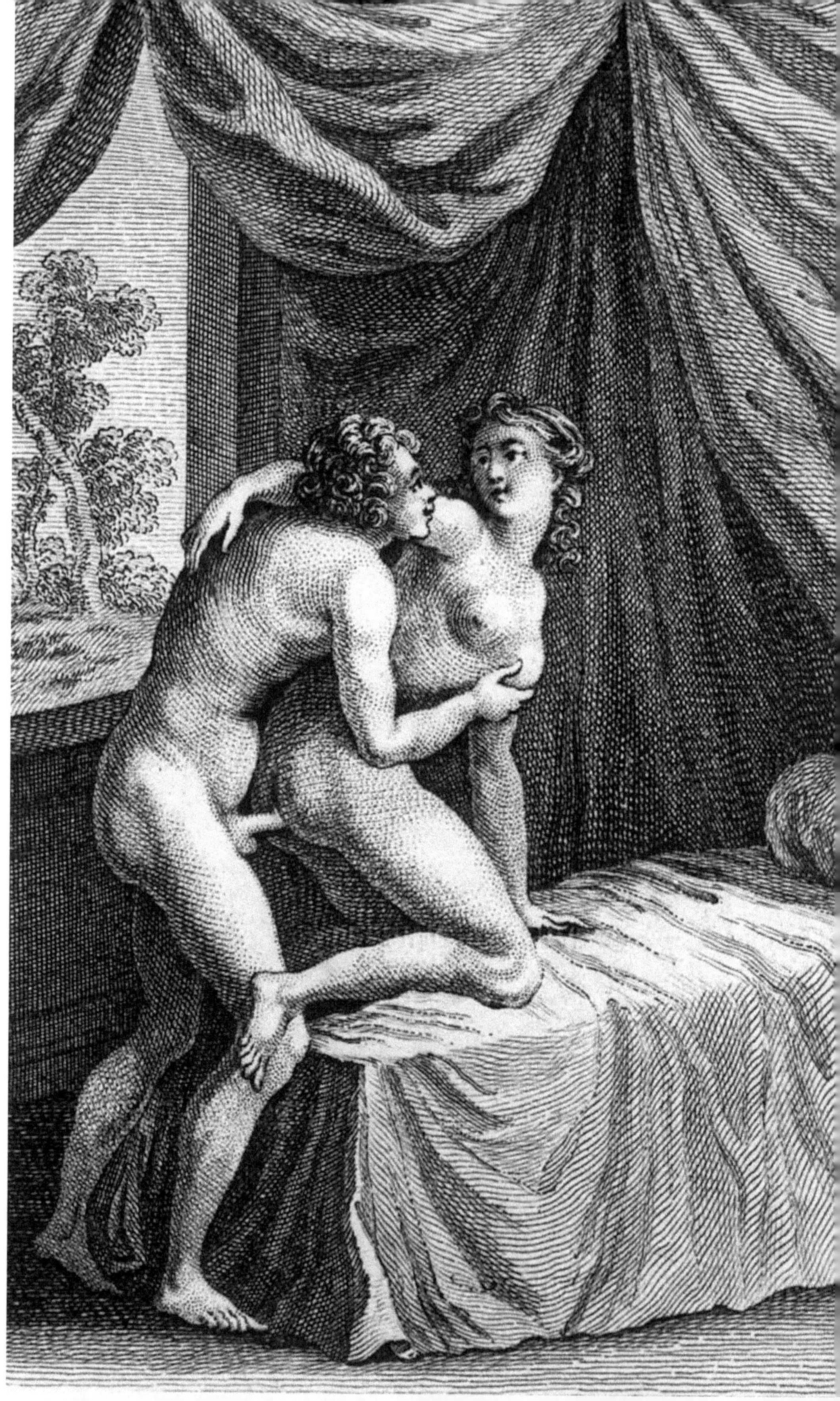

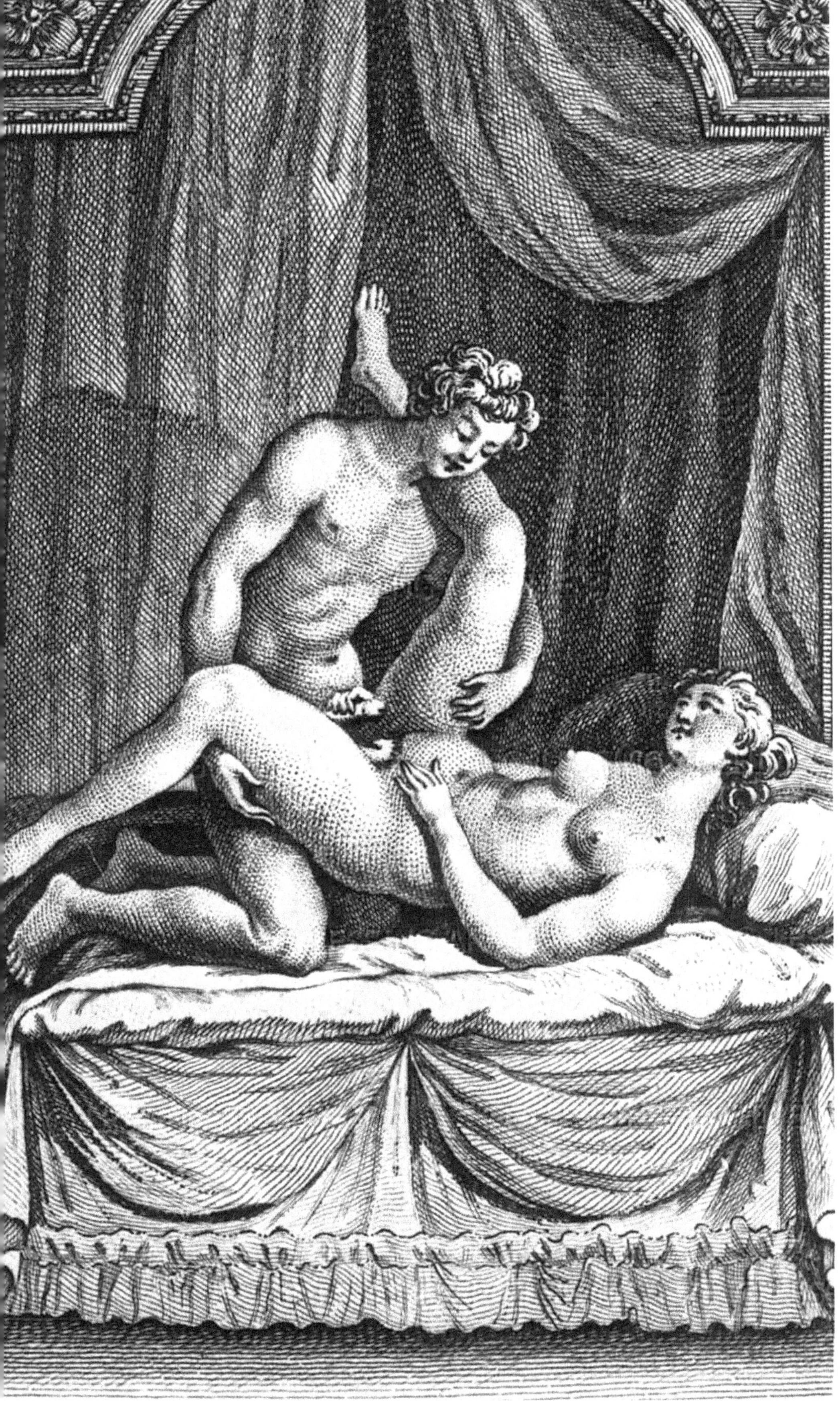

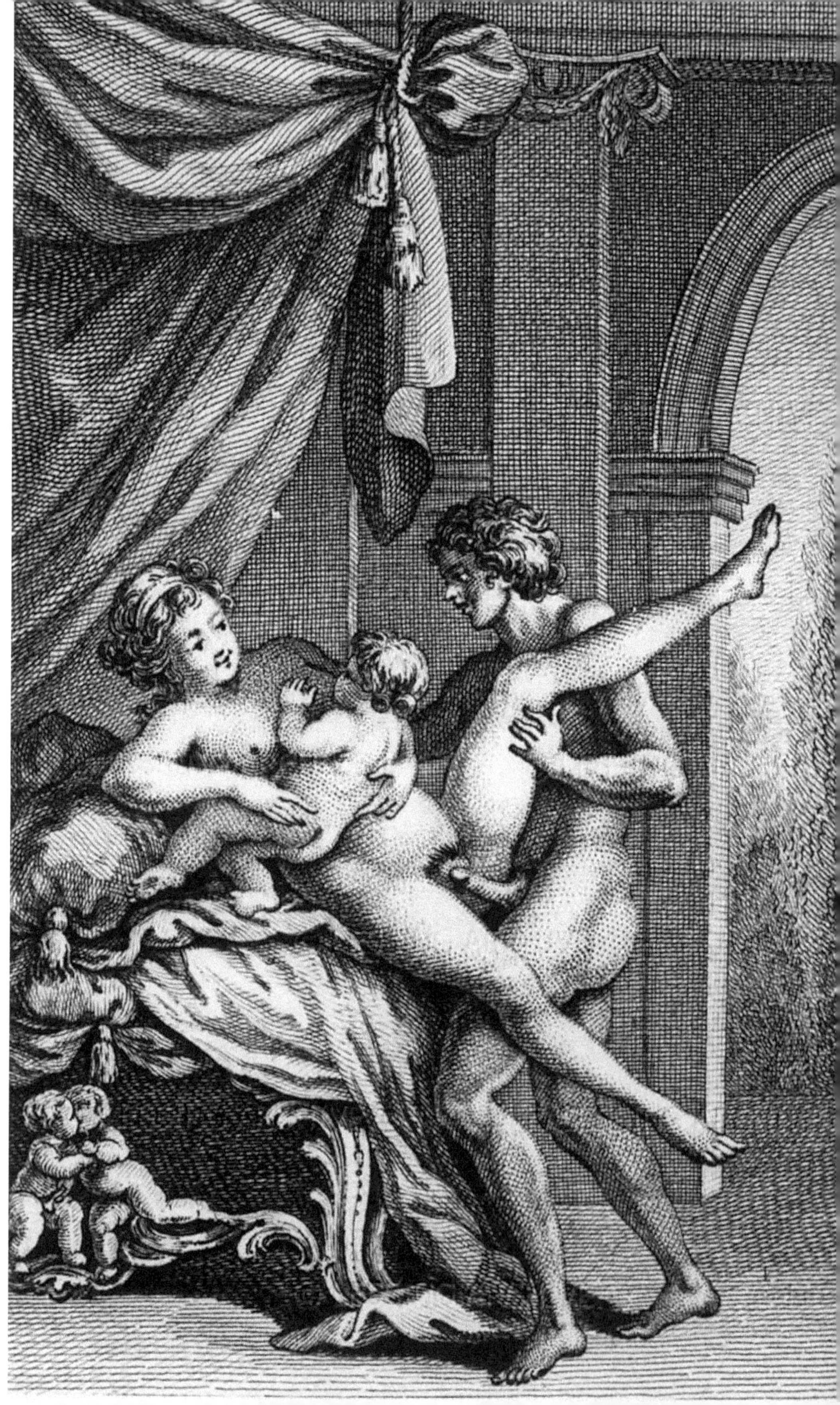

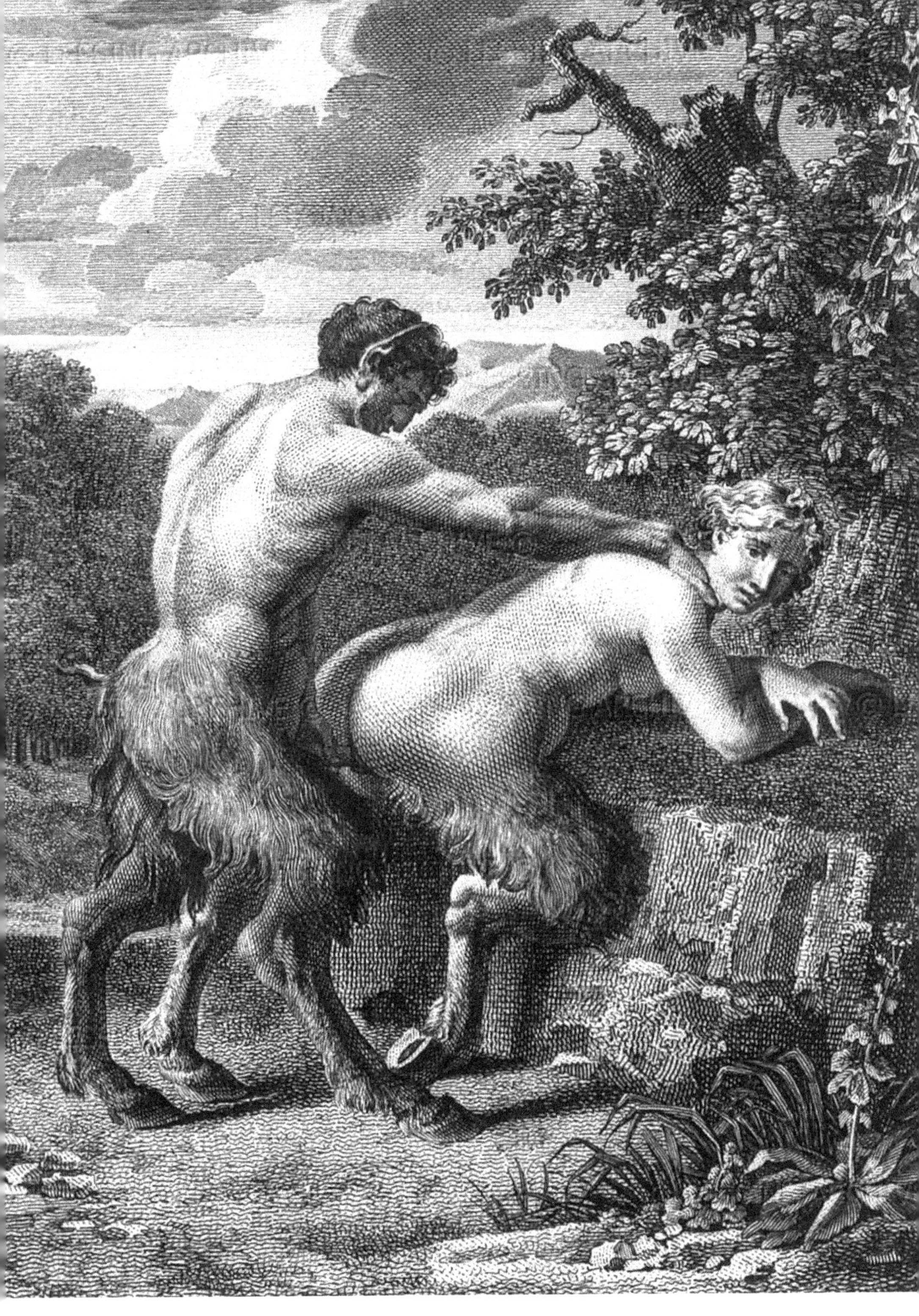

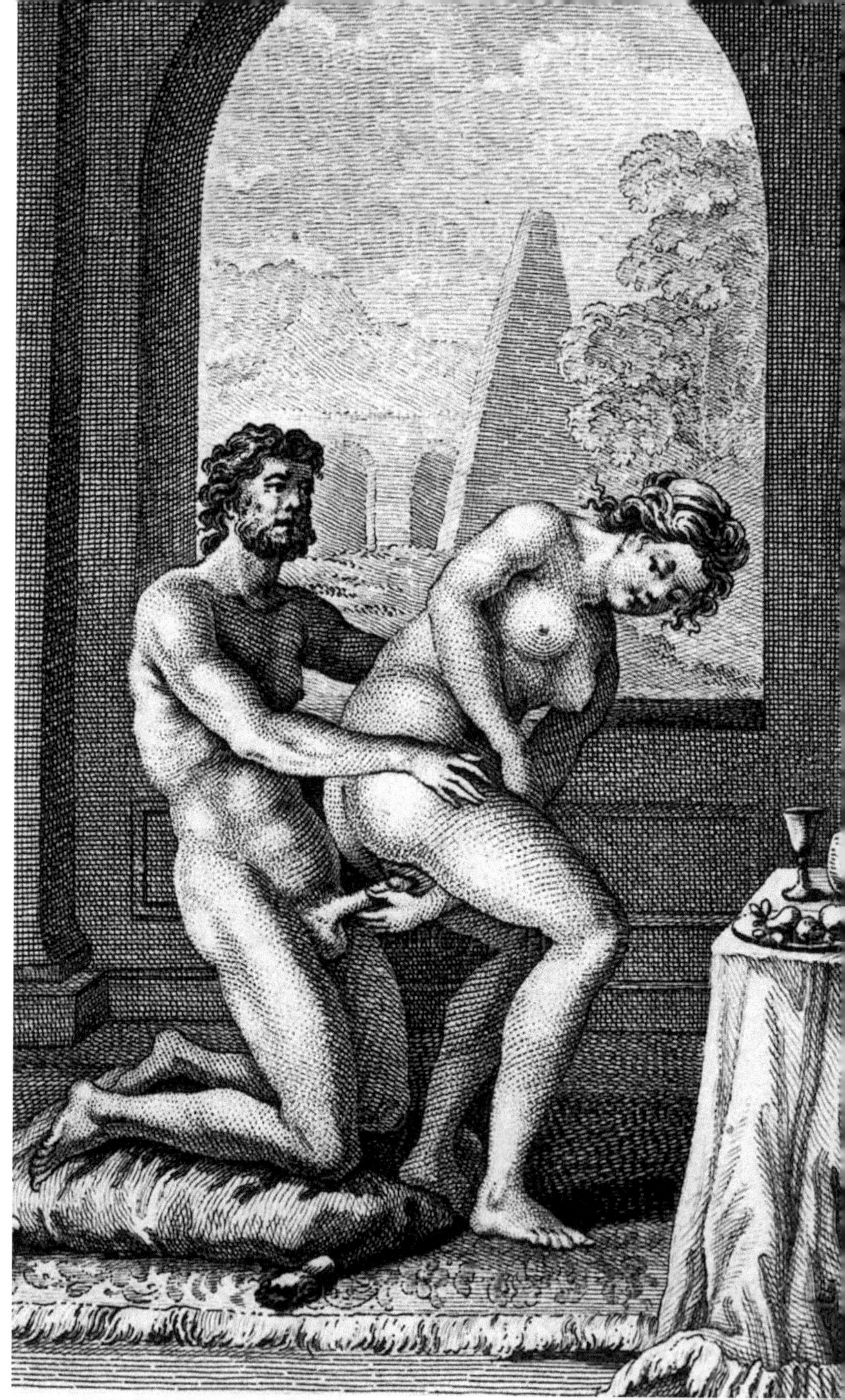

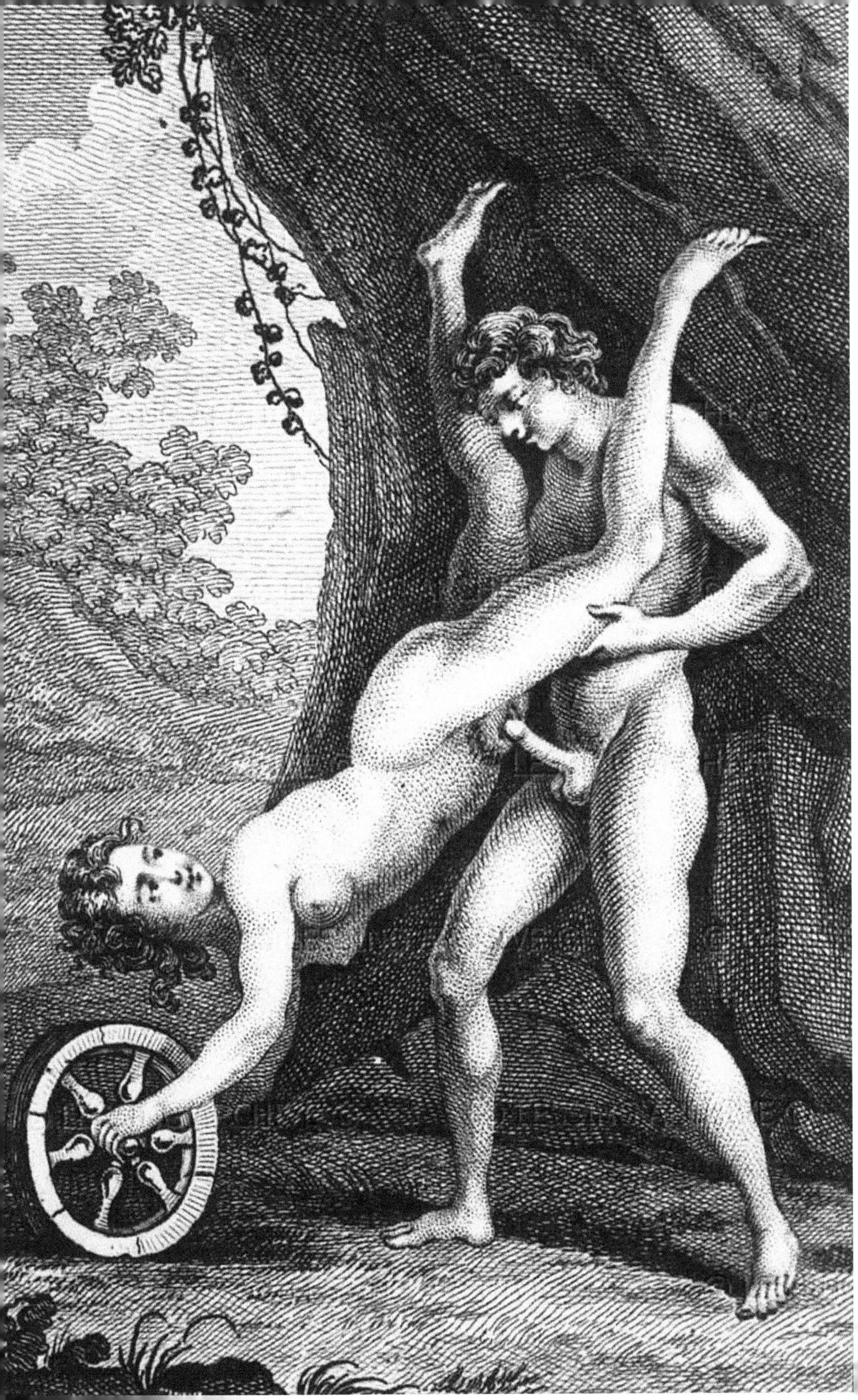

For law-abiding citizens, it seems, the 'line' has to be drawn somewhere. Somewhere between public and private, between sex and love, between visible and invisible, between freedom and control, between secrecy and publicity, between availability and censorship. Indeed, Walter Kendrick said the only definition of pornography is in terms of its forbidden or secret nature.[1]

Pornography brings the secret life of people out into the open. What the Western world holds most dear - the primacy and holiness of the individual, and the primacy and holiness of (heterosexual) love, of marriage, of the family - is cast into doubt by pornography.

Hardcore pornography, in particular, tries to make everything as clear and as visible as possible, and is thus disruptive and unsettling for the establishment. There are, thus, many close-ups of genitals in hard core pornography. Sex is ecstatic, so hard core pornography has to show this ecstasy. It does this by focussing on the genitals.

1 W. Kendrick: *The Secret Museum: Pornography in Modern Culture*, Viking, New York, NY, 1987.

N° 10

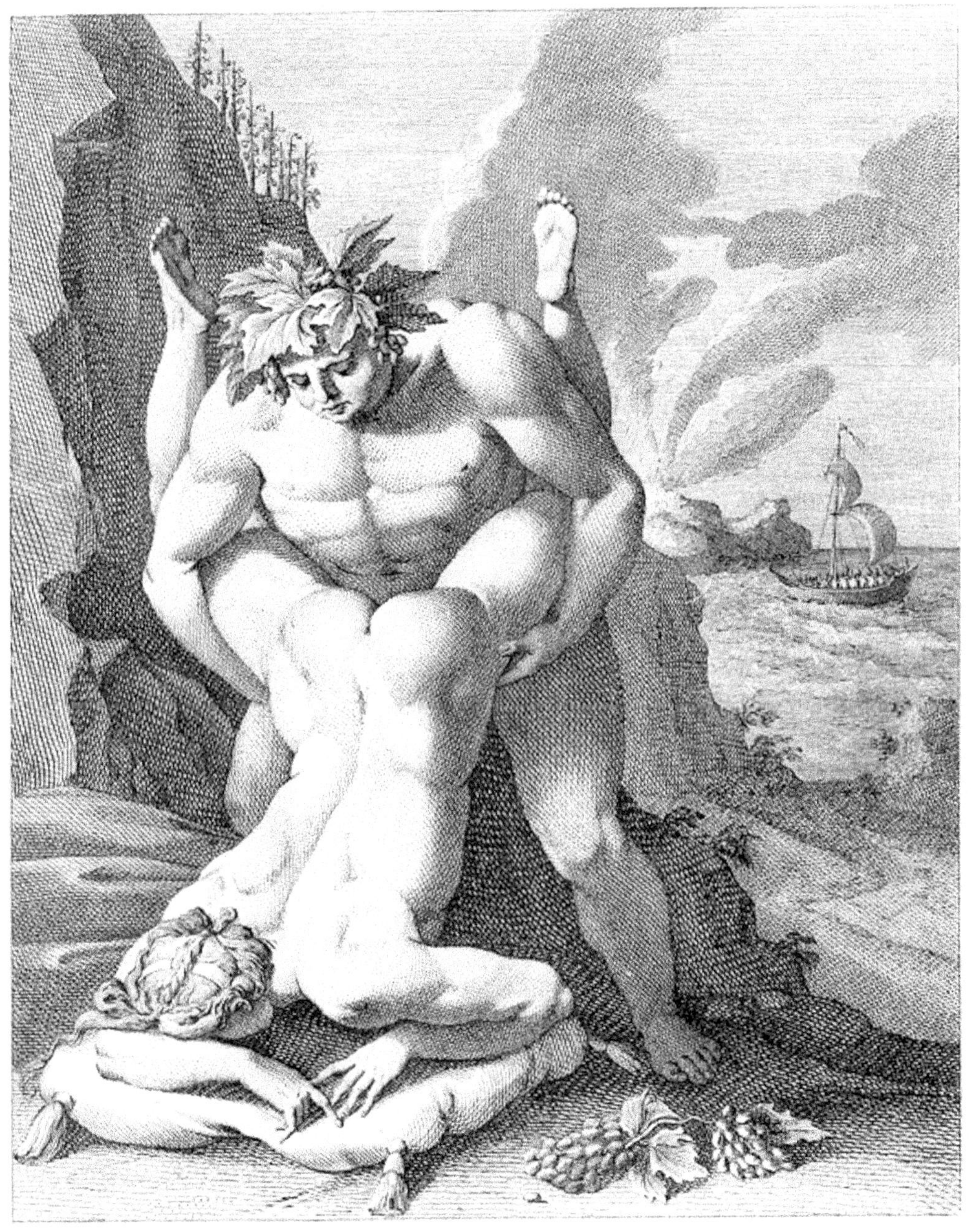

BACHUS ET ARIANE.

After Agostino Caracci, from I Modi

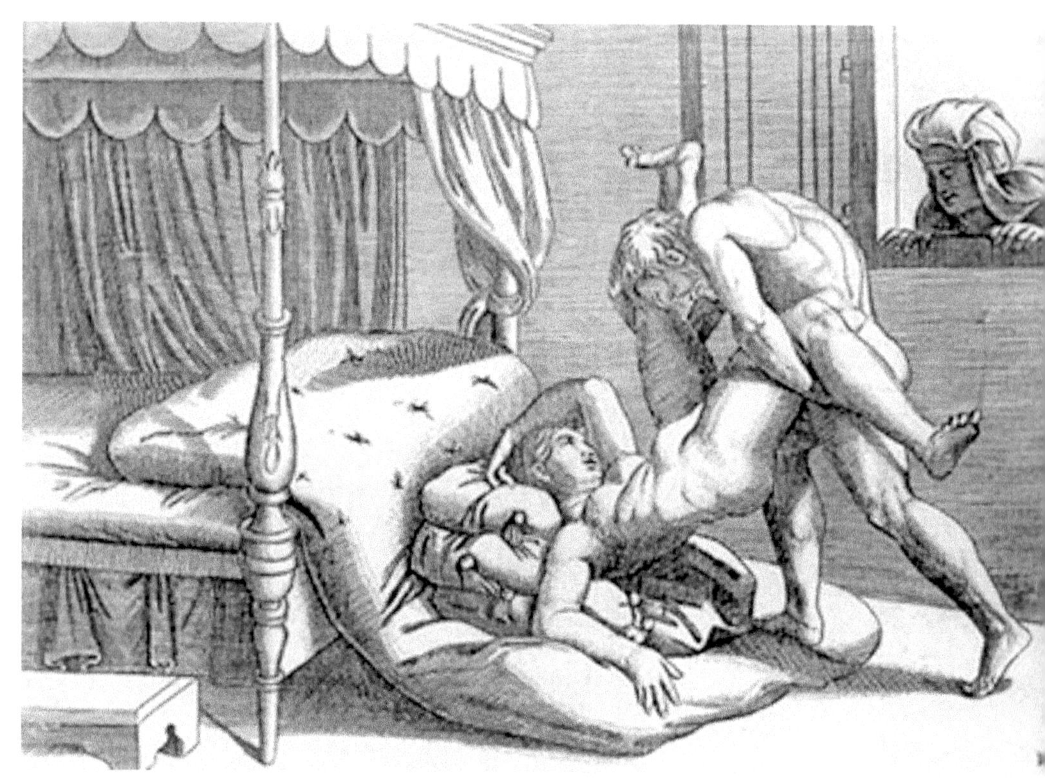

I Modi, by Pietro Aretino, illustrated by Giulio Romano, 16th century

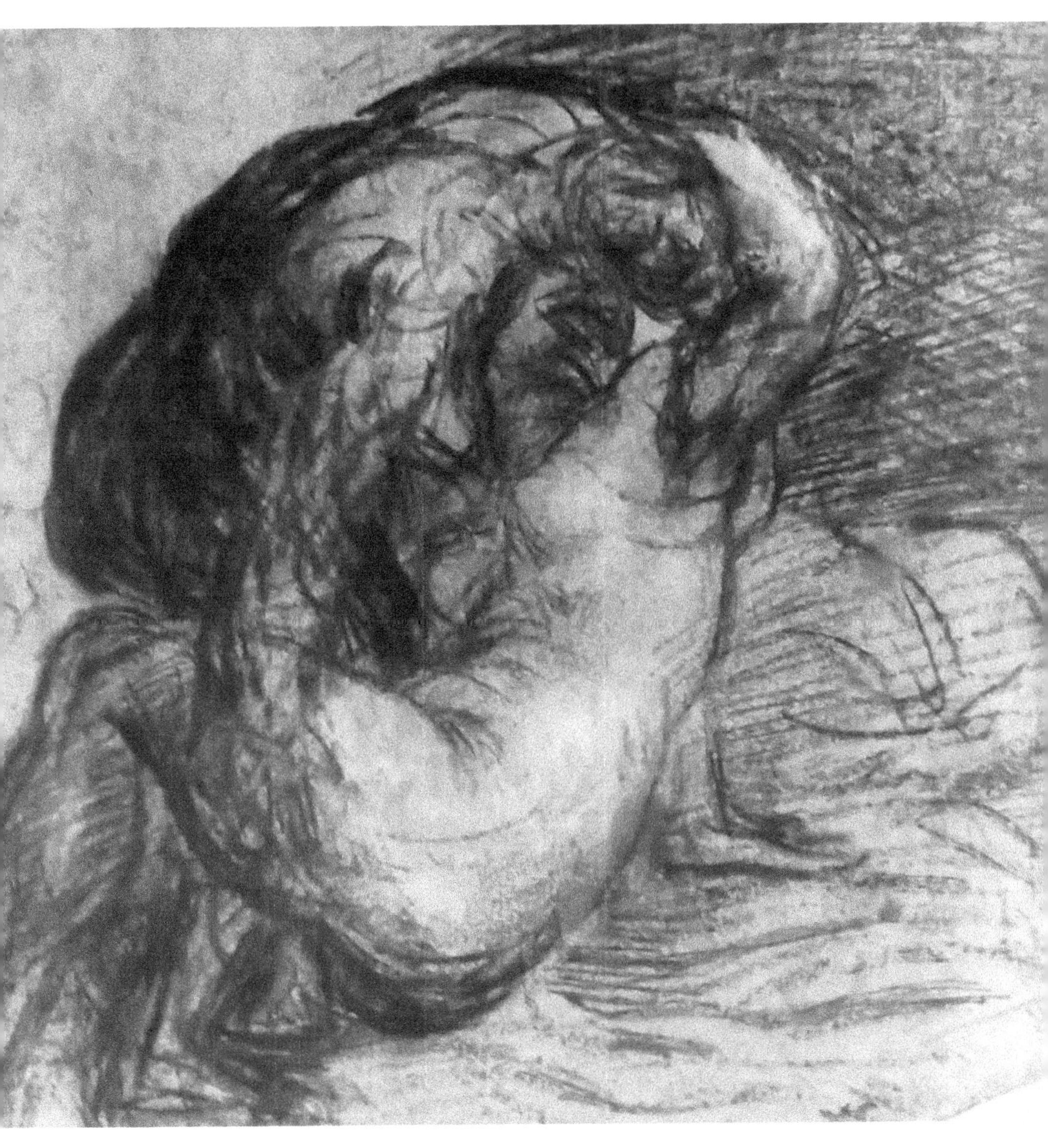

Titian, A Couple, c. 1570, Cambridge

Pornography is the culture of eroticism in the West. There is sex on TV, in fiction, in blockbuster films, in theatre, in pop music, but it is in pornography that erotic feelings are most frequently communicated. Yet pornography is commodified sex, materialist sex, sex manufactured into particular types, genres, roles and modes. There are standard pornographic encounters, standard pornographic camera angles, standard pornographic orgasms. Eroticism, as Freud knew, is powerful, whether emotionally, psychologically, culturally or politically. Pornography, then, deals with really wild eroticism by categorizing it, putting into particular genres or narratives. The visual aspect of pornography helps to deal with the wildness and passion of erotic feeling. Pornography produces images and representations, which are easier to deal with than the real thing. Jane Gallop wrote that the 'visual mode produces representations as a way of mastering what is otherwise too intense'.[1] Experiences such as orgasm and erotic desire can be too overwhelming to be communicated in words. Putting these experiences into visual representations enables them to be controlled, packaged, commodified.

1 J. Gallop: *The Daughter's Seduction: Feminism and Psychoanalysis*, Cornell University Press, New York, NY, 1982, 35.

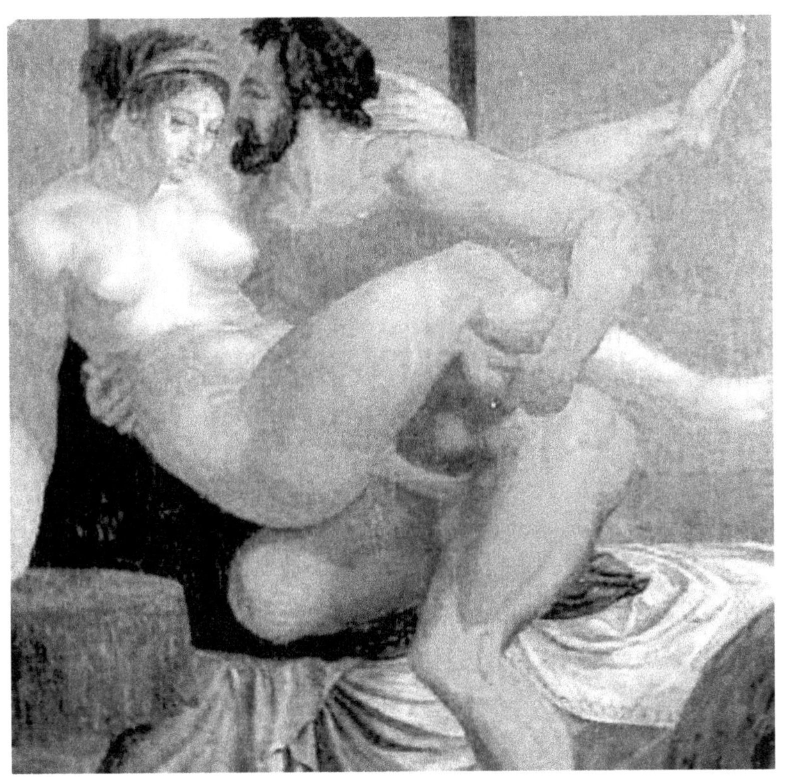

French school, late 18th century

Pornography is *fantasy,* as well as genre, product, system, and materialism. Pornography does not offer the consumer real people, but images, narratives, ideas, suggestions. The visual dimension of pornography helps to create certain kinds of representations of erotic feelings which the consumer can deal with, because they are communicated in recognizable forms. So now we're in an S/M narrative – masters, mistresses and slaves Or, over here we're in the narrative where a sexually frustrated male picks up a female hitchhiker. Or, here we are in the 'bored housewife' scenario: sex-starved, she humps the plumber over the washing machine. The consumer always knows where she or he is with pornography.

Pornography delivers the goods.

It delivers the goods: which's why it's bigger than the movie or pop music industries.

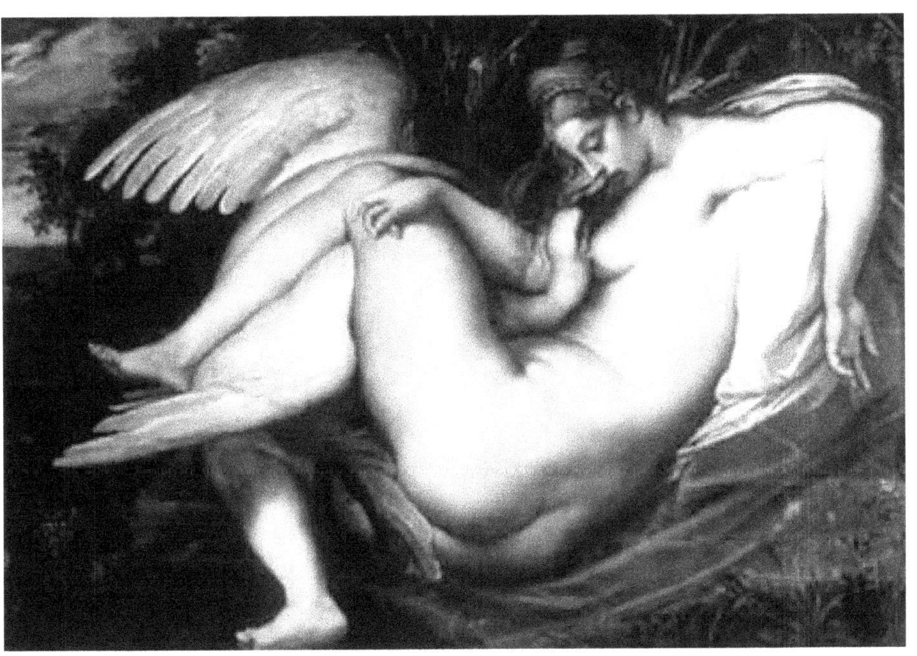

Peter Paul Rubens, Leda and the Swan

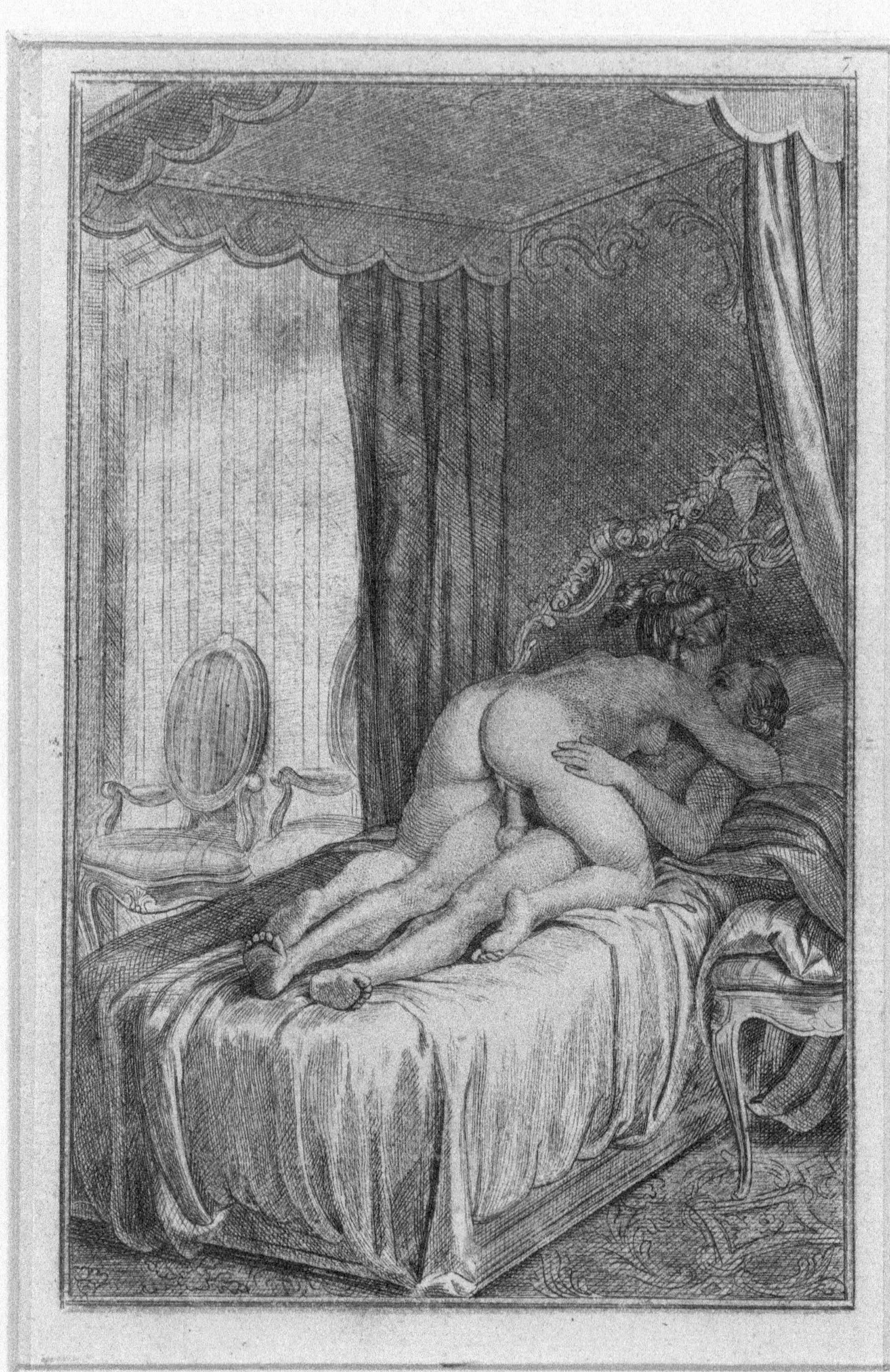

Anonymous, 18th century.

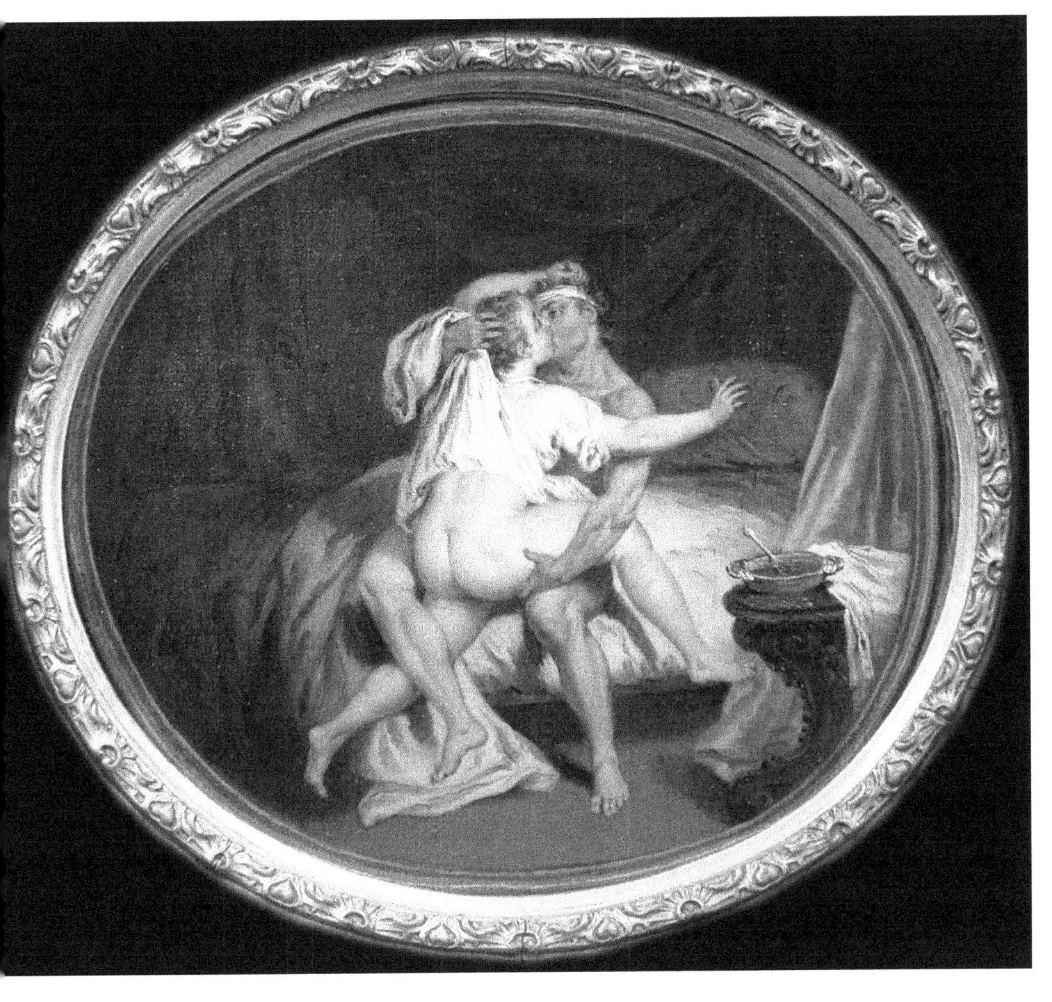

Nicolas Lancret, Scène galante dans une alcôve

If some work is erotic – a scene on TV, a photo, a sculpture, a dance – it's because, in the opinion of some people, you don't 'see' everything. Something is hidden. The 'erotic' in art is about anticipation, waiting, yearning. It's about potential and possibility, hidden but not hidden, partially clothed. As the photographer Grace Lau, who has made many pictures of fetishism, wrote: 'I prefer images that conceal, rather than those that reveal all.'[1]

Pornography, meanwhile, has people doing it now. They undress, and start attacking each other immediately. There's nothing to get in the way, not contraception, not fear, not aversions, not menstruation, not impotence, not interruptions, not anything. In short: it's *fantasy.*

Pornography turns 'what if?' into a reality. What if somebody took their clothes off in this train carriage and started having sex? is a typical question that erotic art suggests but pornography answers. What if this woman at home turns out to be a nymphomaniac and this plumber turns out to be a superstud? What if the wedding guest who just smiled at you turns out to be the fuck of a lifetime? In pornography, people *do* rip their clothes and start mashing each other up.

Pornography presents as a normal, everyday occurrence what is hidden away, what is desired but unspoken. Pornography is the ultimate in fantasy, for in the fairy tale world of pornography, every dream comes true. And it is not only 'true', it is 'real'.

1 Grace Lau: "Confessions of a Complete Scopophiliac", in Gibbons, 195

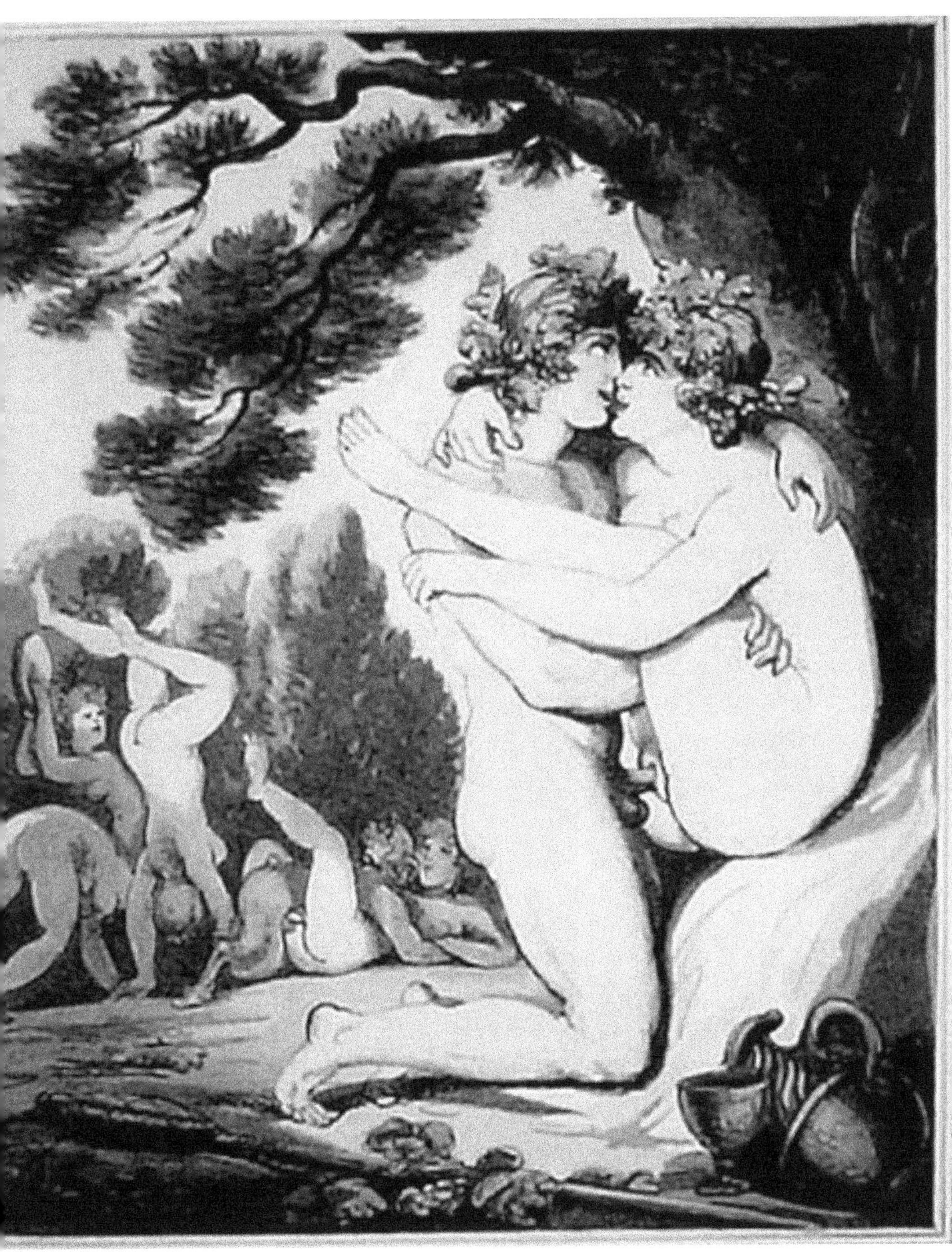

Thomas Rowlandson

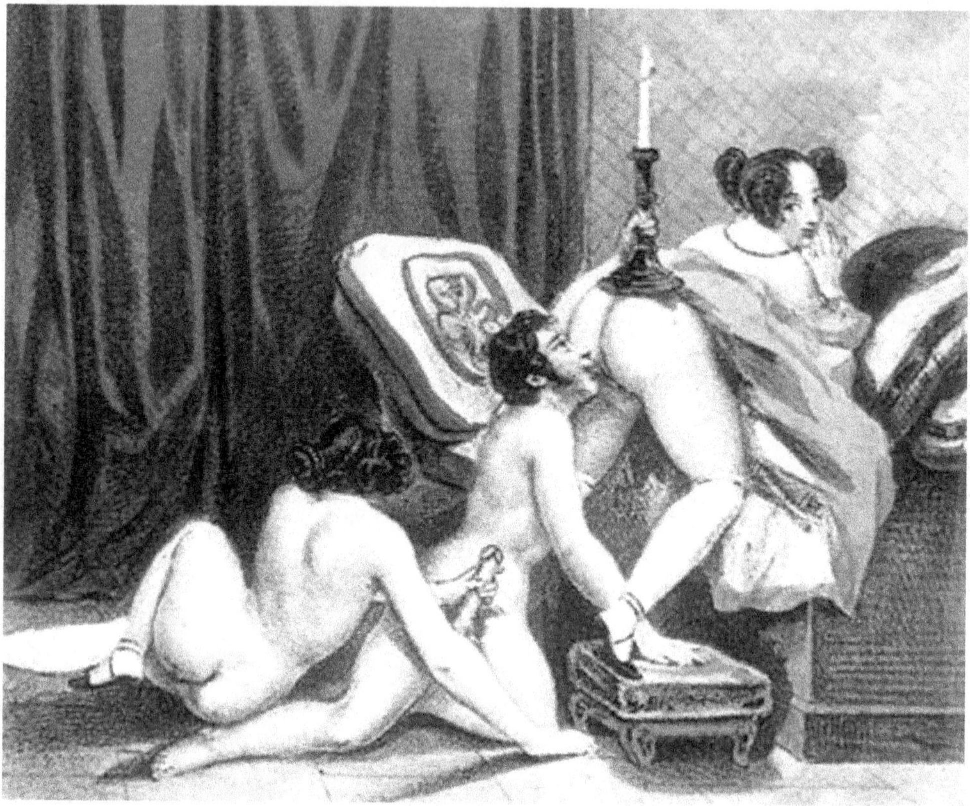

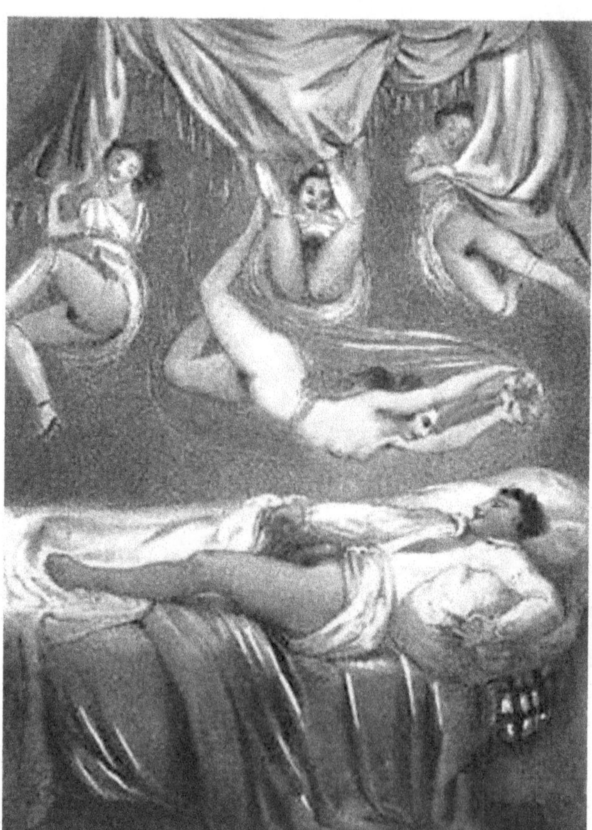

Anonymous, late 1700s

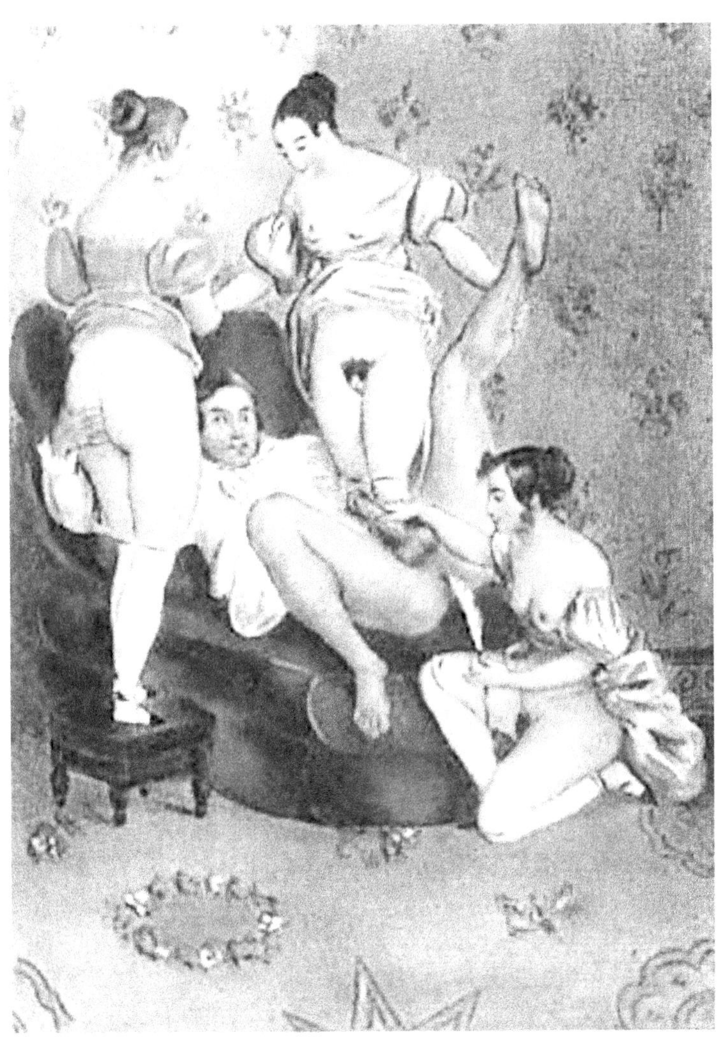

Anonymous, late 1700s

CENSORSHIP

One of the most contentious and fiercely debated aspects of erotic art and pornography is the issue of obscenity, taste and censorship. Throughout the history of art and pornography, different individuals or groups of people have sought to defend certain territories, whether moral, psychological, emotional, spiritual, religious, philosophical, political or ideological. There is always some line between the 'acceptable' and the 'obscene'.

The history of censorship is long and complex. In the 20th century there were many confrontations between artists and the establishment: with D.H. Lawrence's *Lady Chatterley's Lover*, with *Ulysses*, with films such as *Last Tango in Paris, Kids, Natural Born Killers, The Killing of Sister George, Performance, Trash, A Clockwork Orange* and countless others, with the *Oz* trials, with Senator Jesse Helms trying to stop NEA tax payers' money funding 'obscene' work, with reference to the photographer Robert Mapplethorpe (whose photos have created much 'controversy'),[1] with internet porn, with punk rock and gangsta rap, and so on.[2]

1 See M. Schoofs: "Robert Mapplethorpe: Exquisite Subversions", *Windy City Times*, 16 Mch, 1989; H. Kramer: "Mapplethorpe Show at the Whitney: A Big, Glossy, Offensive Exhibit", *The New York Observer*, 22 Aug, 1988; A.C. Danto: *Encounters & Reflections*, Farrar Straus Giroux, New York 1990; E. Kastor & Carla Hall: "Mapplethorpe Aftermath", *Washington Post*, 23 June 1989; T.A. Yasui: "The Mapplethorpe Bonanza", *Washington Post*, 21 Aug, 1989; P. Schjeldhal: "The Mainstreaming of Mapplethorpe: Taste and Hunger", *7 Days*, 10 Aug, 1988; R. Rooney: "The unambiguous stare of Mapplethorpe's lens", *Australian*, 25 Feb, 1986.
2 More Mapplethorpe articles: D. Dominick: "Robert Mapplethorpe's Proud Finale", *Vanity Fair*, Feb, 1989; "Robert Mapplethorpe: Aestheticizing the Perverse", *Artscribe International*, Nov/Dec 1988; J. Ribalta: "Decorative Heroism, The death of Mapplethorpe", *Lapiz*, Apl, 1989.

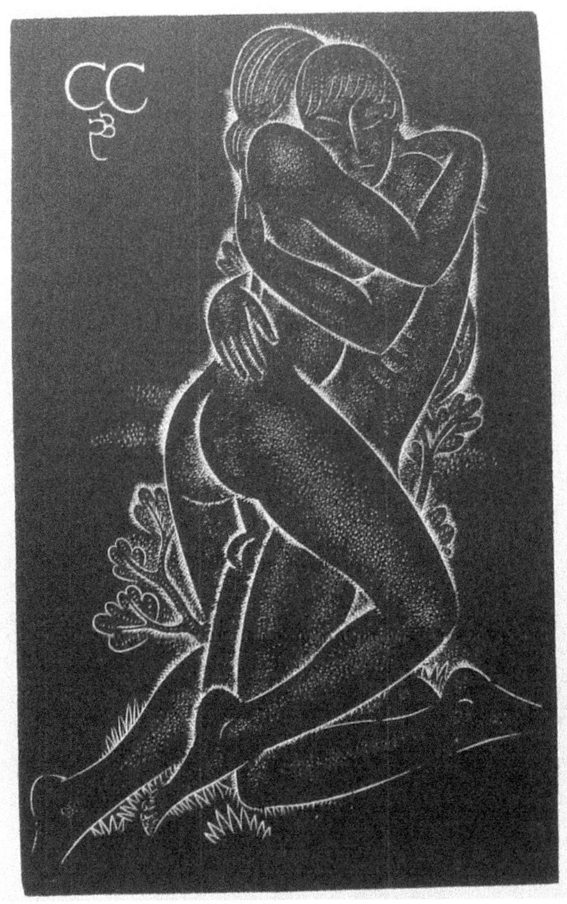

Fucking a flame into being: one of
Eric Gill's illustrations for D.H. Lawrence's book

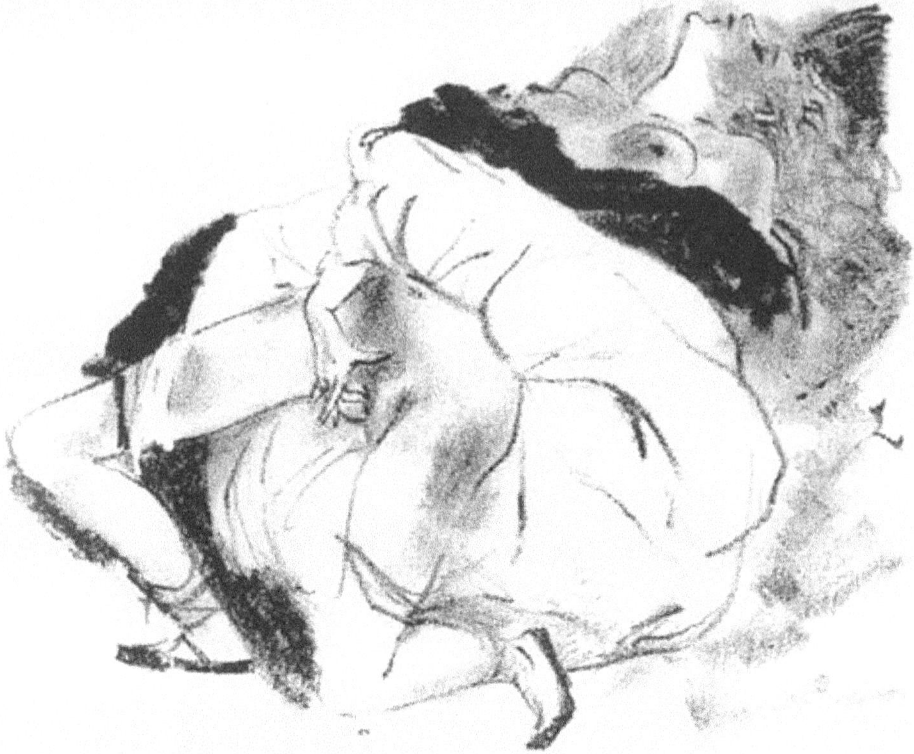

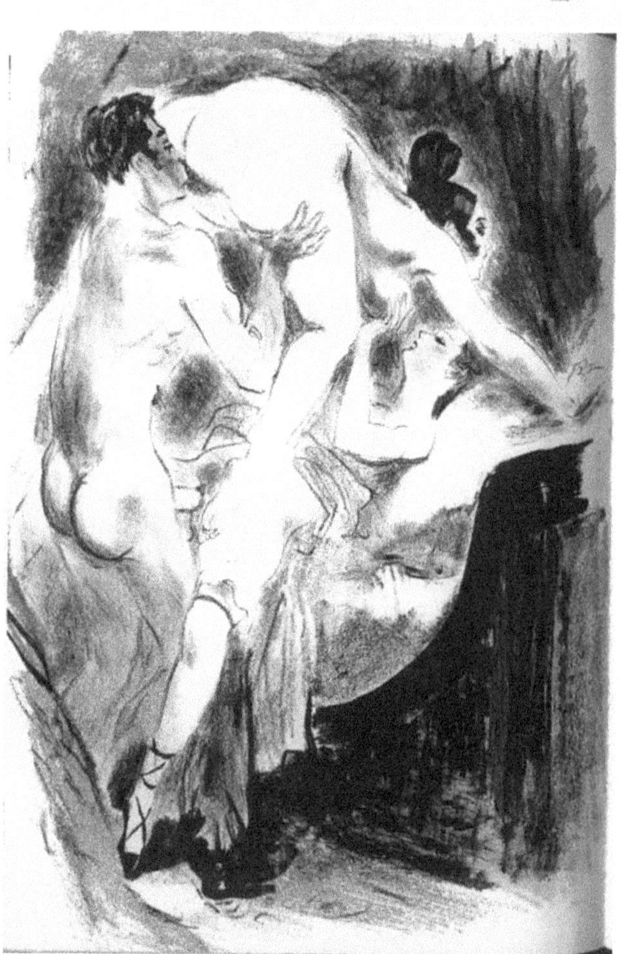

Louis-André Berthomme Saint-André, Gamiani ou Deux Nuit d'Excés, by Alfred de Musset

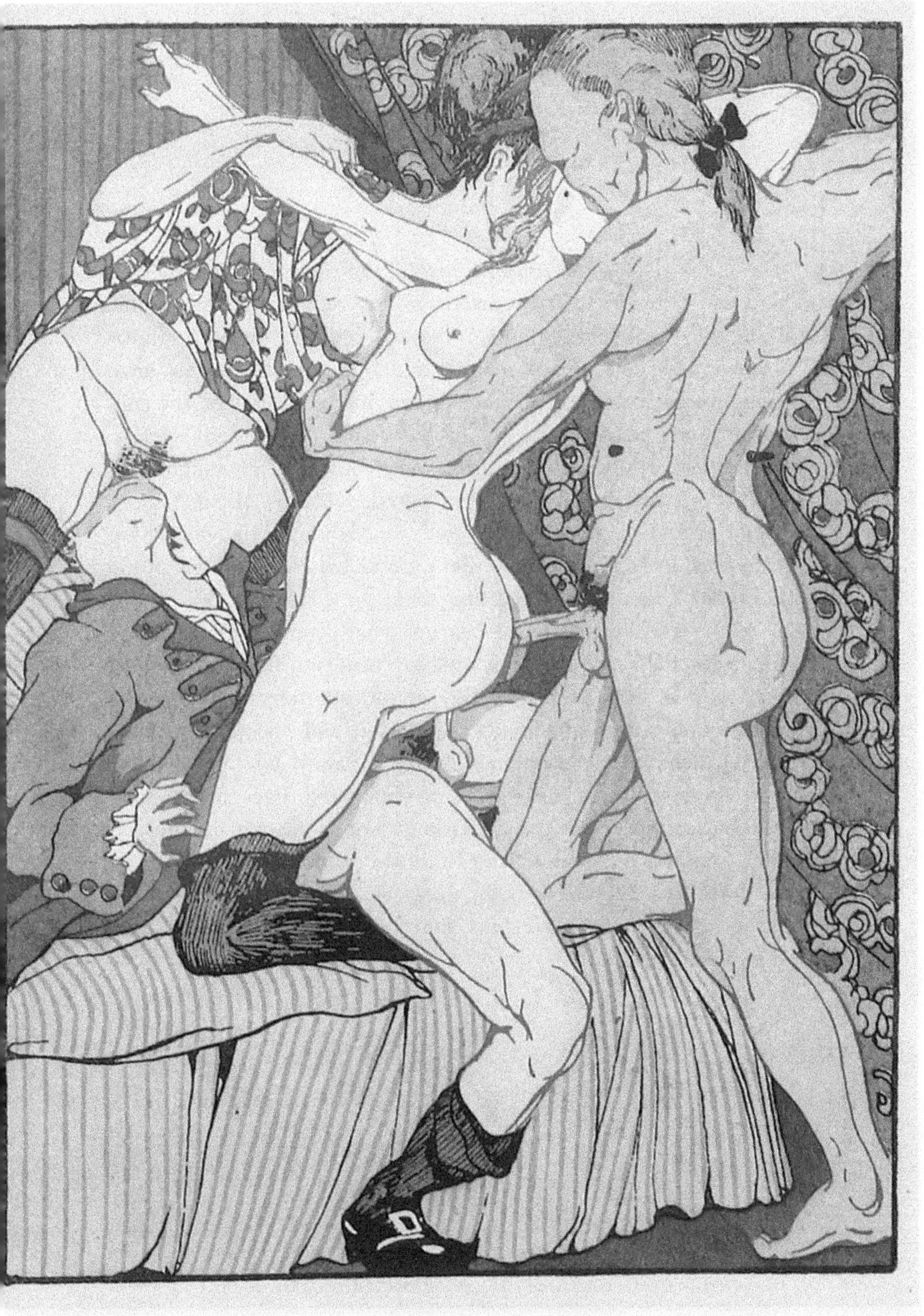

Illustration for the Marquis de Sade,
Le Bordel de Venise, 1921,
by Couperyn (a.k.a. George A. Drains), Paris

CENSORSHIP

The many debates concerning several Obscene Publications Acts and bills, the First Amendment of the American constitution, different regulatory groups, pressure groups, media organizations, publishers, and all manner of intellectuals and artists, have been intense, complex, protracted, and often a shambles. The confusions and ambiguities are at the centre of Western society. Pornography debates produce, very quickly, all manner of confusions and hypocrisies, of a moral, religious, psychological, social and ideological nature.[1] For some, though, the censorship debate is 'in fact, a little internal quibble between sections of the bourgeois community' (according to Suzanne Kappeler).

Pornography goes to the heart of what people hold dear: their identities, their feelings, their philosophical, spiritual and political views, their view of the 'quality of life'. Pornography unsettles these notions and structures. The fervour and uncertainty of the many attempts at legislation and policing show how problematic pornography is. In a case of recent years, five 'homosexual sadomasochists' were convicted in 1990 of inflicting 'injuries on each another's genitals during ritual sex' which involved 'cutting each other's genitals with surgical scalpels, sandpapering scrotums and pushing hooks into penises'. Their appeal was rejected by the courts.[2]

1 See *Art in America*, May 1990; C.H. Rolph: *The Trial of Lady Chatterley*, Penguin, London, 1961; G. Robertson: *Obscenity: an Account of Censorship Laws and Their Enforcements in England and Wales*, Weidenfeld & Nicolson, London, 1979; *The Attorney General's Commission on Pornography – the Meese Commission – Final Report*, US Government Printing Office, Washington DC, 1986; L. Lederer, ed, op. cit.

2 I. MacKinnon: "Lords reject appeals by sado-masochists", *The Independent*, 12 Mch, 1993.

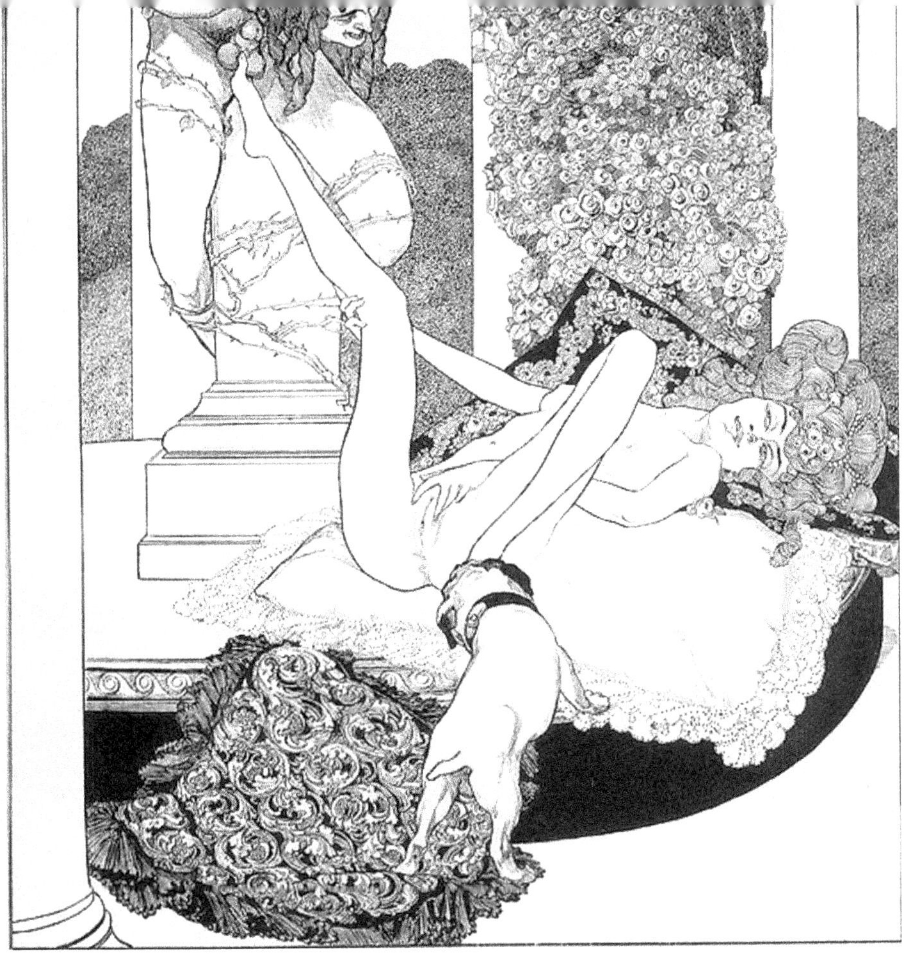

Franz von Bayros (1866-1924),
Der Toilettentisch, Tantalus, 1908

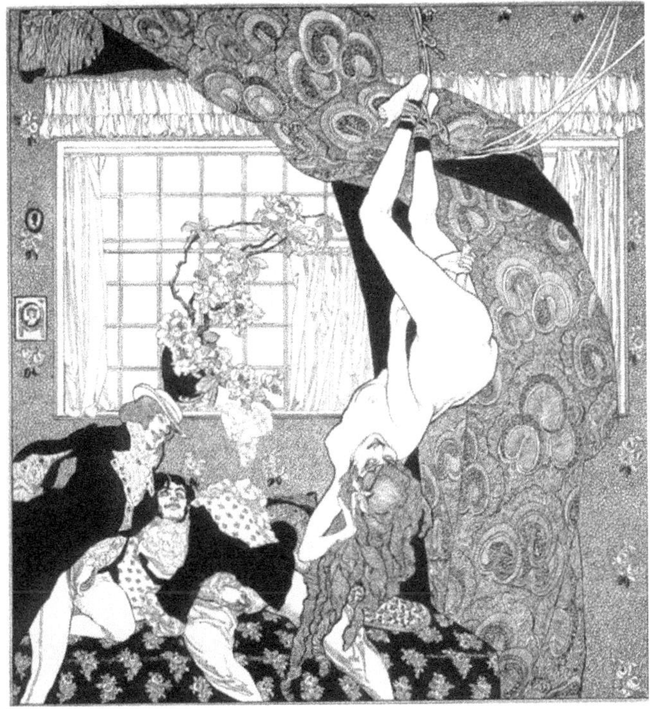

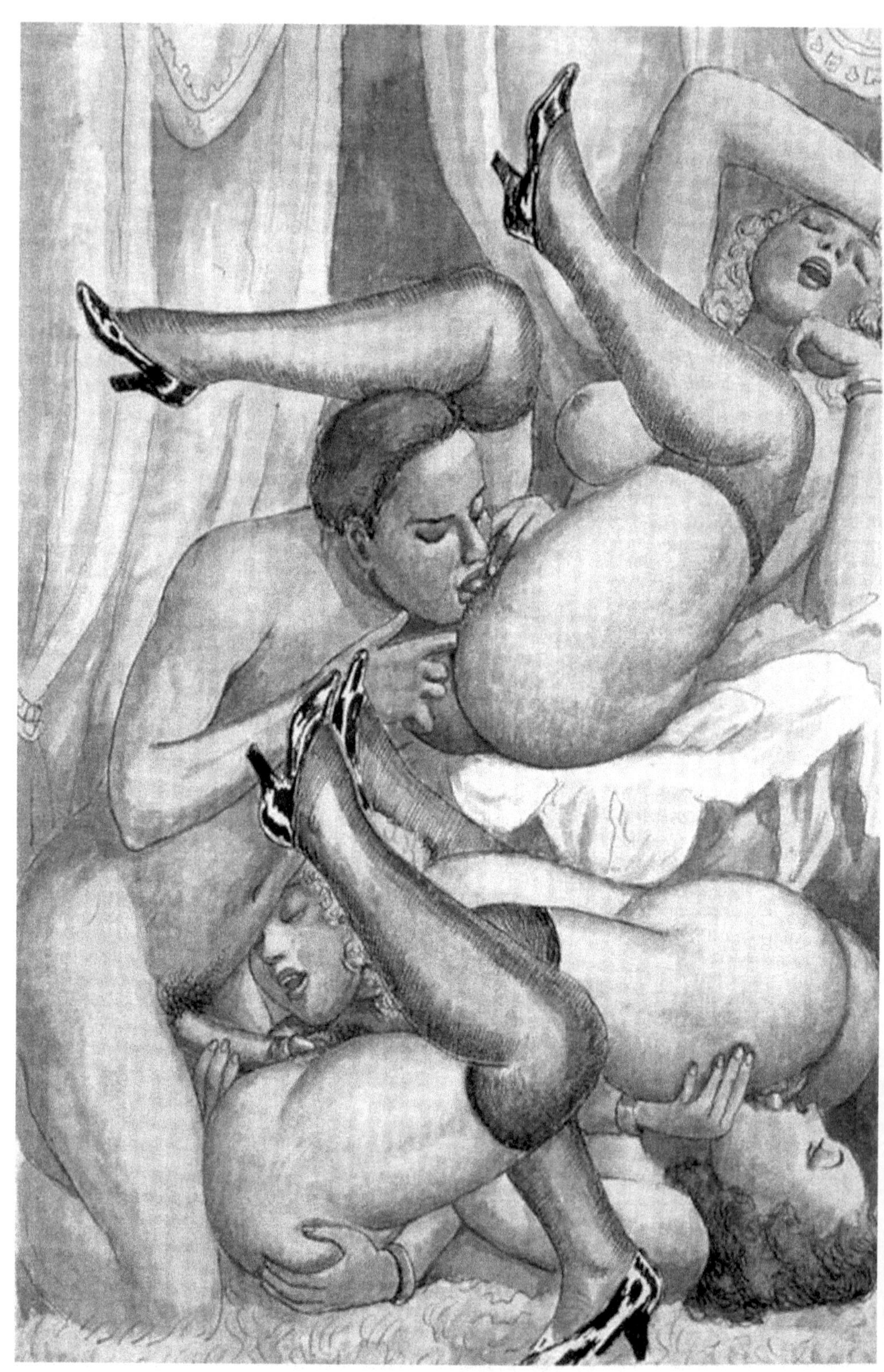

Anonymous, early 20th century

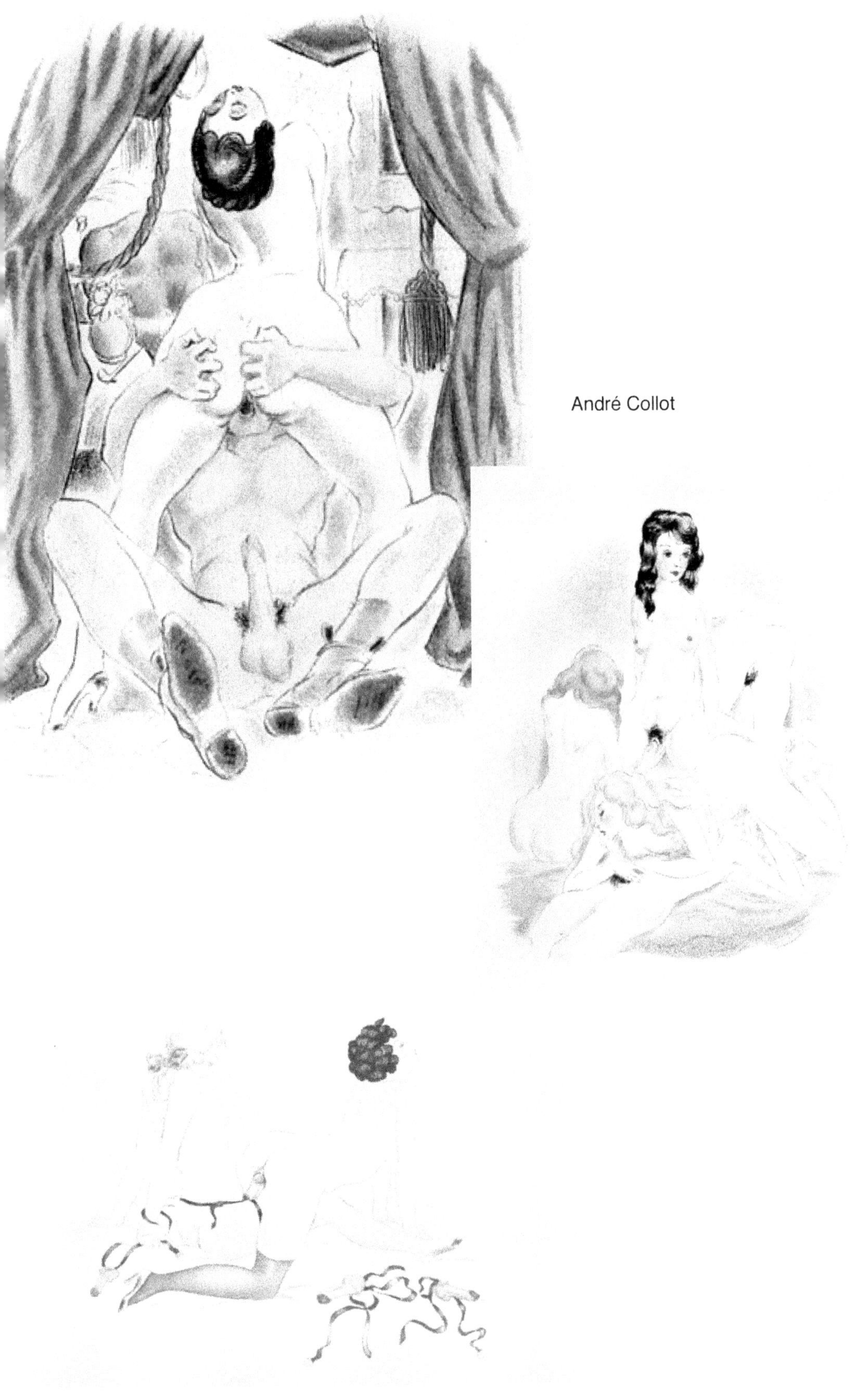

André Collot

FEMALE ORGASM

The female orgasm is 'anatomically invisible', as far as erotica is concerned. So the history of erotica and porn, for some commentators, 'is the history of visual strategies to overcome the anatomical invisibility of the female orgasm'.[1] In erotica, female orgasm is regarded with confusion and ambivalence. What actually is it? eroticists ask, what does it feel like? (Note that most eroticists throughout history have been men, forever excluded from directly experiencing the female orgasm). Thus the controversy over clitoral and vaginal orgasm, over female 'ejaculation', over 'multiple' orgasms. Female 'ejaculation' is 'visible evidence' of orgasm, yet it is censored by pornographers themselves at times.[2]

1 L. Nead, 98; see also L. Williams, 1990.

2 See S. Bell: "Feminist Ejaculations", in Arthur and Marilouise Kroker, eds: *The Hysterical Male: New Feminist Theory*, St Martin's Press, New York, 155-169; also C. Straayer: "The Seduction of Boundaries: Feminist Fluidity in Annie Sprinkle's Art/Education/Sex", in P. Gibson, ed, 168f

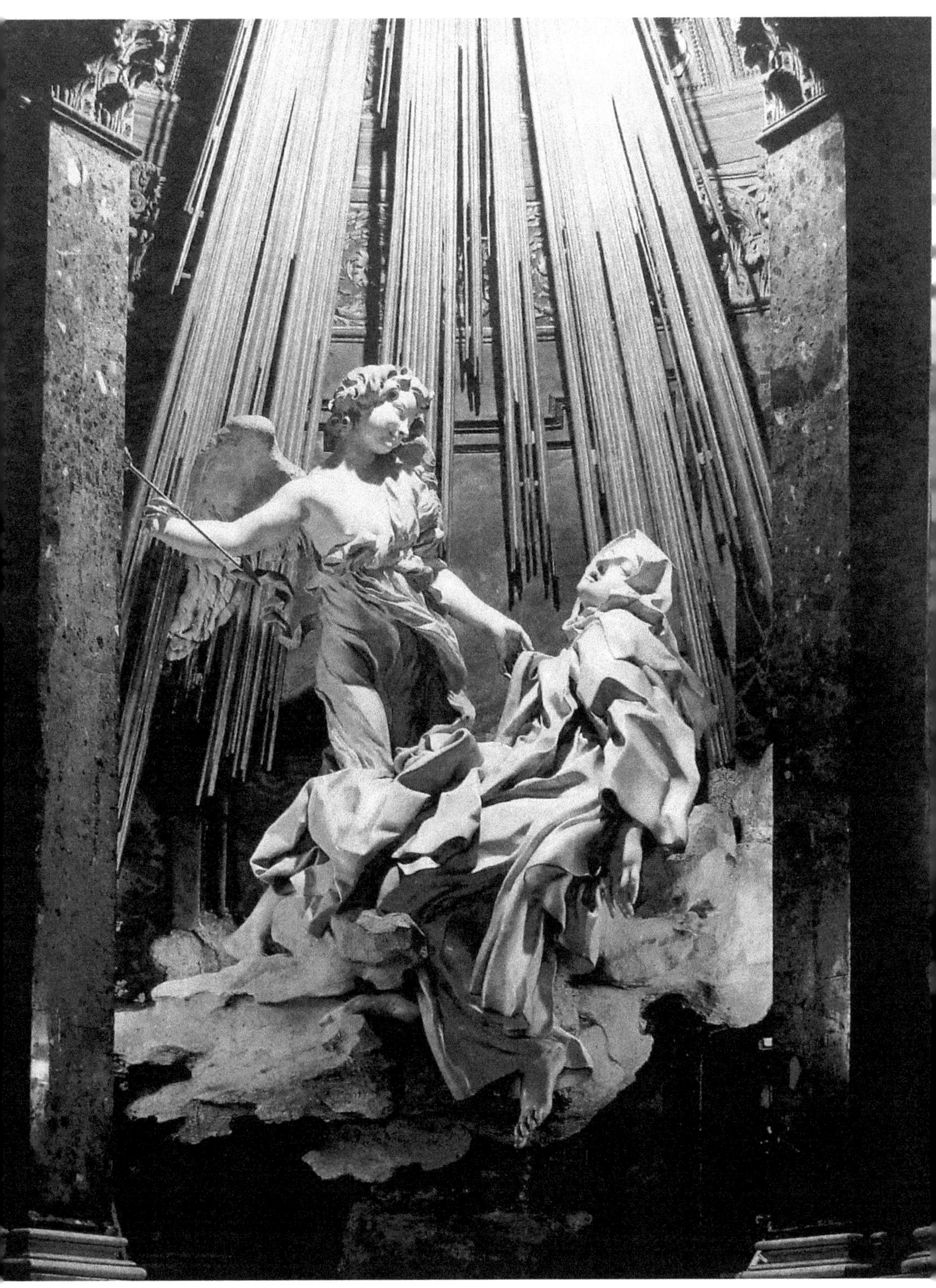

Gianlorenzo Bernini, The Ecstasy of St Theresa, 1652, Rome

ORGASM

Sexuality is not what you *are,* but what you *do.* It is not *who* is fucking *whom,* but *how.*[1] The question is *how is this fucking being done?* Never *why,* always *how.*

For patriarchal people, of either or any sex, it seems it is essential to know *who* is speaking about sex. Is the author male or female (or some other gender)? What is her/ his sexual identity? Patriarchal people are disturbed when their expectations of gender are disrupted. When, say, a male author writes of lesbian sexuality as if from the 'inside', as if in the 'character' of a lesbian. For example, who is the speaker and who is the subject of this poem:

> First, I want to make
>   kiss you...
> I want to make you come
> in my mouth like a storm.[2]

It seems the speaker (Marilyn Hacker) is female and she is describing lesbian sex. But the words could just as apply heterosexual or homosexual eroticism. Only when parts of the body are mentioned – clitoris, nipples, penis, breasts – is it possible to decipher the gender of speaker, text or subject, and sometimes not even then.

---

1 see Valerie Traub, in V. Wayne, 83

2 Marilyn Hacker: 'Noces', from *Love, Death and the Changing of the Seasons,* Arbor House 1986

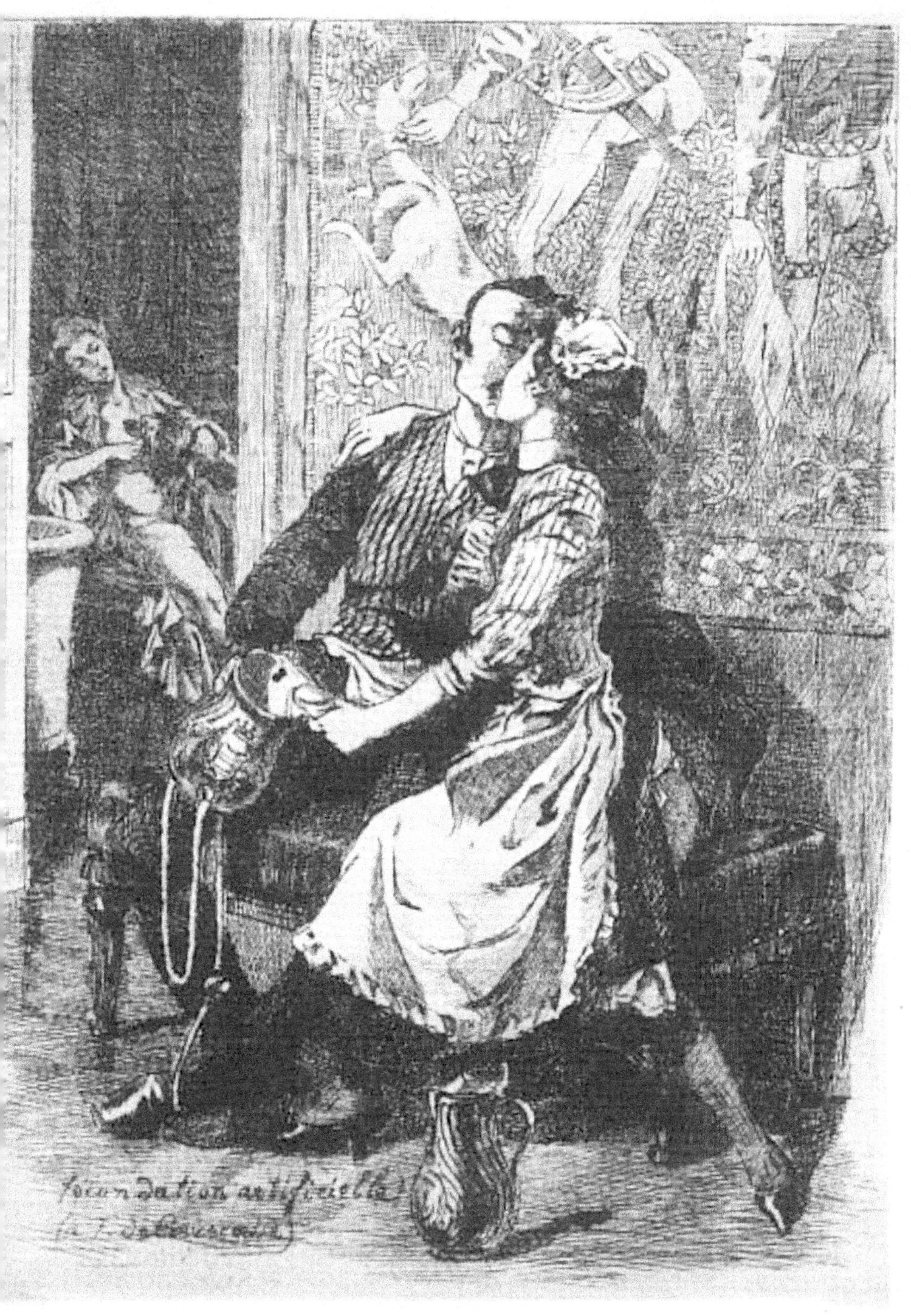

Martin van Maele

THE PHALLUS

In pornography, the great signifier is the phallus, while the site of pleasure is the woman's body. Reclining on a million couches in artists' studios, the female nude offers itself up as a country to be colonized. It is both a pleasure machine and a fantasy. The orchestrator of pleasure in this pornographic scenario is that little slip of flesh, the penis. The phallus is good, whole, true, unifying, as opposed to the bad, fragmented, impure, chaotic vagina.[1] The phallus is the emblem of male power, as many commentators, not only feminists, note: '[t]he supreme power is the power that prevails over mortality', and this power is 'reasonably equated with the phallus'.[2] For feminists, the West is a phallic/ phallocentric/ phallogocentric society, where the phallus, the sublime signifier, the most censored image in the West, is the beginning and the end of sexual pleasure. For Madeleine Gagnon, the phallus is an emblem of male narcissism:

> The phallus... represents repressive capitalist ownership, the exploiting bourgeois... The phallus means everything sets itself up as a mirror. Everything that erects itself as perfection.[3]

1 See T. Moi: *Sexual/ Textual Politics*, 66f; S.M. Gilbert & S. Gubar: *The Madwoman in the Attic: The Woman Writer and the Nineteenth Century Literary Imagination*, Yale University Press, New Haven, CT, 1979.
2 L. Steinberg: *The Sexuality of Christ in Renaissance Art and in Modern Oblivion*, Pantheon, New York, 1984, 90.
3 M. Gagnon: "Corps I", *La venue à l'écriture*, UGE, 10/18, Paris 1977; in E. Marks, 180.

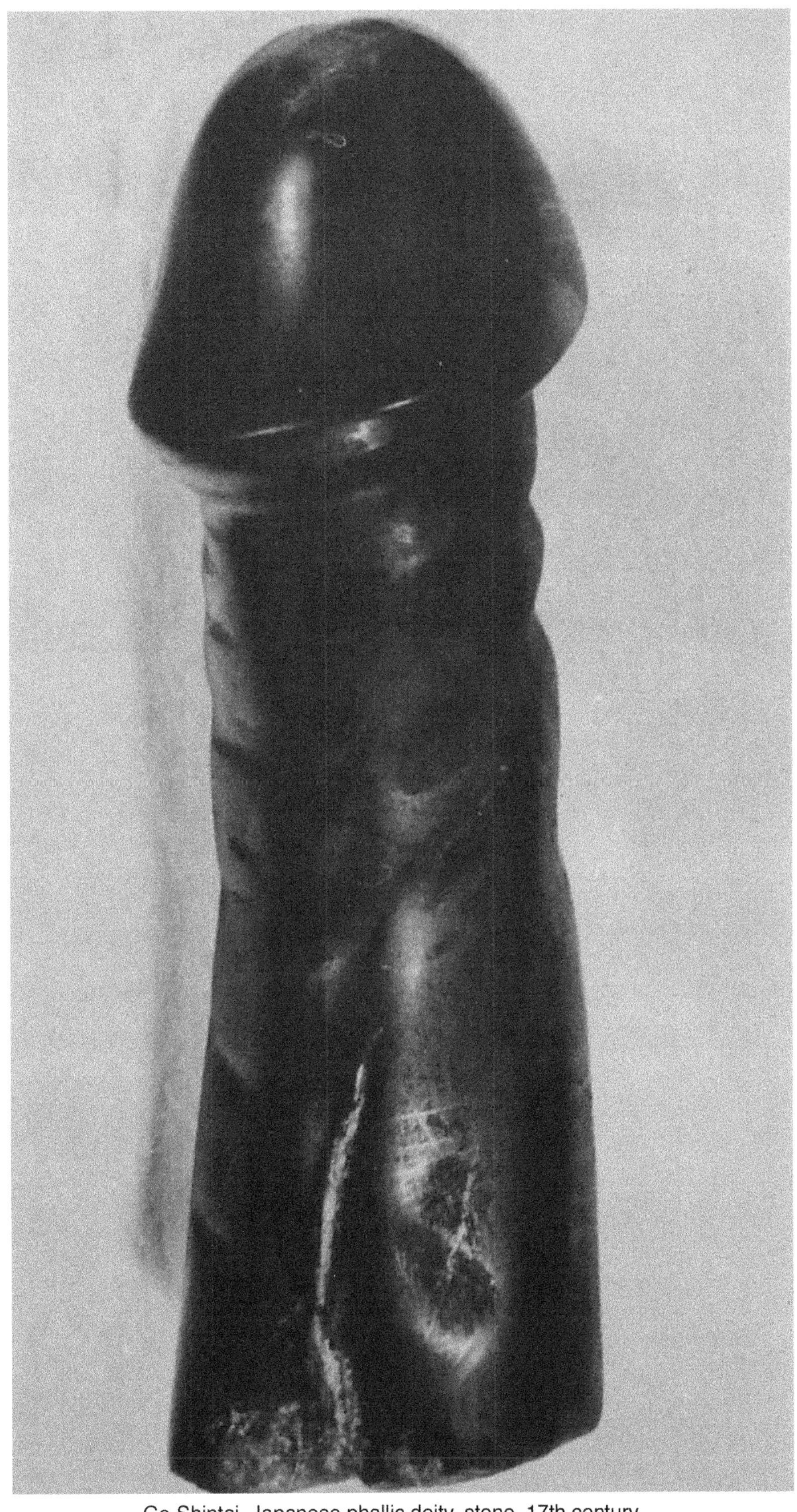

Go-Shintai, Japanese phallic deity, stone, 17th century

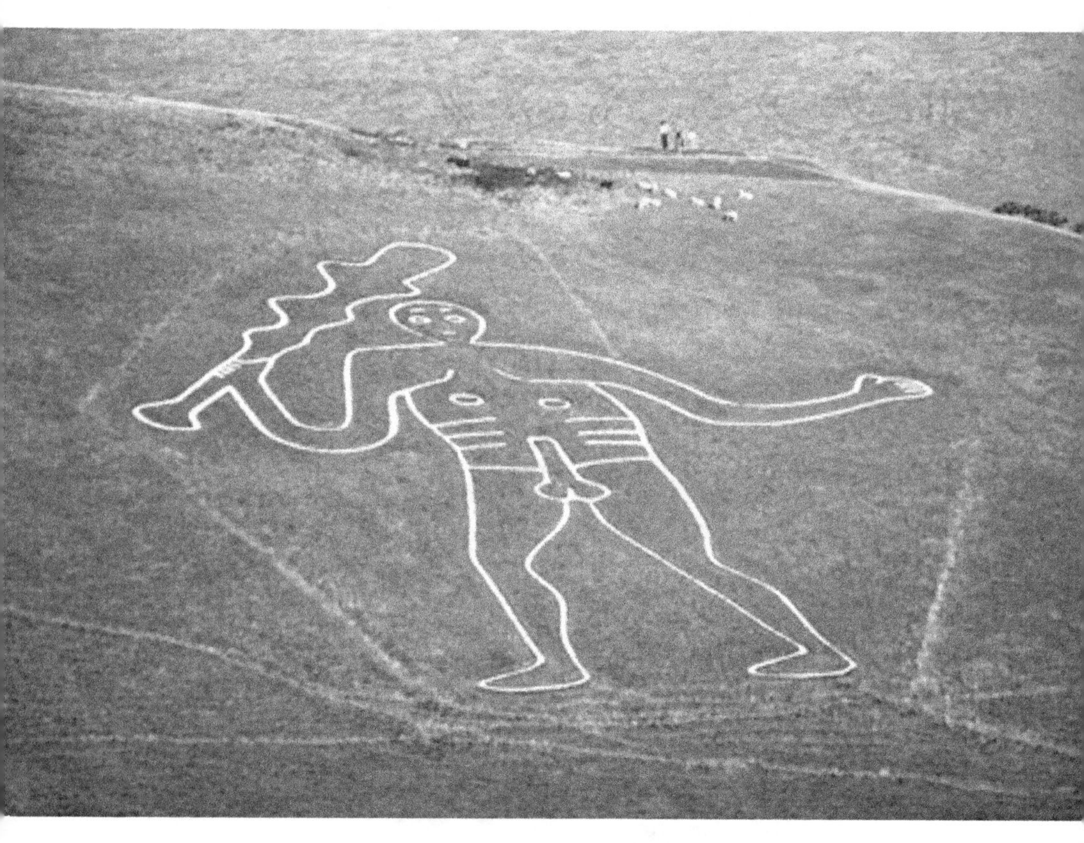

Cerne Giant, Dorset, England

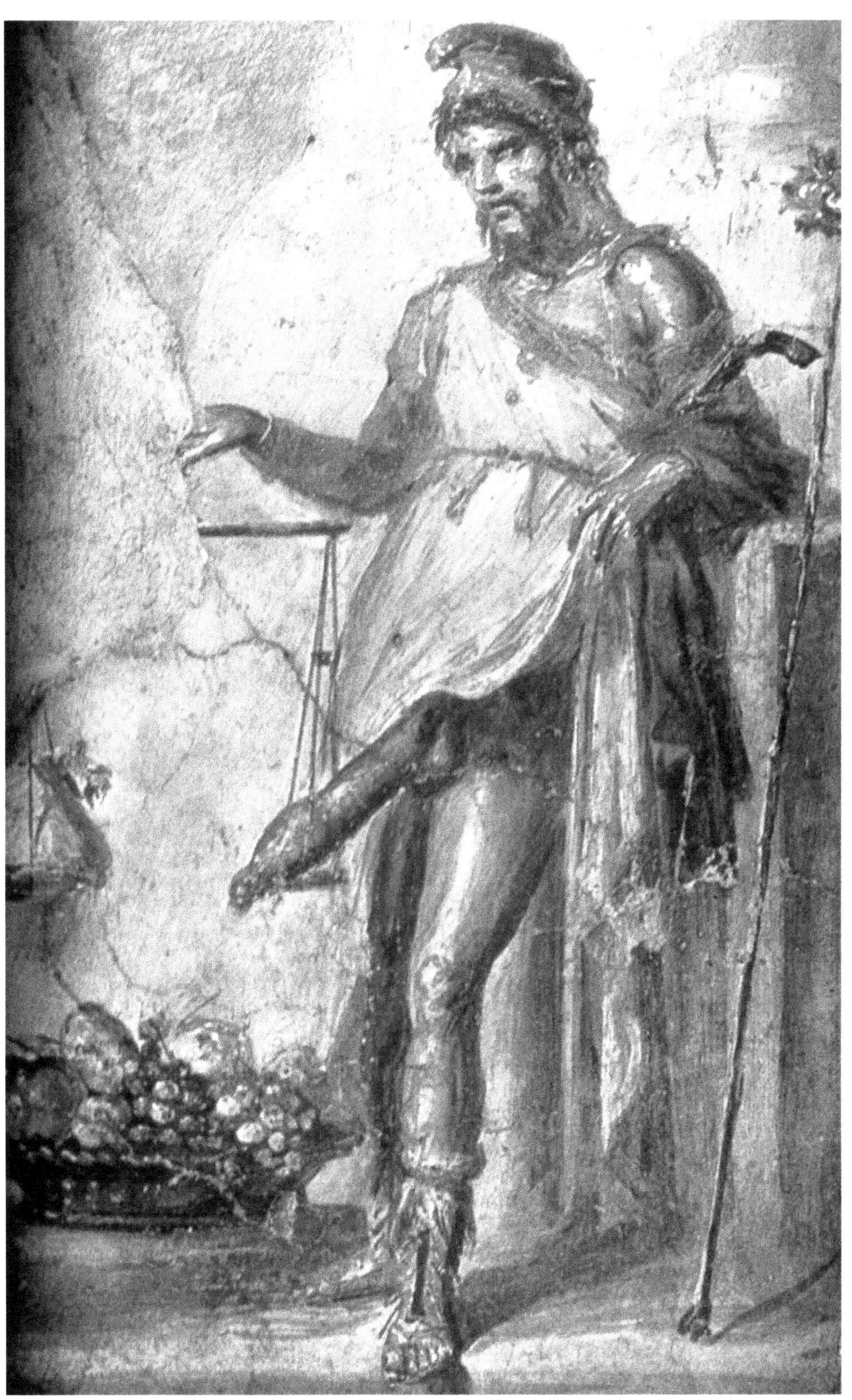

Fresco, Ancient Roman

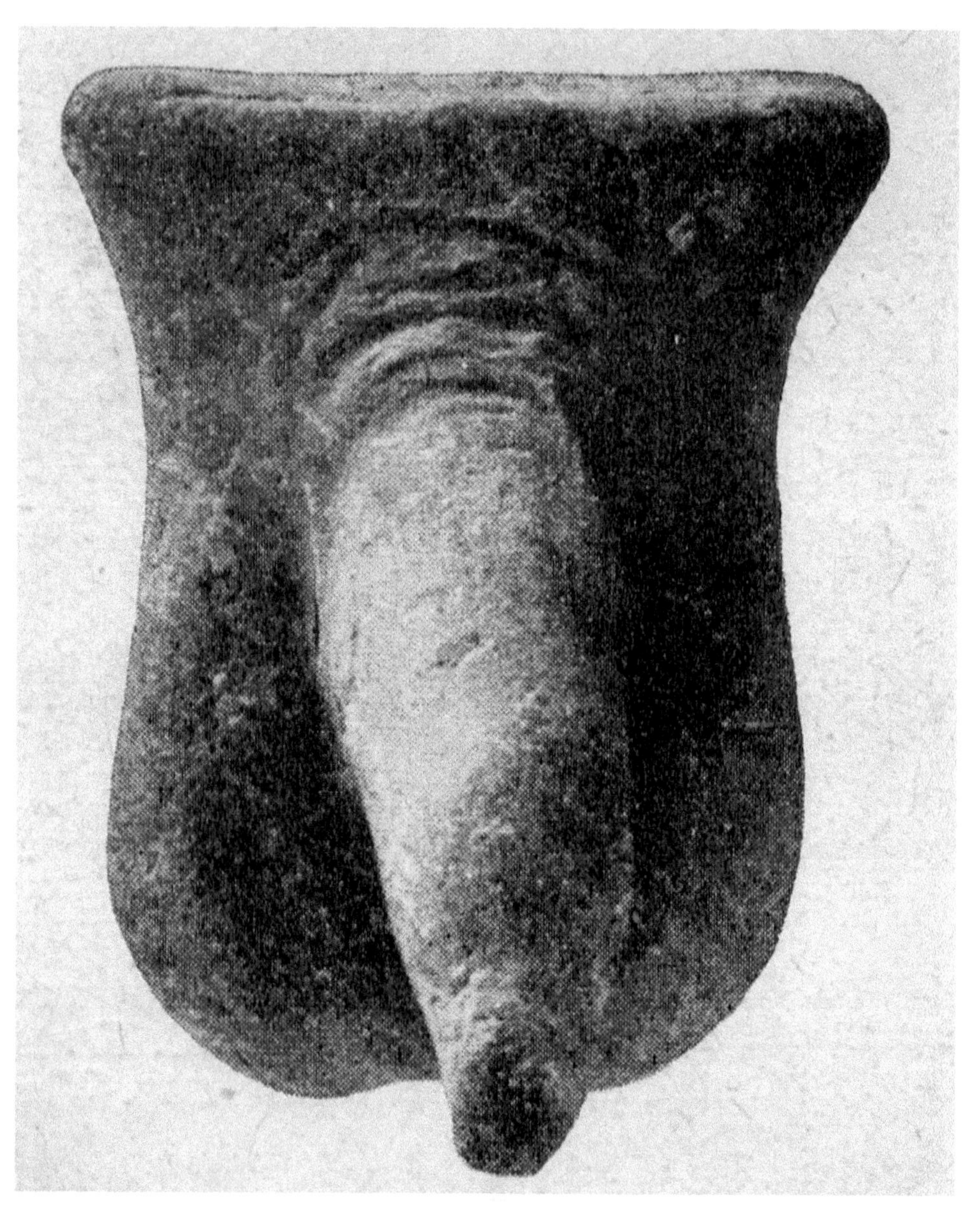

Ancient Votive Phallus, from Albert Moll, Handbuch der Sexualwissenschaften, Verlag Von F.C. Vogel, Leipzig, 1921

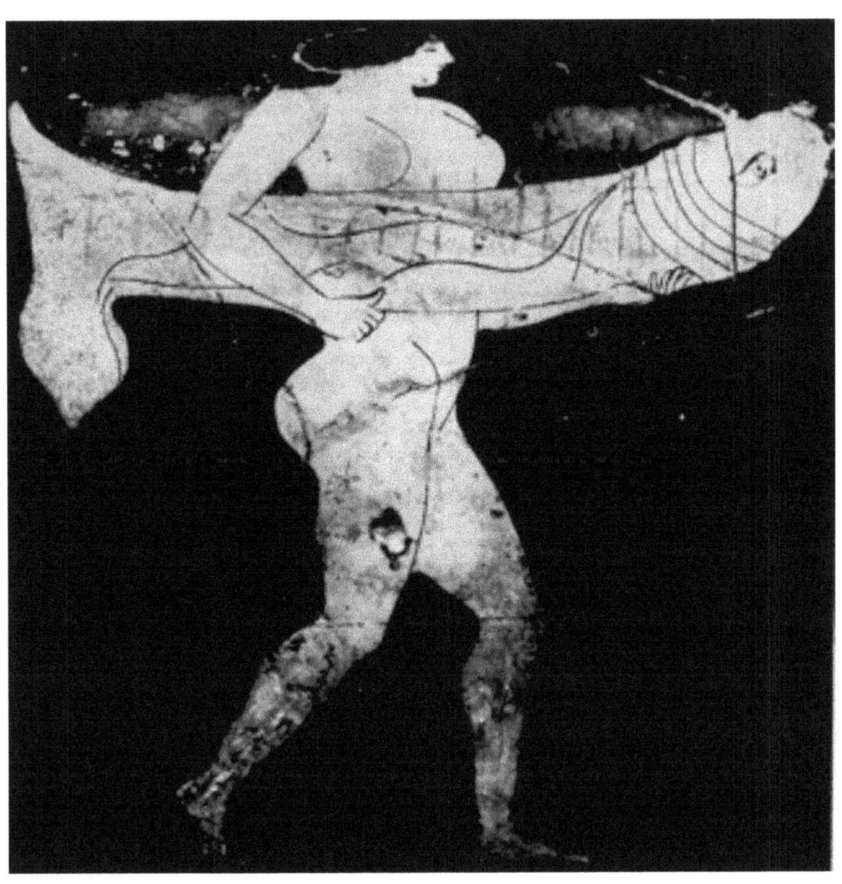

Vase, Ancient Greek

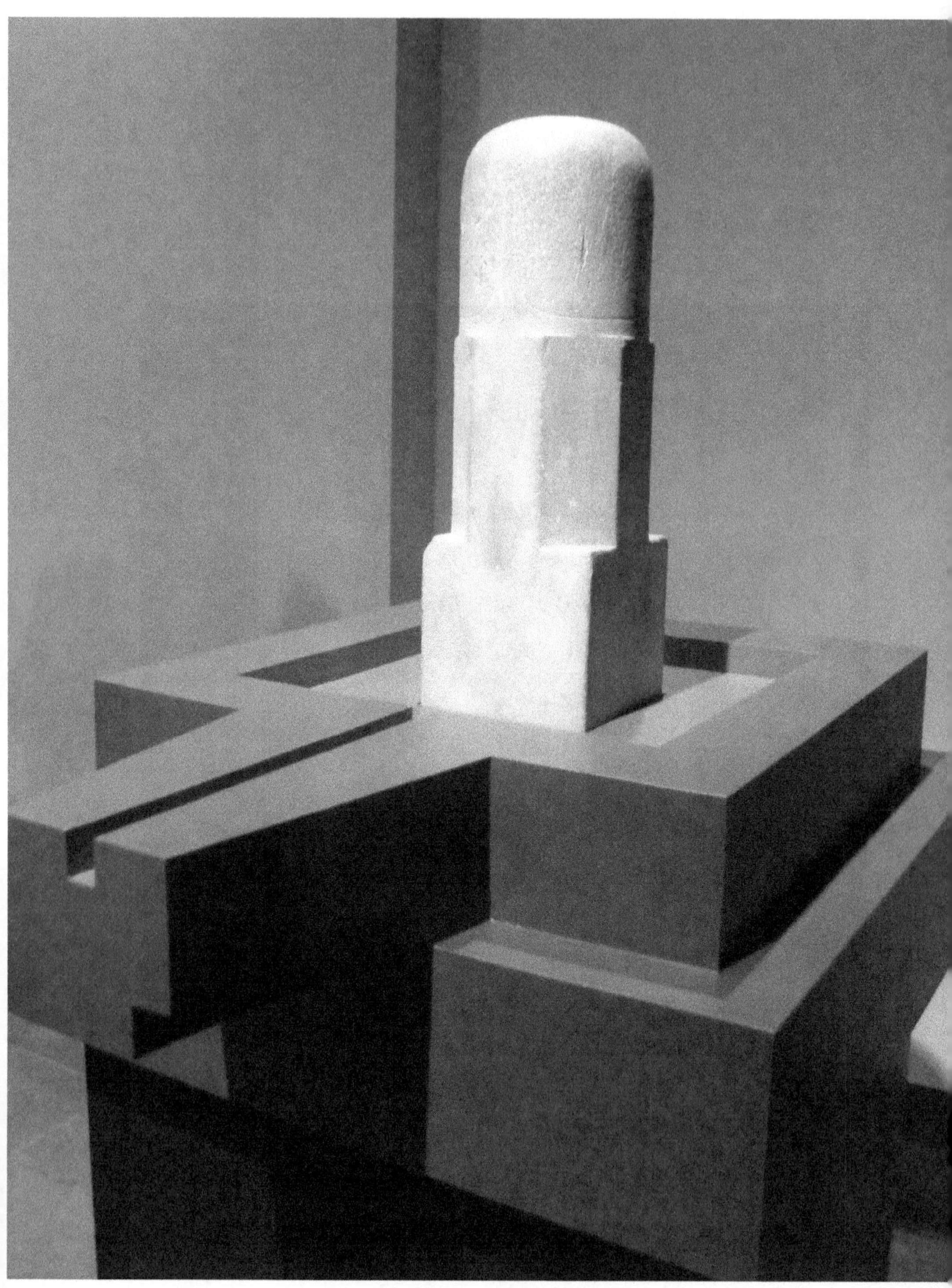

Lingam and Yoni, Cambodian, Norton Simon Museum, Pasadena, CA

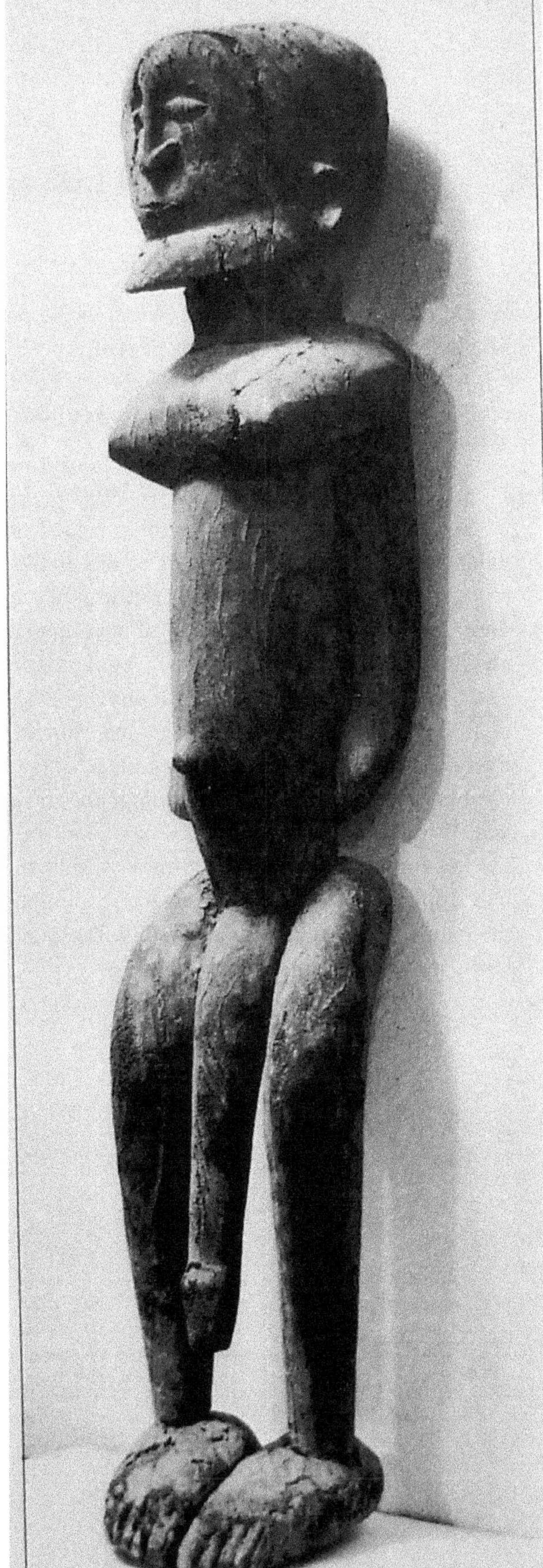

Wood figure, Ivory Coast

THE PHALLUS

Whole philosophic systems are based on the phallus, yet, as Juliet Mitchell remarked in "Feminine Sexuality':

> It's extraordinary what happens when you get rid of the centrality of the concept of the phallus. I mean, you get rid of the unconscious, get rid of sexuality, get rid of the original psychoanalytic point.[1]

If men reduce people to their sexual identities, as some feminists claim, then at the heart of this is the penis. Women are reduced to 'cunt', as Kate Millet put it, while men are all phallus. There are certainly no shortage of phallic symbols and artifacts about. The real thing, the real penis, is censored, carefully guarded – it's not much to look at anyway – so men displace their phallic sexuality onto thrusting cars, lorries, missiles, bombs, towers, cameras, computers, guitars, cigarettes, telephones, swords, guns, eyes, etc. These things abound in (patriarchal) art, and throughout the history of art (and pornography adds a million further fetishes). The trouble is that the penis ain't much of a thing, after all. As Richard Dyer commented: 'the fact is that the penis isn't a patch on the phallus. The penis can never live up to the mystique implied by the phallus'.[2]

---

1 J. Mitchell: "Feminine Sexuality: Interview with Juliet Mitchell and Jacqueline Rose", *m/f*, 8 (1983), 15.
2 R. Dyer: 'Don't Look Now", *Screen*, vol. 23, 3/4, 1983, and in A. McRobbie, 206.

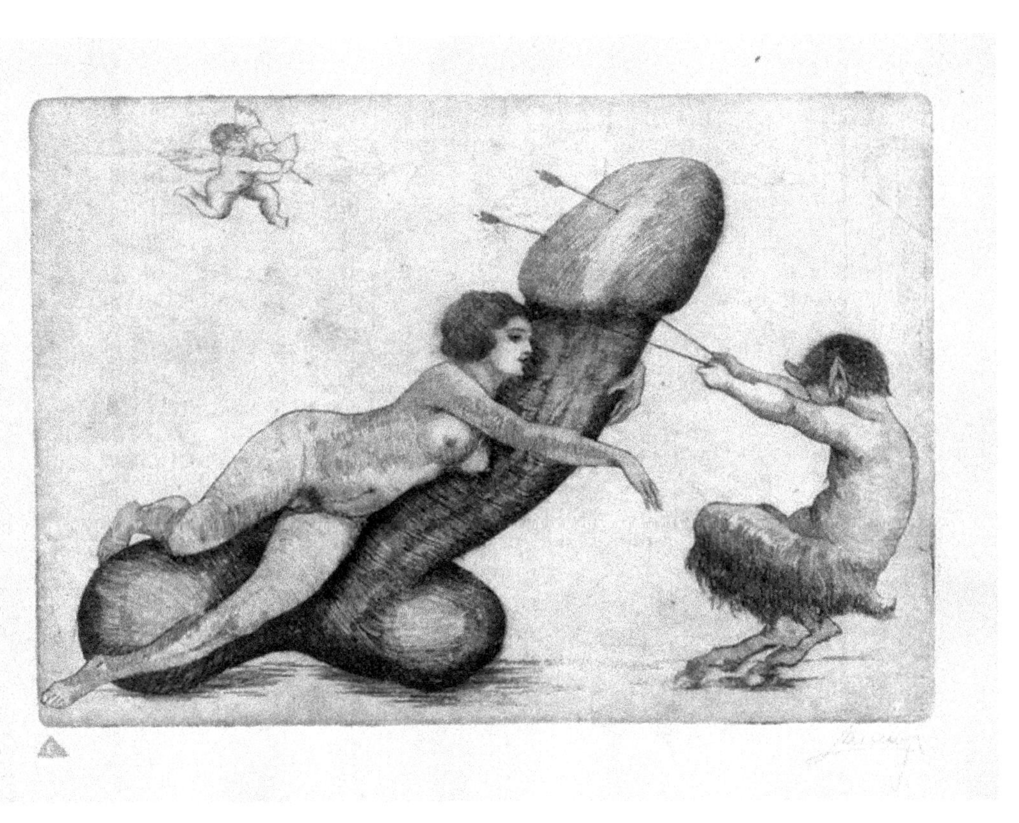

After Max Klinger (1857-1920)

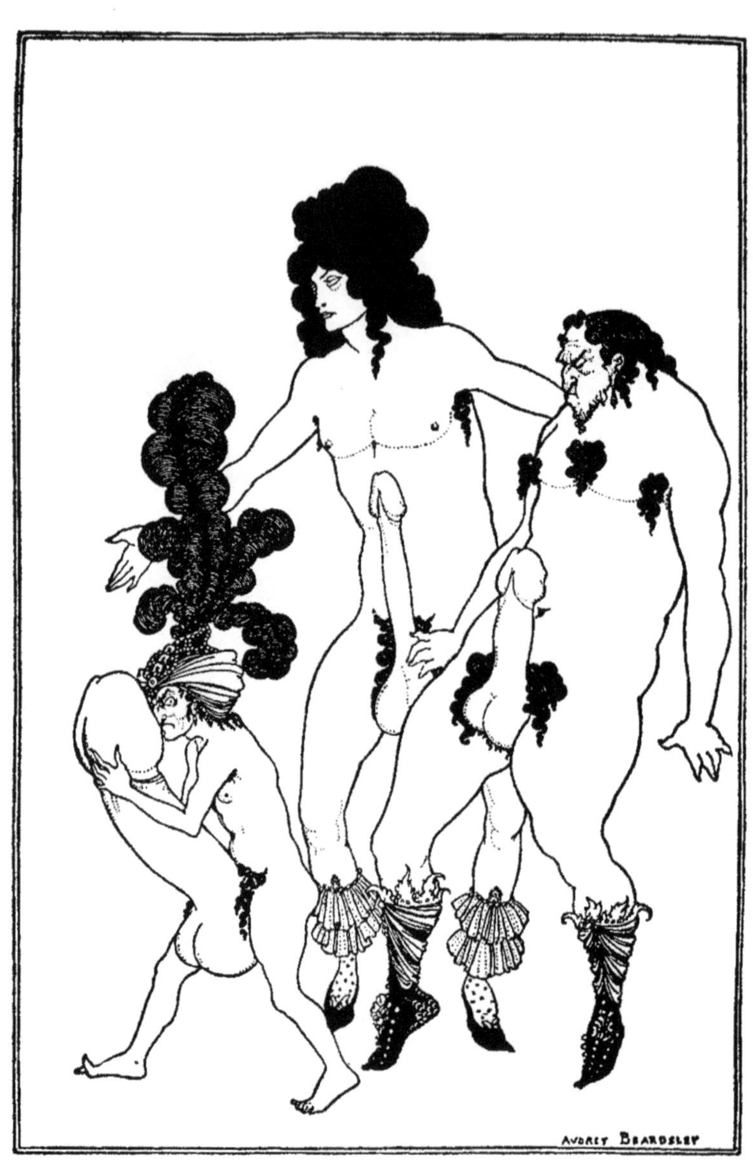

Aubrey Beardsley, Aristophanes, Lysistrata, 1896

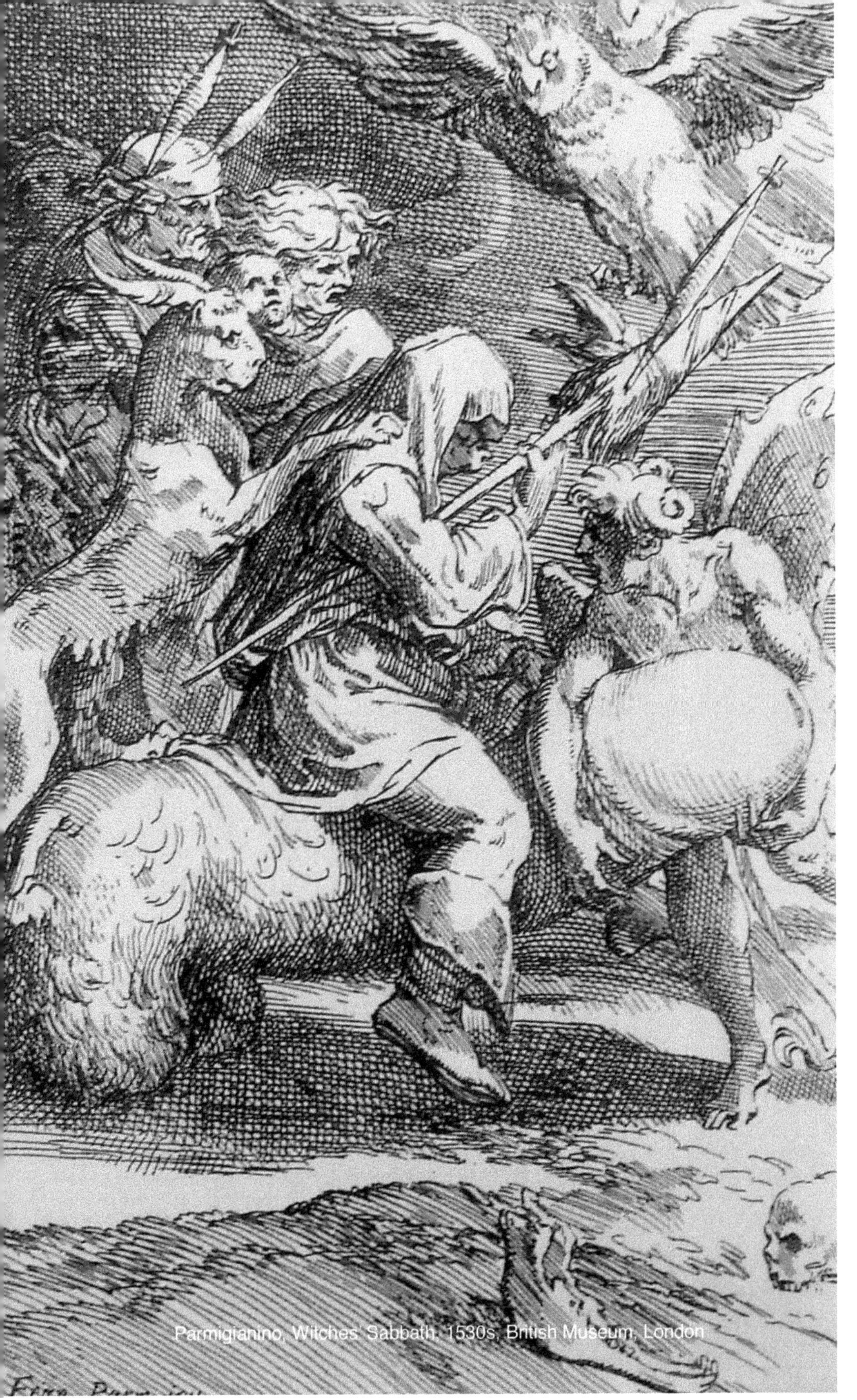

Parmigianino, Witches' Sabbath, 1530s, British Museum, London

In the (second wave) feminist view, the pornographer creates with his penis – the paintbrush, camera, computer or pen – these things are called 'tools', a common euphemism for the penis (there are thousands of other phallic control devices, such as game consoles, TVs, digital cameras, hi-fis, factory machinery, aeroplanes, etc). The quill, stylus or 'sharp projective' is a crucial element in the male's manufacture of art and pornography.[1] When Pierre Renoir was asked how he painted when he hands were crippled by arthritis he replied, '[w]ith my prick'.[2]

In pornography, the eye becomes the phallus, and looking is equated with caressing the obscure object of desire with the phallus (in the Lacanian system). Throughout Western art the phallus has been that visually absent but psychologically and ideologically present object. It is central in erotic art. Look at the Western art nudes – by Titian, Picasso, Ingres, Boucher: the phallus is there even though one doesn't see it. It's the same in any number of books, poems, sculptures, plays, operas, installations.

1 See J. Derrida: *Spurs: Nietzsche's Styles*, tr. B. Harlow, University of Chicago Press, Chicago 1979, 37-9; on the penis as a paintbrush, see Carol Duncan: "The Esthetics of Power in Modern Erotic Art", *Heresies*, 1, 1977, 46-50.
2 In J. Hobhouse, 135.

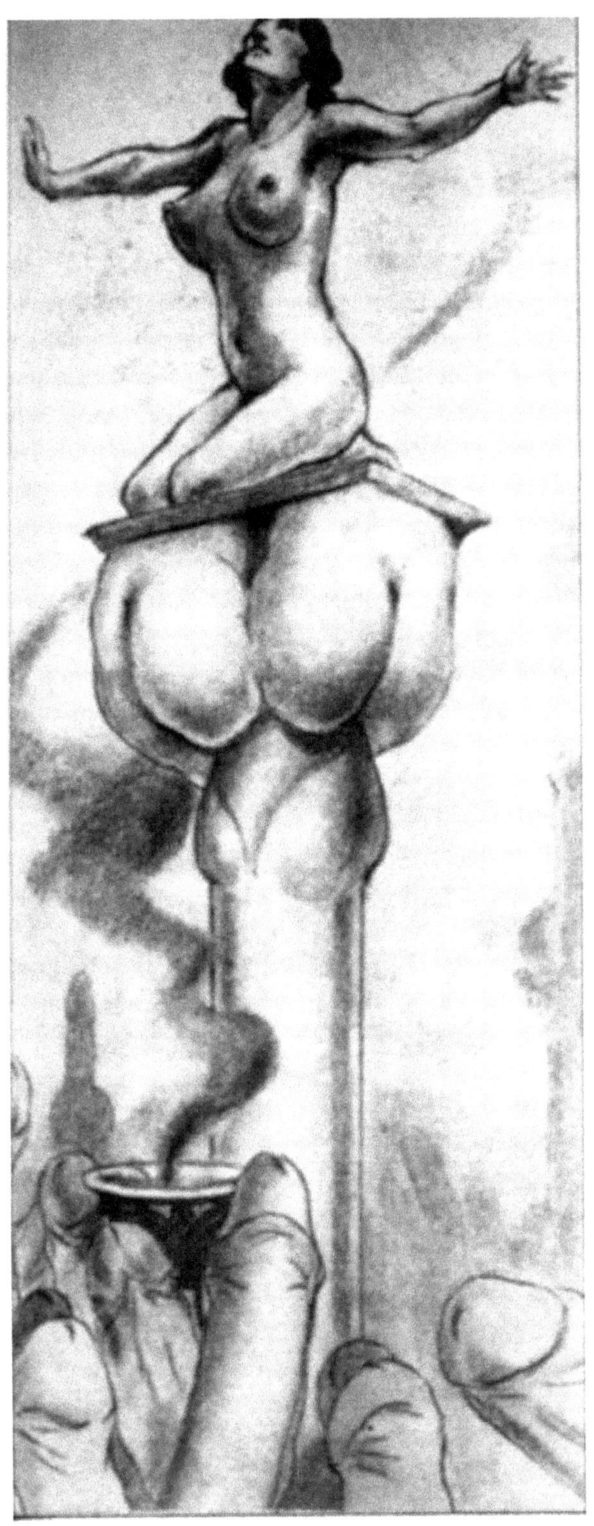

Anonymous, 19th century

LESBIAN EROTICA

In heterosexual pornography, lesbian eroticism is often introduced, but always controlled by a patriarchal force. Typically, in a soft porn scenario, two bisexual women cavort on a bed overseen by a male ('I've always wanted to see ya with another woman' drools the man to his wife/ girlfriend; or, frequently, 'I got back from work an' saw my wife and her best friend writhin' on the bed'). Towards the end of the scene, the man makes love to both women. Why? Because they needed the phallus, they needed a man to be fulfilled. Variations on this scenario occur endlessly in pornography. The male presence (the phallus) is seen as necessary for the true satisfaction for women (for valorization, for authenticity: i.e., it's not *true* sex without the phallus).

Lesbian or women's pornography, made by women for women, disappoints some feminists. Elizabeth Carola, who called herself as a 'radical feminist lesbian', described magazines such as *On Our Backs, Bad Attitude, OW! – Outrageous Women: A Journal of Woman-to-Woman SM, Yellow Silk, The Power Exchange*:

> Like all porn, this new 'woman's' porn is neither about nor for women. Like all porn it is, in a most basic sense, *against* women and *about* male fantasy – the basic male fantasy of Woman as Wholly Sexual Object whose Purpose is To Be Fucked – which feeds men's egos, fuels their violence...

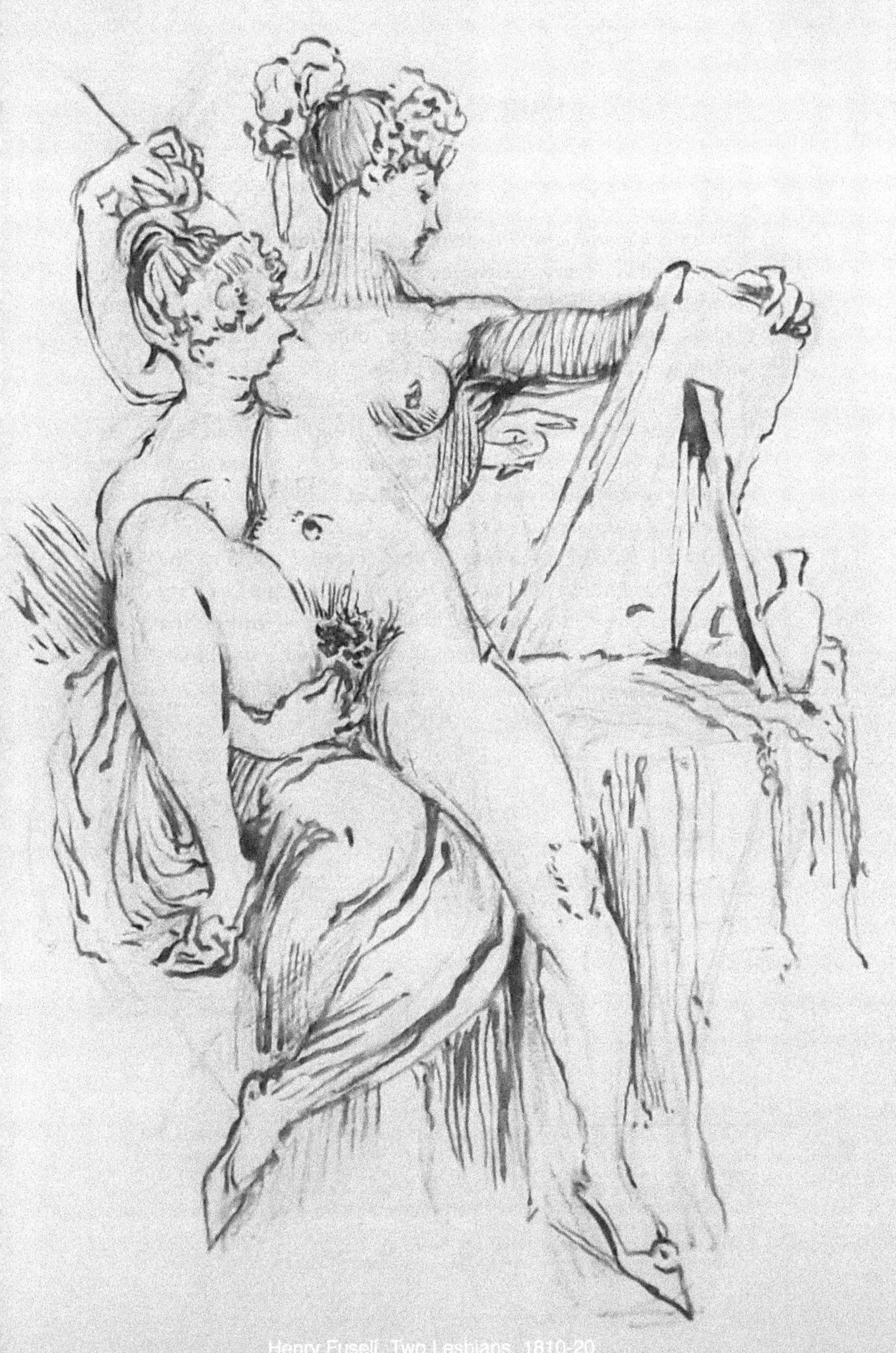

Henry Fuseli, Two Lesbians, 1810-20
private collection

LESBIAN EROTICISM

Lesbian sex is marked in contemporary cultural theory by the *lack* of the phallus. Hence, lesbian eroticism must always be 'deviant', because it departs from the patriarchal norms which exalt the phallus. Lesbianism must always be 'other', sexually, and many feminists note that the otherness of lesbian sexuality is one of the reasons that men and their patriarchal institutions are very threatened by lesbianism.[1] Lesbian attacks patriarchy at its powerbase. Men cannot control lesbians: '[l]esbians, by loving women and not men, pose a direct threat to the very basis of male supremacy', write Alice, Gordon, Debbie and Mary.[2] The lesbian is crucial, argued Monique Wittig, because she 'is the only concept that I know of which is beyond the categories of sex (man and woman)'.[3] Wittig moved towards a view of culture that goes beyond gender, beyond 'biological dimorphism', and biology.

1 T. Atkinson: *Amazon Odyssey*, Links Books, New York 1974; Alice, Gordon, Debbie and Mary: "Separatism", in S.L. Hoagland & J. Penelope, eds: *For Lesbians Only: A separatist anthology*, Onlywomen Press 1988, 31-40; A. Rich: "Towards a woman-centred university", in *On Lies, Secrets and Silence*, Novotny, New York 1979; J. Johnston: *Lesbian Nation: The Feminist Solution*, Simon & Shuster, New York 1974; S. Rowbotham: *Beyond the Fragments: Feminism and the making of Socialism*, Merlin 1979.

2 Alice, Gordon, Debbie and Mary, op. cit., 31-40.

3 M. Wittig: "One is not born a woman", in S. Hoagland, op. cit., 446-7.

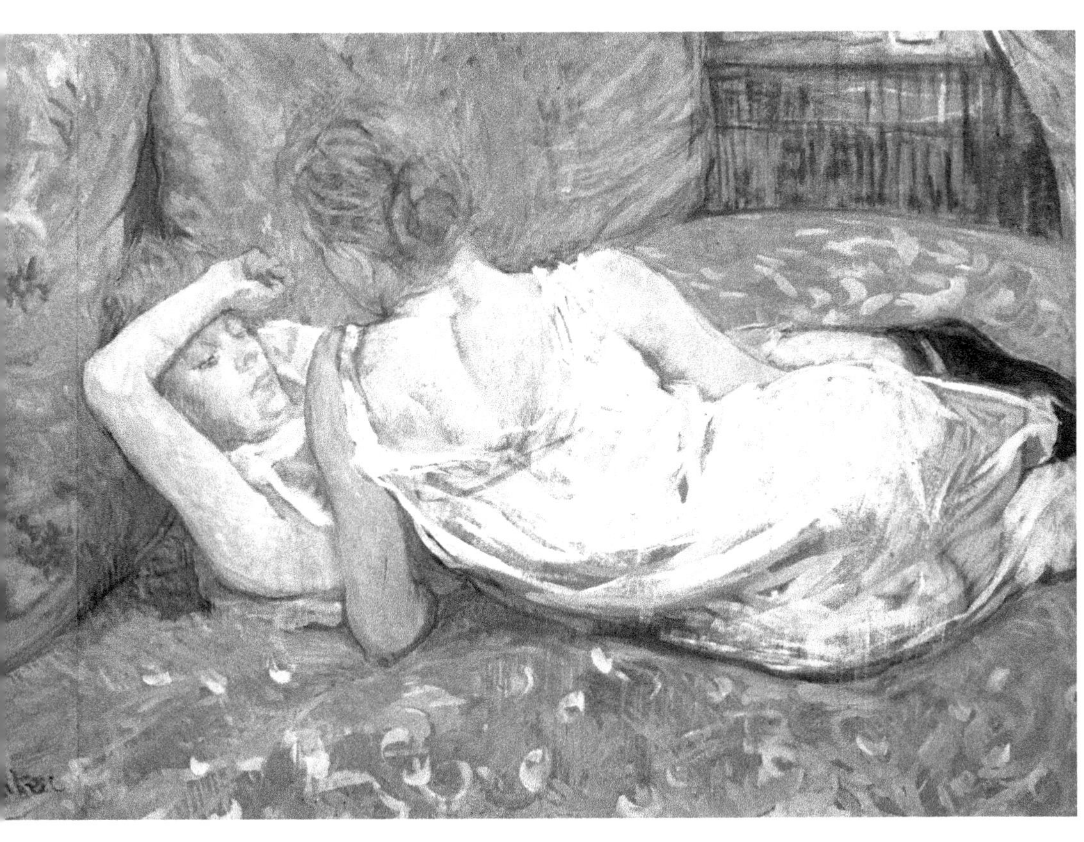

Henri de Toulouse-Lautrec (1864-1901), Two Friends

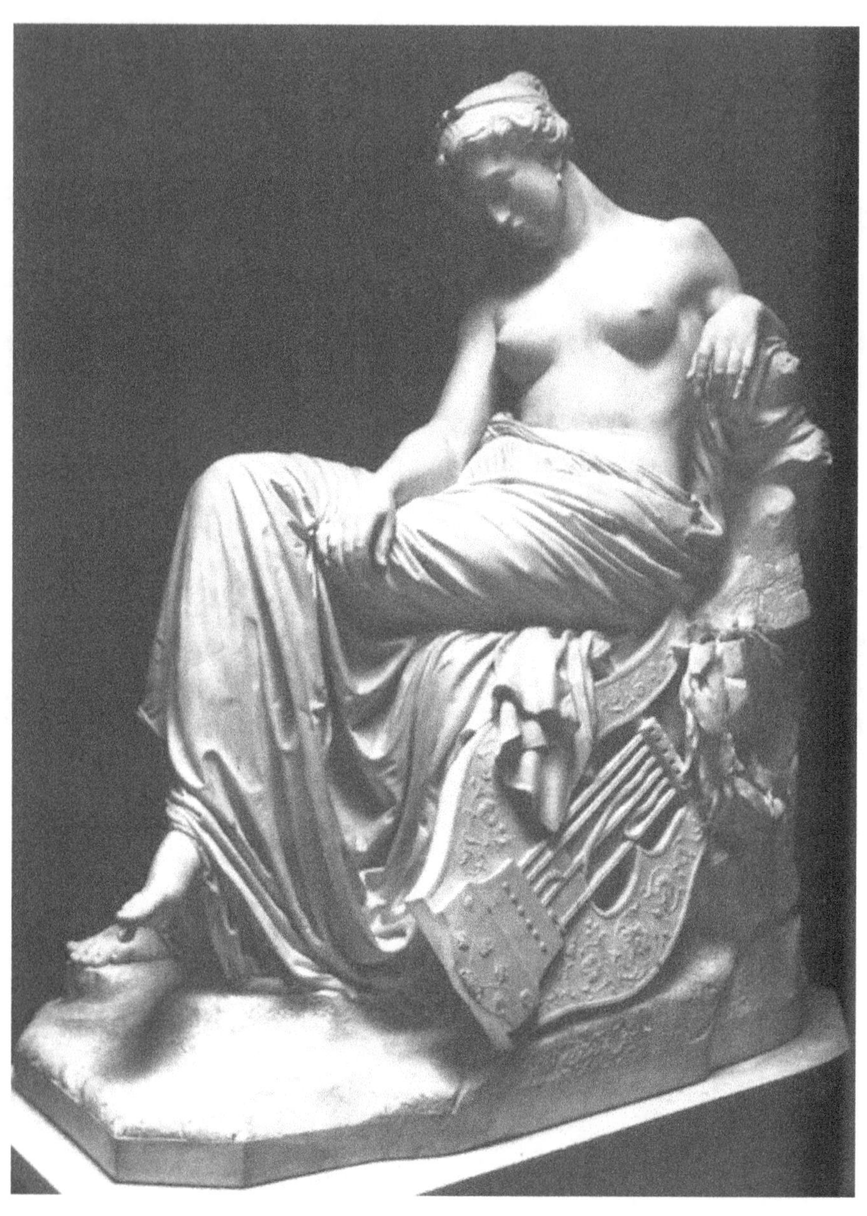

Giovanni Dupré, Sappho, 1857, Rome

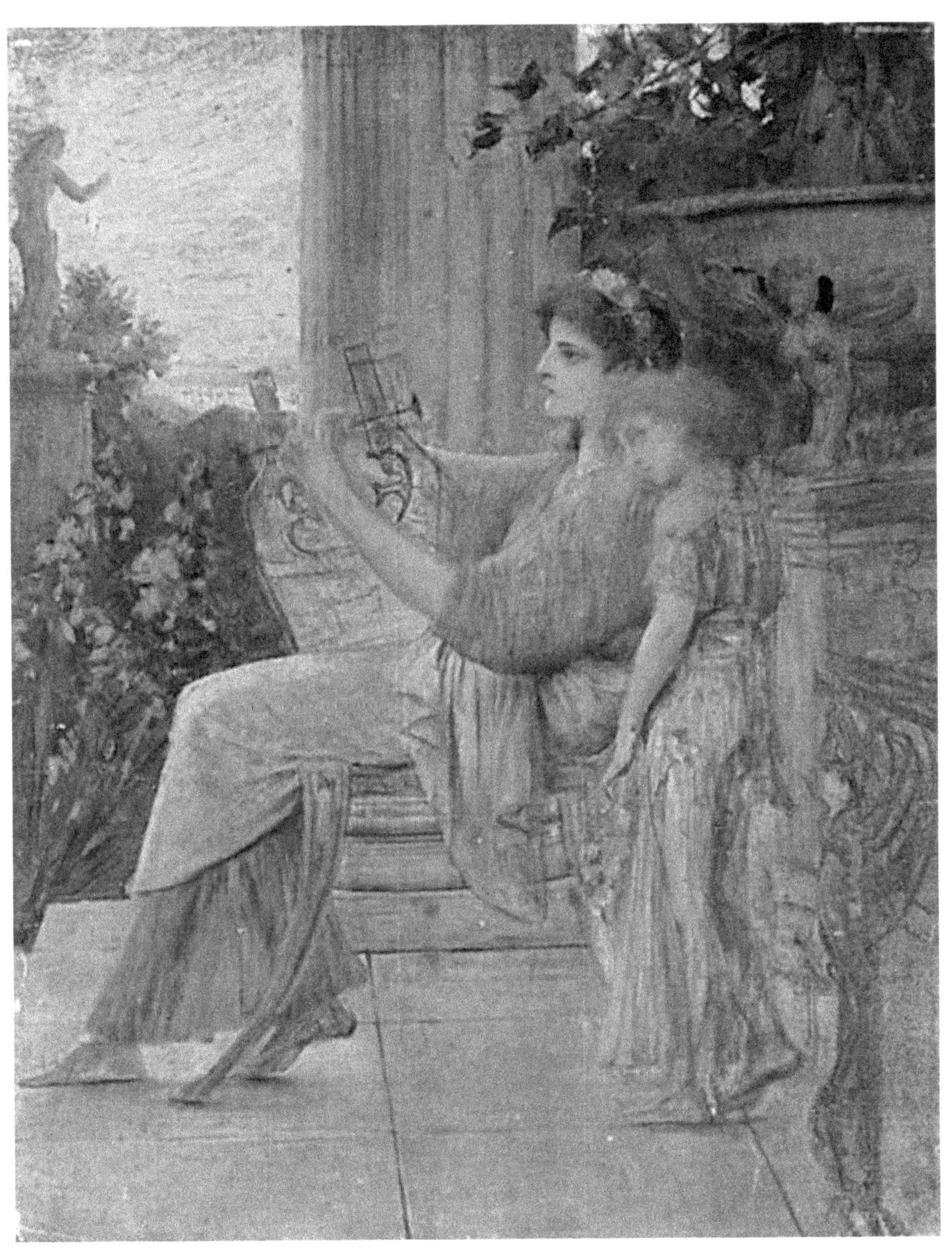

Gustav Klimt, Sappho, 1888-90

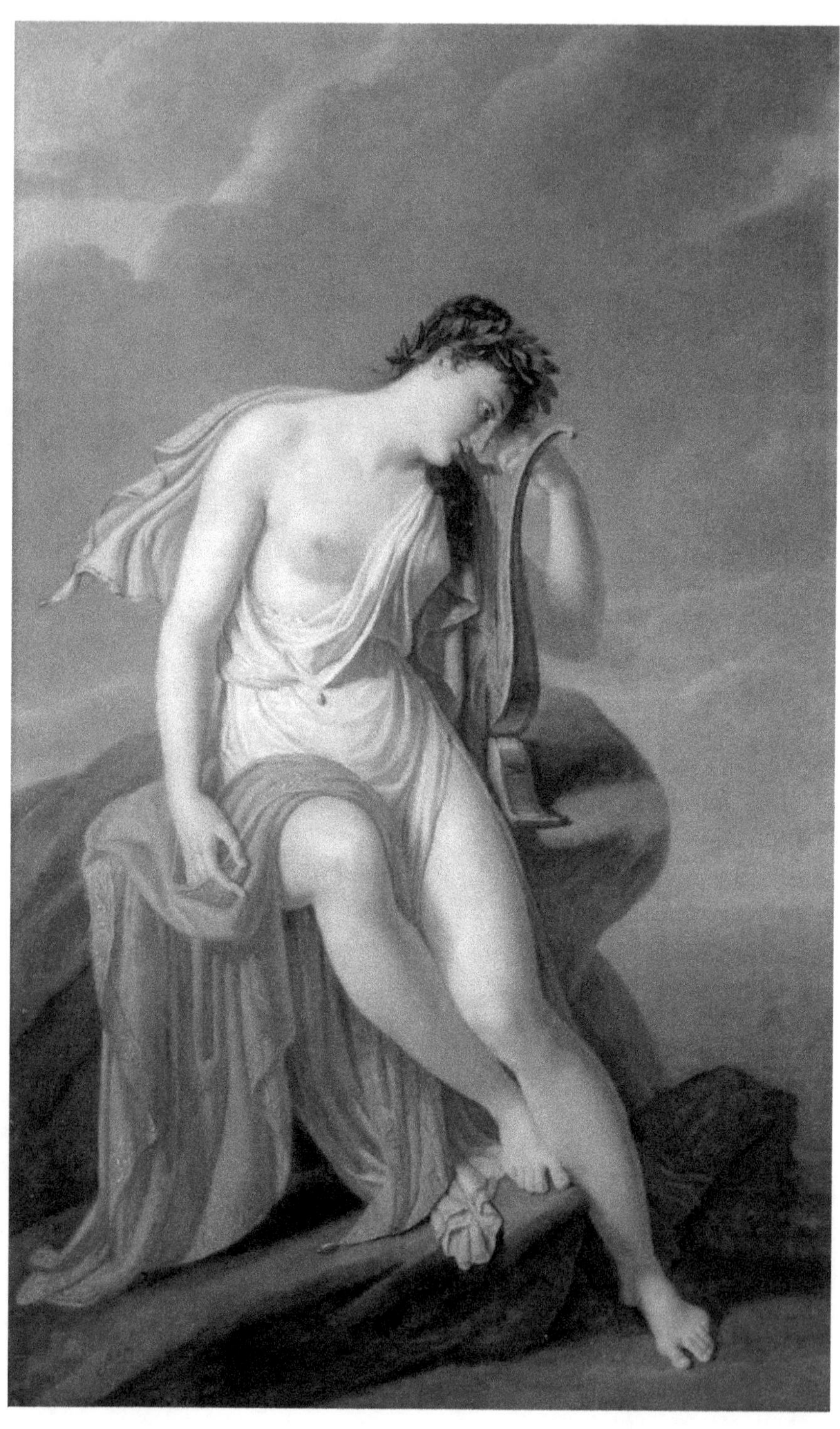

Pierre-Narcisse Guérin, Sappho On the Leucadian Cliff, 1800

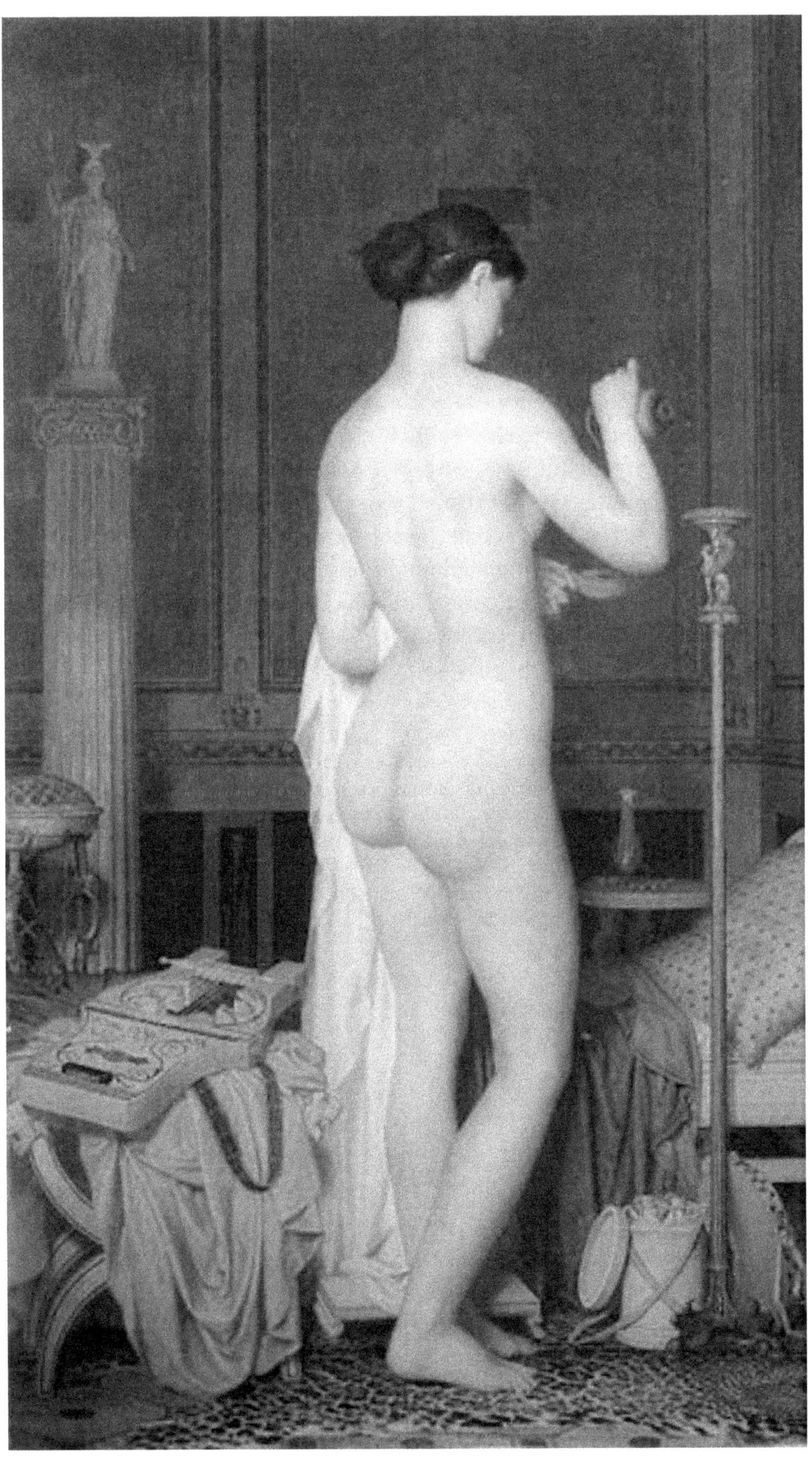

Marc-Charles-Gabriel Gleyre, Le Coucher de Sappho, 1867, Lausanne

LESBIAN EROTICA

Men are excluded from lesbian erotica: '[p]ornography for lesbians is unique in that it presumes a *female* gaze, and a lesbian one at that,' wrote Barbara Smith. But although 'lesbian' and 'women's' erotica and porn is for made for and by women, it still works within patriarchy, within male-made structures, values, ideologies and attitudes, just as lesbianism itself, according to some feminists, is not truly 'outside' of heterosexuality and patriarchy. The view is that '[l]esbians who engage in consensual S/M are thus merely imitating and even colluding in patriarchal structures,' according to Clare Whatling.[1] Clare Whatling suggests that lesbian S/M practice can parody and subvert patriarchal values and systems. She wrote:

> S/M is never *intrinsically* revolutionary. Like all sexual practice, it is a product of its time and context. As with other sexual practices, it may be oppositional under certain conditions, but it is never always so... S/M is constructed in relation to the society in which it is played out and cannot be understood without reference to the structures that exist there... Where S/M does perhaps differ from more conventional sexual practices is in the self-consciousness it brings to encounters. For S/M as a practice does much to foreground the constructedness of all sexuality.[2]

1 C. Whatling: "Who's read *Macho Sluts*", in J. Still, 193.
2 C. Whatling, op.cit., 194.

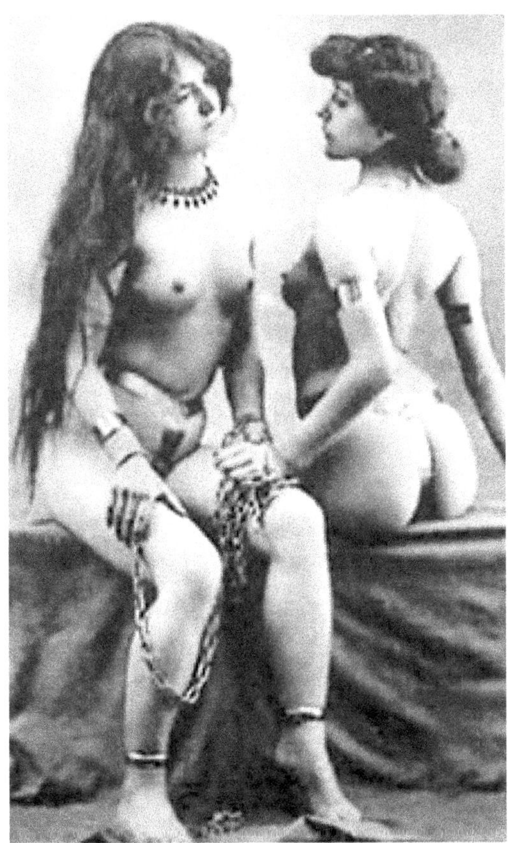

Anonymous, lesbian photograhs, 19th century

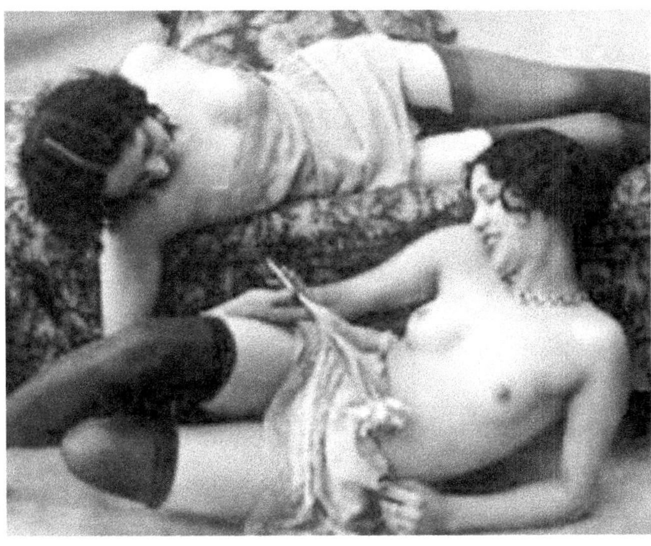

LESBIAN EROTICISM

Not all feminists agree about the revolutionary potential of lesbianism, if it is a lesbianism that keeps defining itself in terms of patriarchy. Elizabeth Mees reckoned that 'lesbianism, as an attack on hetero-relations, takes (its) place within the structure of the institution of heterosexuality. The lesbian is born of/ in it.'[1] There is no escape, it seems, from patriarchal and heterosexuality: the world is permeated with these ancient structures. As Sheila Jeffreys wrote: '[e]very woman grows up in a heteropatriarchal world',[2] while Ann Barr Snitow remarked in "Mass Market Romance':

> One of our culture's most intense myths, the ideal of an individual who is brave and complete in isolation, is for men only. Women are grounded, enmeshed in civilization, in social connection, in family and in love (a condition a feminist culture might well define as desirable) while all our culture's rich myths of individualism are essentially closed to them.[3]

1 E. Mees, in K. Jay & J. Glasgow: *Lesbian Text and Contexts: Radical Revisions*, New York University Press, New York, NY, 1990, 82.
2 S. Jeffreys: "The Censoring of Revolutionary Feminism", in G. Chester, 139.
3 A. Snitow: "Mass Market Romance: Pornography for Women Is Different", *Radical History Review*, no. 20, Spring/Summer, 1979.

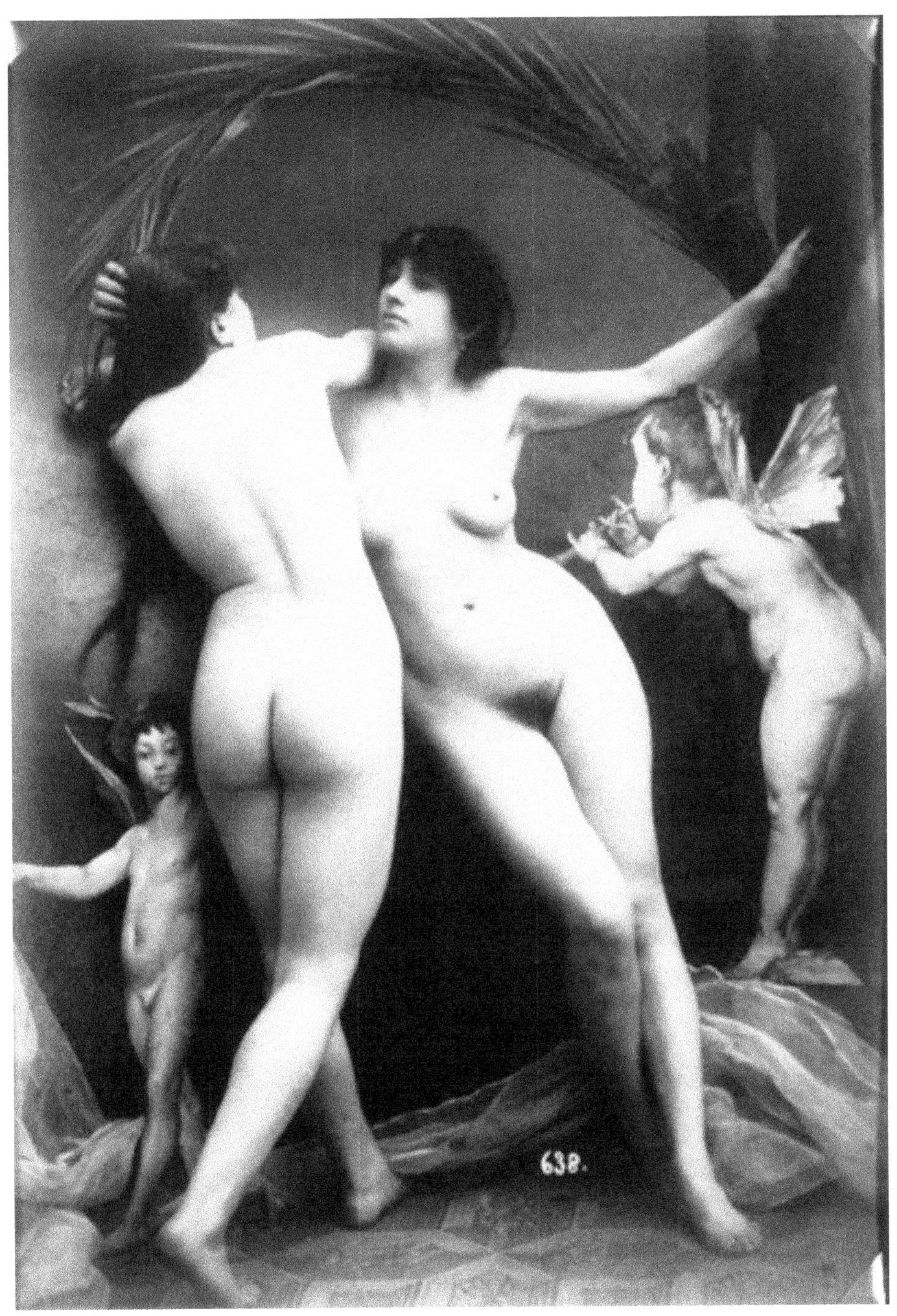

Gaudenzio Marconi (1841-85), Nudes and Angels, 1880s

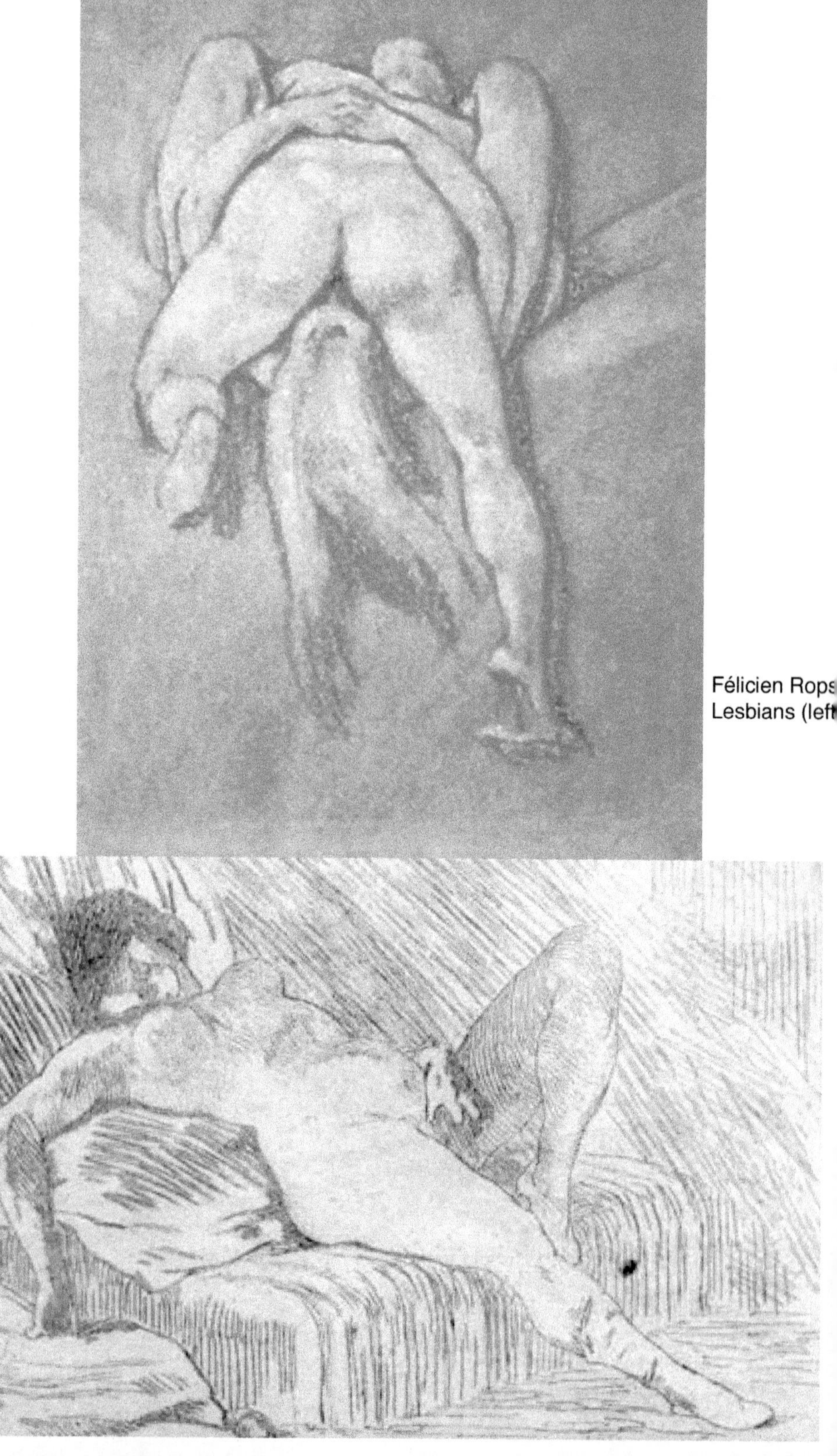

Félicien Rops
Lesbians (left

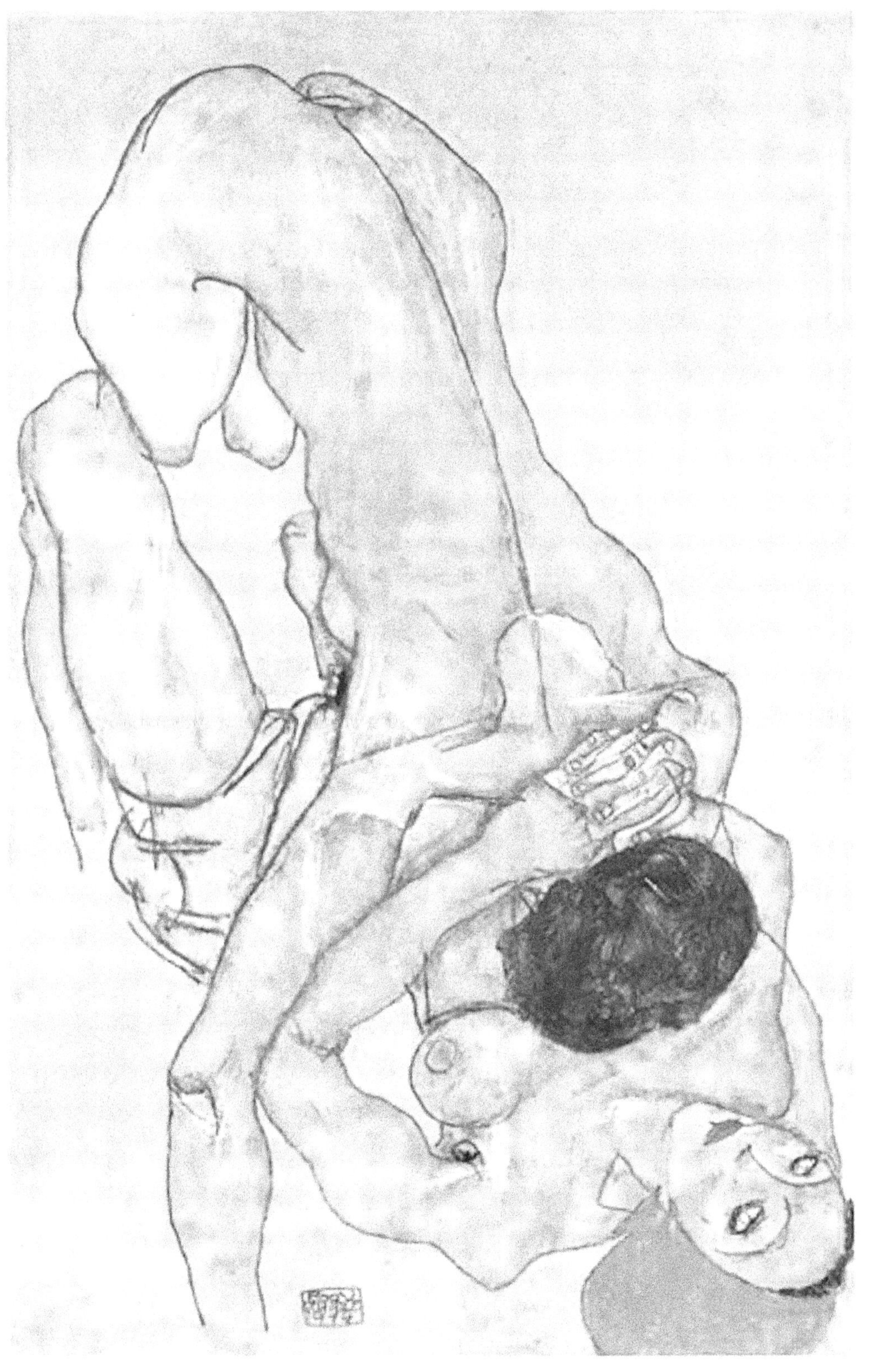

Egon Schiele, Two Women Lovers, 1914

VOYEURISM

The Lacanian Look emphasizes eroticism. Seeing is erotic, the eye becomes a kind of phallus, caressing the obscure object of desire, which it can never 'possess'. As the poet Rainer Maria Rilke wrote '[g]azing is a wonderful thing.'[1] The act of looking eroticizes the object. Jack Zipes describes it thus in *Don't Bet On the Prince*:

> For him [Lacan], seeing is desire, and the eye functions as a kind of phallus. However, the eye cannot clearly see its object of desire, and in the case of male desire, the female object of desire is an illusion created by the male unconscious. Or, in other words, the male desire for woman expressed in the gaze is auto-erotic and involves the male's desire to have his own identity reconfirmed in a mirror image.[2]

The look is an assertion of male power and sexuality. For the gaze is male, and feminists have grappled with the notion of a 'female' gaze, whether there can be such a thing as a 'female' or 'feminine' gaze.[3]

---

1 R. Rilke, letter to Clara Rilke, 8 March 1907, in *Gesammalte Briefe 1892-1926*, Insel Verlag, Leipzig 1940, II, 279f

2 Jack Zipes: *Don't Bet on the Prince: Contemporary Feminist Fairy Tales in North America and England*, Gower, Aldershot 1986, 258

3 Maggie Humm: "Is the gaze feminist? Pornography, film and feminism", *Perspectives on Pornography*, eds G.Day & C. Bloom, Macmillan 1988; Lorraine Gamran & Margaret Marshment, eds: *The Female Gaze*, Women's Press 1988; E.D. Pribram, ed: *Female Spectators: looking at film and television*, Verso, 1988

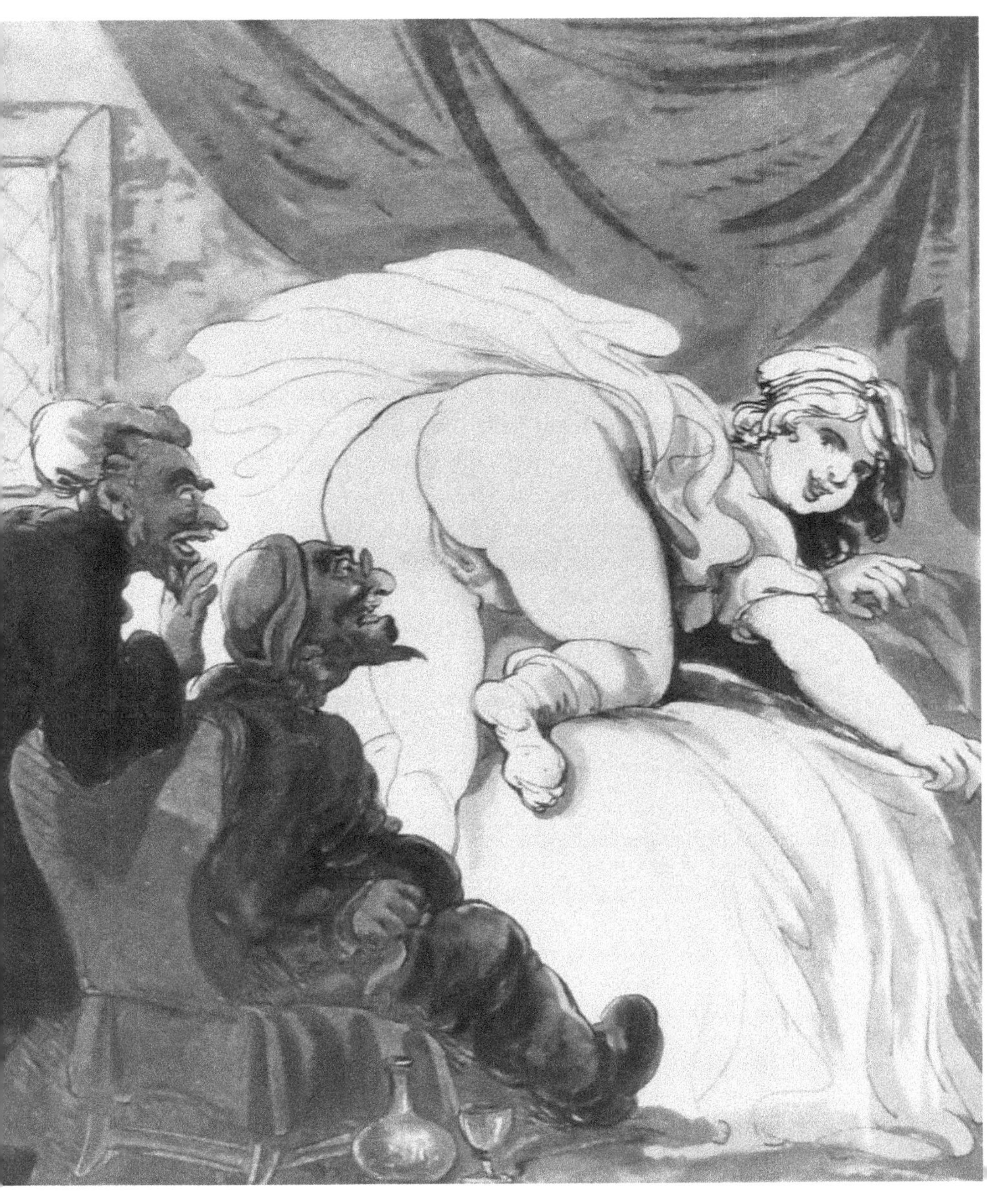

Thomas Rowlandson, Susannah and the Elders, 1820, London

SEX AND DEATH

Pain is good, because it means you are fully alive. This is the Existential view of patriarchal culture. 'Sensual pleasure is agony in the strictest meaning of the word', says C. Mauclair in a Freudian tone.[1] Suffering is holy, in the Christian tradition. The journey from martyrdom to sainthood and beatification is swift. The West exalts pain. Christ *suffered*, say theologians, so he must have been right, he must have lived hard, because he died hard. Death becomes heroic. Death transfigures people. Suicide is even better, if you can manage it. Hence Marilyn Monroe, Vincent van Gogh, Johann Wolfgang von Goethe's Werther, Virginia Woolf. Die young, and become famous (many artists have followed this equation: Egon Schiele, Frédéric Chopin, Wolfgang Amadeus Mozart, Georges Seurat, James Dean, Paula Modersohn-Becker, D.H. Lawrence, Jimmy Hendrix, Jim Morrison, Arthur Rimbaud, Raphael, John Keats, Percy Shelley, and Novalis.

1 C. Mauclair: *Magie de l'amour,* 145, quoted in Julius Evola, 84

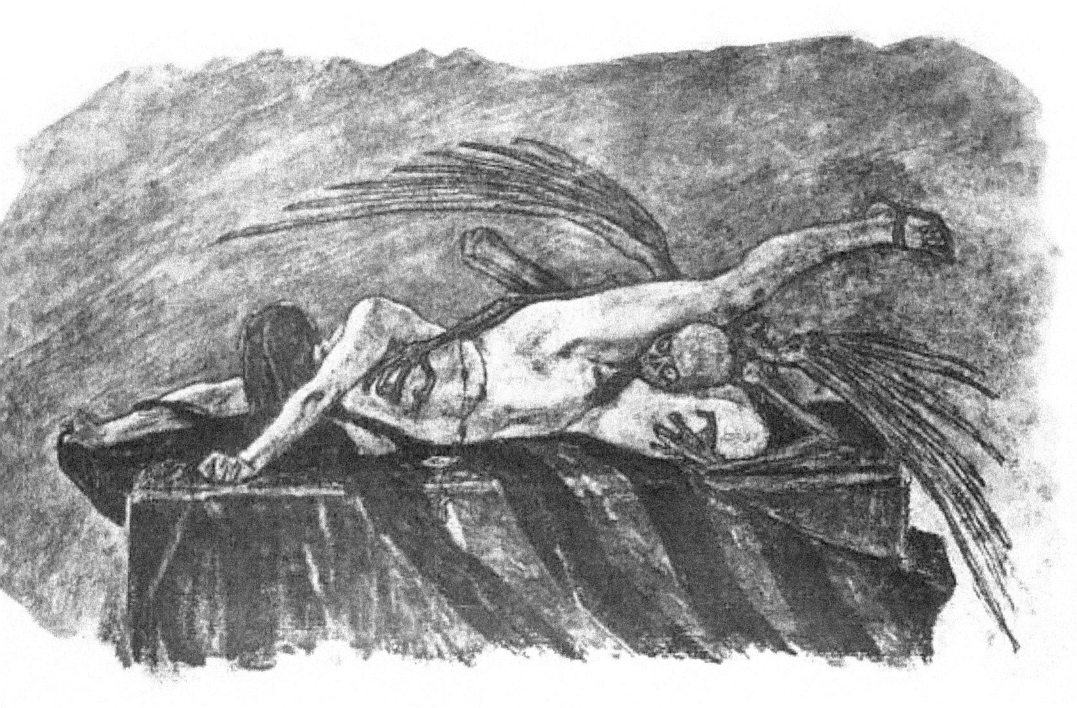

Félicien Rops

Part Two

Erotic Art In the 18th Century

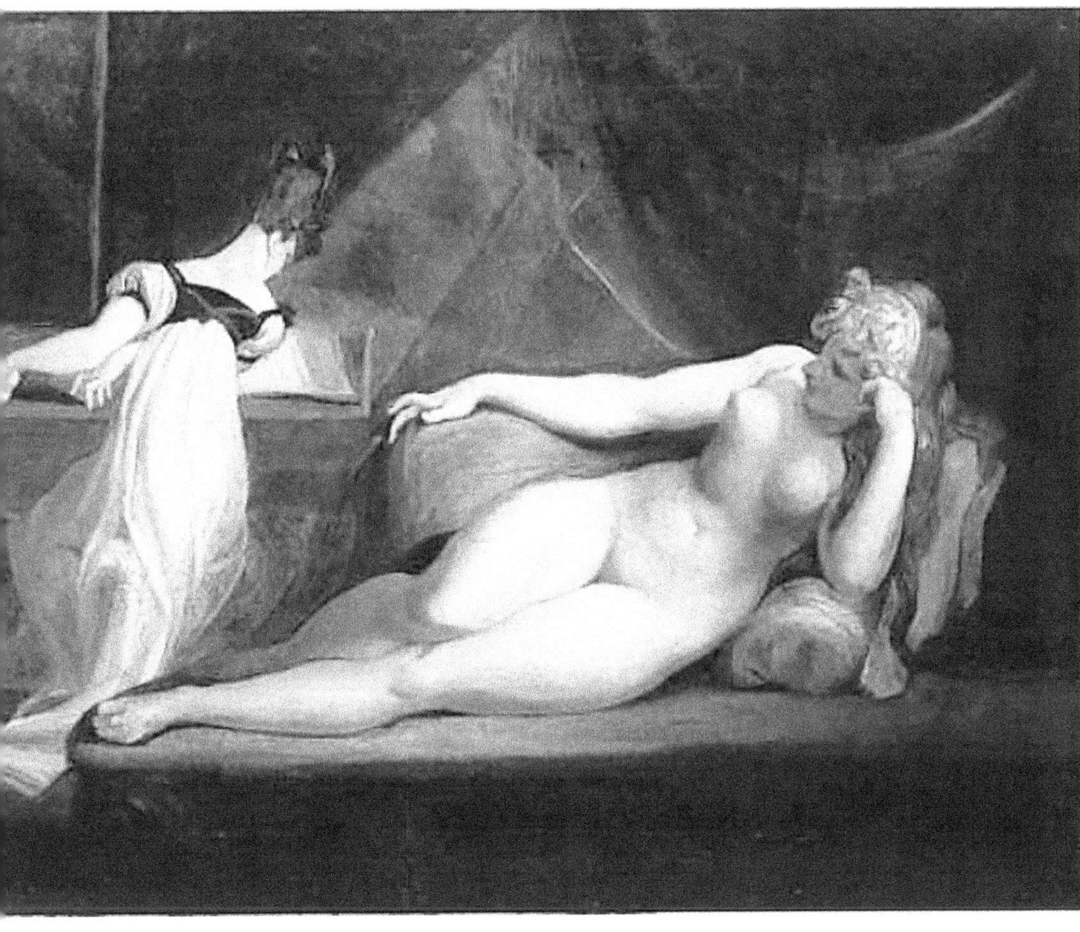

ANIMA

In the Jungian system, Beatrice, Laura, Cleopatra, Isolde, Eurydice, Ariadne and all those women of myth, poetry and legend, are incarnations of the *anima,* which is, as Carl Jung explains, something all males possess: '[e]very man carries with him the eternal image of woman, not the image of this or that particular woman, but a definitive feminine image.'[1] The *anima* is 'a personification of the unconscious in a man, which appears as a woman or a goddess in dreams, visions and creative fantasies', write Emma Jung and Marie-Louise von Franz, glossing Jung's *anima* concept.[2]

Male painters throughout history have depicted their version of the *anima,* it seems. Each (male) painter has a version of the 'inner feminine figure', as Carl Jung calls it.[3] For painters, this idealized *anima* figure seems to be another manifestation of that obscure object of desire, the eroticized woman, a mirror for male lust. The equation is: the more sublime and voluptuous the woman is painted, the more sublime and voluptuous is the artist's desire. The artist's model, then, can be seen as a Jungian *anima,* heavily eroticized, a Lacanian phallic mirror.

---

1 C. Jung: *The Development of Personality,* vol. 17, Routledge, 1954, 198; Marie-Louise von Franz: *The Psychological Meaning of Redemption Motifs in Fairy Tales,* Inner City Books, Toronto 1980, 39f

2 Emma Jung & Marie-Louise von Franz: *The Grail Legend, tr.* Andrea Dykes, Sigo Press, Boston, Mass., 1980, 64

3 C. Jung: *Memories, Dreams, Reflections,* Collins 1967, 210-1

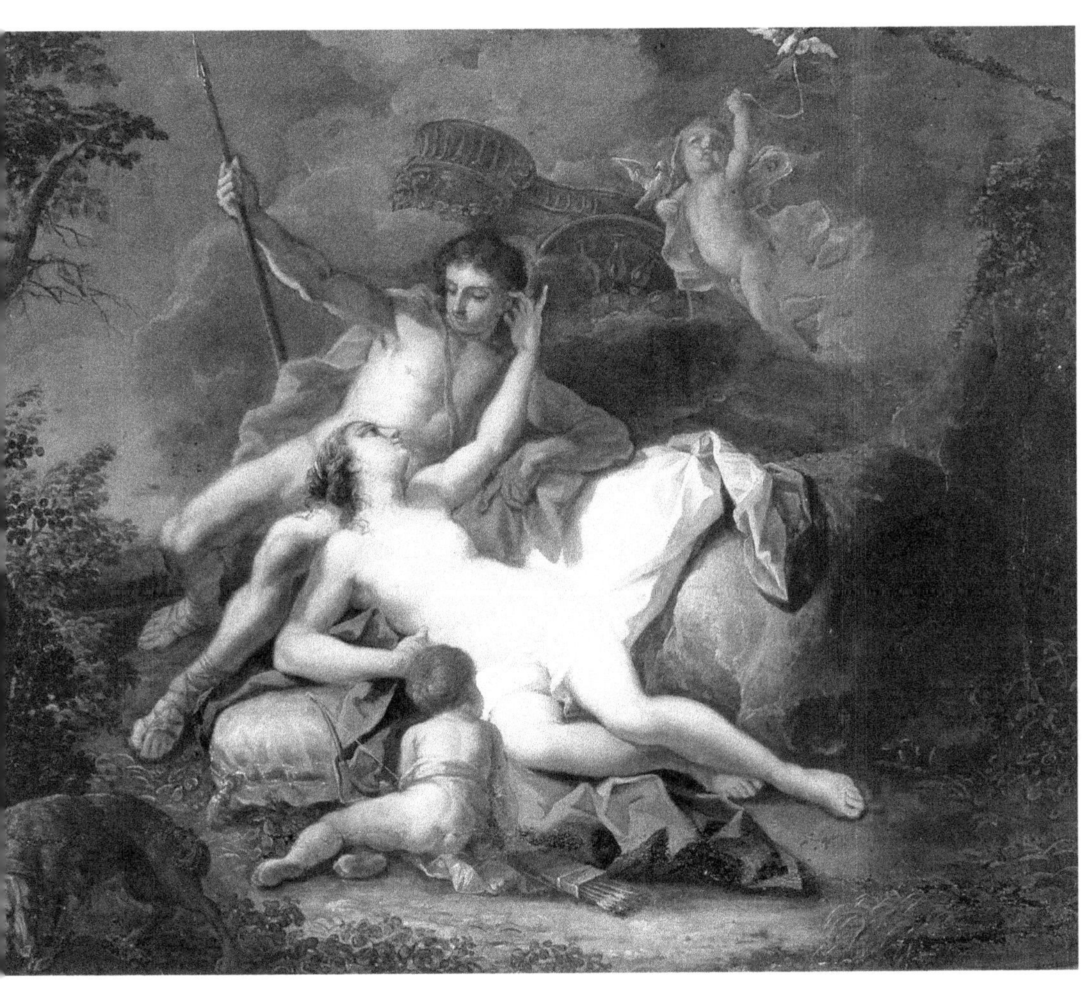

Louis de Silvestre (circle of), Venus and Adonis, 18th century.

Seen in Lacanian theory, the female model becomes the 'obscure object of desire' feared and desired, ever unreachable, the manifestation of eternal loss.[1] We can see elements of the Lacanian lack, desire, repression, mirror stage, Symbolic Order and œdipal anxiety in the modern artists who create specifically erotic images. In the output of artists such as Pierre Renoir, Henri Matisse, Jules Pascin, Aristide Maillol, Auguste Rodin, Gustav Klimt, Amedeo Modigliani and Pablo Picasso, one finds loss, desire, repression and anxiety quite clearly. The art they produced is fiercely heterosexual, glorifying women, even as, in some cases (Picasso) the paintings seem to denigrate women. Renoir, in paintings such as *Bather Arranging Her Hair*, Pascin in *The Prodigal Son*, and Lawrence Alma-Tadema in *In the Tepidarium*, produced works that exalt women as sexual objects. The soft flesh is available but also distinctly not available; there is acres of skin, especially in Pascin's painting, but it is not touchable either.[2] These nude paintings remain chimeras, never to be possessed, always to be yearned for. As Nicolas Poussin wrote of painting: '[p]ainting is nothing but an imitation of human actions, which alone are, properly speaking, inimitable'.[3] Poussin recognizes that painting is always an imitation, a mirror; the real thing can never be possessed in art. It is the same in erotic art - indeed, it is most dramatically expressed in erotic art - this paradoxical fear and desire, this simultaneous desire and loss, this ambiguous conflict between possession and dispossession.

1 Toril Moi: *Sexual Textual Politics*, 99f; Anika Lemaire: *Jacques Lacan*, Routledge & Kegan Paul 1977; Elizabeth Wright: *Psychoanalytic Criticism*, Methuen 1984
2 Pierre Renoir: *Bather Arranging Her Hair*, 1885, canvas, 92 x 73cm, Sterling and Francis Clark Institute, Williamstown, Mass.; Lawrence Alma-Tadema: *In the Tepidarium*, 1881, wood, 24 x 33cm, Lady Lever Art Gallery, Port Sunlight; Jules Pascin: *The Prodigal Son*, 1928, oil on board, 15 x 18in, private collection, Switzerland
3 In R. Goldwater, 154.

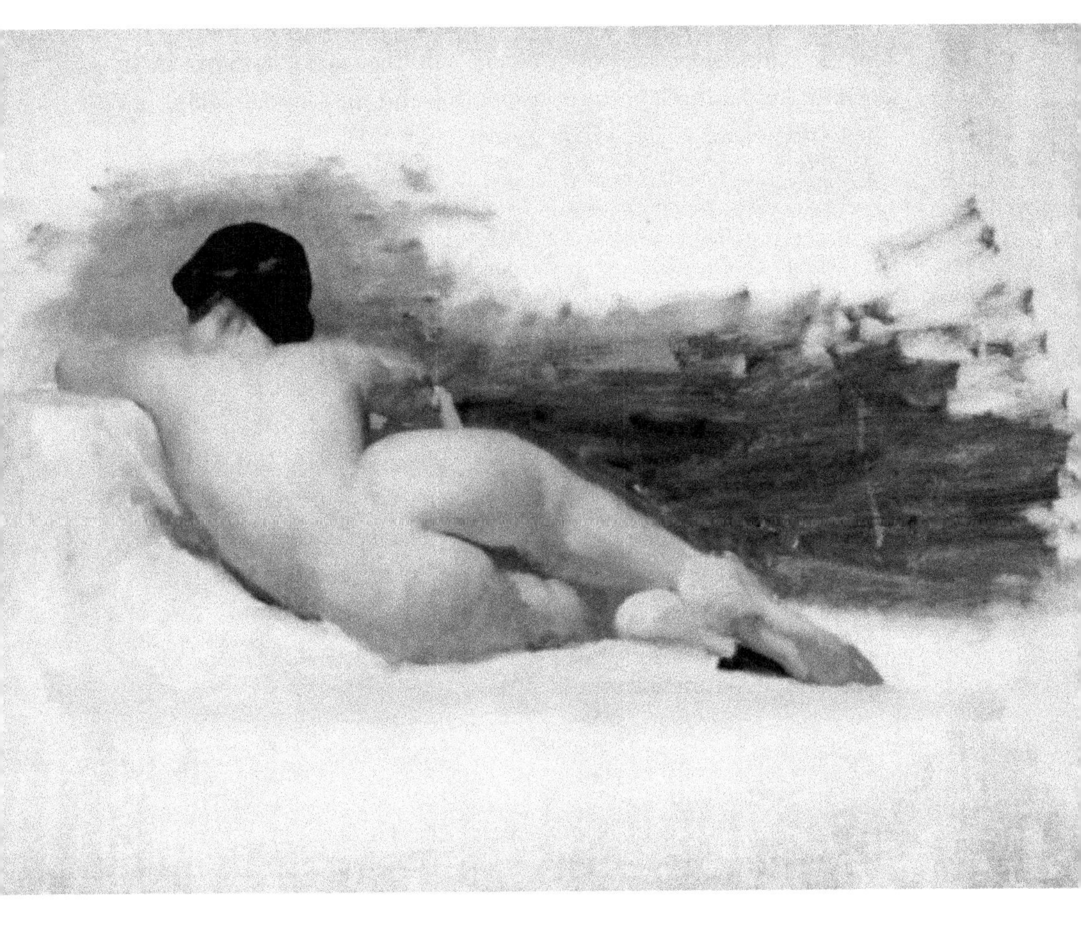

Henry Fuseli

THE FEMALE NUDE - 18TH CENTURY

The female nude is the apotheosis of 'high art', yet it constantly wavers around the borderline between art and pornography. The female nude is erotic *and* obscene, in the male system, both desired and loathed, both representable and un-representable.

Lynda Nead writes in *The Female Nude* (71):

> The body is, therefore, central in the formation of individual identity and is the site of the subject's desires and fantasies, actions and behaviour. Once one rejects the perception of the body as a biologically determined and pre-cultural given and moves towards the conception of 'embodied' subjects, the way is opened for feminist interventions within the definition of the female body.

The 18th century developed the portrayals of nudes in painting of the post-Renaissance period, particularly linked to the emerging academies and art schools. This rise in nude painting reflected the social changes of the 18th century, which exploded in the 19th century with a huge increase in population, the rise of mercantile capitalism, the increase in prostitution, the decline of authoritarian institutions such as organized religion, and the increasing dependence on technology,

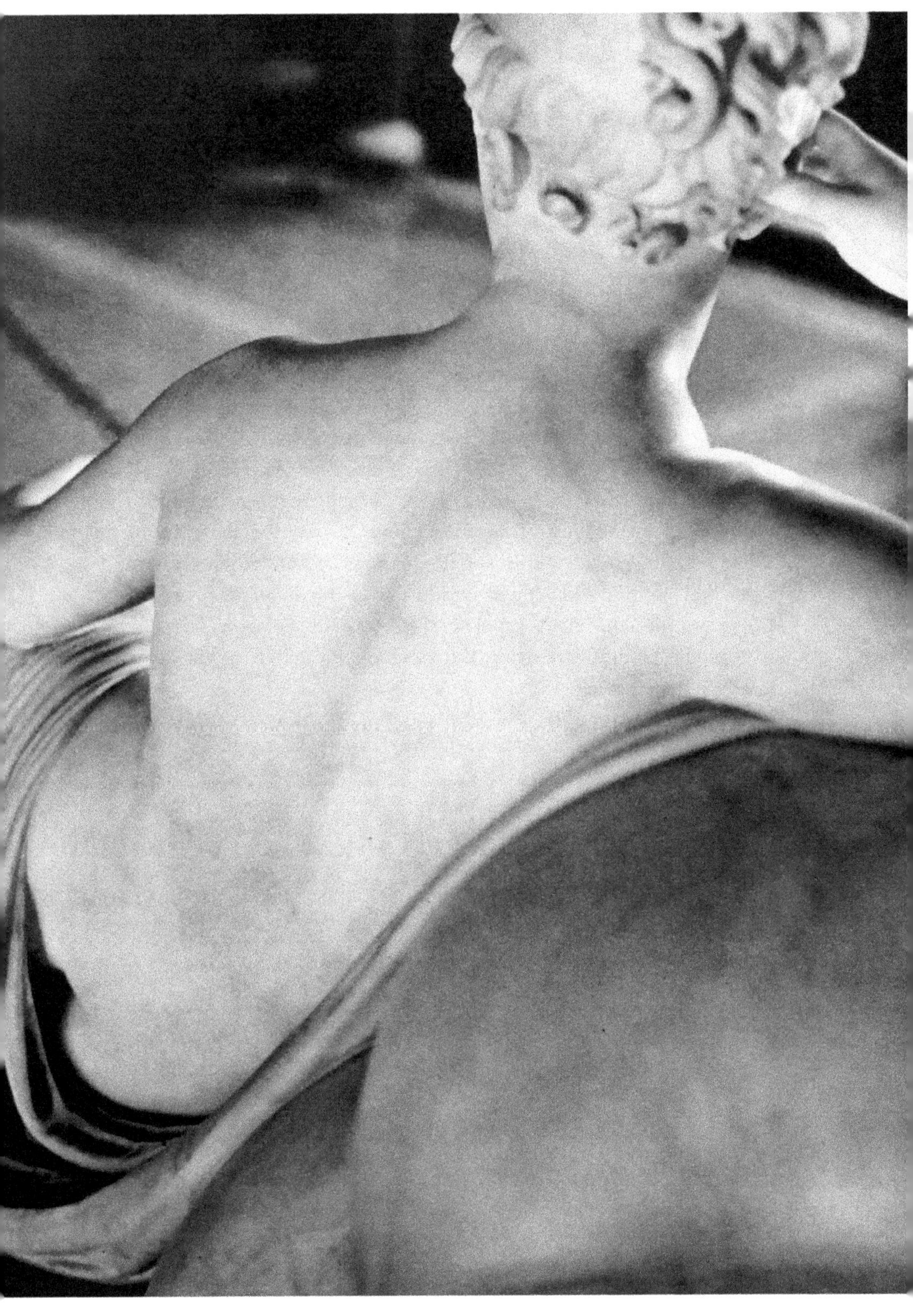

Antonio Canova, Venus Victorious, 1808

LEDA AND THE SWAN

Like Michelangelo Buonarroti, Leonardo da Vinci produced an erotic version of *Leda and the Swan*. Both Michelangelo's and Leonardo's images are lost. We know both, though, because they were copied.[1] Michelangelo's picture is explicitly erotic: the huge swan lies between the deity's legs, the feathers of his wing over her vulva, a touch that expresses male 'possession' of the woman's sexuality.

Leonardo da Vinci made his *Leda and the Swan* as erotica is made; at the request of a (male) client: 'I executed the painting... for a lover. He wished to see the features of his goddess mirrored so that he might kiss them without arousing suspicion', Leonardo wrote.[2] In Antoine Coypel's (?) picture of *Leda and the Swan*, Jupiter's genitals are again the focus of the image, as the woman sits astride his legs.[3]

1 After Michelangelo: *Leda and the Swan*, 16th century, Royal Academy, London
2 quoted in Peter Webb, 112
3 Antoine Coypel (?): *Jupiter with Leda and the Swan*, from *Histoire Universelle*, c. 1750, British Museum

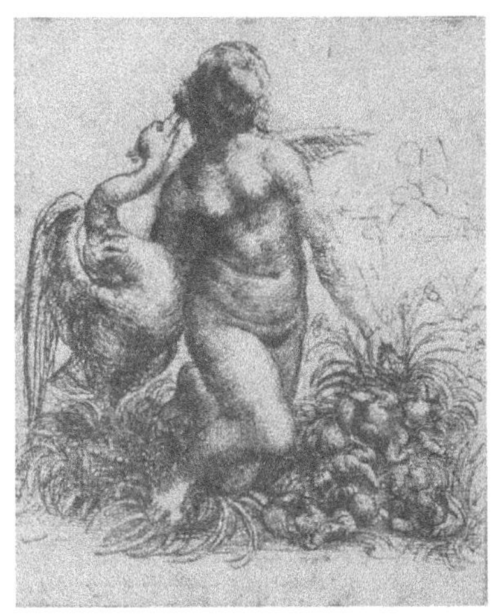

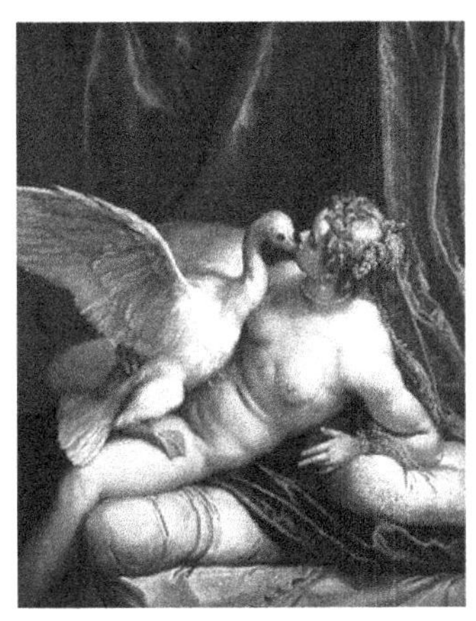

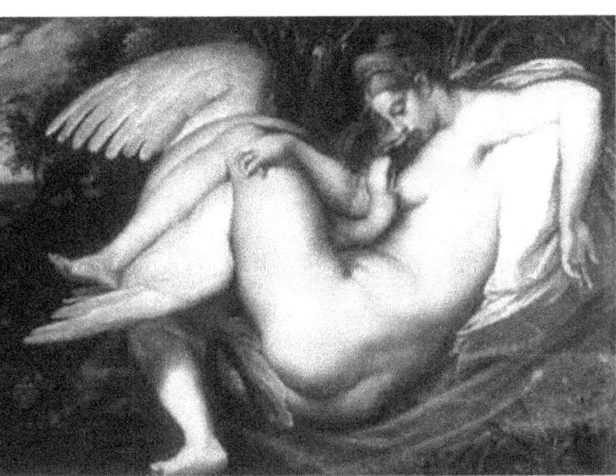

Images of Leda and the Swan by
Leonardo da Vinci (top),
Veronese (top right),
Peter Rubens (left),
Giovanni Boldoni (bottom left),
And Luciano Castelli (below).

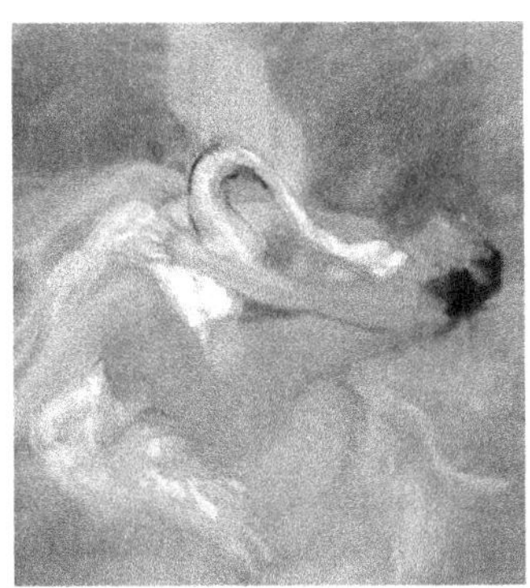

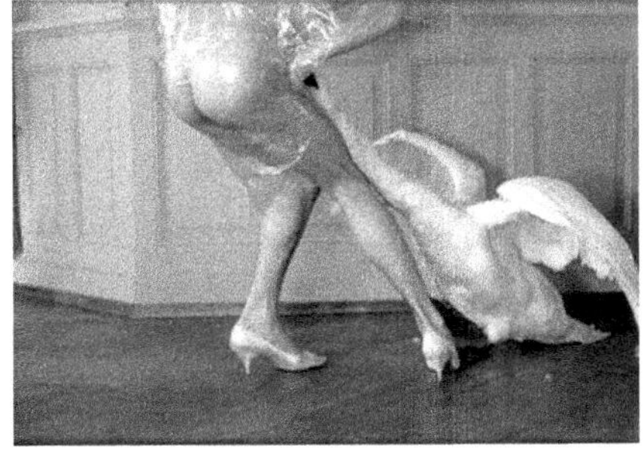

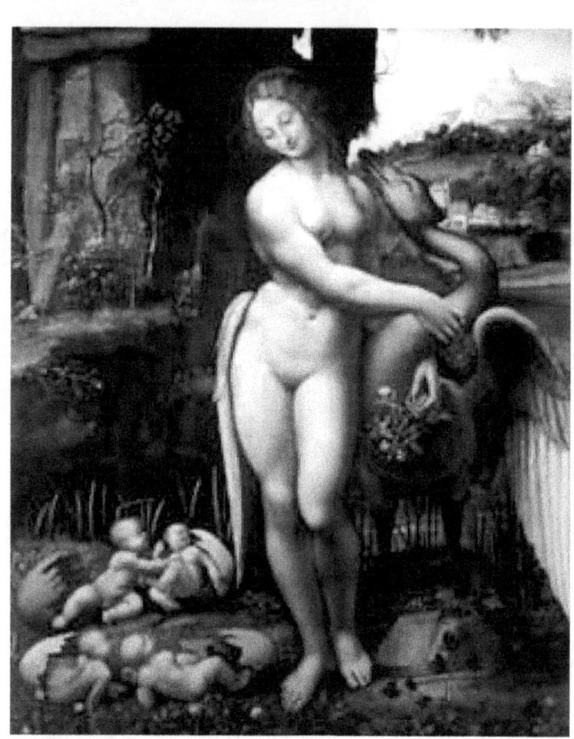

Leda and the Swan.
After Leonardo da Vinci (right).
After Paolo Veronese (below).

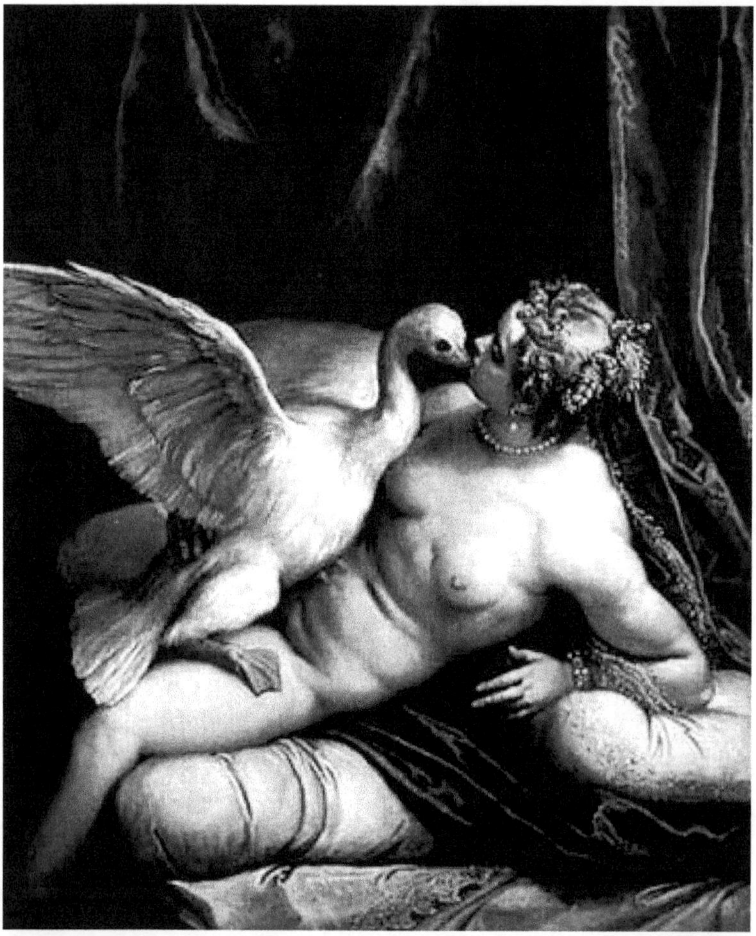

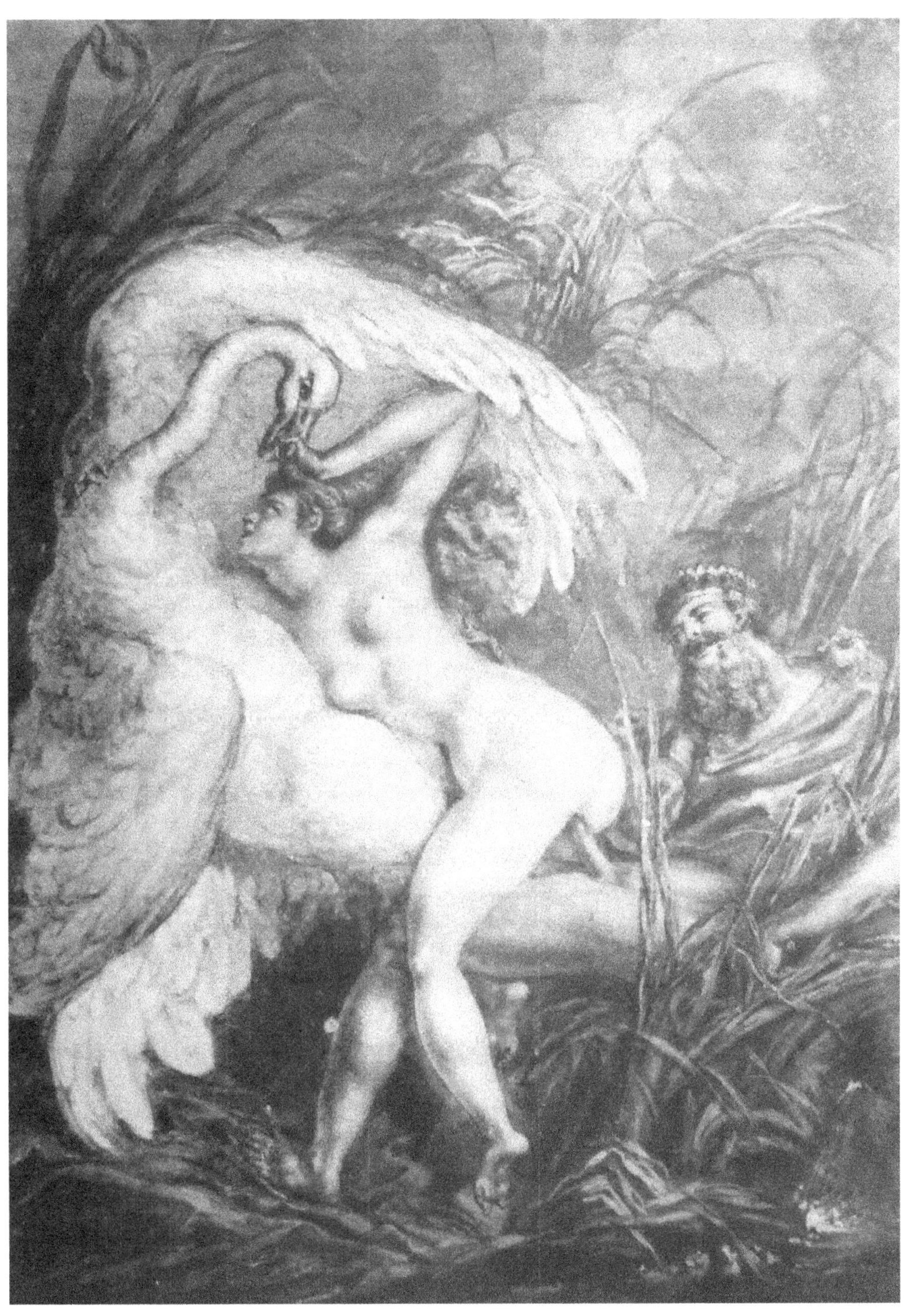

Antyoine Coypel, Jupiter With Leda and the Swan, c. 1750

CHRISTIANITY AND PORNOGRAPHY IN THE 18TH CENTURY

Pornography subverts the laws of Christianity, but it is based on the same laws. Porn comes out of the same world, the same politics, the same culture, as Christianity. Not only is there much of Christianity in pornography, there is much of pornography in Christianity. For instance, Christian history is a catalogue of sadomasochistic events and acts, some really horrific scenes of torture and oppression. More acts of terror have been carried out in the name of God than in the name of 'freedom' or 'truth' or 'honour'.

Painters throughout Western history have reflected the violent acts of Christianity, portraying them as heroic gestures: many painters portrayed St Sebastian full of arrows (Andrea Mantegna, Antonella da Messina, Pietro Perugino, Henrick Terbruggen, and, more recently, Eric Gill and Egon Schiele). In the 18th century, the obsession with portraying the suffering in Catholicism continued.

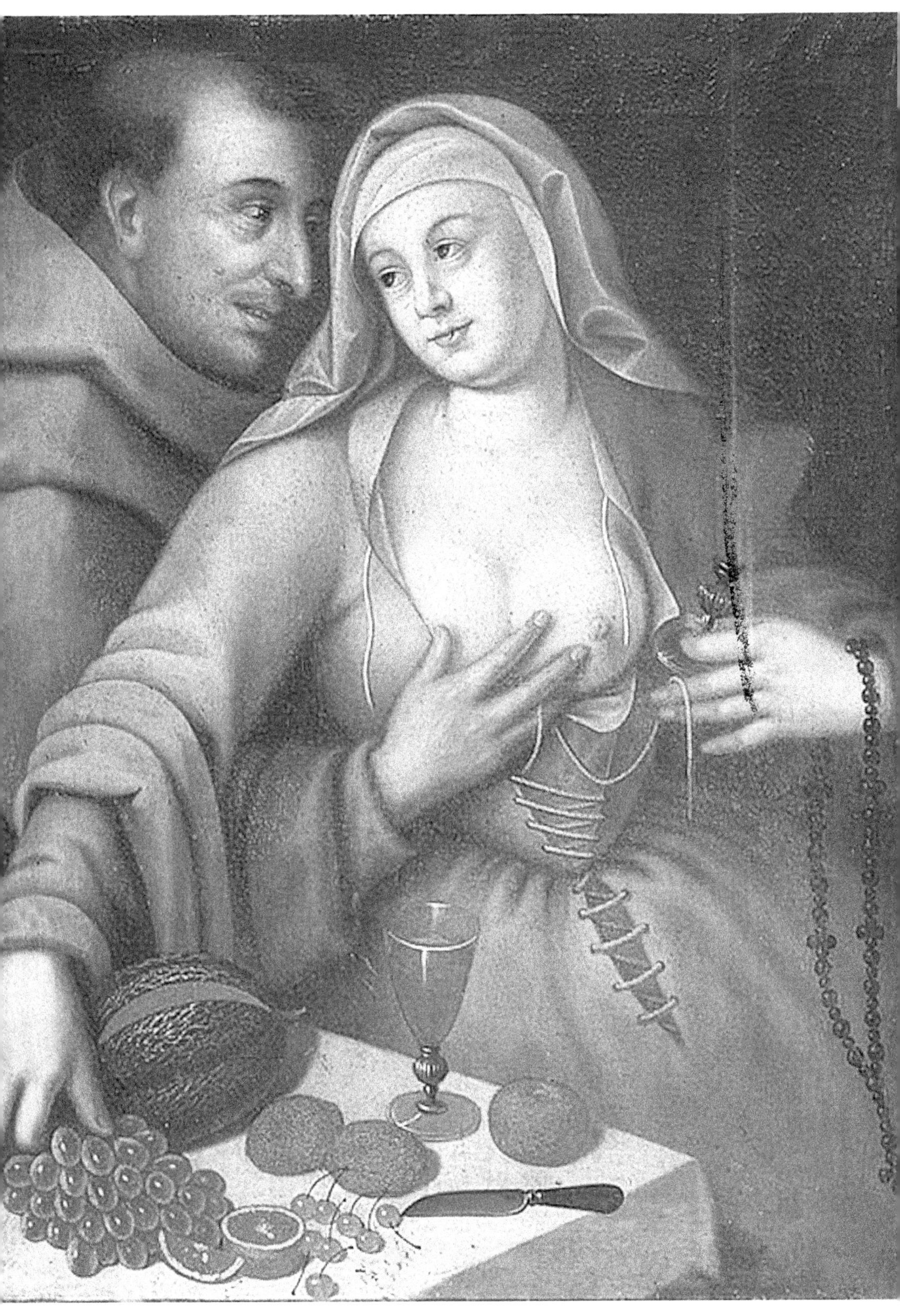

Anonymous, Dutch, 18th century.

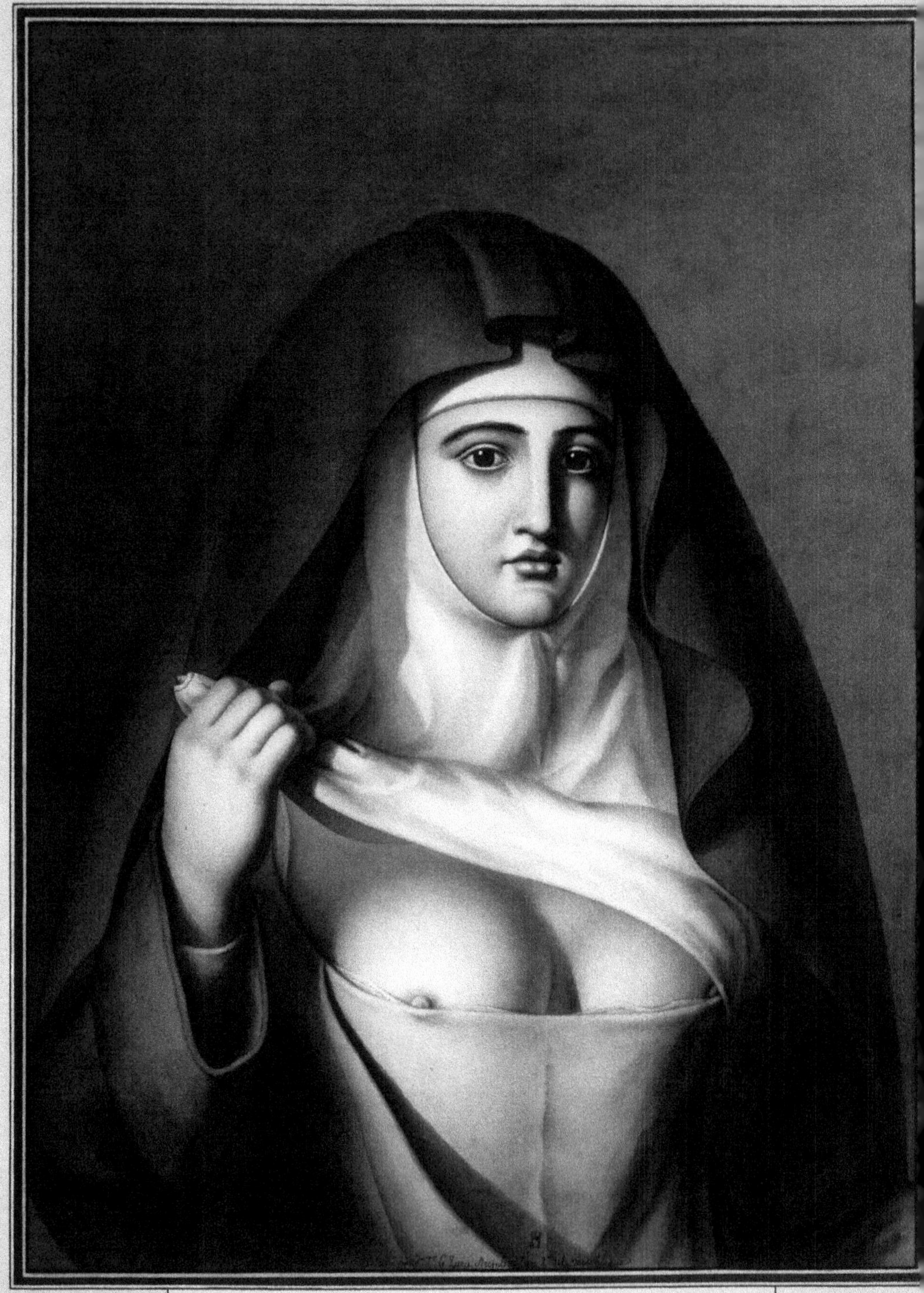

Jean-Jacques Lequeu, Et nous aussi nous serons meres, 1794.

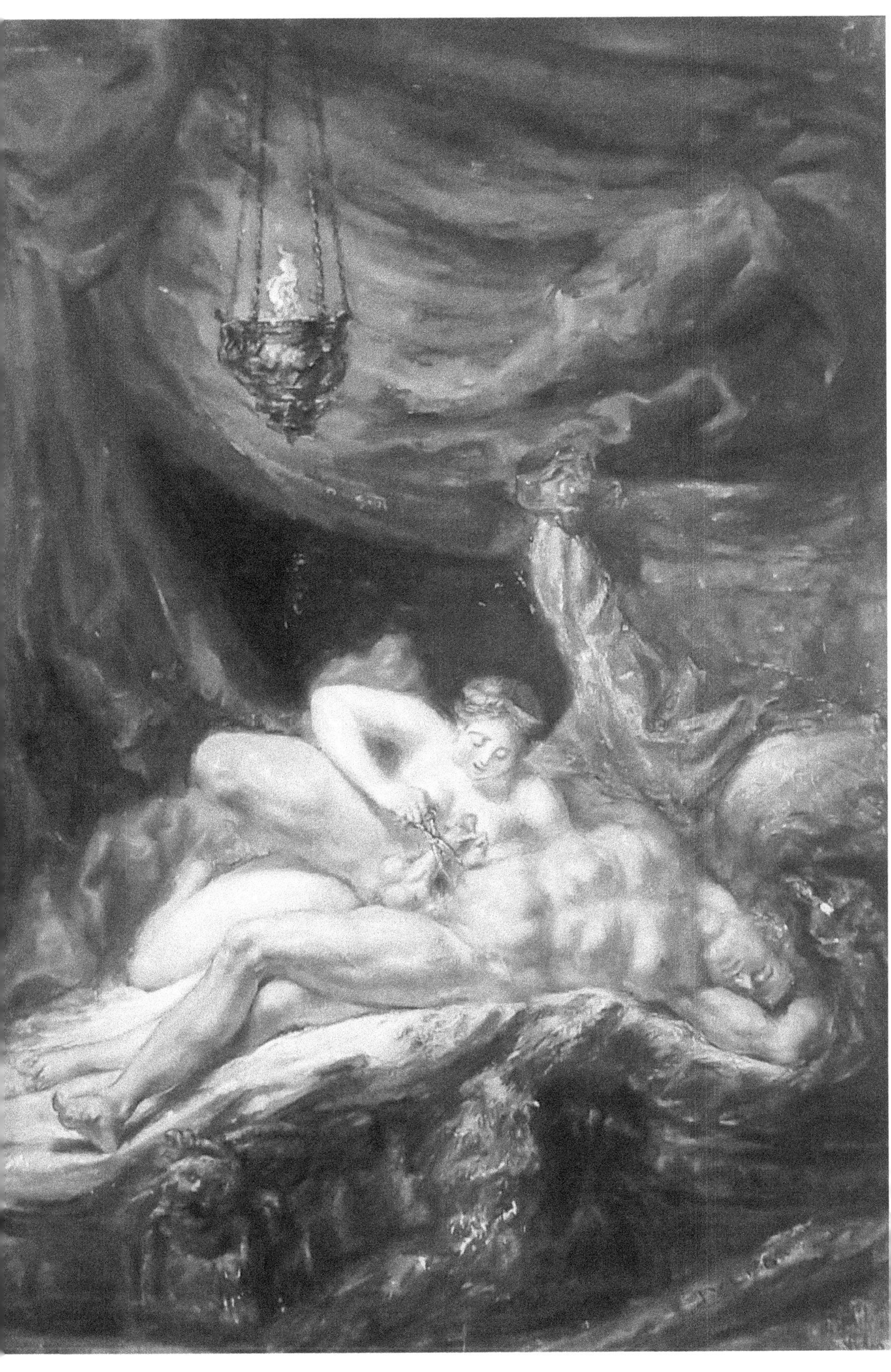

Anonymous, Samson and Delilah, 18th century, French, British Museum

CHRISTIANITY

In the patriarchal view, religion is sexy, and sex is religious. Artists in the 18th century often combined sexual and religious imagery (it was another way of exploring eroticism - and could be powerful precisely because the repression and exertion of power in the social realm was so strong). Western art, like pornography, draws on the Judæo-Christian insistence on sin, death, vice, fornication, dirt and suppression. The father of Christianity is not Jesus but St Paul. Jesus wrote nothing; St Paul wrote everything, setting down the views of Christianity in that fanatical prose in the *Corinthians* and *Galatians* and *Romans,* which gets so many things wrong about flesh and spirit and marriage. Michael Foucault writes of some of the strictures of Christianity:

> Christianity associated it ['the sexual act'] with evil, sin, the Fall, and death, whereas antiquity invested it with positive symbolic values.[1]

In Christianity, women are the 'gateway to Hell' as the early theologian Tertullian poetically put it; women are evil, sinful, lustful ('the Devil is a woman' is a common theme in mediæval philosophy as well as pop songs). From Eve in the *Old Testament* to the Virgin and Magdalene in the *New Testament,* women are definitely second class citizens in the eyes of Western religion. Women-hating is startling in its violent manifestations - not just in wife-beating, which occurs everywhere and, one supposes, at every moment of human history, but also in the mass movements, such as the fight against witchcraft in the Middle Ages and later, when, armed with the *Malleus Maleficarum*, the Witchfinder Generals hunted down and tortured and killed hundreds or thousands, some say millions, of women.

1 M. Foucault: *The Use of Pleasure,* 14

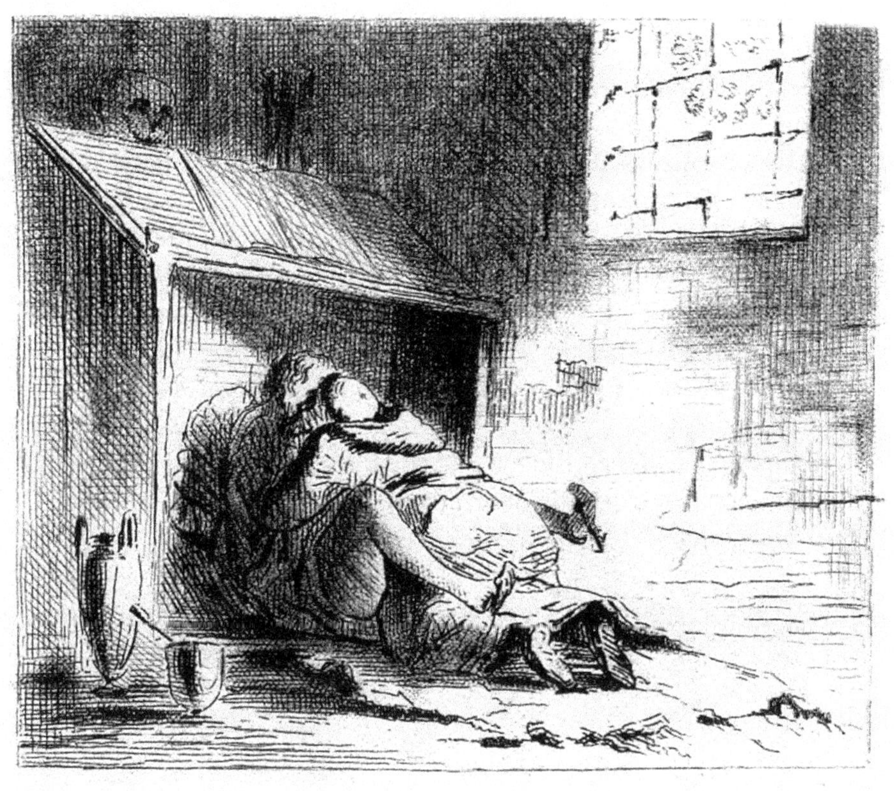

Dominique Vivant Denon, Oeuvre priapique de Denon, 1793

EROTIC ART AND PORNOGRAPHY

The establishment art historical view of erotic art and pornography is that true erotic or high art engenders quiet contemplation, a detached ravishing of the senses, a meditation on Platonic, Aristotlean and Kantian ideas of 'beauty' and æsthetics. 'High art', which is legitimate art, art which justifies itself by its 'genius' or obvious 'greatness', is about distance and disinterested pleasure. The high art nude, in painting or sculpture, in the patriarchal view, justifies its existence by the brilliance of its production, the sumptuousness of its colour and form, the marvel of its human touches, the grandeur of its design, the loftiness of its ambition, the dynamism of its structures, and so on. As that producer of exquisite bodies, French Neo-Classical artist J.A.D. Ingres, wrote:

> There are not two arts, there is only one: it is the one which has as its foundation the beautiful, which is eternal and natural.[1]

1 Ingres, quoted in Goldwater, 216

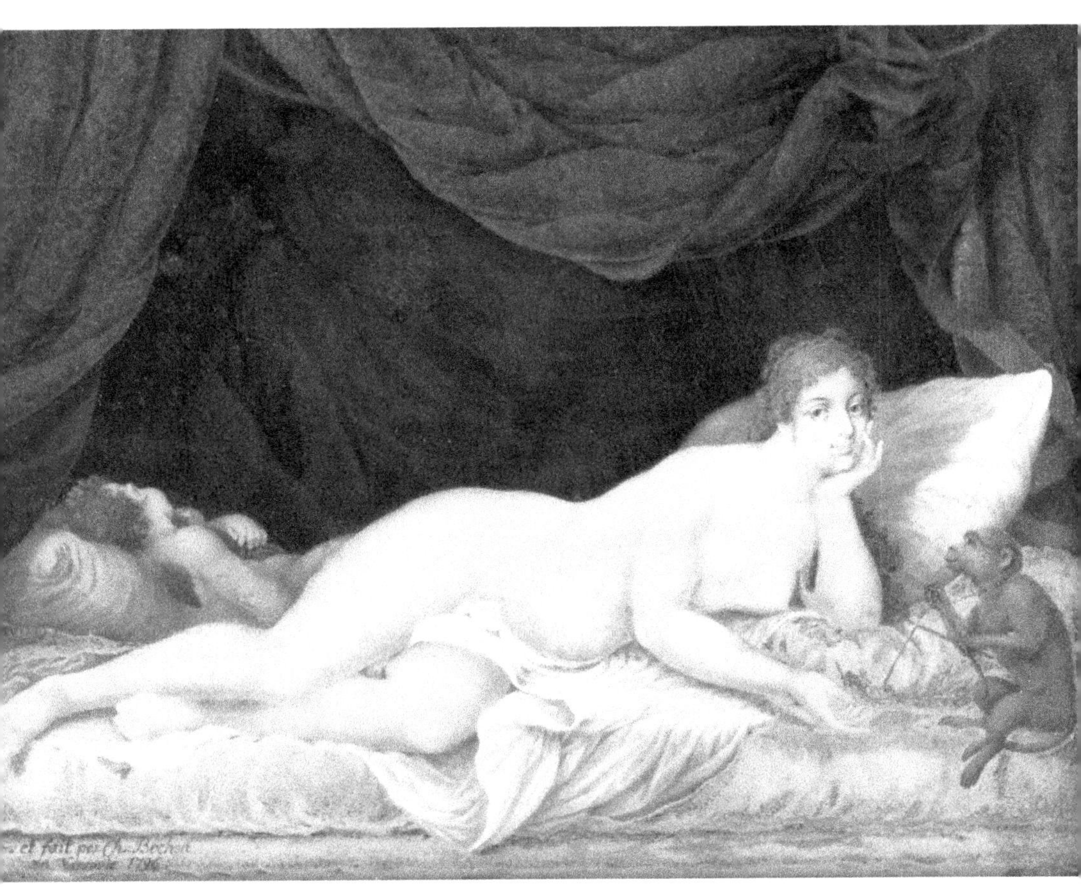

Charles Bechon, Reclining Venus With Cupid and a Monkey, 1796.

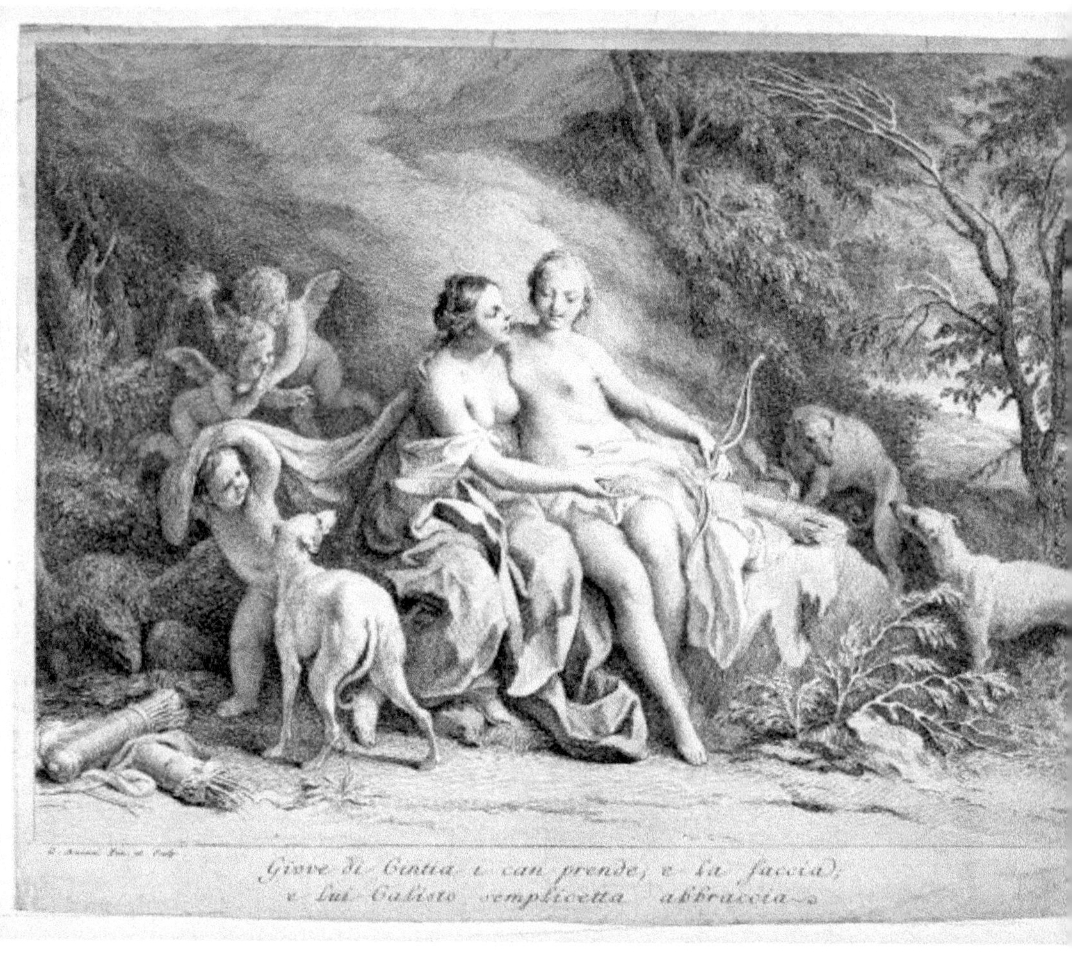

Jacopo Amigoni, Giove and Callisto, c. 1740-1750

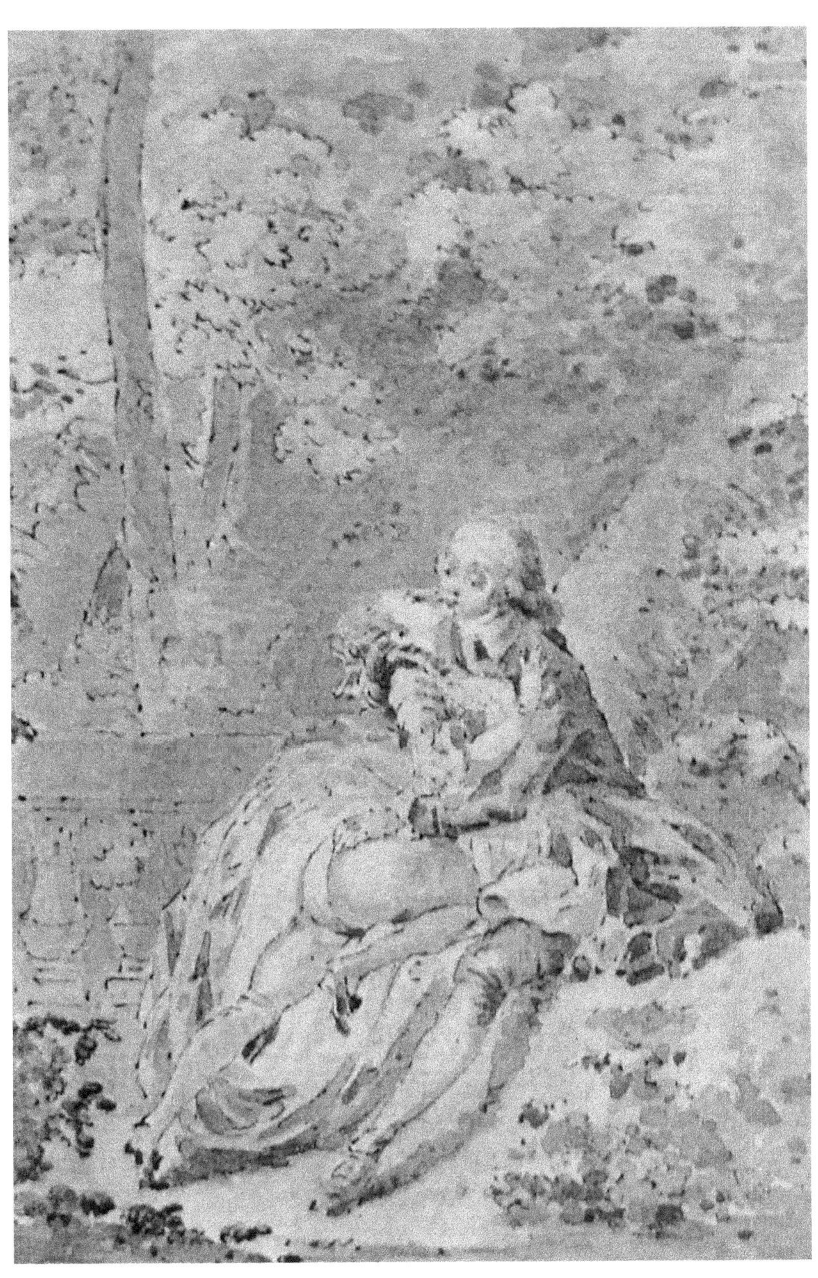

Nicolas Lafrensen, 18th century, Sweden

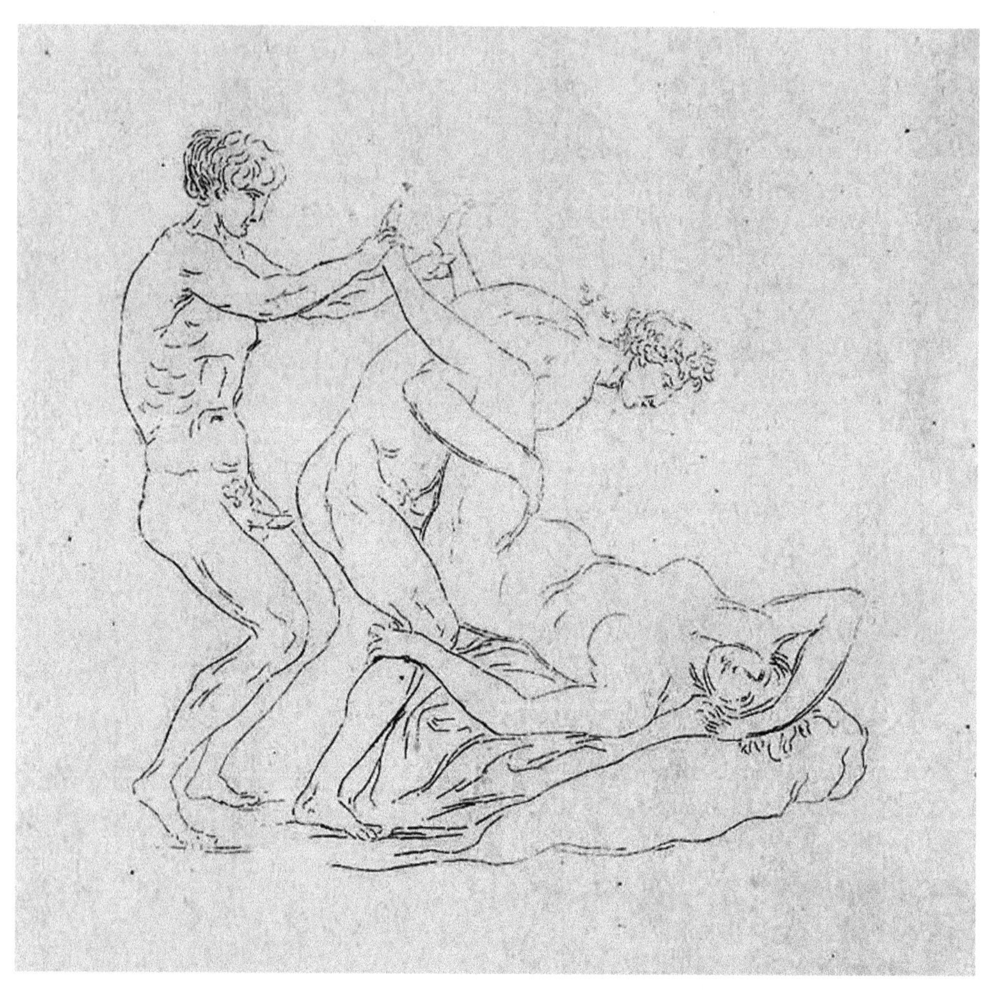

Dominique Vivant Denon, Oeuvre priapique de Denon, 1793
(This page and over).

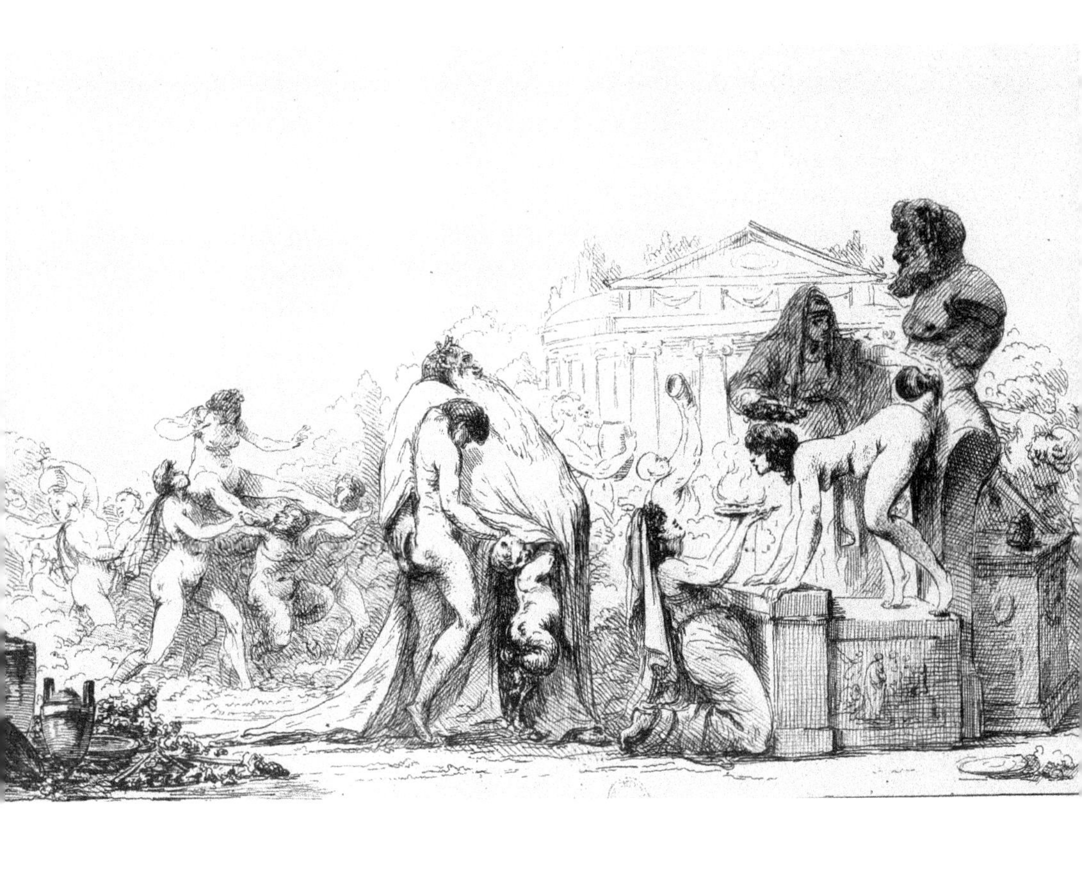

FEMME FATALES

The *femme fatale* type neatly melds sex and death, desire and fear, contact and loss, for the (male) artist. She appears in Medusa, Salomé, Delilah, Jezebel, Judith, Lilith, Ninuë (the lover of Merlin), Venus, Helen of Troy, La Belle Dame Sans Merci, and Cleopatra. These female 'types' combined beauty with death, immense power and all manner of sadistic, masochistic and fetishistic fantasies. These are the women who will whip you to death, if you wish, as in Leopold Sacher-Masoch's *Venus in Furs.* Figures such as Cleopatra provided the longed for combination of socio-political, religious sovereignty, wild eroticism, intrigue, magnificent settings and gory love-deaths. As Max Lake informs us:

> The amatory skills of Cleopatra passed into legend while she lived. Apart from the rapid seduction of both Julius Caesar and Mark Antony, she is reported to have fellated one hundred noblemen in a single evening. Her Greek nickname was *meriochane*, 'she who parts wide for a thousand men.'[1]

1 Max Lake: *Scents and Sensuality: The Essence of Excitement*, John Murray 1989, 58

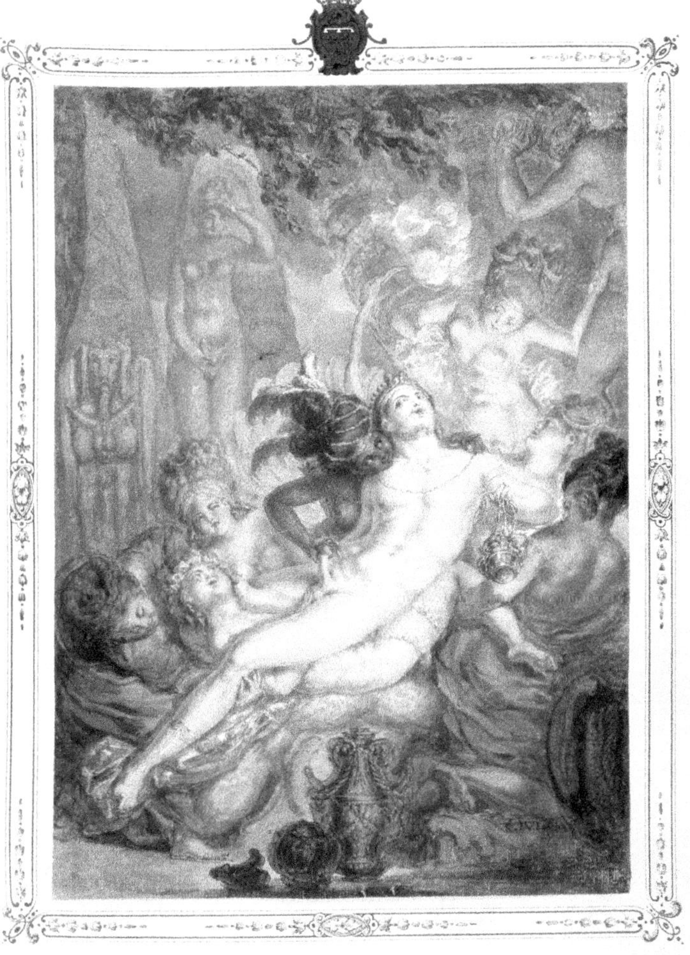

Salomon sacrifiant aux Dieux étrangers.

Anonymous, L'Histoire Universelle

ANDRÉ-ROBERT DE NERCIAT

André-Robert de Nerciat (1739-1800) was the author of several forms of literature, including poetry, plays, music and erotica. His best-known erotic book was *Le Diable au corps,* which was illustrated by Antoine Borel. In it, the Marquise and her freiend the Countess pursue sexual pleasure, including lesbian sex.

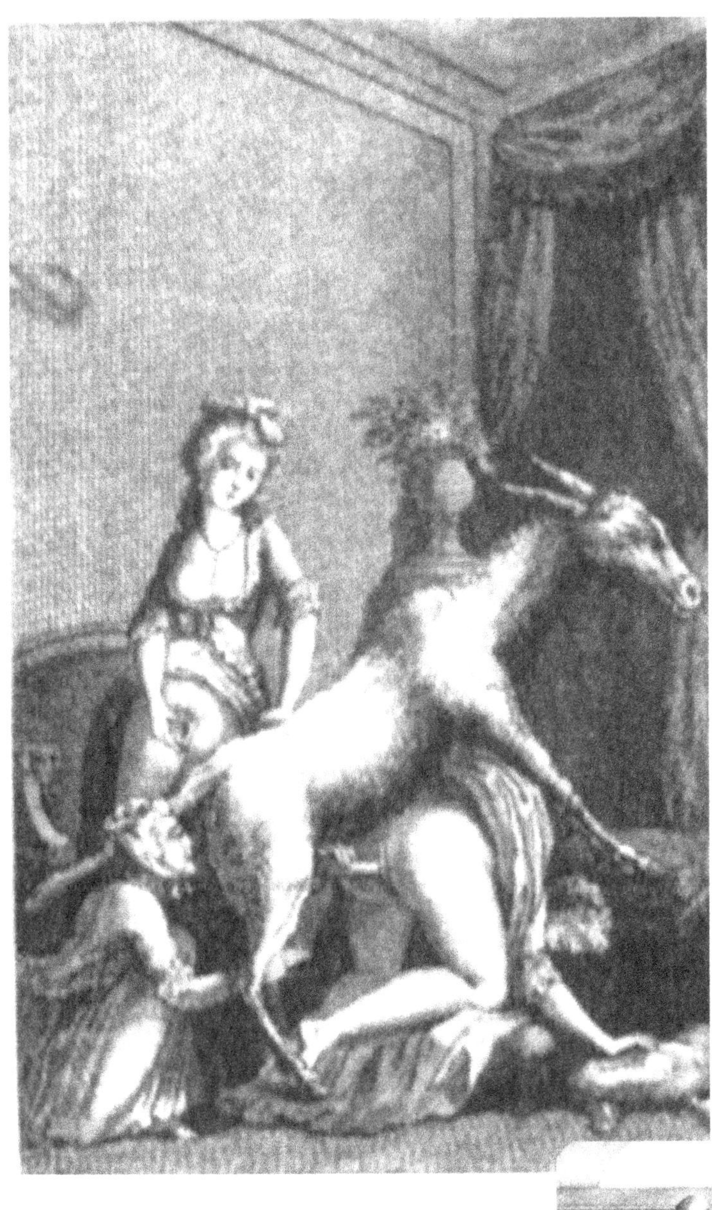

From Le DIable du corps,
by André-Robert Andréa de Nerciat, 1786
this page and following pages.

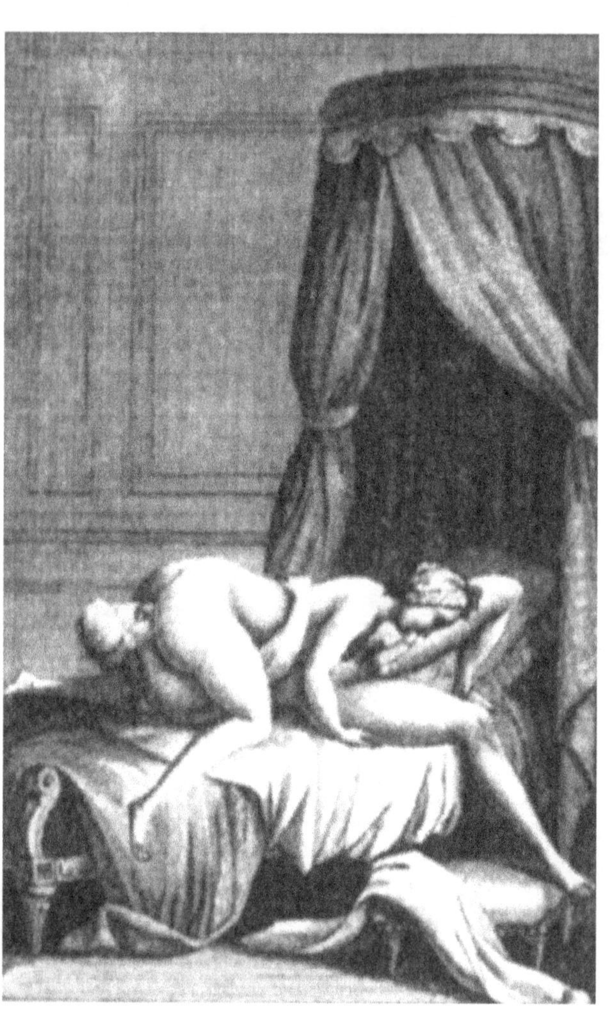

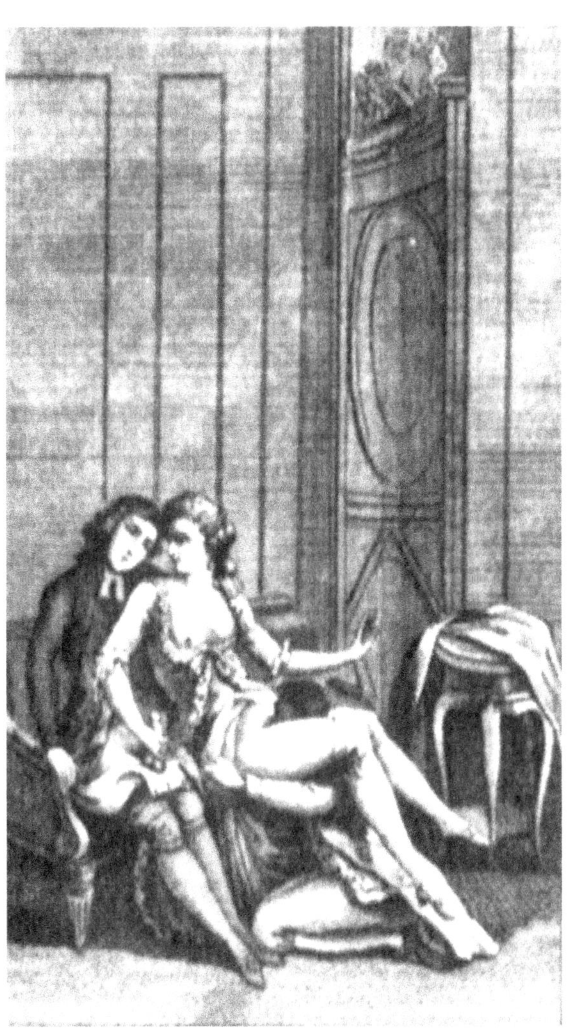

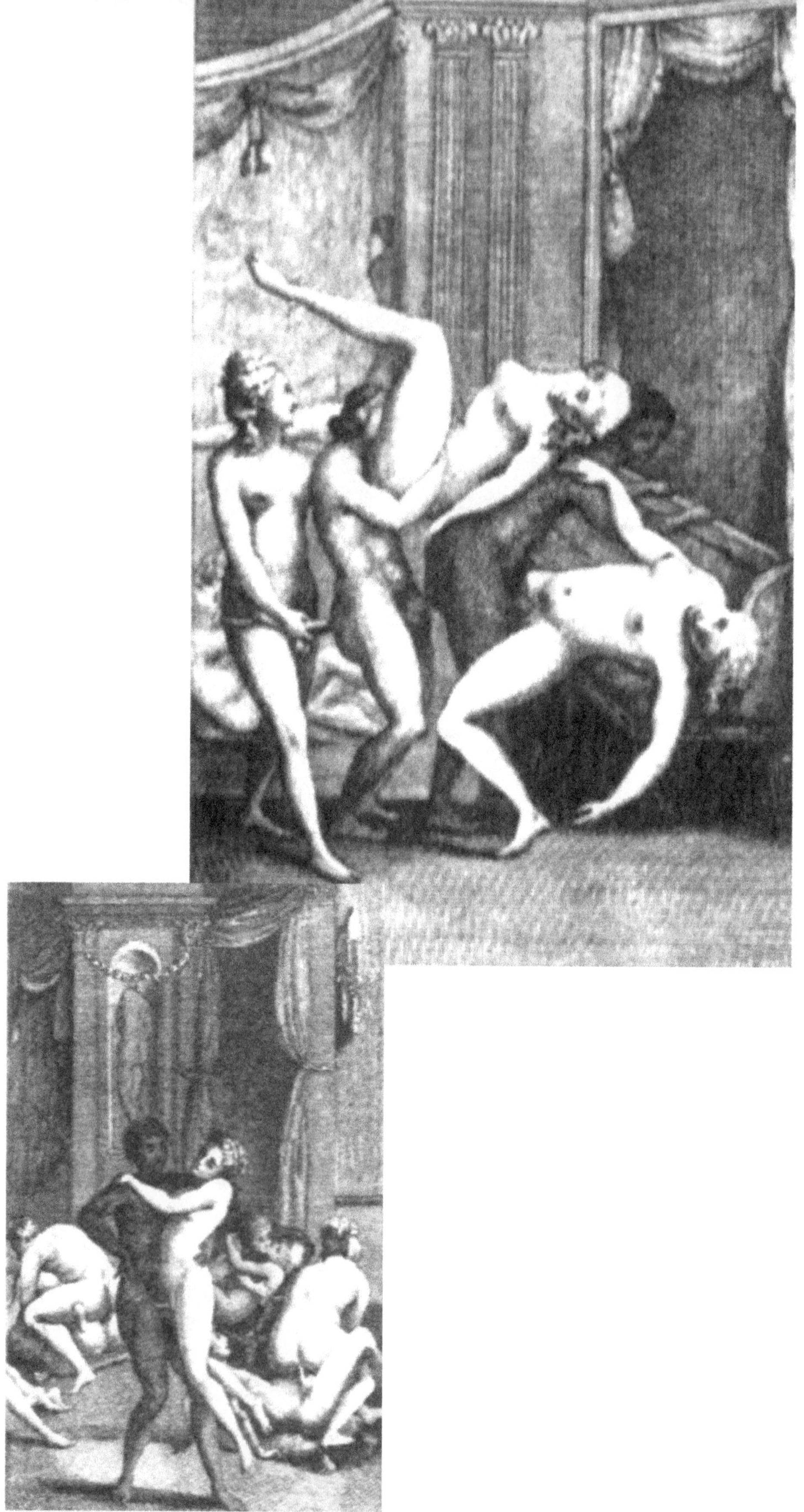

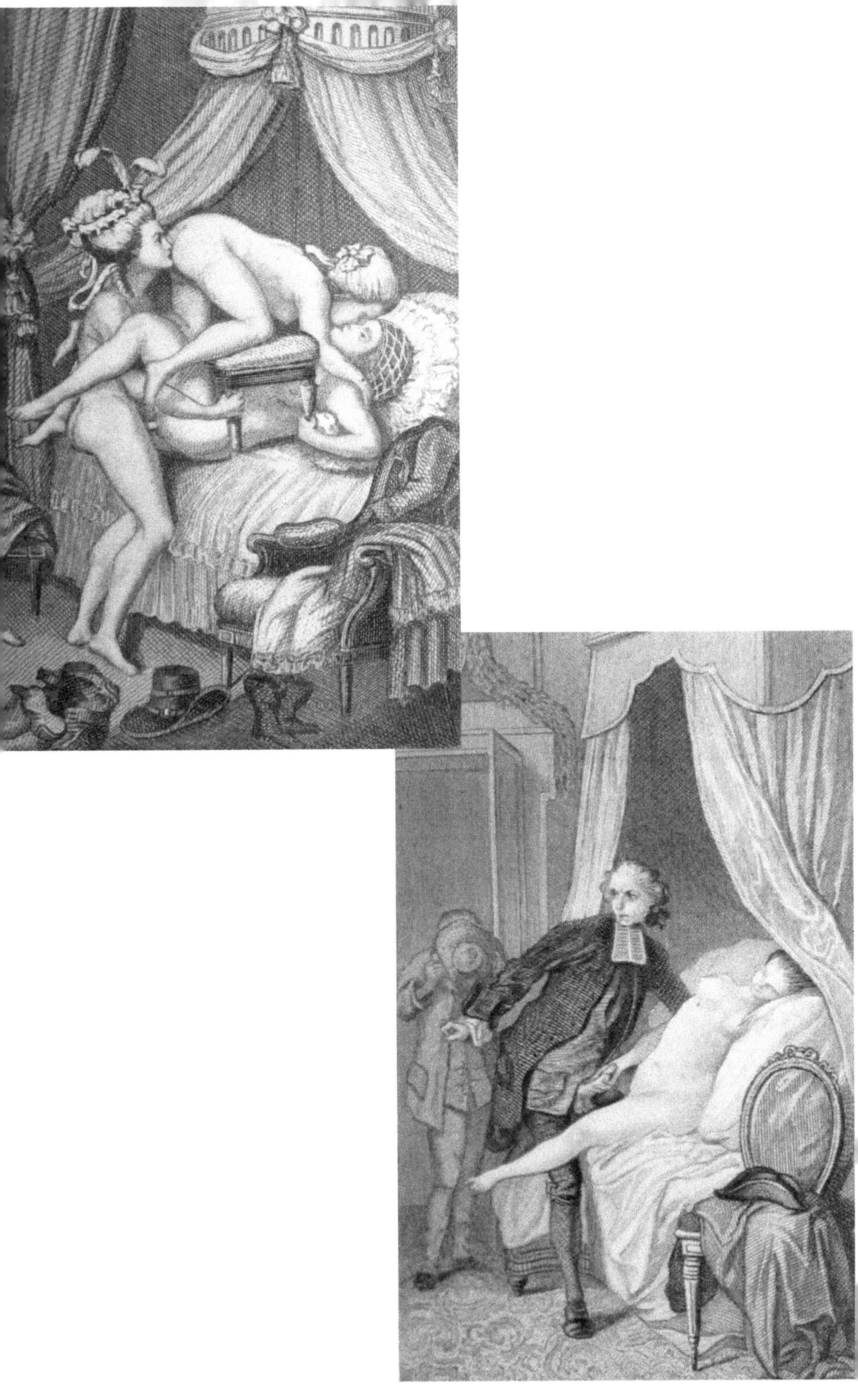

ANTOINE BOREL

Antoine Borel (1743-1810) is best-known in the history of erotica as the highly accomplished illustrator of important works of erotic fiction of the 18th century, including *Thérèse Philosophe, Fanny Hill, Justine, Juliette, The Indiscreet,* and *Le Diable.* (Many of these books were published in Amsterdam, to avoid censorship). Borel worked with engraver François-Rollan Elluin, who produced engravings from Borel's drawings.

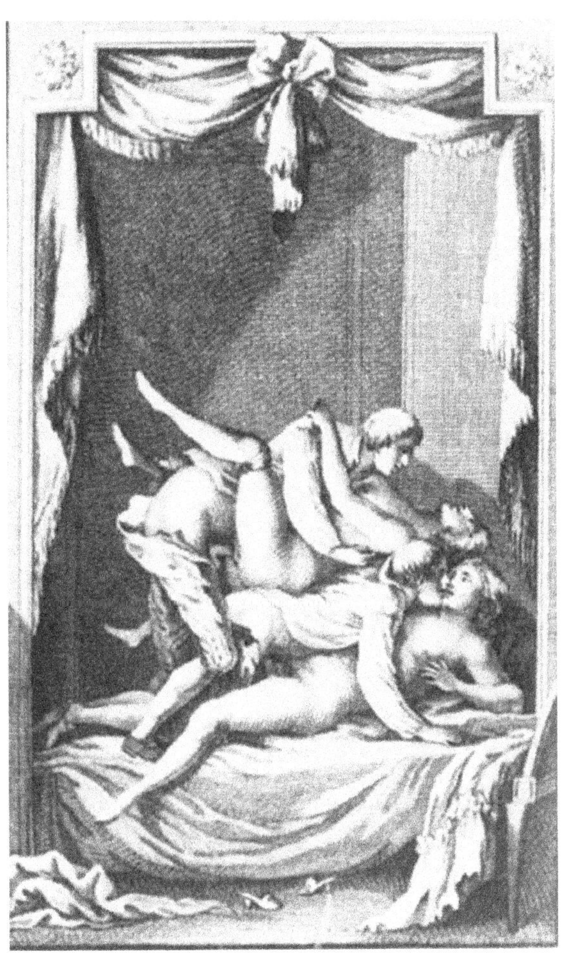

Antoine Borel, illustration for Mémoires de Saturnin
by Jean-Charles Gervaise, 1787.

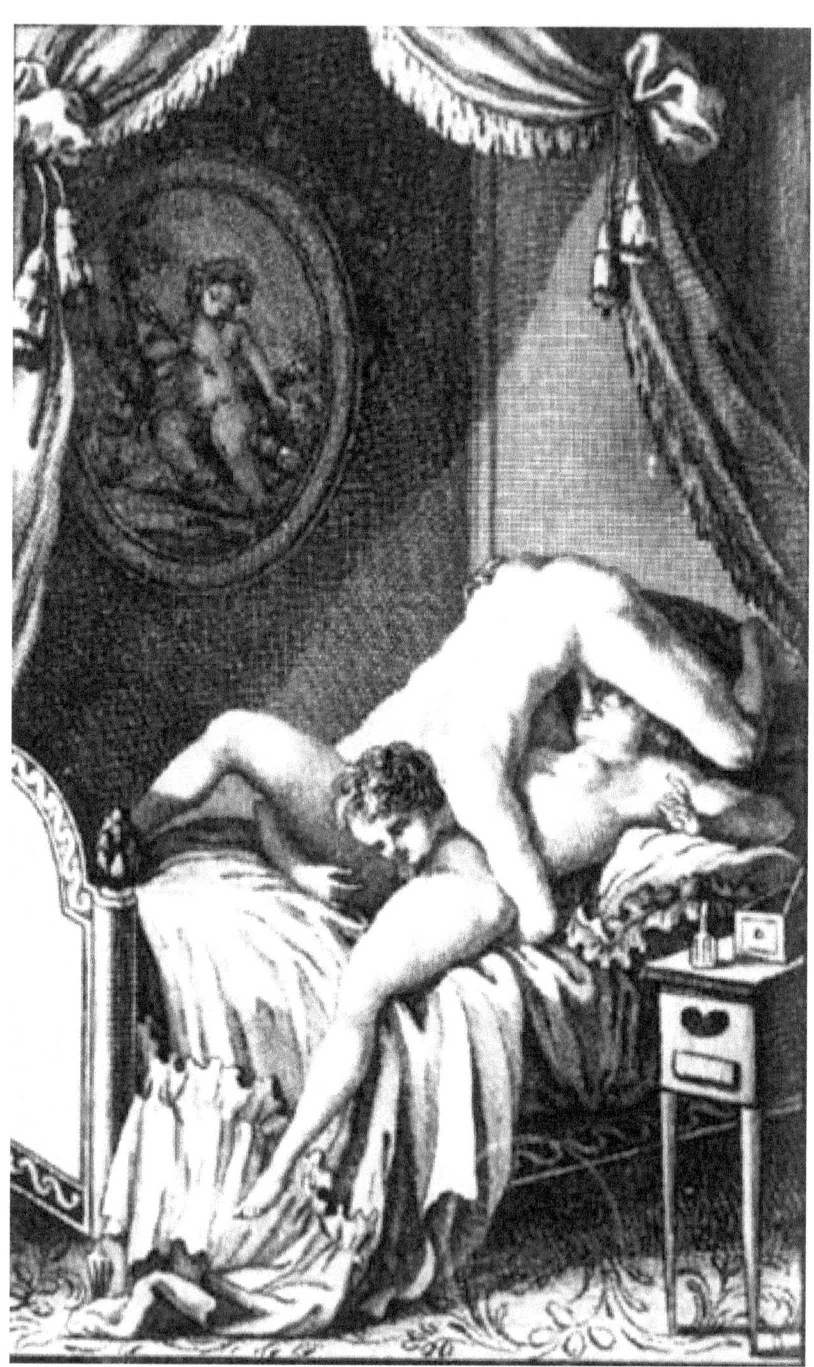

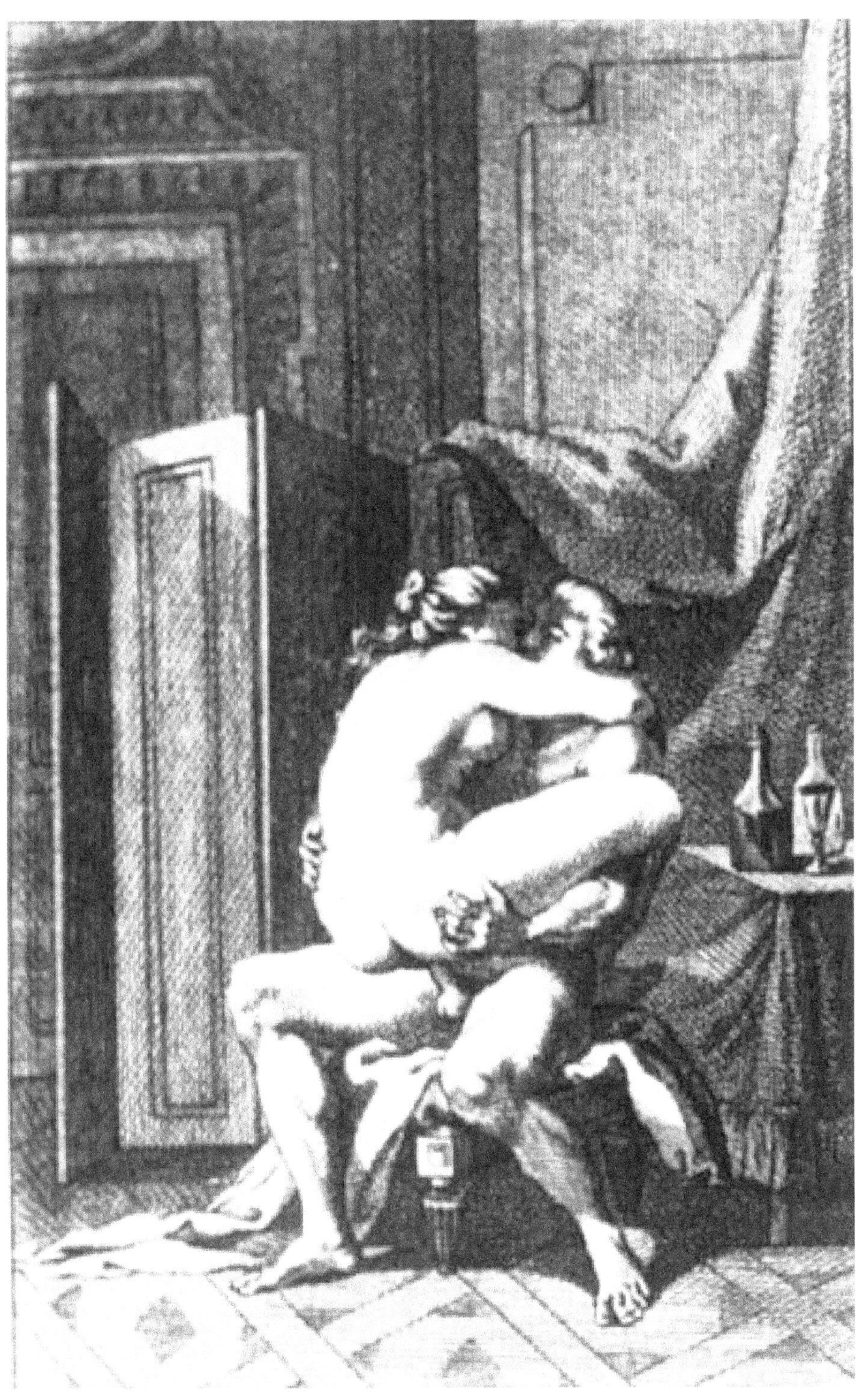

Antoine Borel, from Le Mersius François ou Entretiens Galans d'Aloysia,
by François Roland Elluin

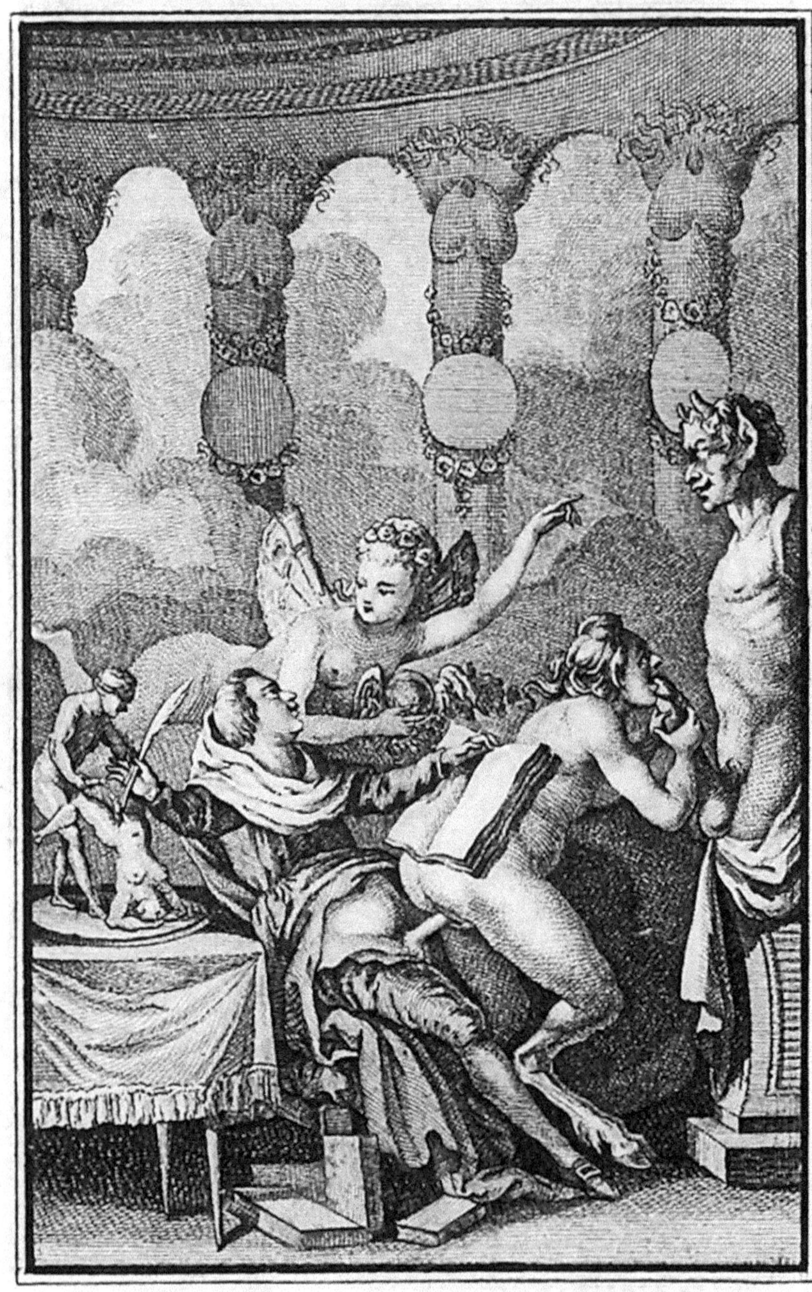

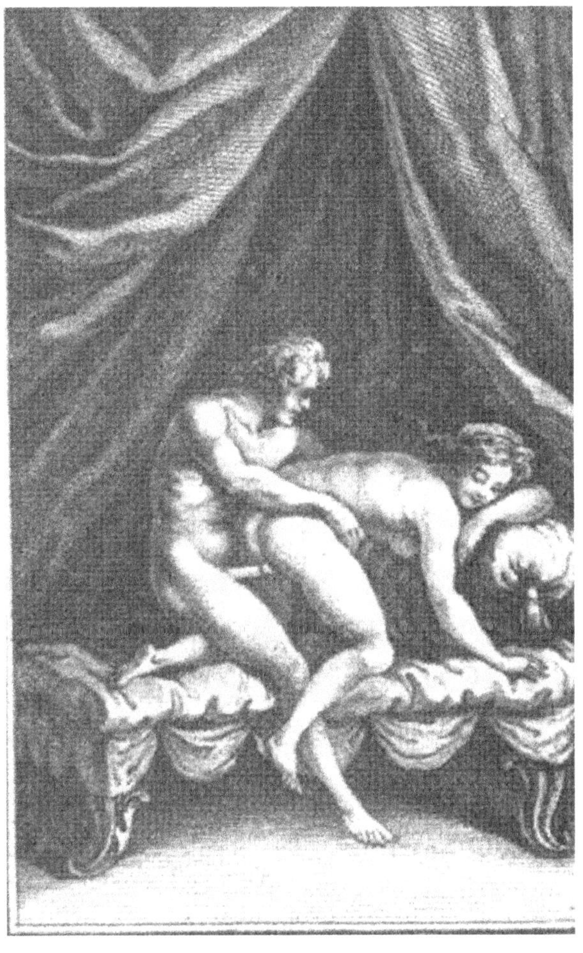

Antoine Borel, illustration for L'Arétin François, 1778, by Félix Nogaret (this page and over).

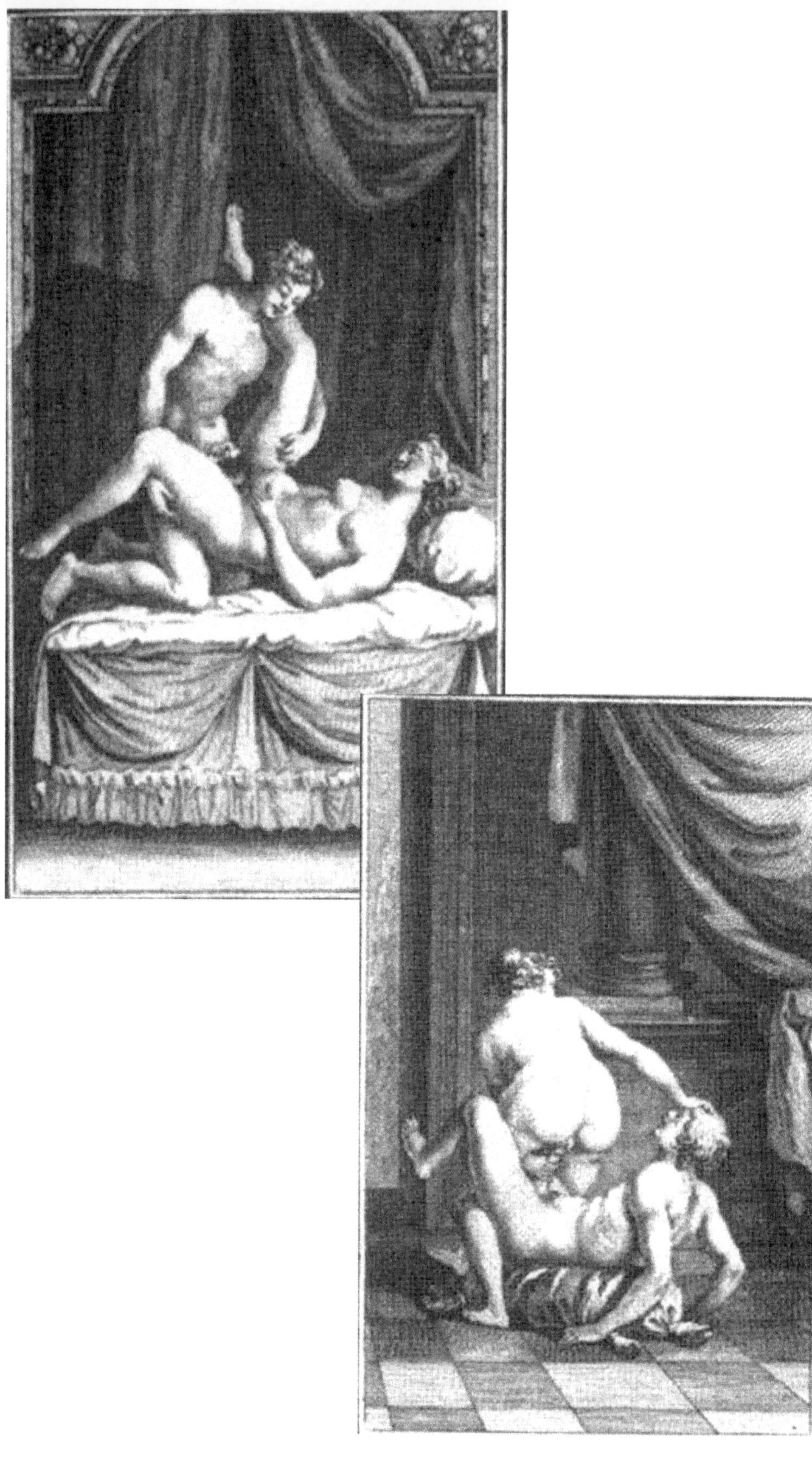

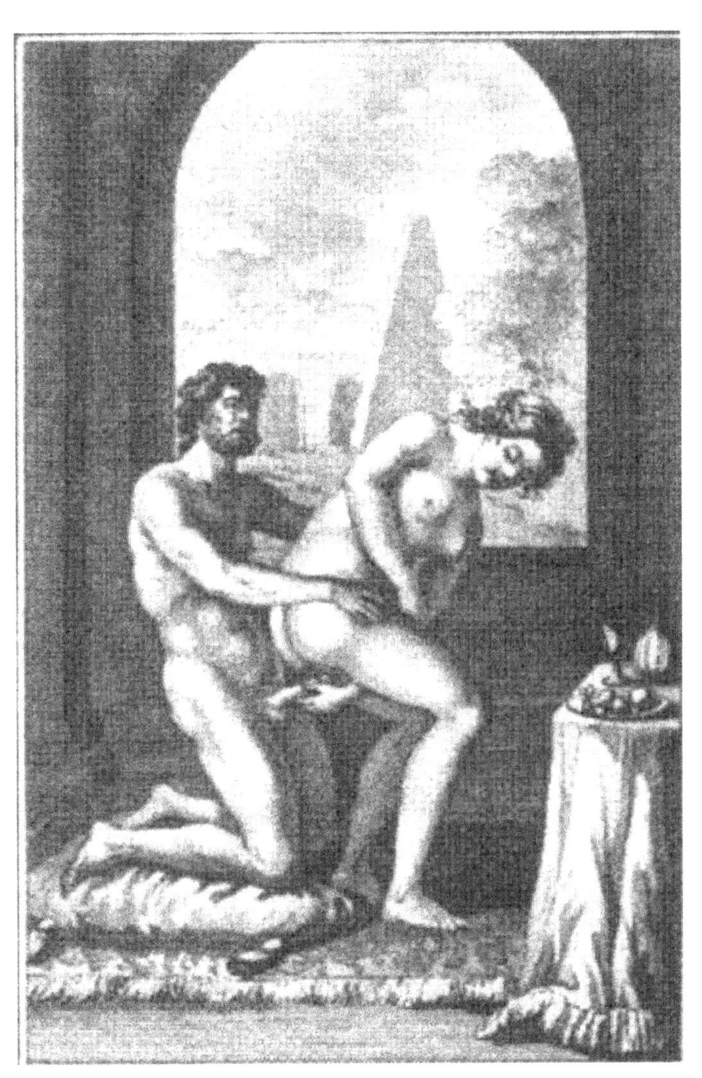

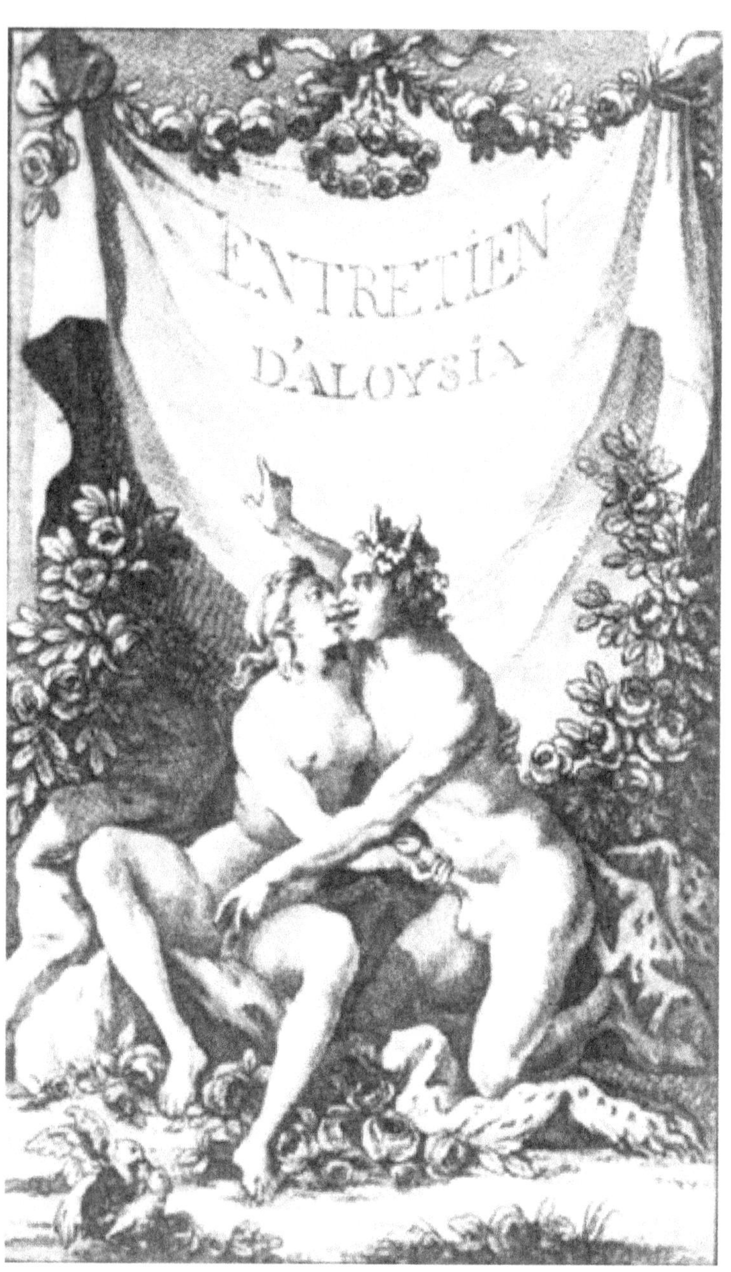
ENTRETIEN
D'ALOYSIA

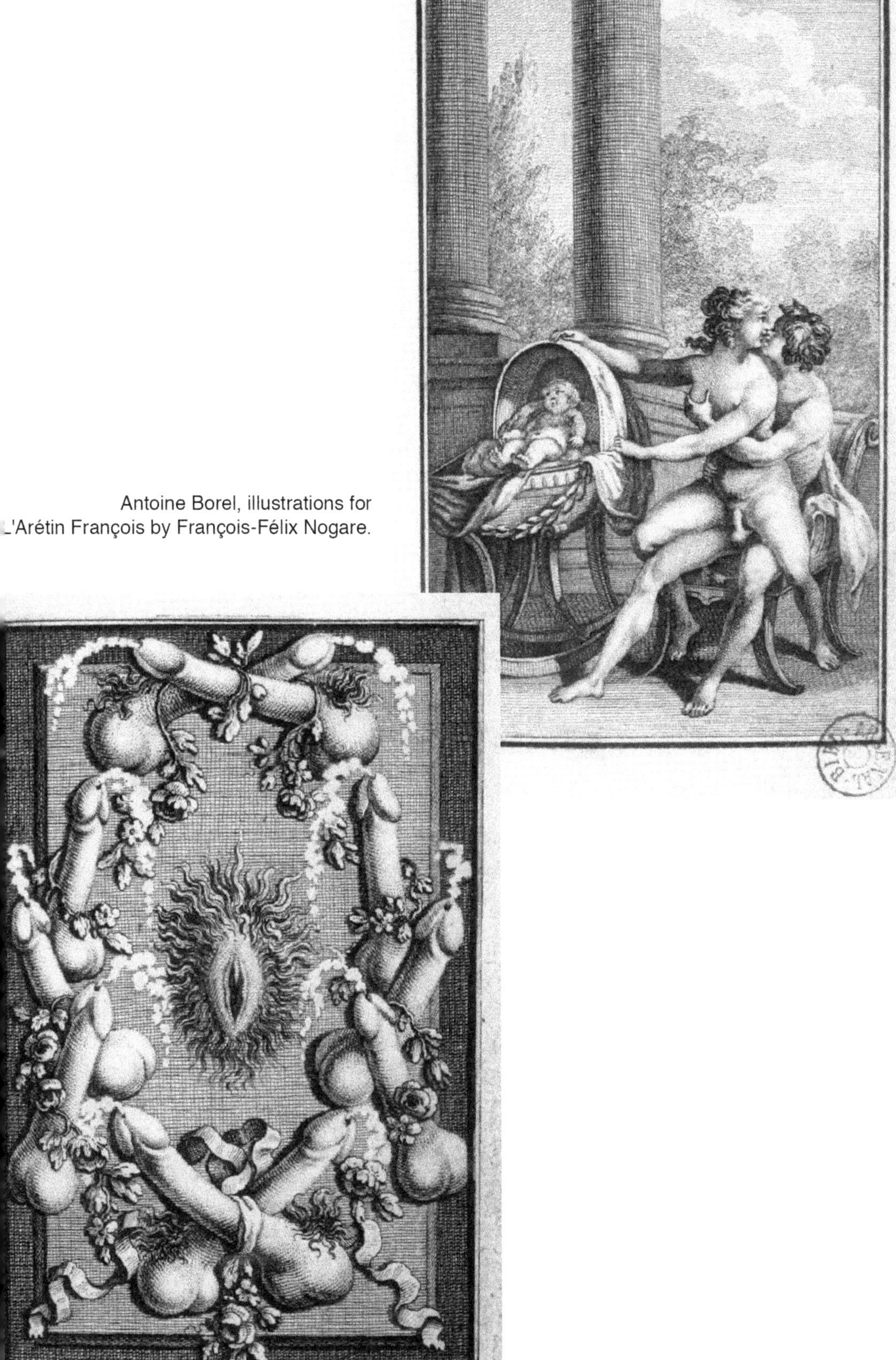

Antoine Borel, illustrations for L'Arétin François by François-Félix Nogare.

THÉRÈSE PHILOSOPHE

Thérèse Philosophe, ou Mémoires pour servir a l'histoire du Père Dirrag et de Mademoissel Éradice was an 18th century novel by Jean-Baptiste de Boyer, Marquis d'Argens (first published in 1748). It was an erotic version of the philosophical novel (popularized by Diderot, Voltaire, Rousseau *et al*). Antoine Borel illustrated one of the early editions (with 20 engravings).

Pl. 7

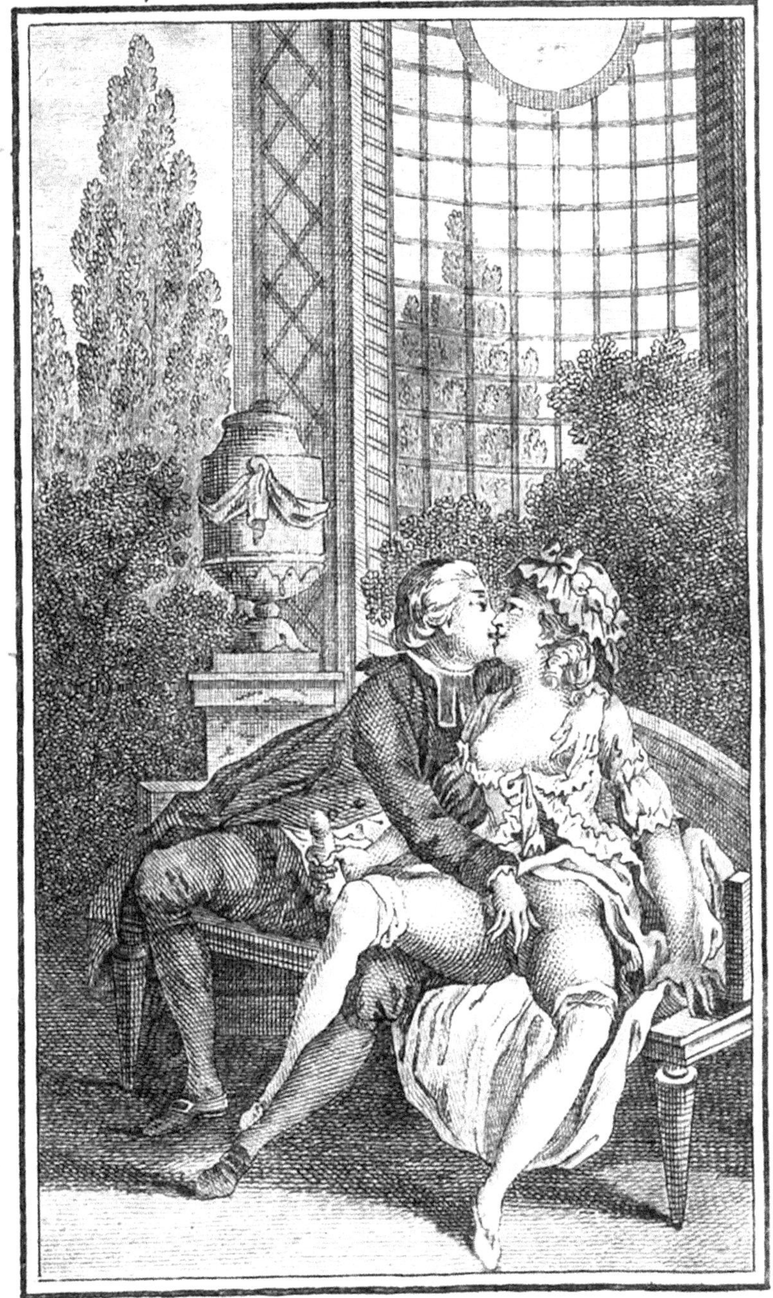

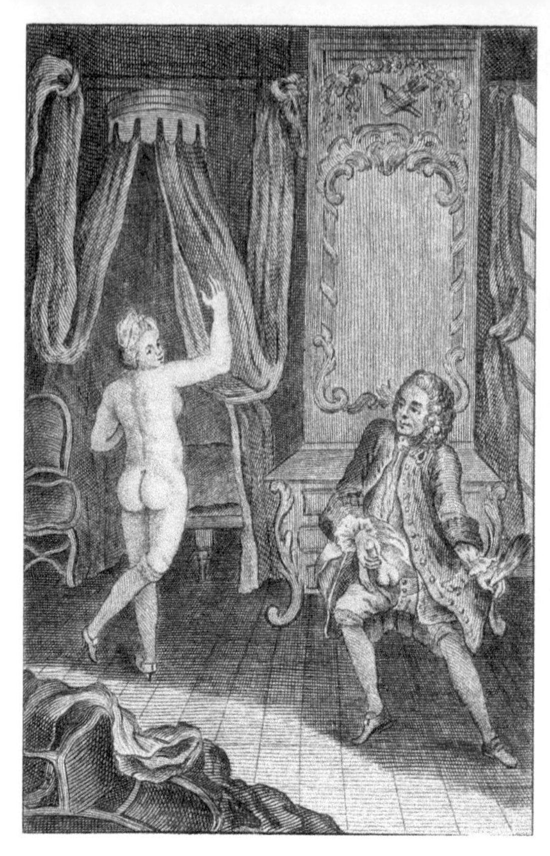

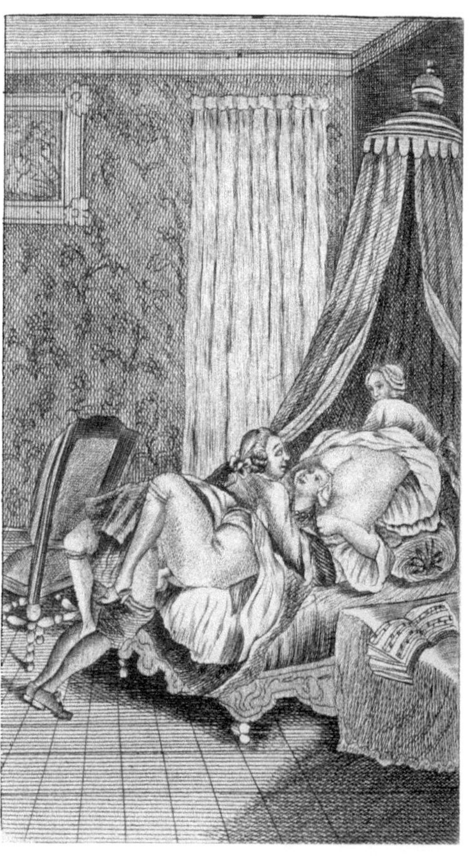

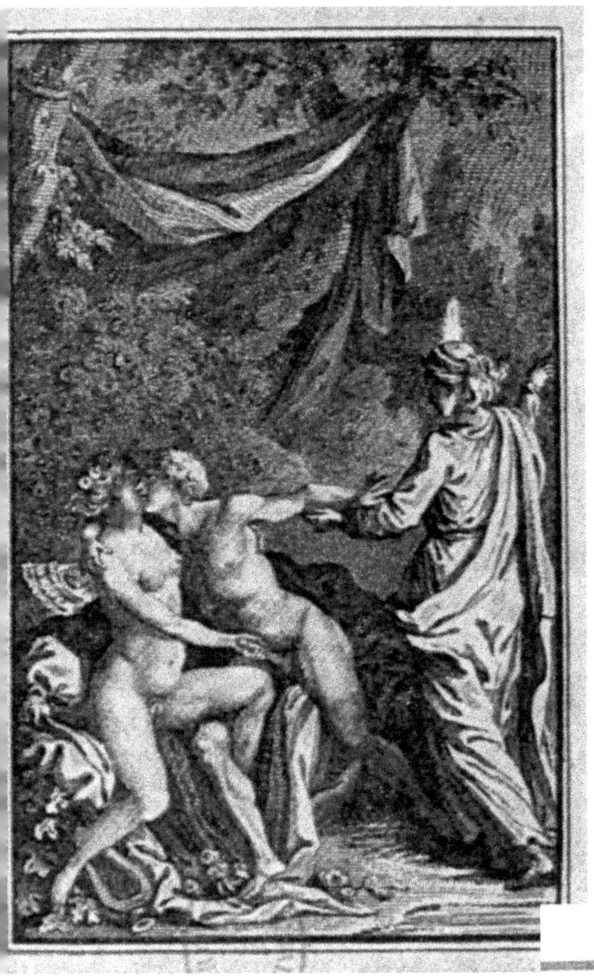

Thérèse Philosophe, 1785.

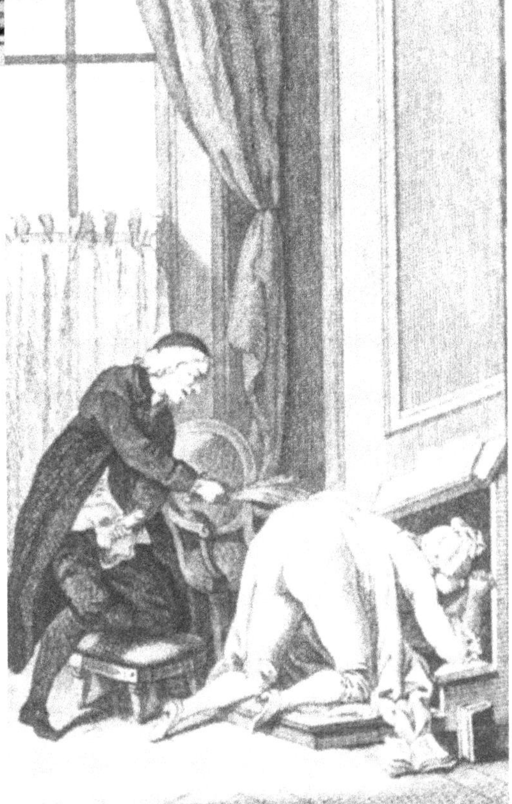

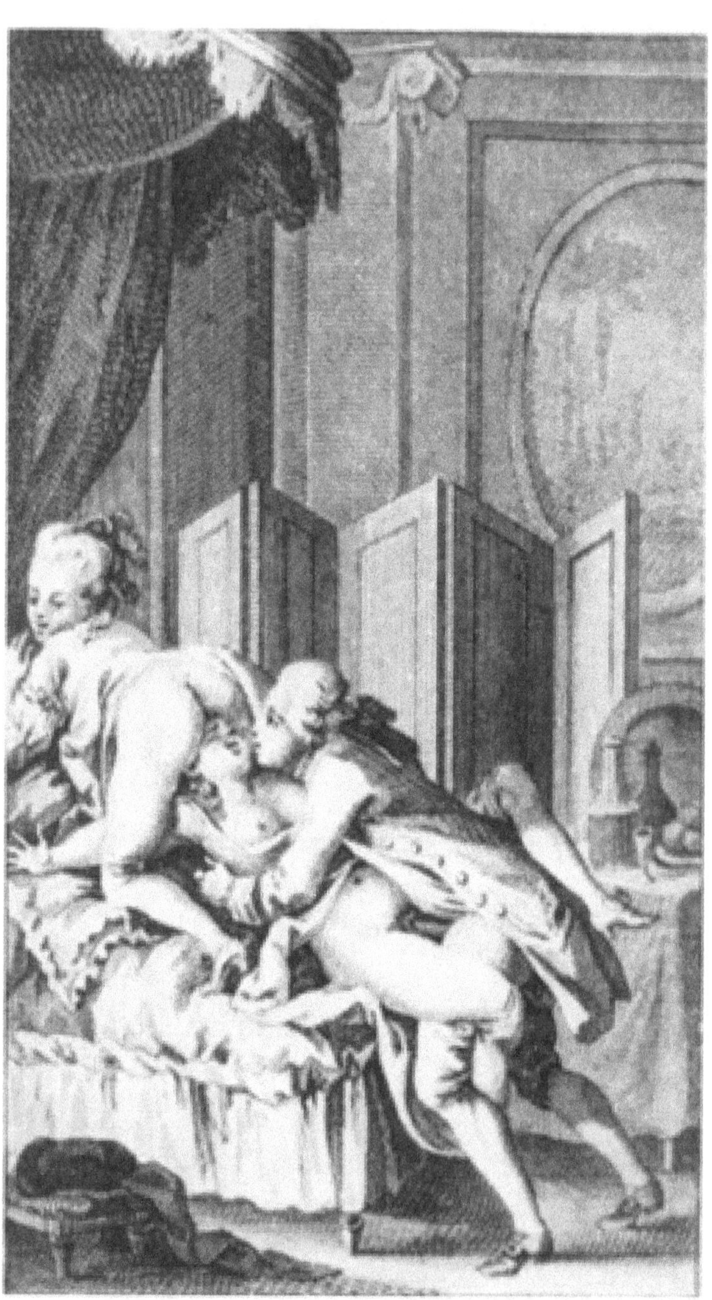

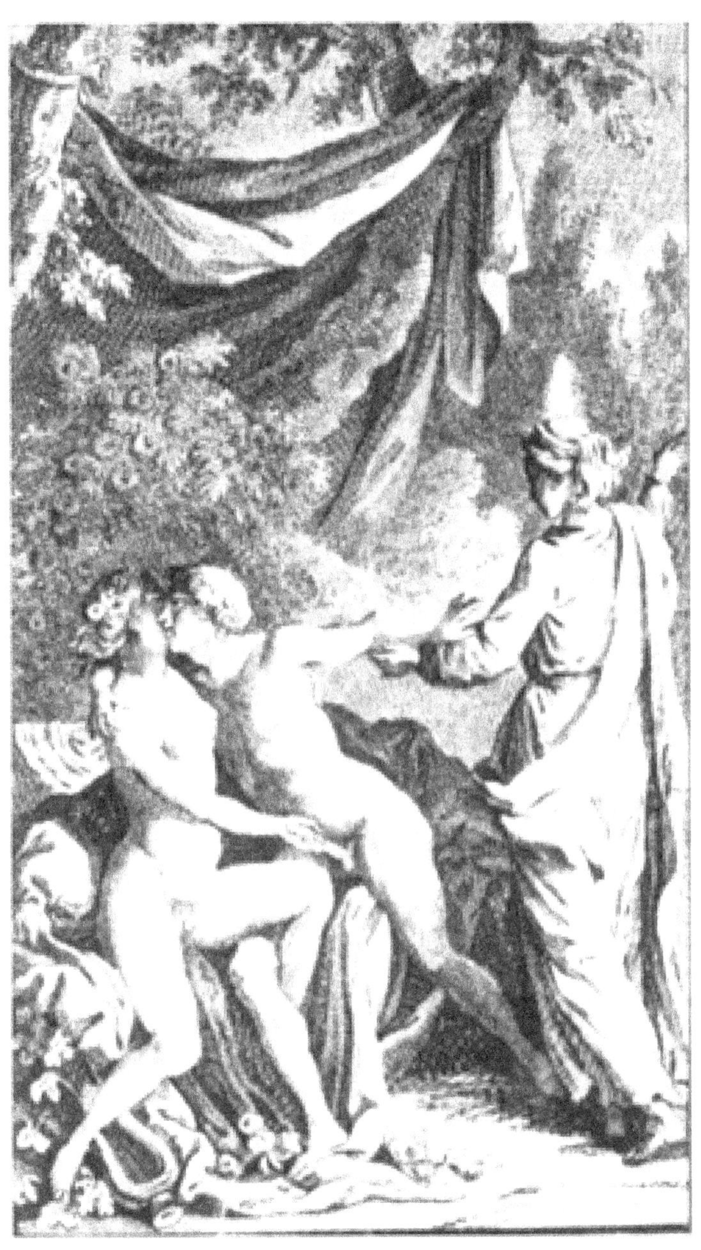

FANNY HILL

Fanny Hill: Memoirs of a Woman of Pleasure, by John Cleland (1709-89), published in 1748, is a classic of English erotica. Antoine Borel was one of the first illustrators of the book. This extract frfom *Fanny Hill* is typical:

> By this time his machine, stiffly risen at me, gave me to see it in its highest state and bravery. He feels it himself, seems pleased at its condition, and, smiling loves and graces, seizes one of my hands, and carries it, with gentle compulsion, to this pride of nature, and its richest master piece.
>
> I, struggling faintly, could not help feeling what I could not grasp, a column of the whitest ivory, beautifully streaked with blue veins, and carrying, fully un-capt, a head of the liveliest vermilion: no horn could be harder or stiffer; yet no velvet more smooth or delicious to the touch. Presently he guided my hand lower, to that part in which nature, and pleasure keep their stores in concert, so aptly fastened and hung on to the root of their first instrument and minister, that not improperly he might be styled their purse-bearer too: there he made me feel distinctly, through their soft cover, the contents, a pair of roundish balls, that seemed to play within, and elude all pressure, but the tenderest, from without.

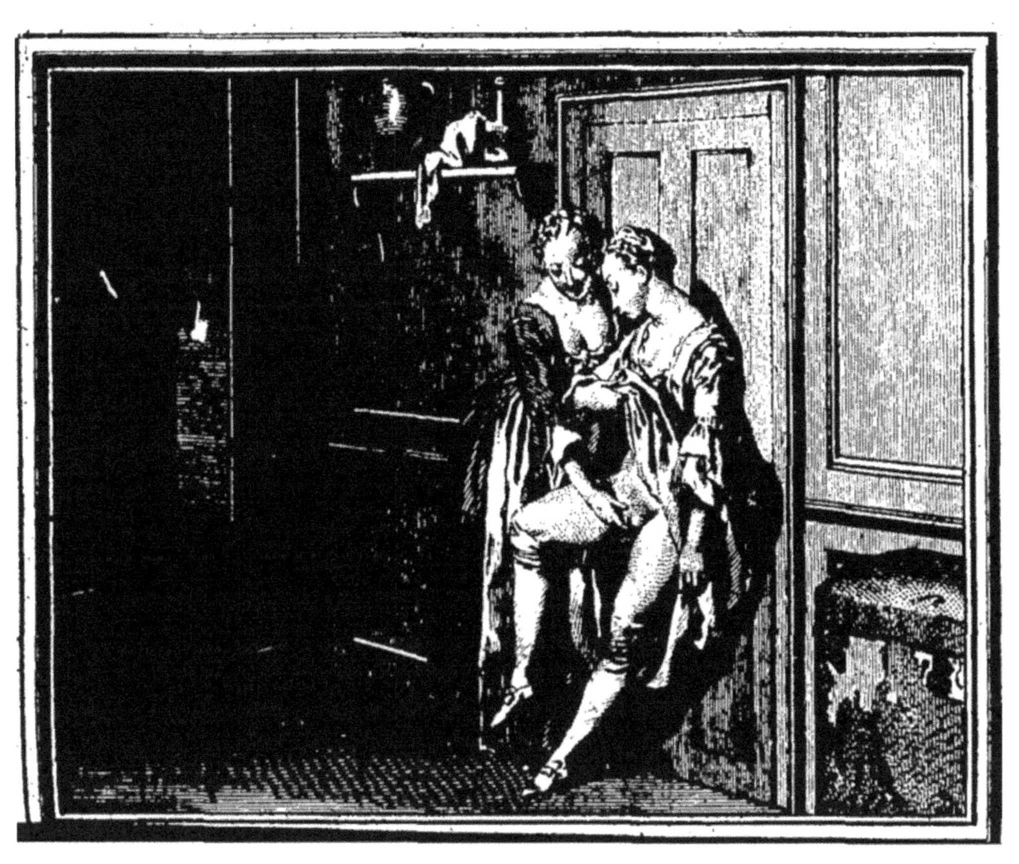

Illustration from the 1766 original edition of Fanny Hill

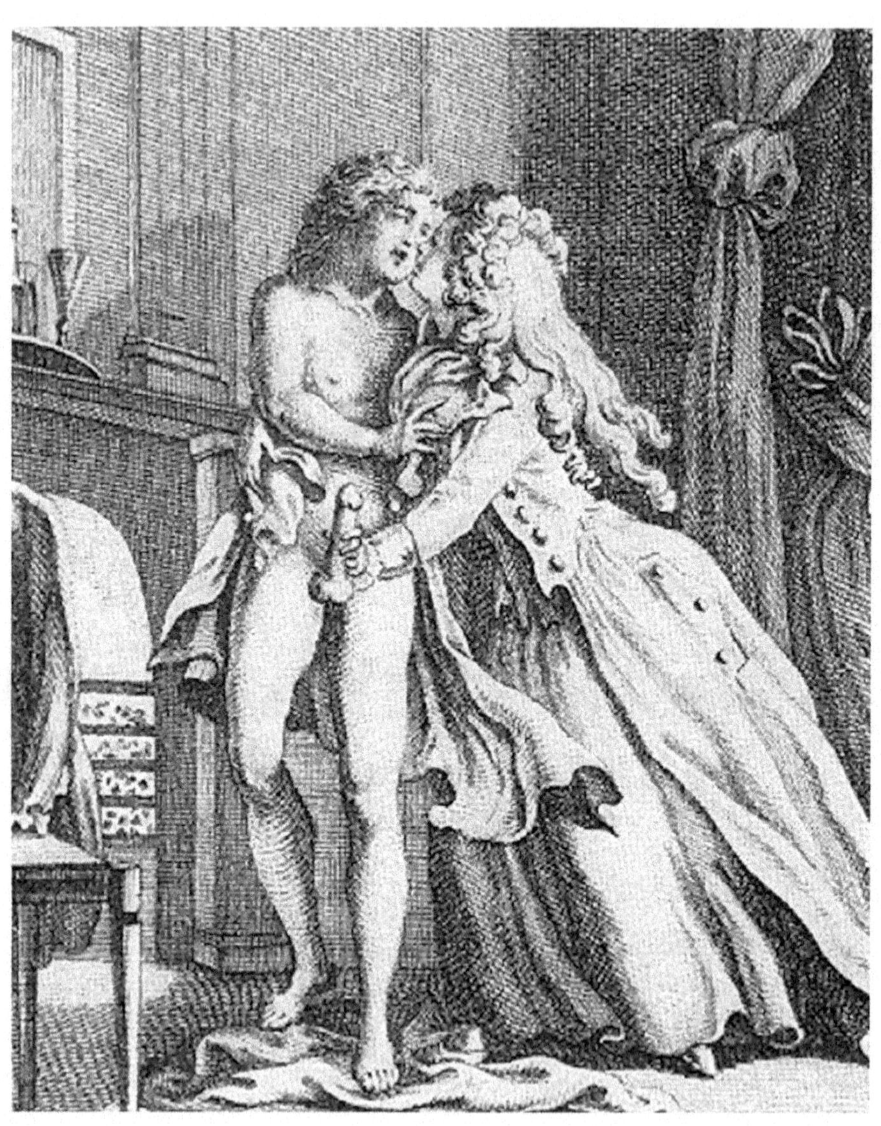

Fanny Hill illustrated by Antoine Borel (this page and over).

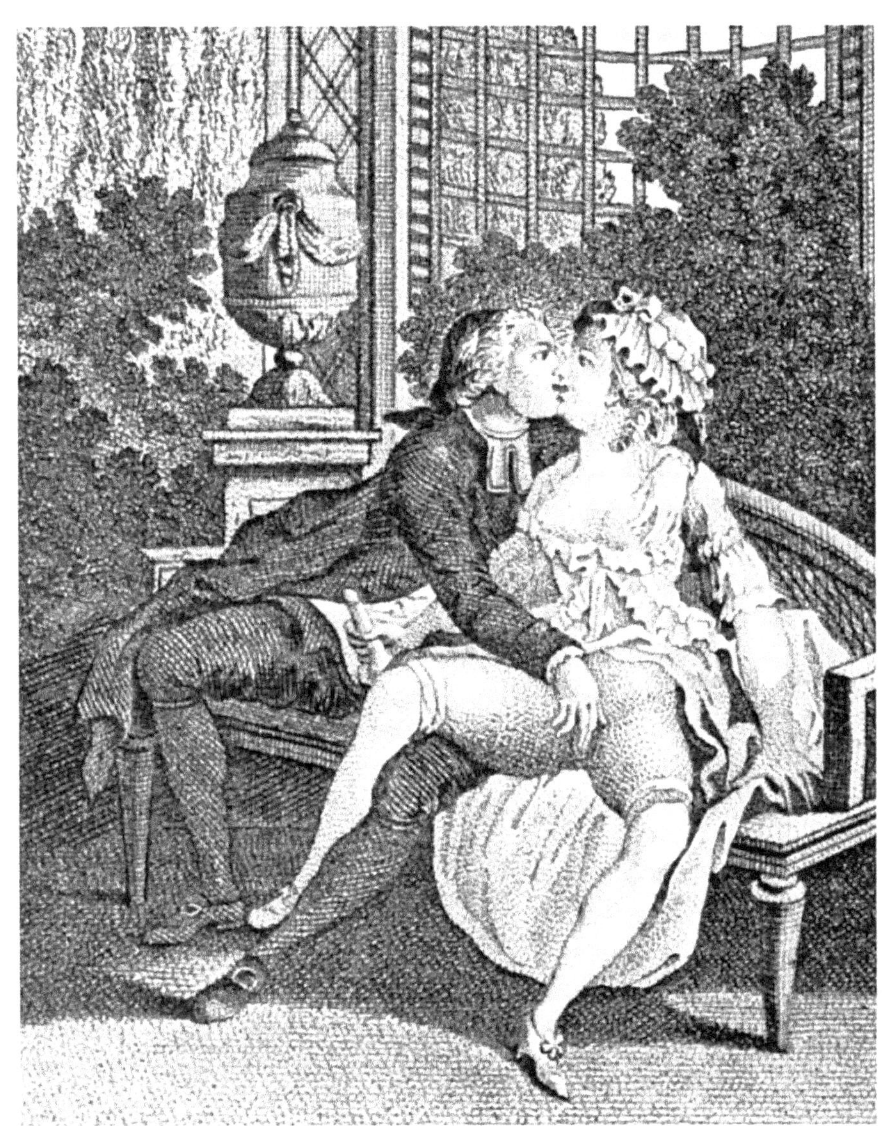

VOLTAIRE - *CANDIDE*

In *Candide*, Voltaire (1694-1778) satirized French society in one of the funniest novels of the era. Voltaire sent up the cult of beauty and desire, as this extract illustrates:

> This pause recalls Candide to himself. The fire of love takes possession of his breast: he darts the most ardent looks on all around him; imprints warm kisses on lips as warm, and eyes that swim in liquid fire: he passes his hands over globes whiter than alabaster, whose elastic motion repels touch; admires their proportion; perceives little vermilion protuberances, like those rose buds which only wait the genial rays of the sun to unfold them: he kisses them with rapture, and his lips for some time remained as if glued to the spot.

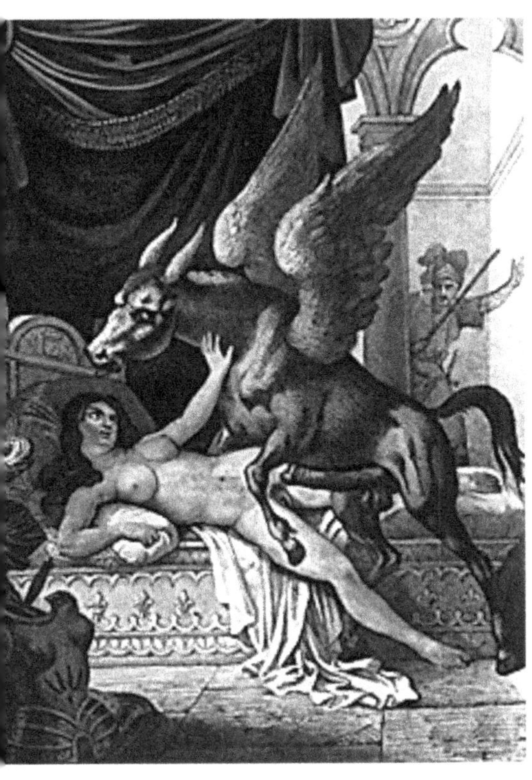

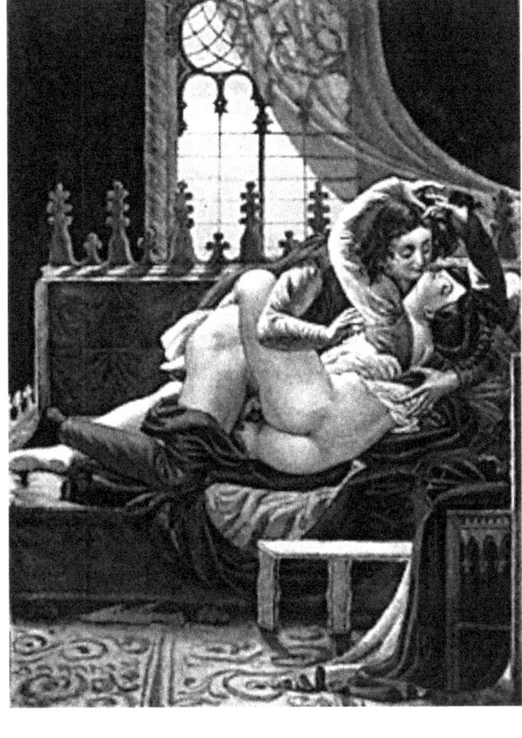

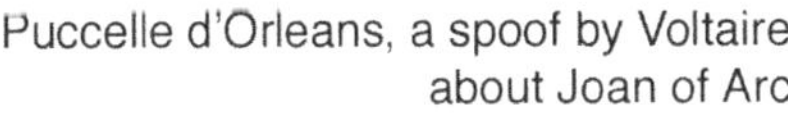

Puccelle d'Orleans, a spoof by Voltaire about Joan of Arc

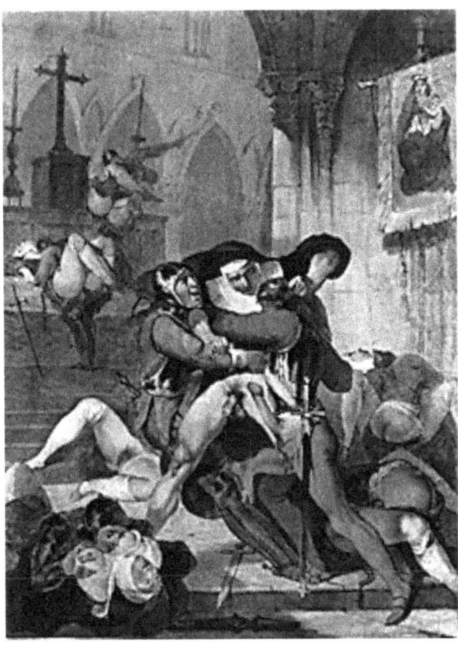

JACQUES JOSEPH COINY

Jacques Joseph Coiny (1761-1809) was the artist of an edition of etchings based on Agostino Carracci's famous set of sexual postures (*I Modi*). It was published in Paris in 1798 as *Augustine Carracci's The Arentin or Collection of Erotic Postures* (*L'Arétin d'Augustin Carrache ou Recueil de postures érotiques*).

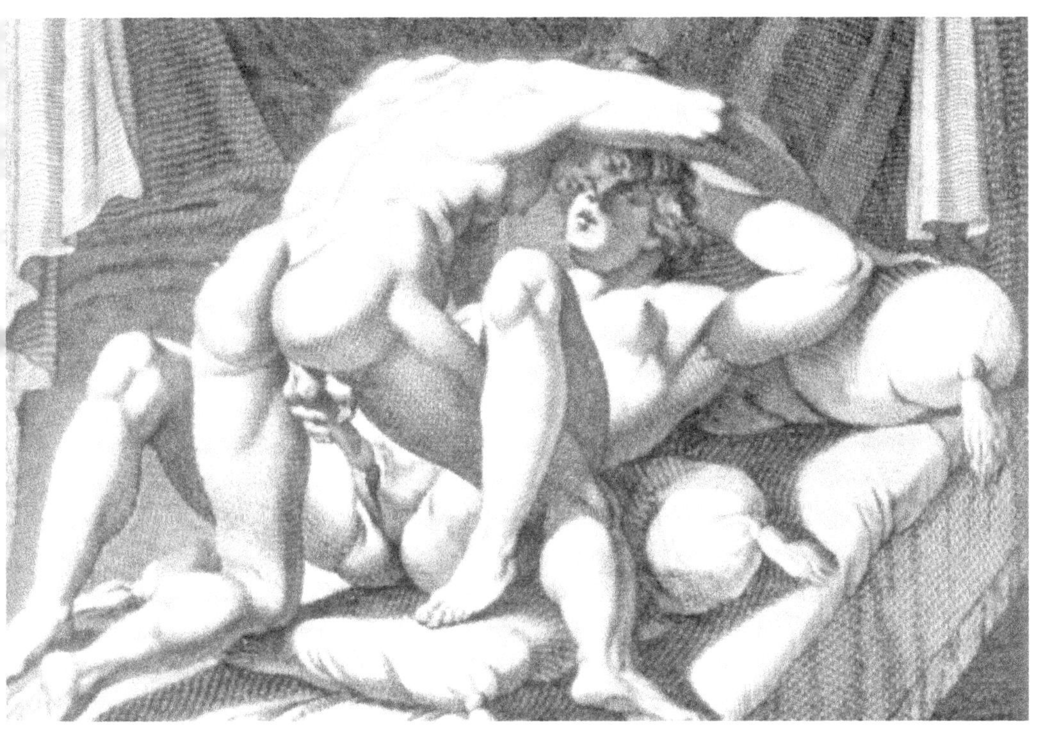

Jacques-Joseph Coiny, after Agostino Caracci, 1798

Nº 18.

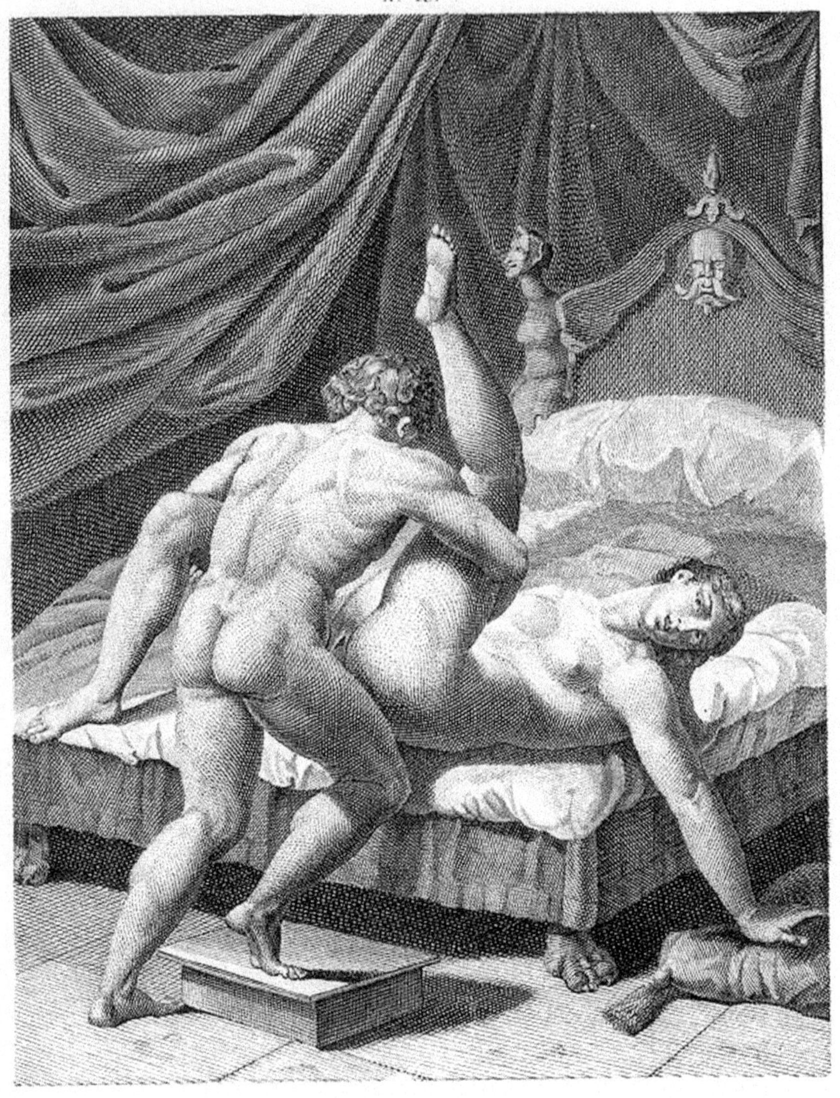

ALCIBIADE ET GLYCERE

N.° 15

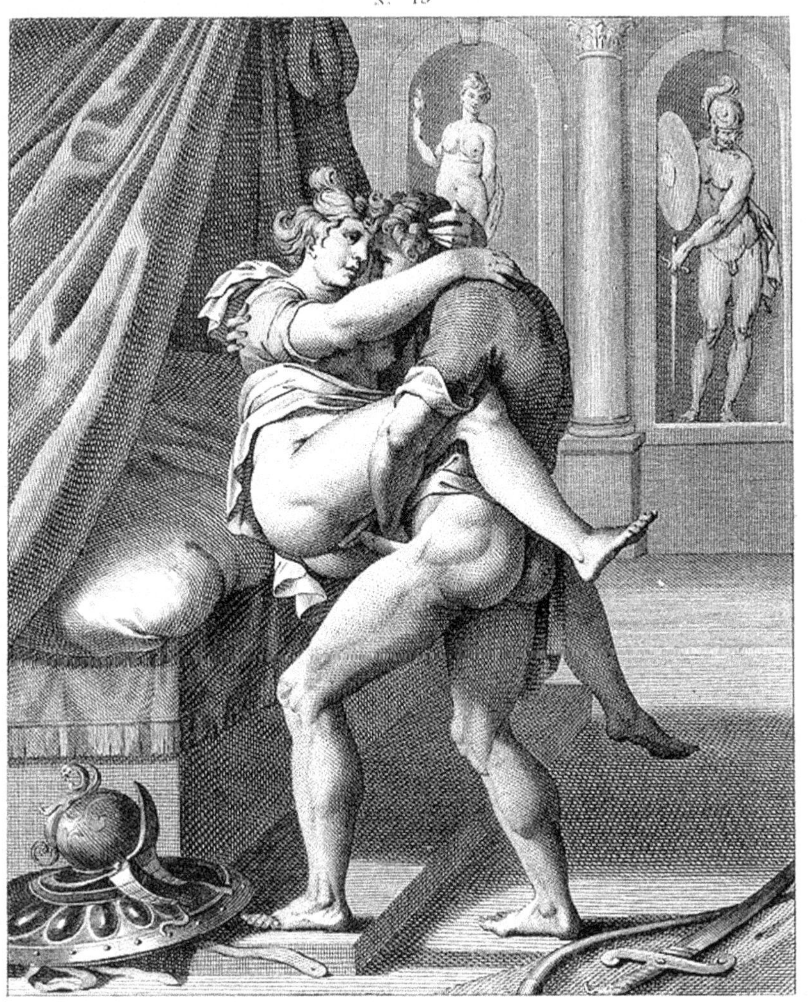

ACHILLE ET BRISEIS

JOHAN TOBIAS SERGEL

Johan Tobias Sergel (1740-1814) was a Swedish sculptor, who was born and lived in Stockholm. He drew his caricatures and erotic pictures which were possibly inspired by Thomas Rowlandson and other erotic artists.

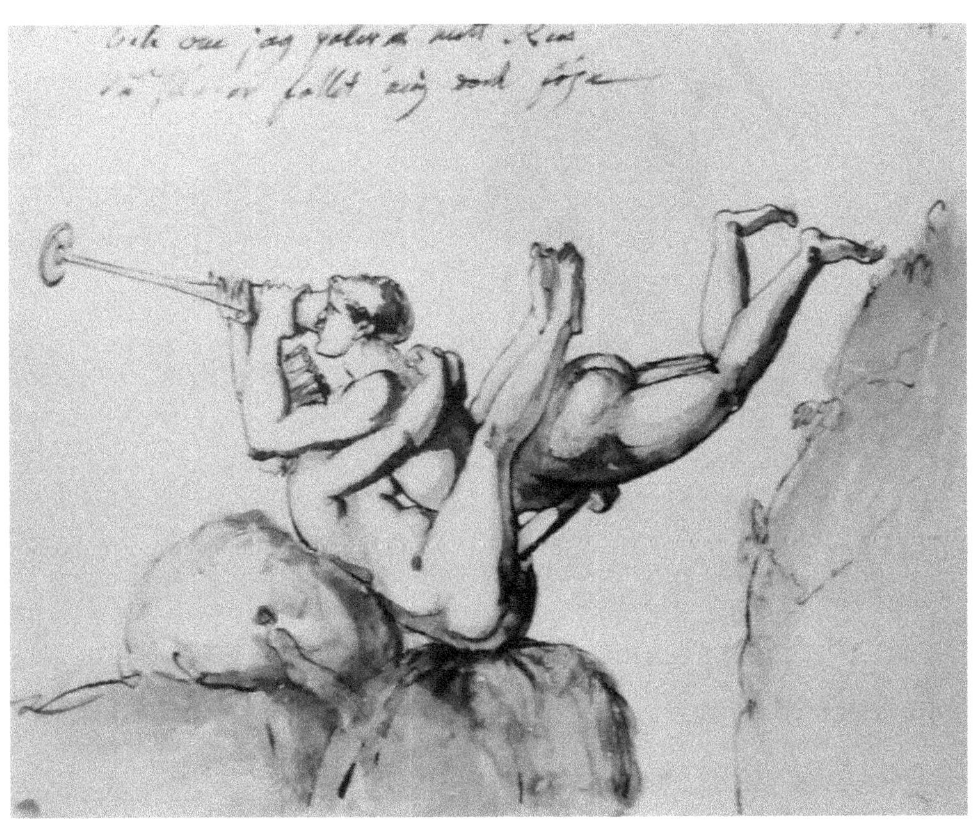

Johan Tobias Sergel, 18th century, Seden

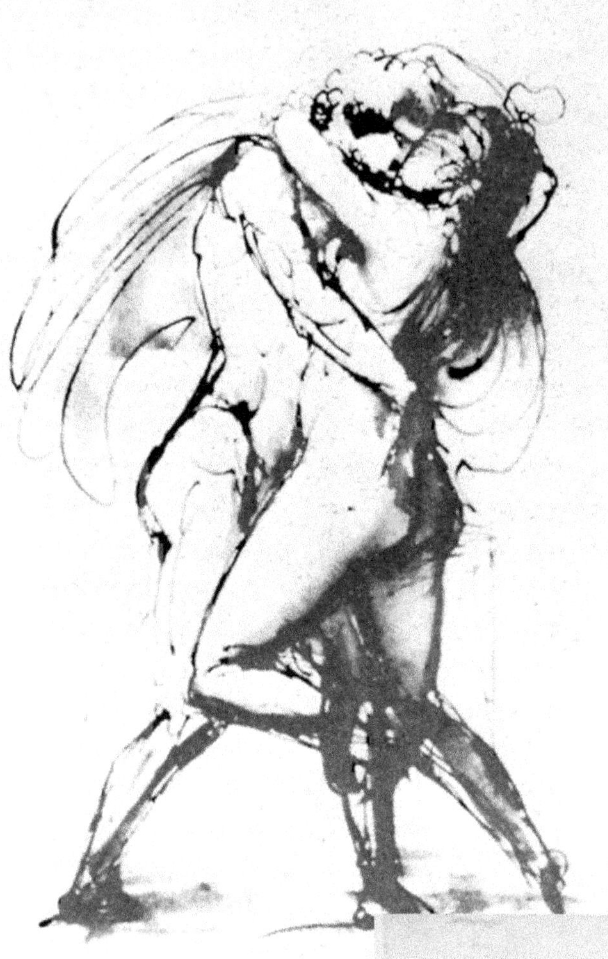

Johan Tobias Sergel

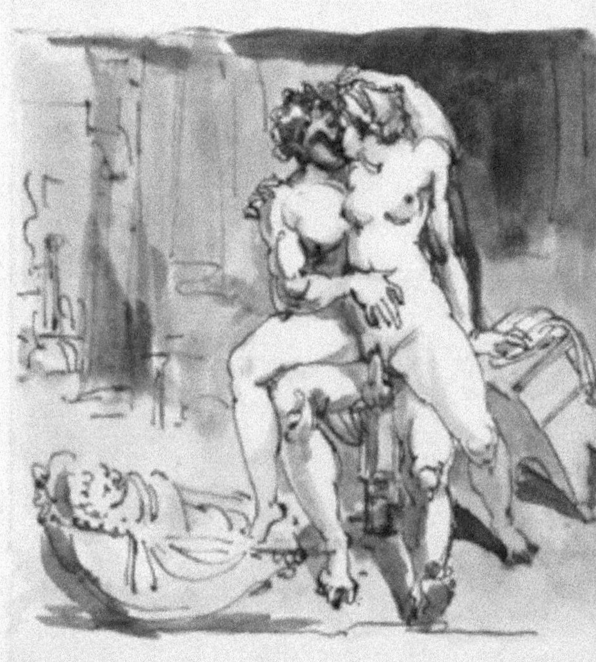

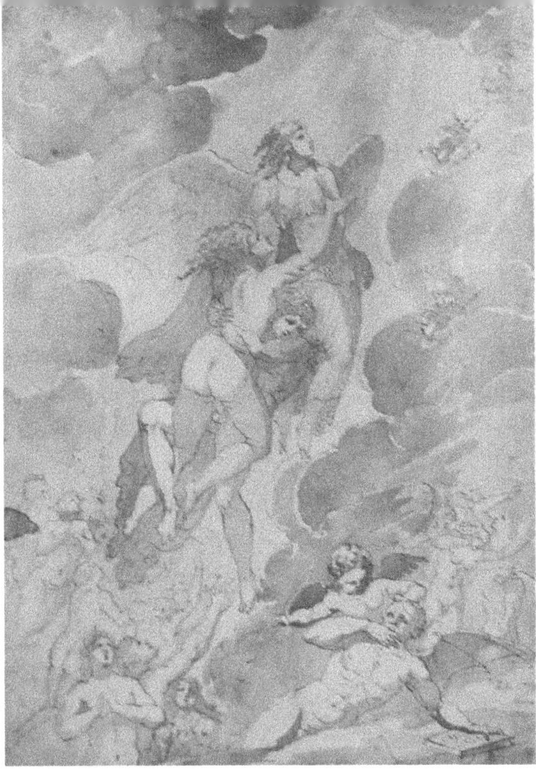

Two drawings by
Johan Tobias Sergel,
Sweden, late 18th century

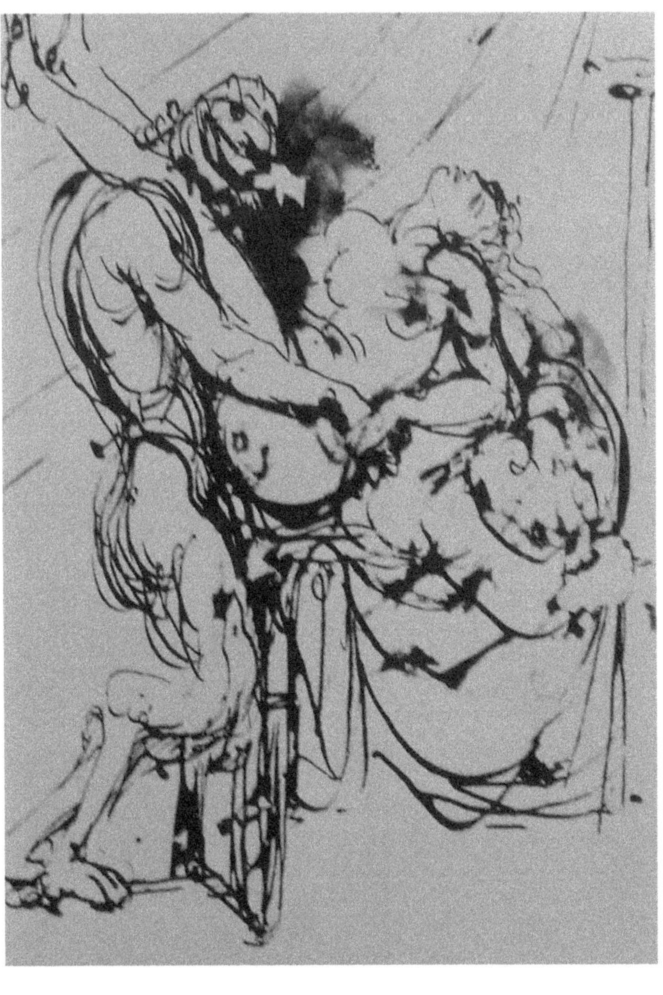

THOMAS ROWLANDSON

Thomas Rowlandson (1756-1827) is one of the great social commentators among British artists, capturing in a sprawling, vivacious and often humorous manner the variety of life in early modern Britain. His erotica is well-known, and a clear ancestor of saucy British postcard humour, of *Carry On* movies, of the nudge-nudge, wink-wink, *Monty Python* style of British comedy.

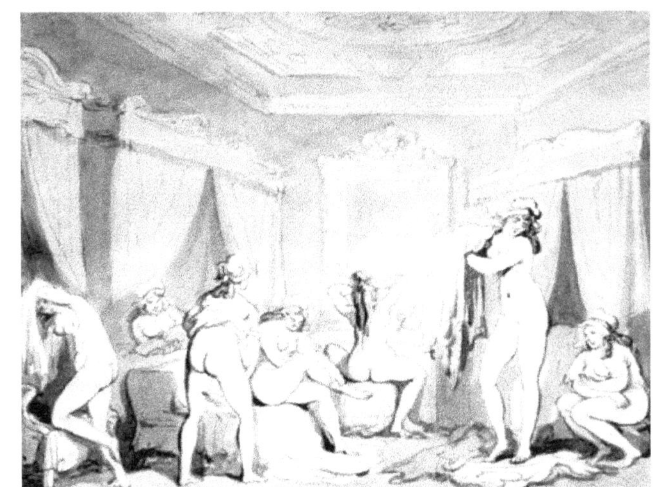

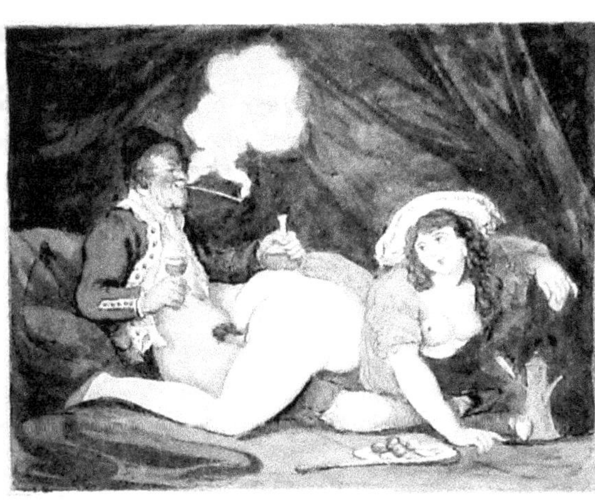

Thomas Rowlandson.
This page and following pages

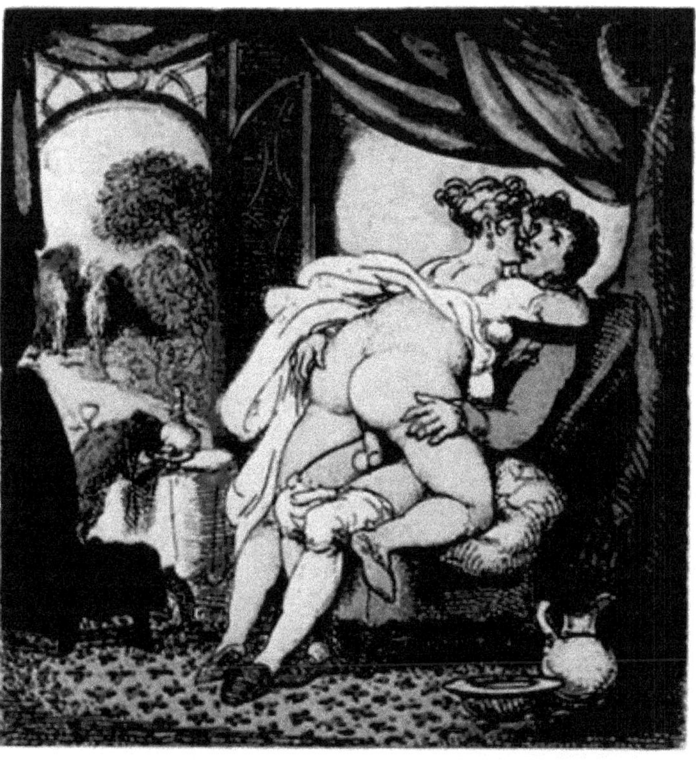

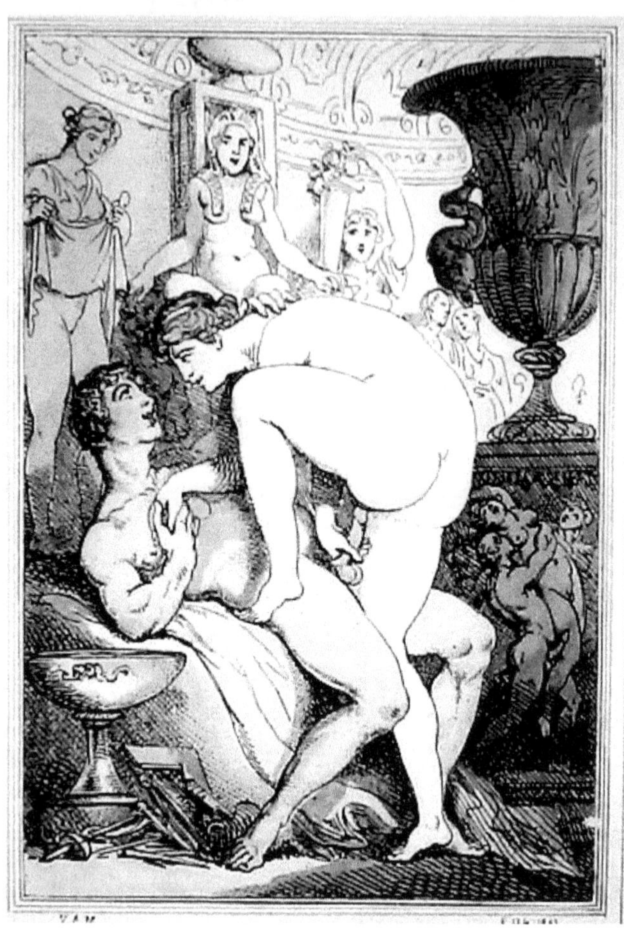

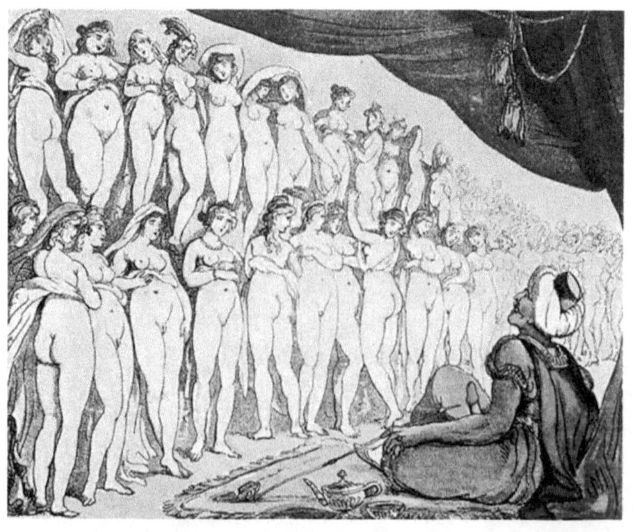

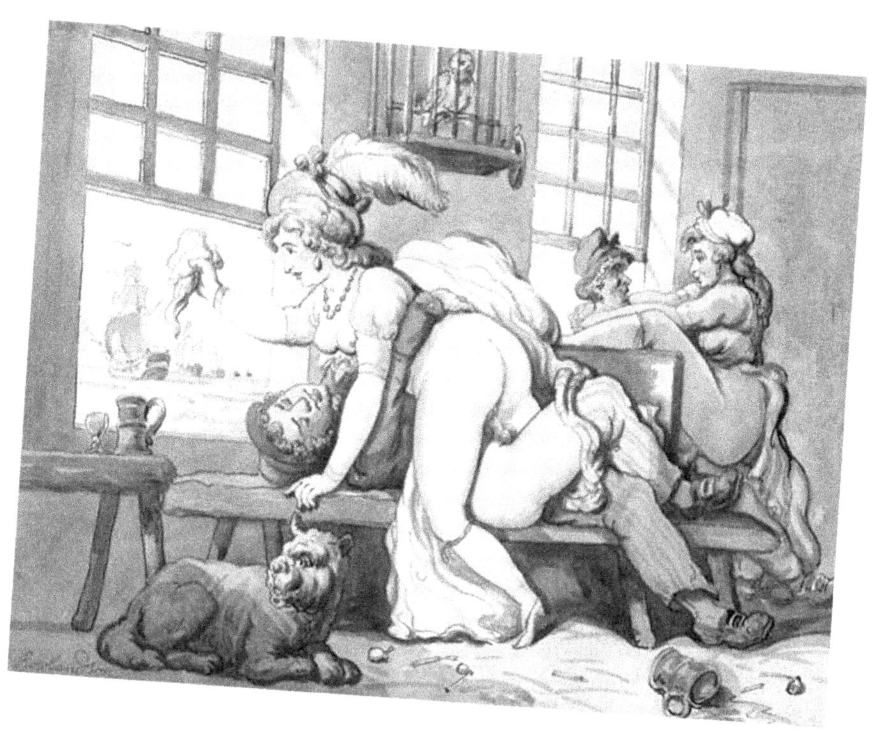

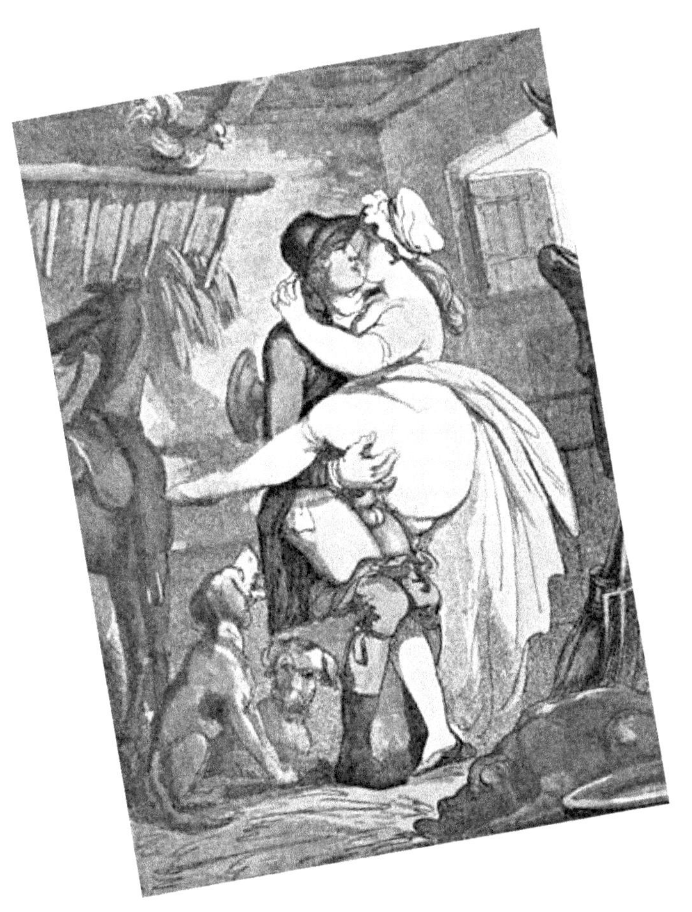

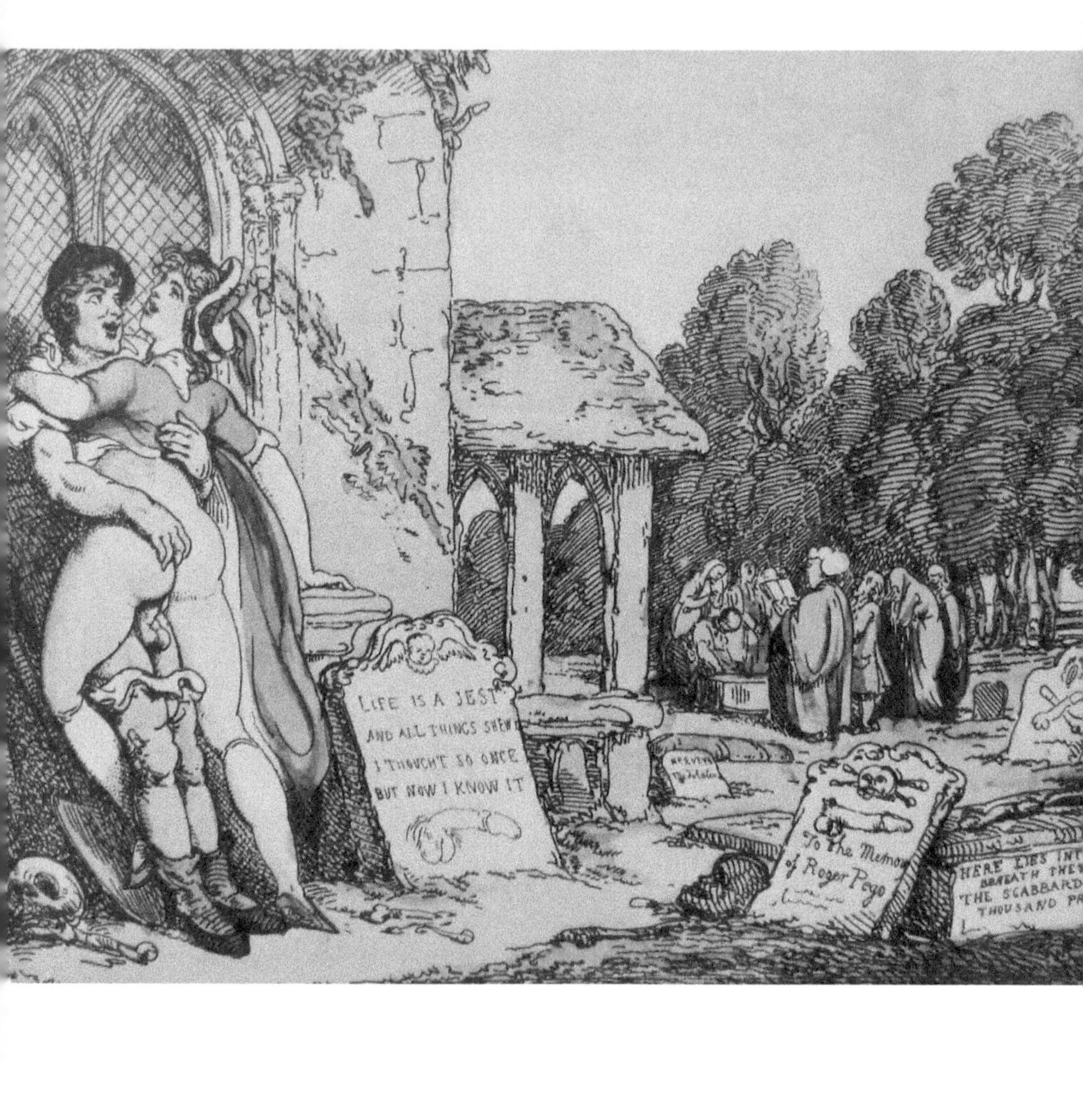
LIFE IS A JEST
AND ALL THINGS SHEW
I THOUGHT SO ONCE
BUT NOW I KNOW IT
To the Memo
of Roger Pego
HERE LIES IN
BENEATH THE
THE SCABBARD
THOUSAND

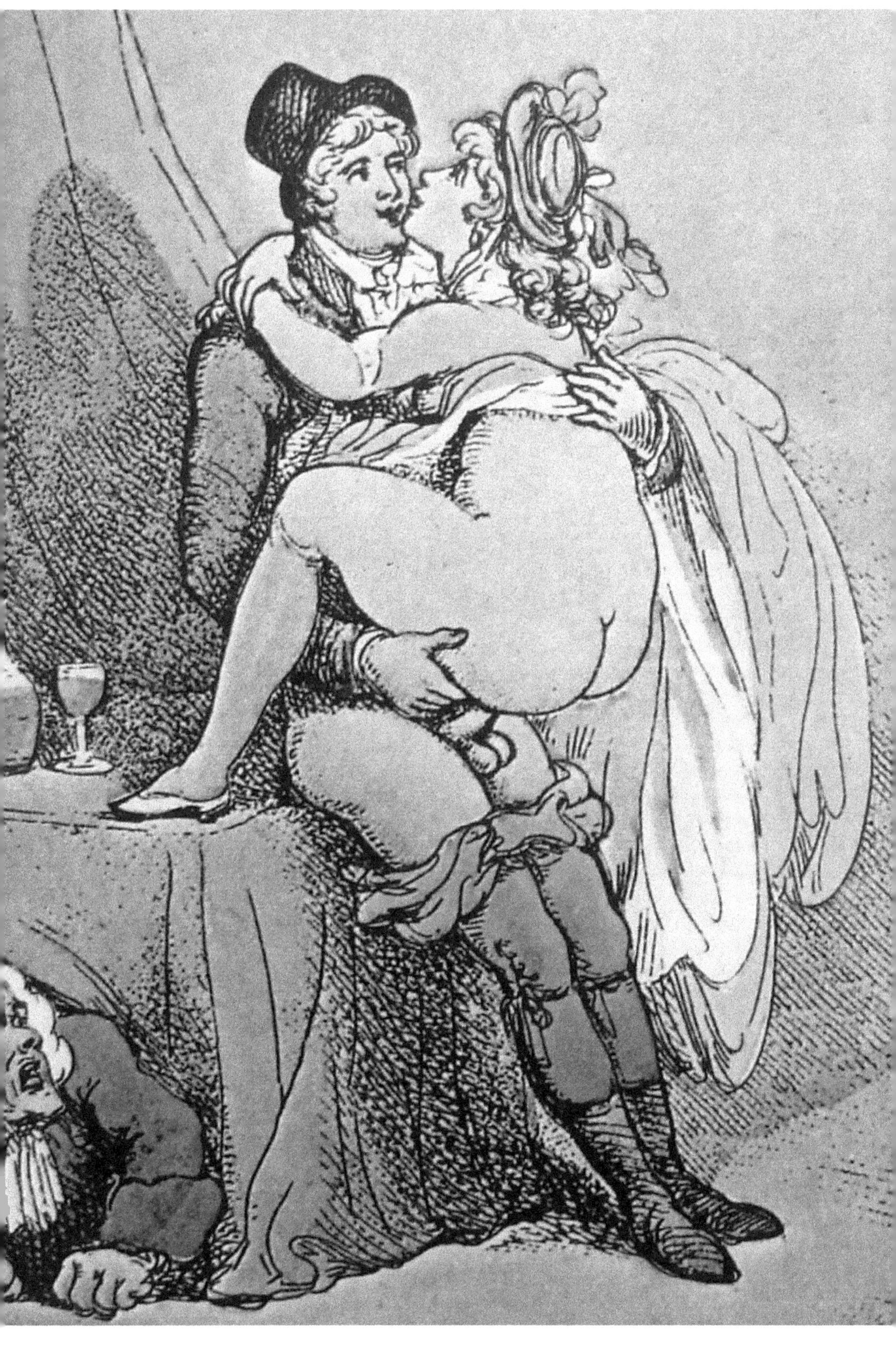

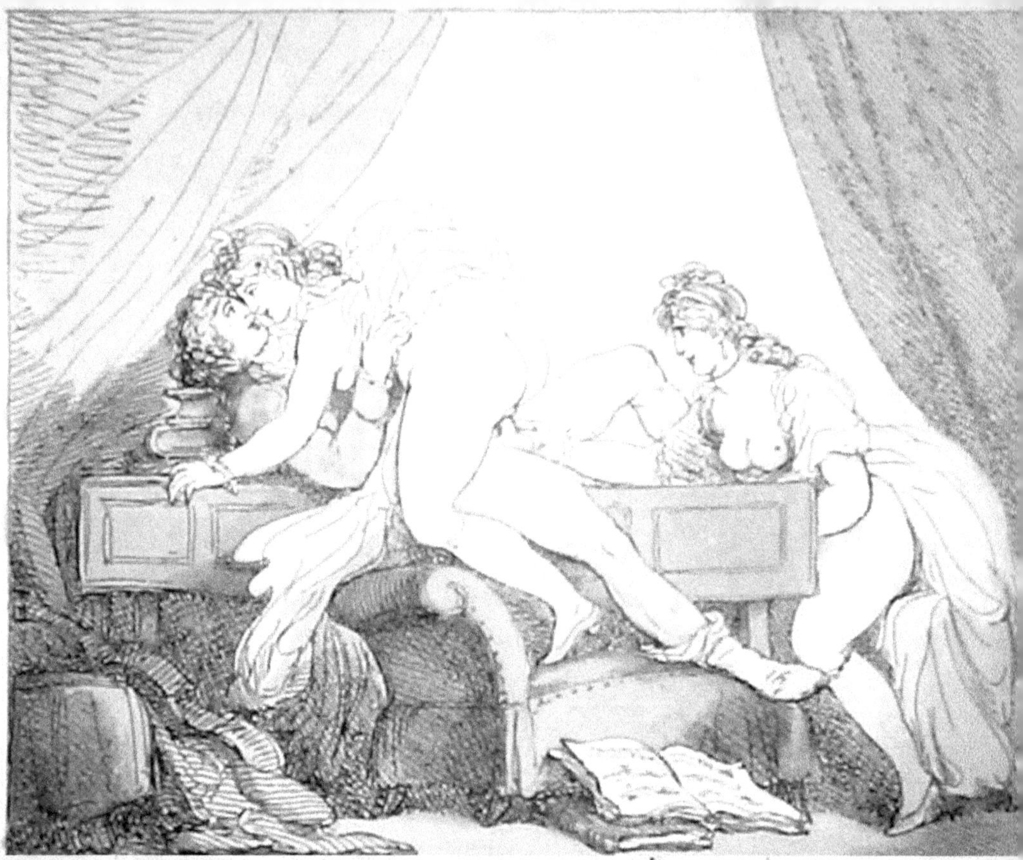

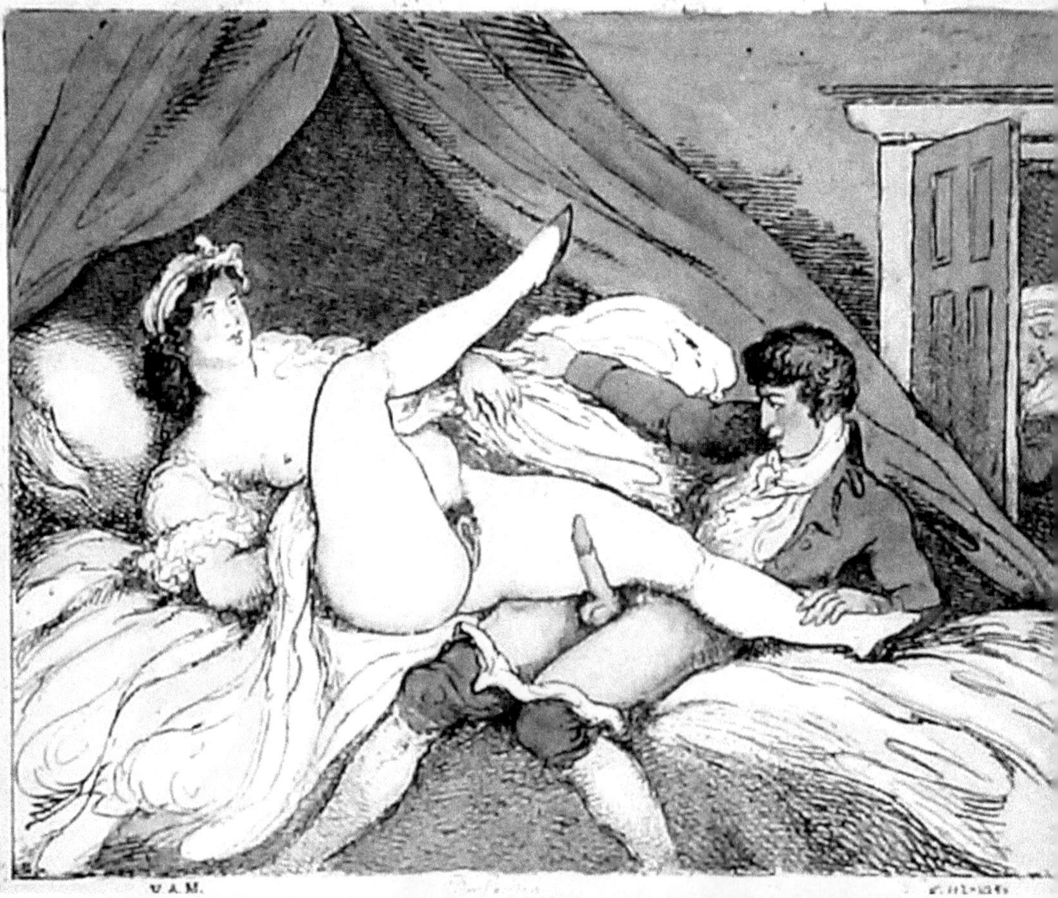

V.A.M.

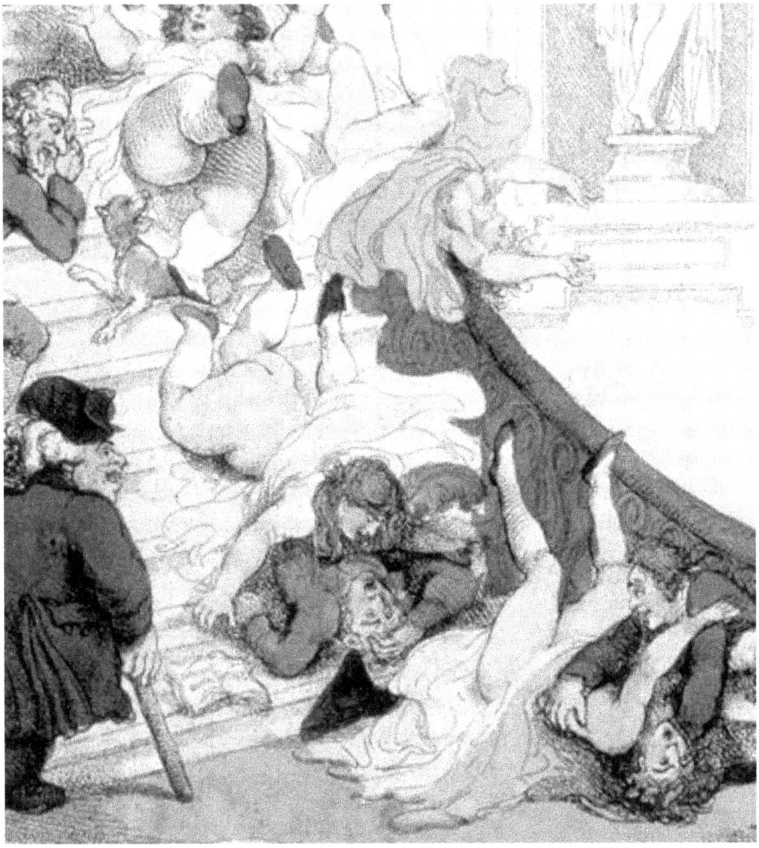

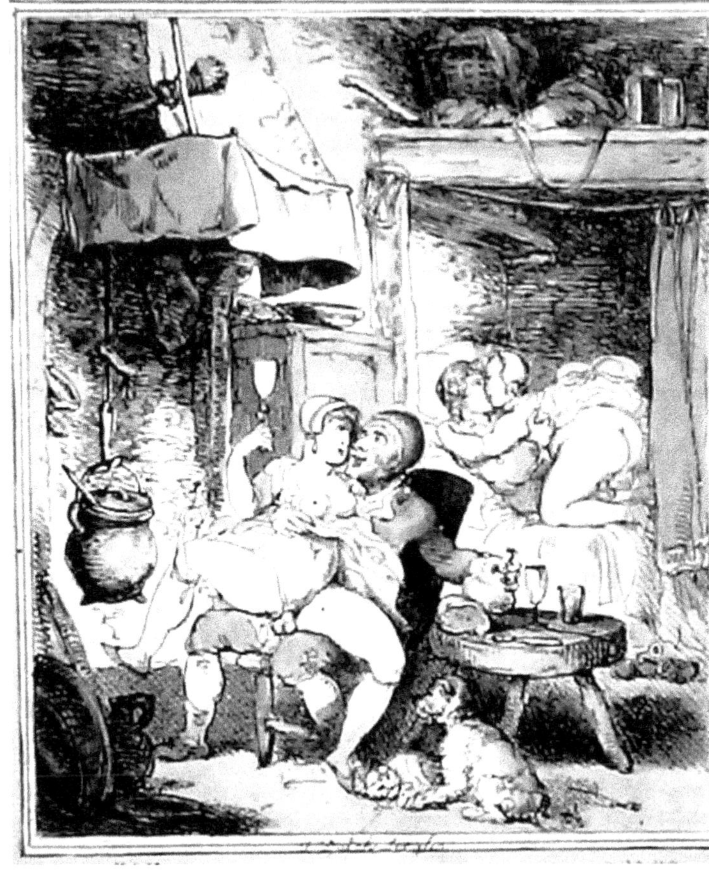

THE MARQUIS DE SADE

Donatien-Alphonse-François de Sade, a.k.a. the Marquis de Sade (1740-1814), was the controversial author of 4 novels, short stories, plays, dialogues, letters, journals and pamphlets (including *Justine, Philosophy of the Bedroom, The Story of Juliette* and *Les Cent Vingt Journés de Sodome*). De Sade's was a notorious life, leading to a number of spells in prison (prostitutes, attempts on his life, run-ins with the police, accused of poisoning Marseilles hookers, etc).[1] He apparently indulged in some of the sadomasochistic practices described in his fiction (some of which led to his imprisonment); that's part of the Sadean Legend, of course.[2]

1 According to Gérard Zwang, 'it is because of excessive imprisonment and vindictive and cowardly censorship that Sade has been put on a pedestal and consecrated a martyr, great philosopher, major writer and specialist in eroticism' (quoted in B. Groult: "Les portiers de nuit", in *Ainsi soit-elle,* Grasset, Paris, 1975, and in E. Marks, 69).

2 We want to believe that notorious writers are *really* notorious! And not like everybody else.

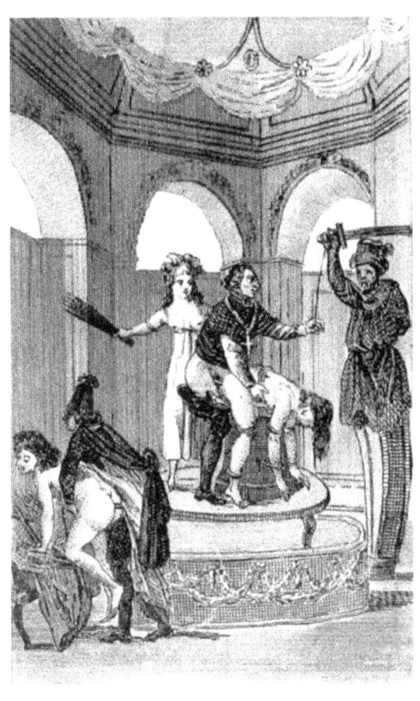

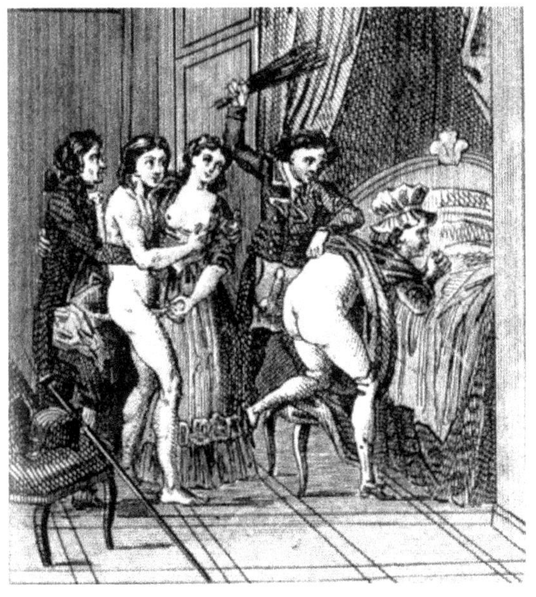

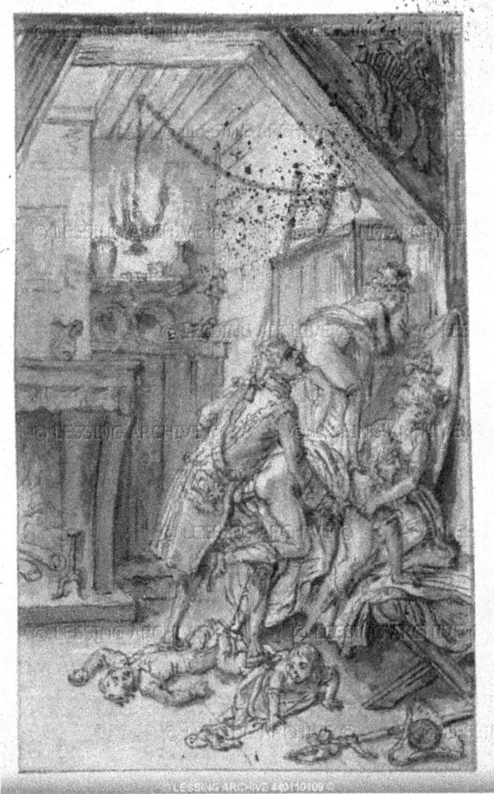

Illustrations from Justine, late 18th century

THE MARQUIS DE SADE

The Marquis de Sade is the high priest of metaphysical eroticism, as championed by the European artistic élite, such as Charles Baudelaire, Jean Cocteau, the Surrealists, Algernon Swinburne, Lautréamont, Fyodor Dost-oievsky and John Cowper Powys. Among visual artists, the inheritors of the Sadeian pornographic ethic include Pablo Picasso, Hans Bellmer, Jean Cocteau, Max Ernst, Allen Jones, and David Salle. Many artists have had a go at illustrating de Sade's work.

The Marquis de Sade also possessed the childish urge to shock society – in common with the Surrealists and so many other avant gardists (and a good many filmmakers, too). There is undoubtedly a yen to startle audiences, a conscious effort to find *something* that will wind up someone in the audience. After de Sade, the fiction of Henry Miller, Jean Genet, Georges Bataille and William Burroughs seems a mere postscript. This extract from *The 120 Days of Sodom* is typical:

> Curval, who had not been experiencing such an onslaught, blasphemed with joy. He quivered in excitement, opened his legs wide and prepared himself. At that moment the youthful sperm of the charming boy he was masturbating dripped down to the enormous tip of his frenzied instrument. This warm sperm which drenched him, the repeated shuddering of the duke who was beginning to discharge also, everything led him on, everything brought on his climax and floods of foaming sperm flooded Durcet's arse.[1]

1 Quoted in M. Crosland, 2000, 37.

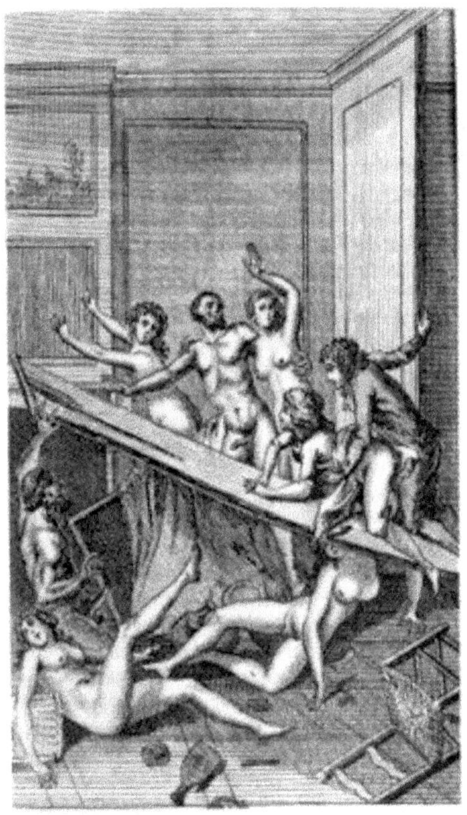

Illustration from Histoire de Juliette,
Marquis de Sade, 1797

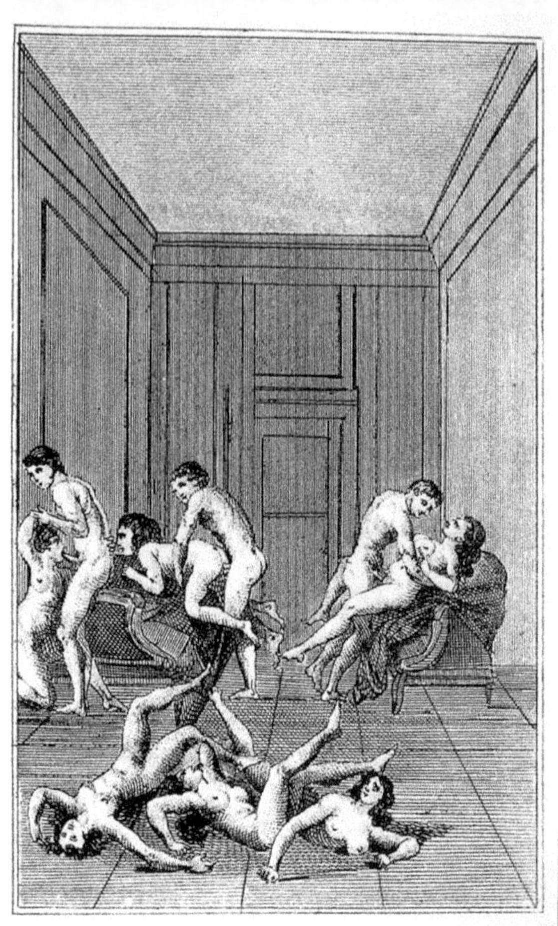

Justine illustrated by Antoine Borel.

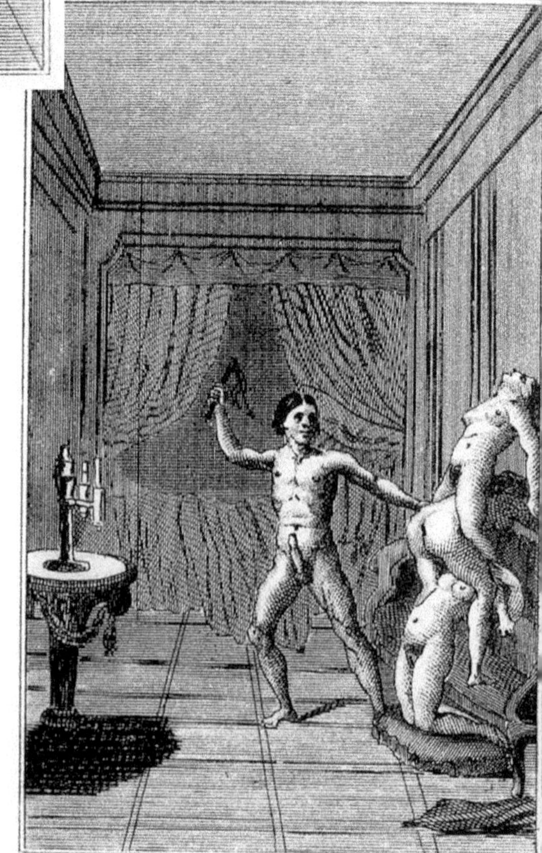

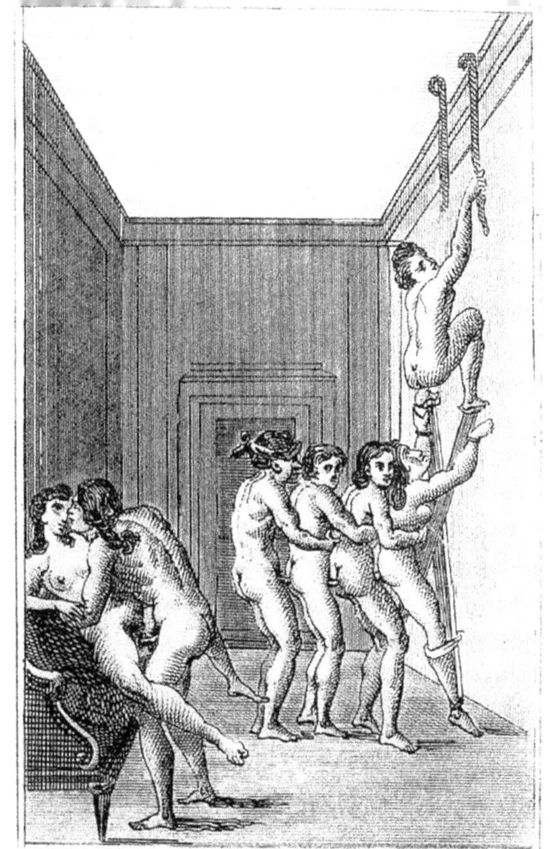

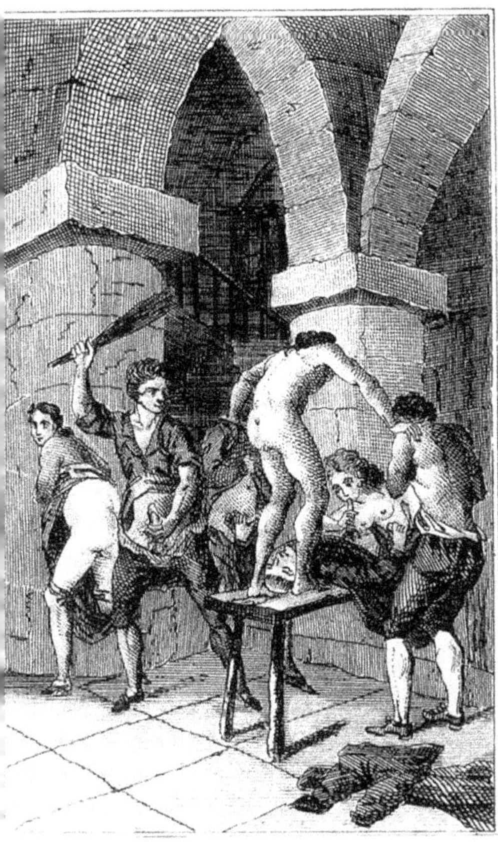

FRANCOIS BOUCHER

François Boucher (1703-70) was one of the key French artists of the 18th century, alongside Fragonard and Watteau. De Goncourt described Boucher as 'one of those men who typify the tastes of a century, who express it, personify it, and incarnate it'.

François Boucher developed a lighthearted, decorative and sensual approach to art (which some derided as superficial). But Boucher was the favourite painter of Madame de Pompadour, and decorated Versailles, Fontainbleau, Bellevue and Marly, designed ballets and operas, and tapestries.

Erotic art may defined as simply 'æstheticized sexual representation' (L. Nead, 103); that is, erotic feelings processed through the mechanisms of 'high culture'. For some feminists, there is no doubt that the enjoyment of the female nude is pornographic, and is largely inseparable from the lustful consumption of pornography. The boundaries between 'art' and 'pornography' are being constantly blurred, constantly reset and rewritten.

None of that would have mattered to François Boucher, who happily celebrated the frivolous pursuit of pleasure in his paintings.

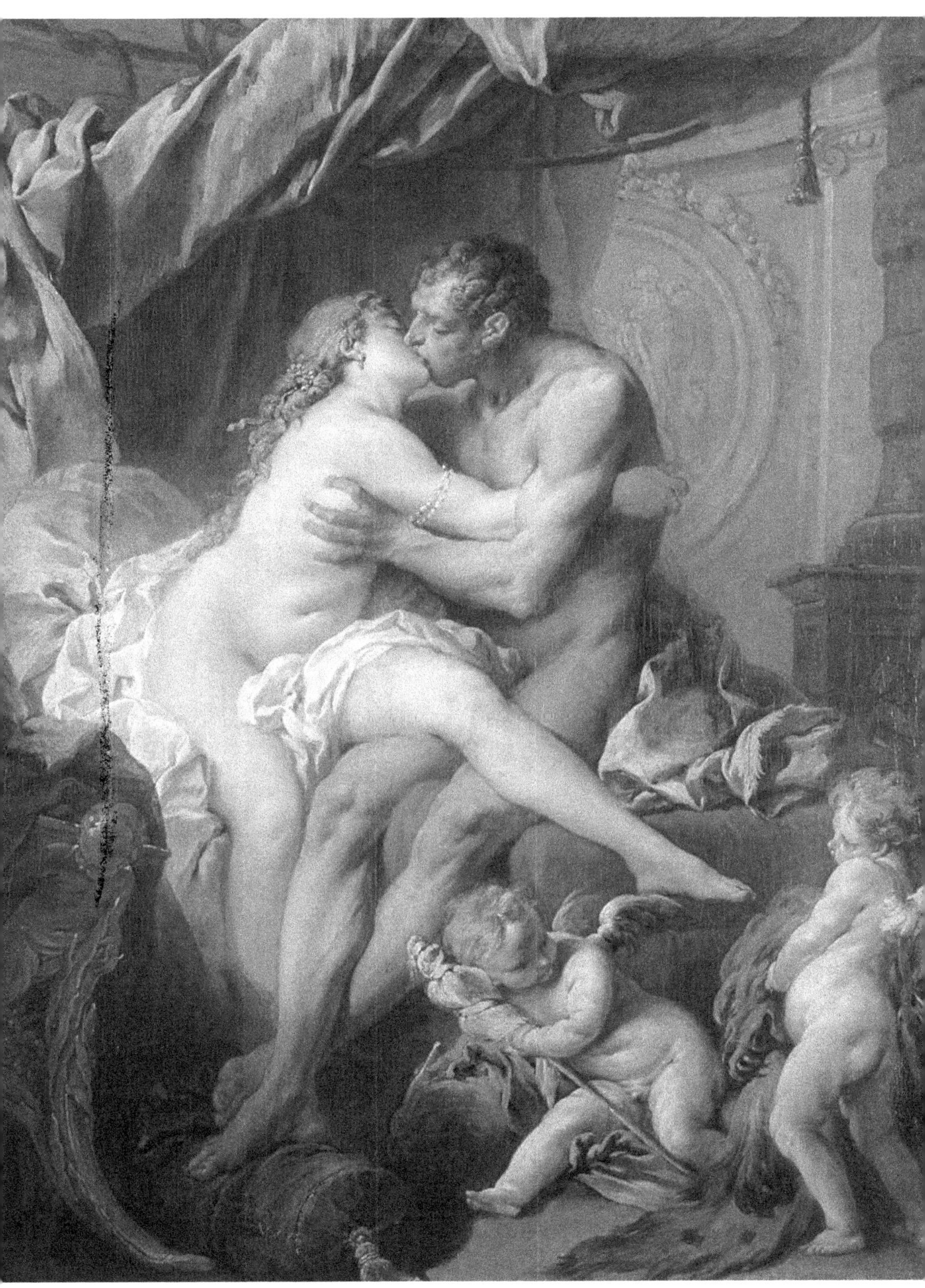

François Boucher, Hercules and Omphale

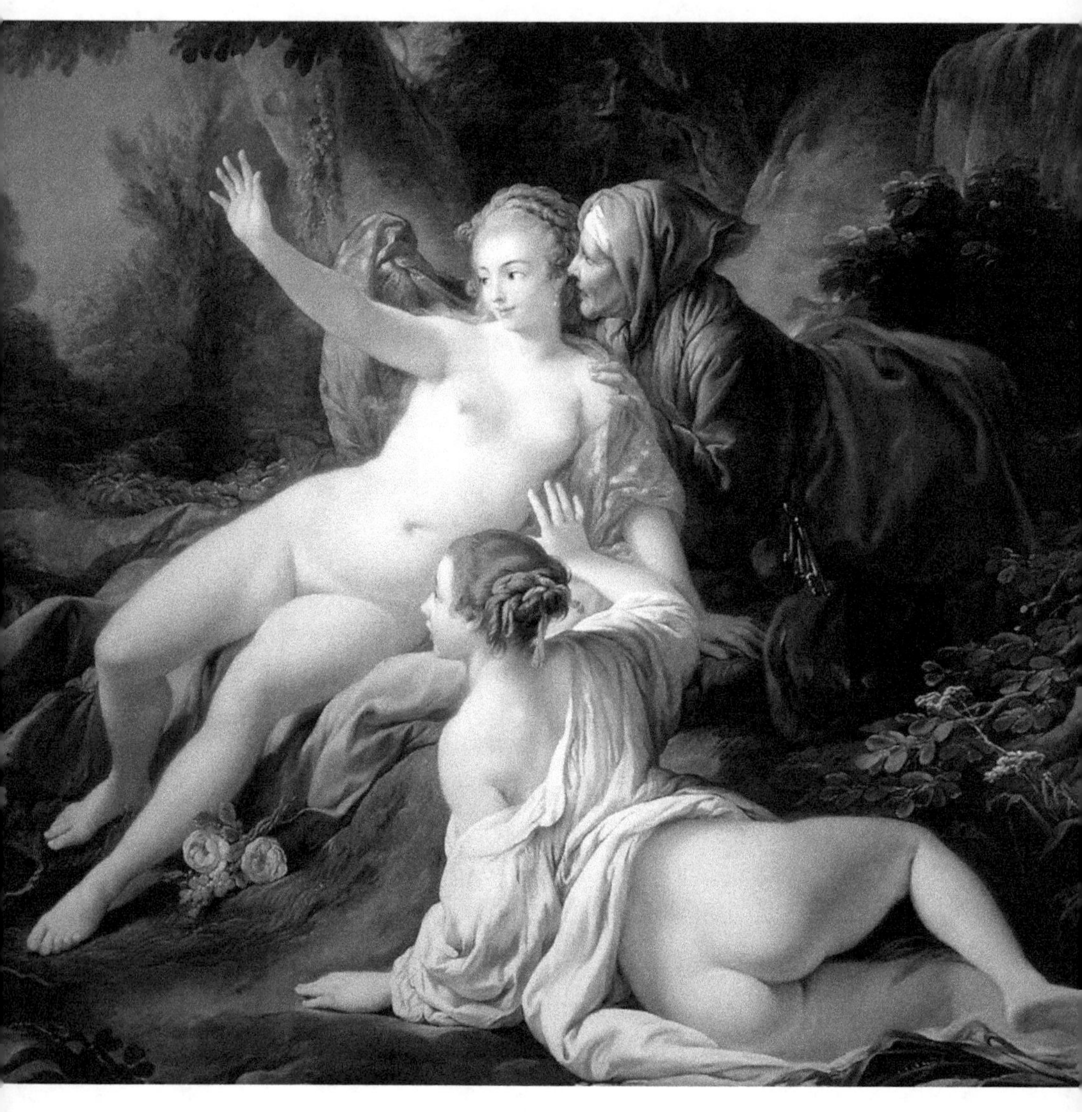

François Boucher, Vertumnus and Pomona, 1740

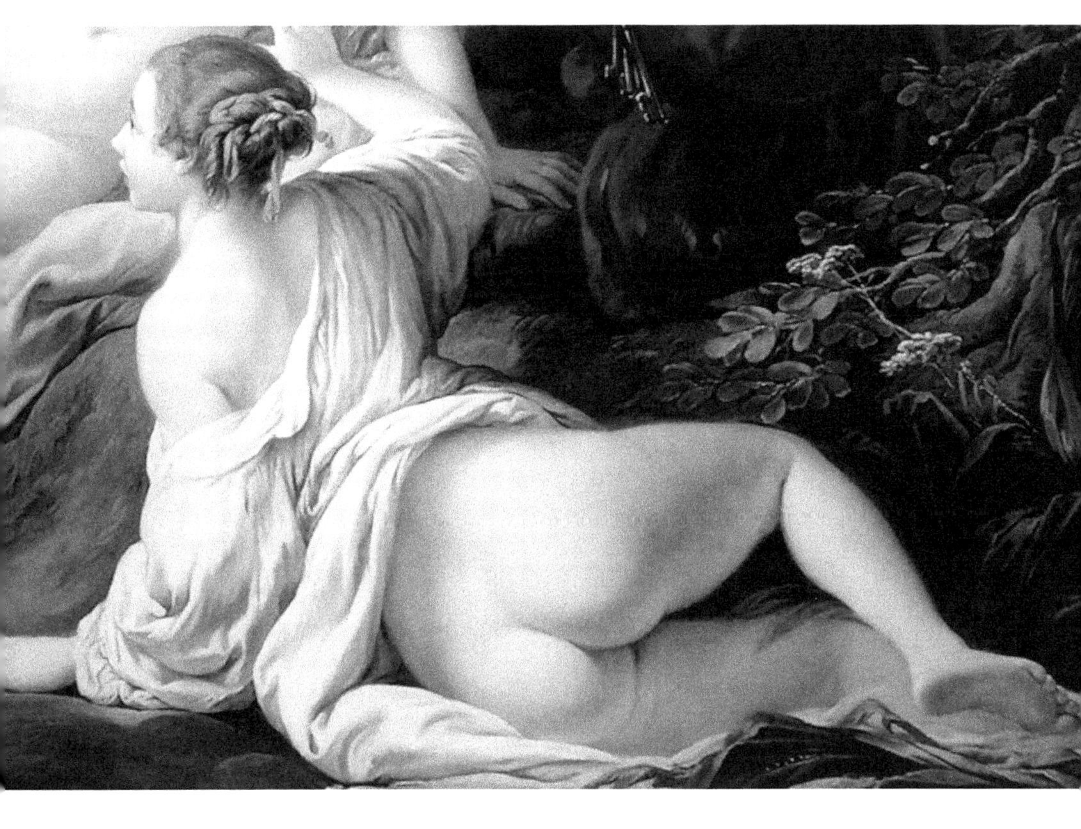

FRANCOIS BOUCHER

Louise O'Murphy, the model for François Boucher's famous nude *Mademoiselle O'Murphy*, became King Louis XV's personal prostitute (his 'mistress', as critics call them) after the King saw Boucher's painting. The high art 'possession' or pleasure of the female nude in Boucher's painting became the real 'possession' of Louise O'Murphy's body. Clearly, kings can 'buy' what they like: they can have the best art, and 'have' the best women.

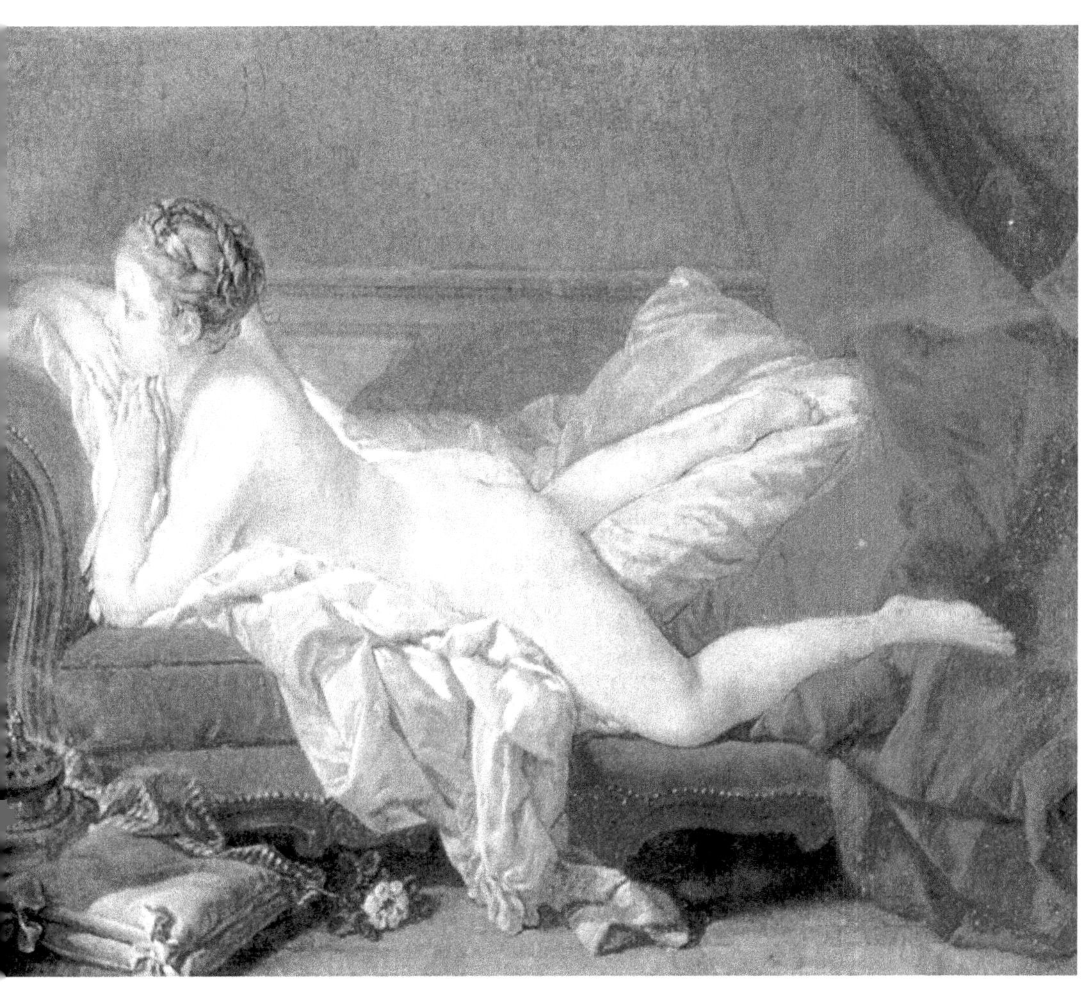

François Boucher, Madamoiselle O'Murphy, 1751

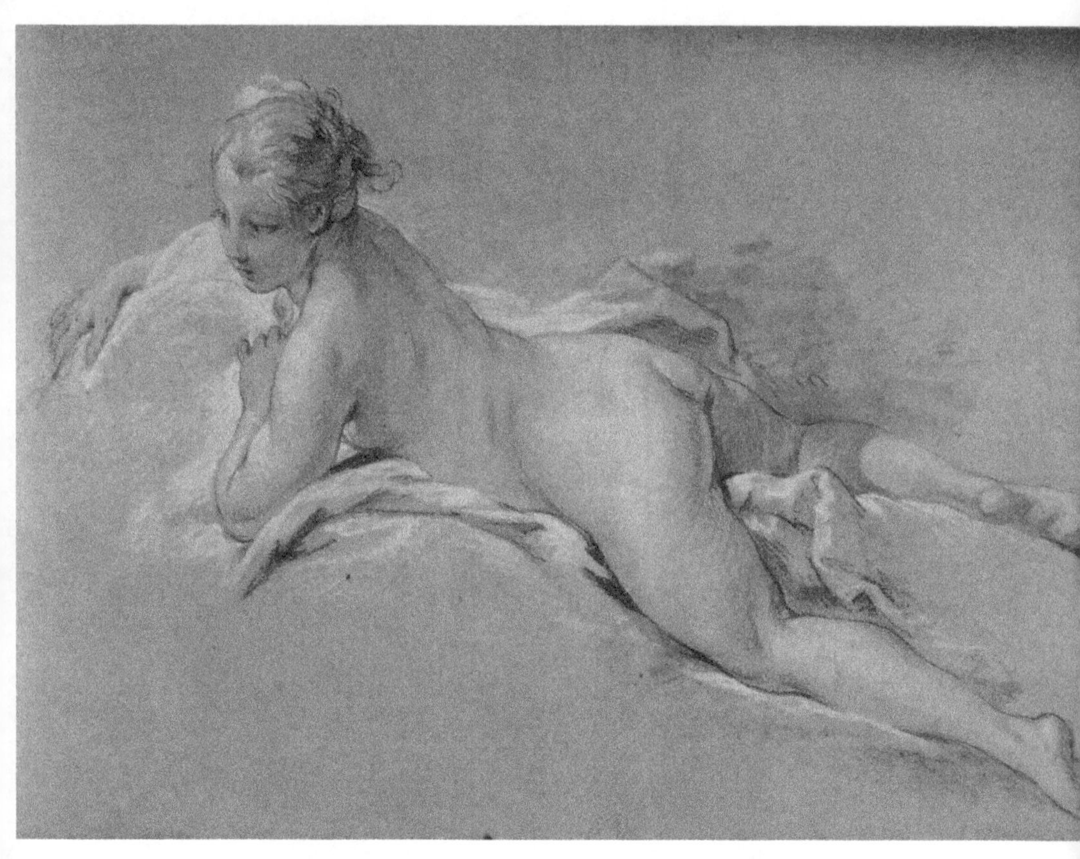

François Boucher

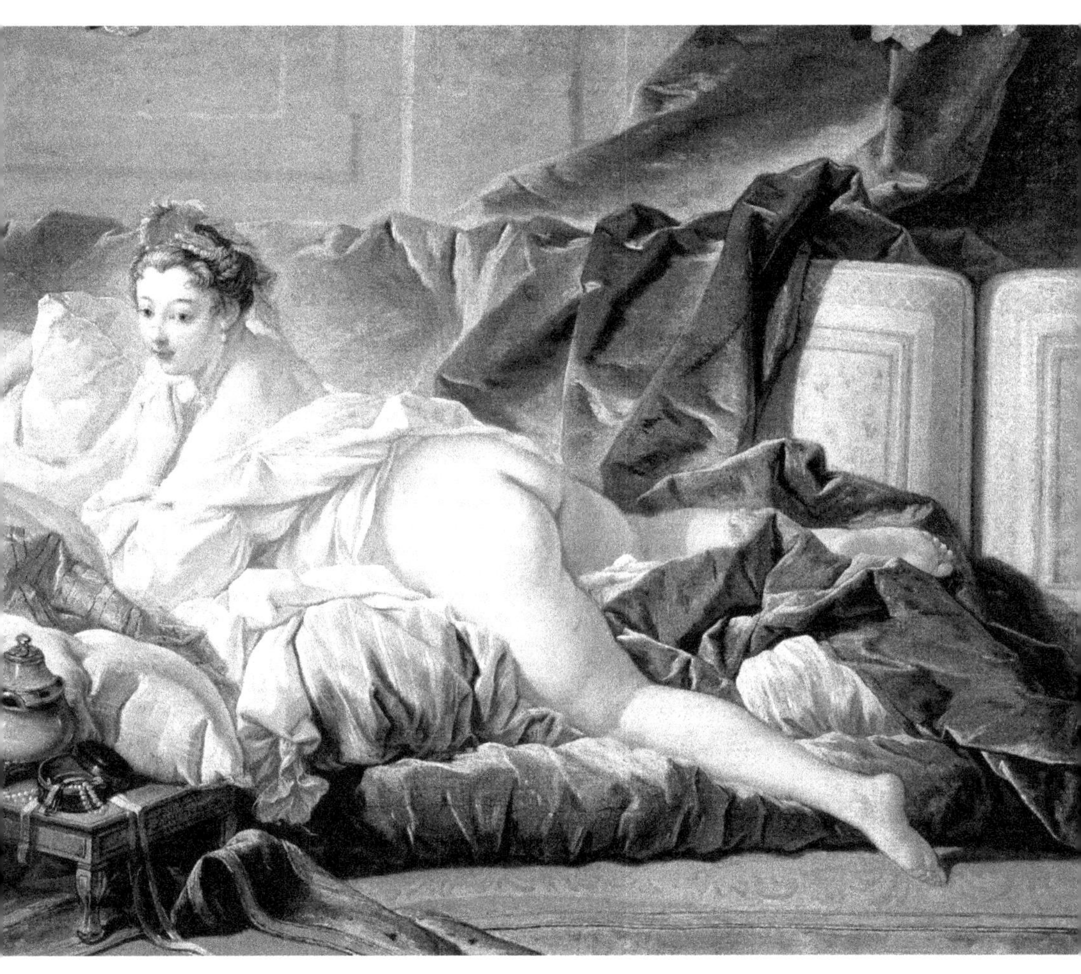

François Boucher, Brown Odalisque

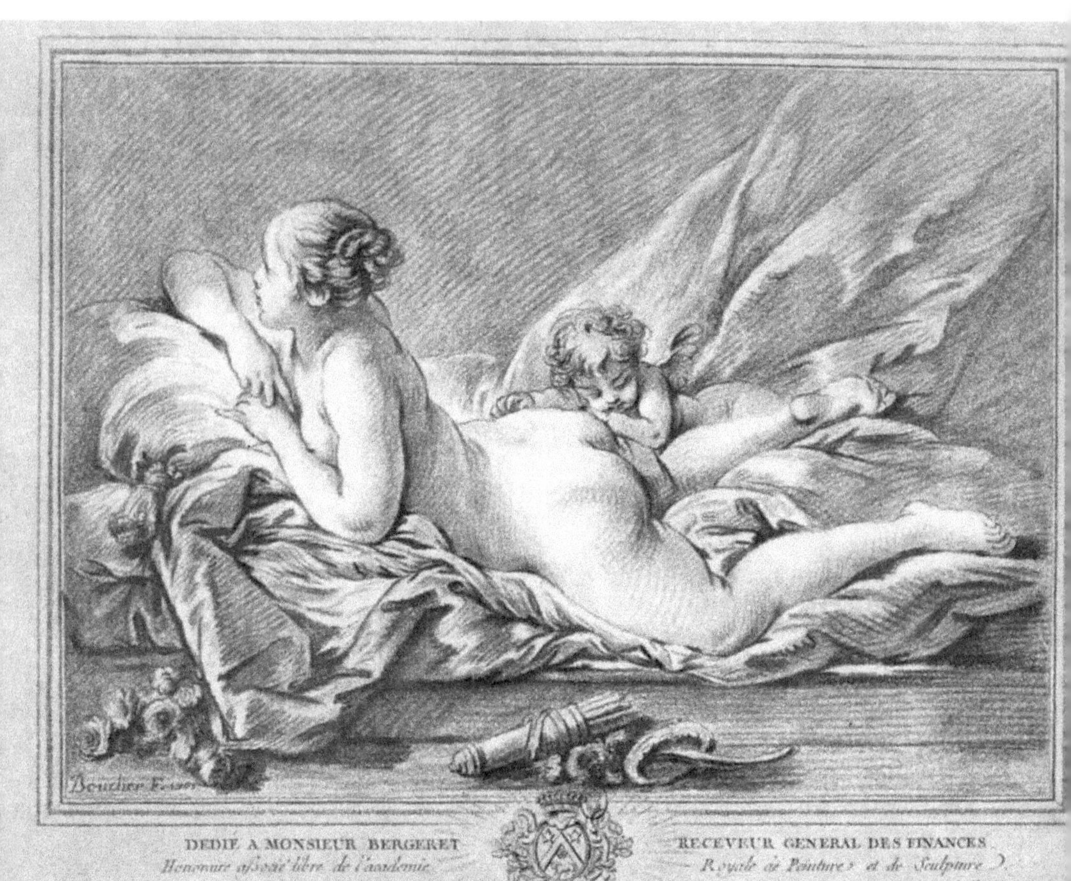

After François Boucher

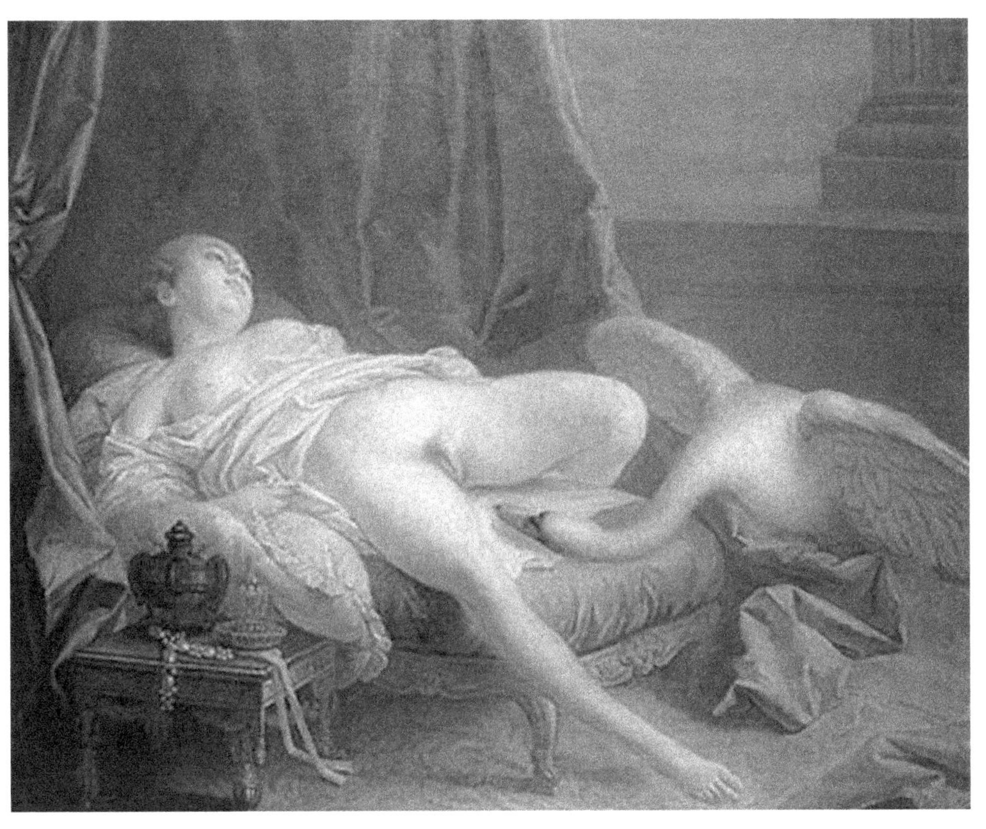

François Boucher, Leda and the Swan

JEAN-BAPTISTE GREUZE

Jean-Baptiste Greuze (1725-1805) was a French Academy painter best-known for his historical works and portraits. His most famous work is *The Broken Vessel.* Historical and mythological subjects enabled Greuze to portray suggestive scenes, such as *Cupid Crowned By Psyche* (1785-90) and *The Two Friends*.

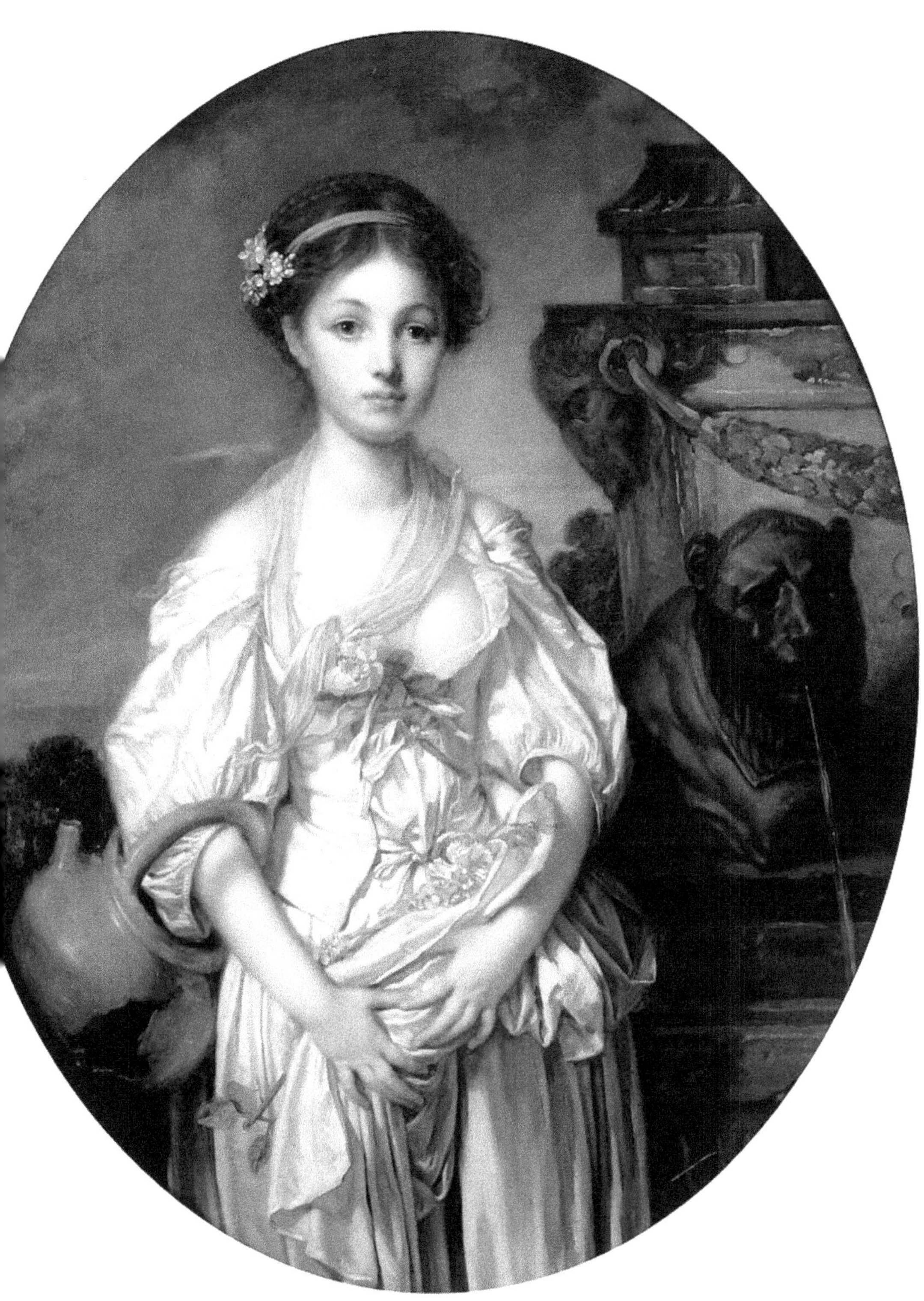

Jean-Baptiste Greuze, The Broken Pitcher, Louvre, Paris

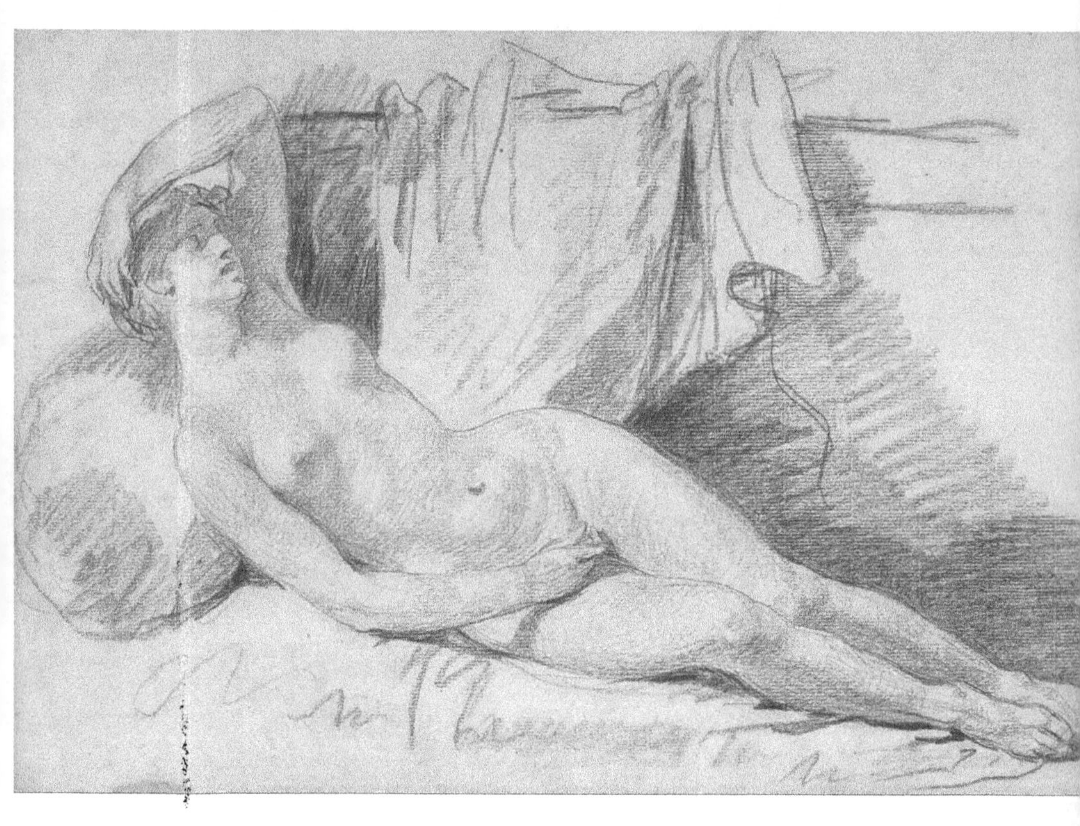

Jean-Baptiste Greuze, Reclining Female Nude,
Study For Aegina Visited By Jupiter, 1762-82

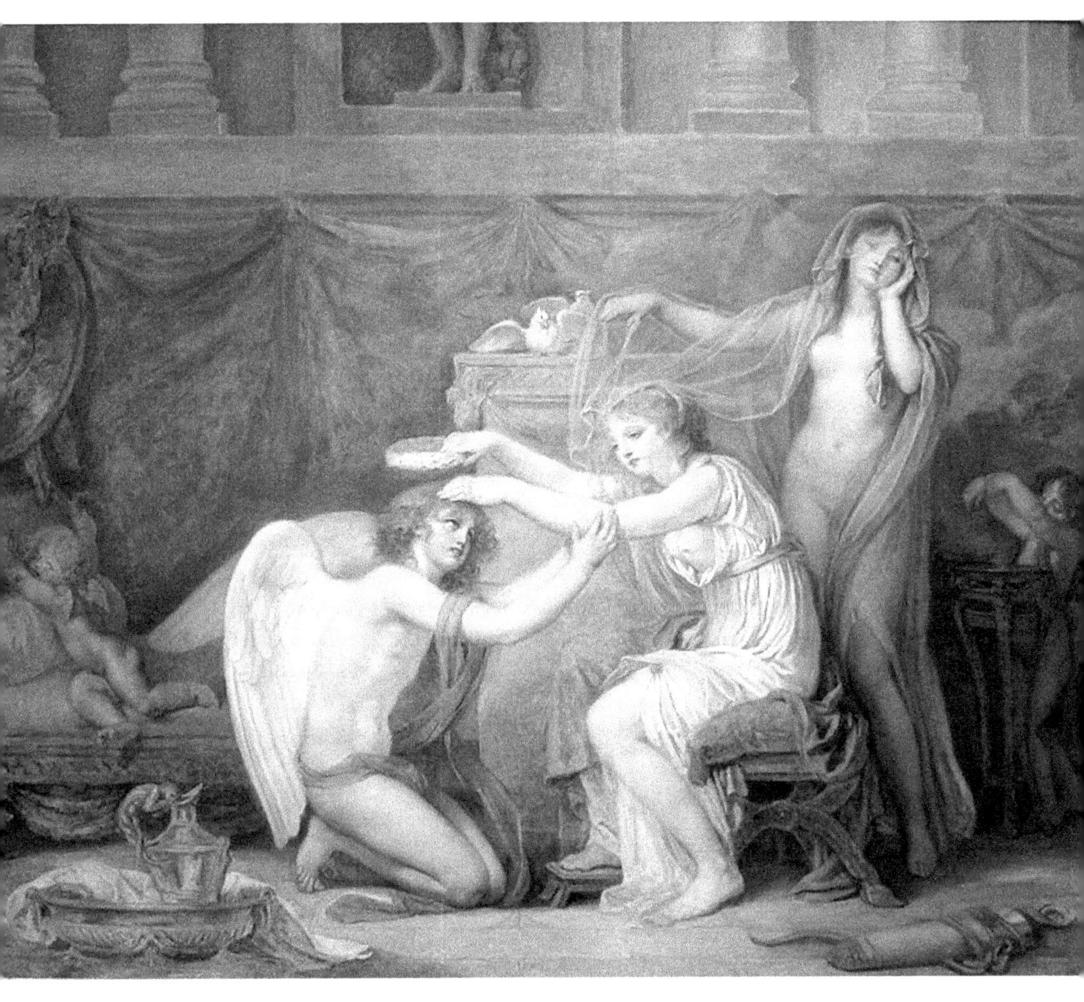

Jean-Baptiste Greuze, Cupid Crowned by Psyche, 1785-90.

JEAN-ANTOINE WATTEAU

Jean-Antoine Watteau (1684-1721) was one of the most celebrated artists of the 18th century, the embodiment of the pursuit of sophisticated, cultured leisure, frivolity and pleasure (as in *Les Champs Elysées*). Watteau was a master colourist, his pictures of fashionable, well-off figures are painted in light, pastel hues.

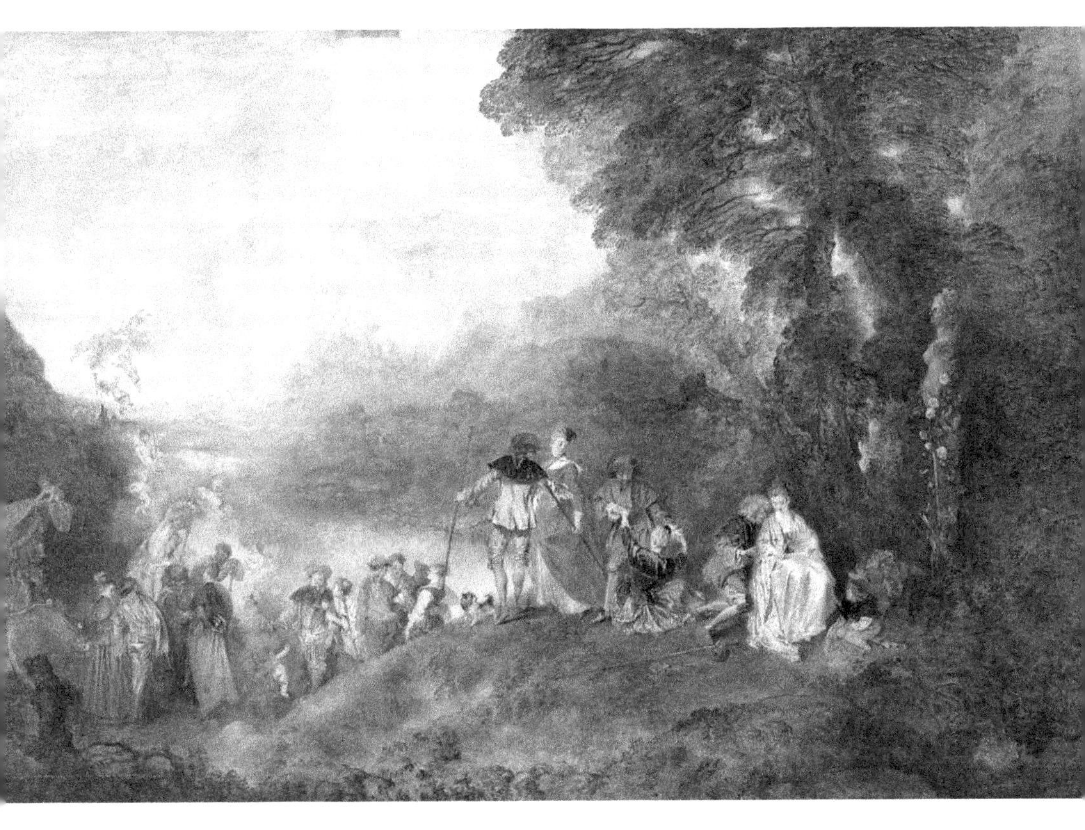

Jean-Antoine Watteau, L'Embarquement pour l'Ile de Cythere, 1717, Louvre, Paris

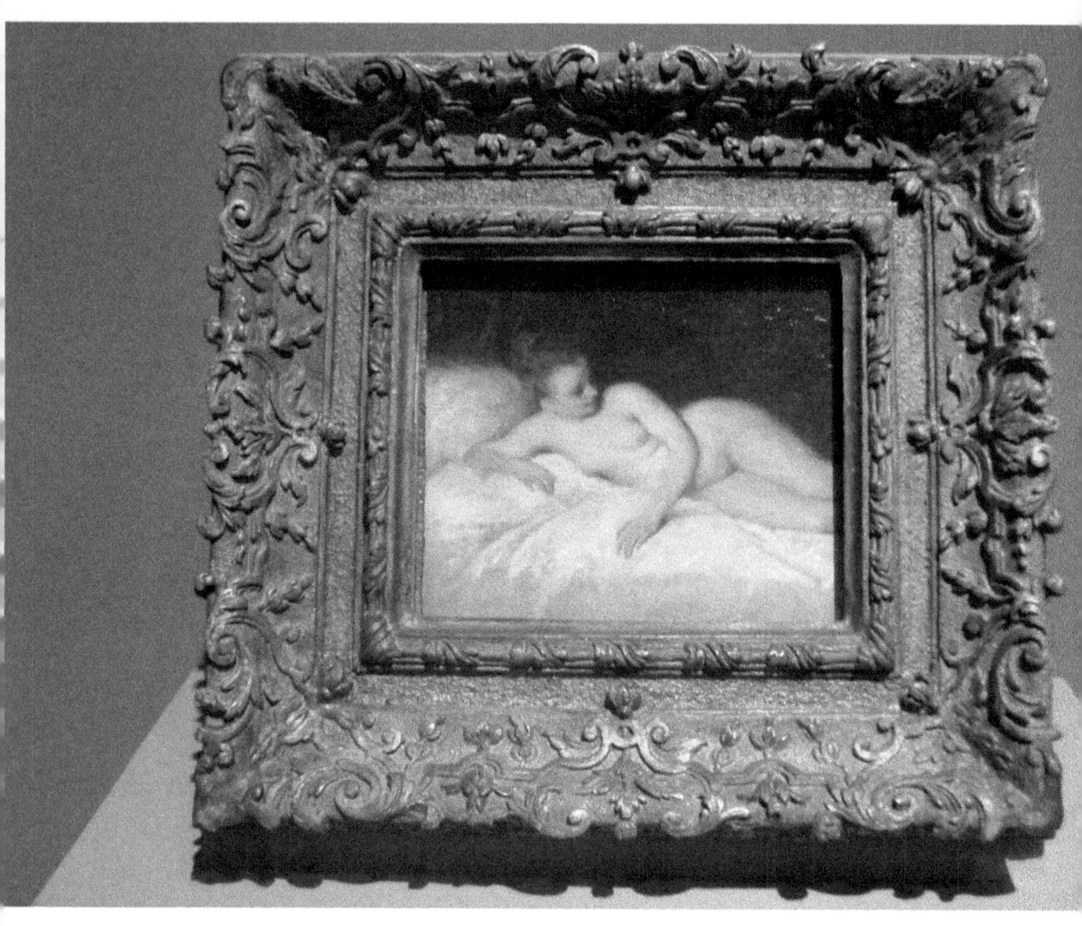

Antoine Watteau, Reclining Woman, 1713-17

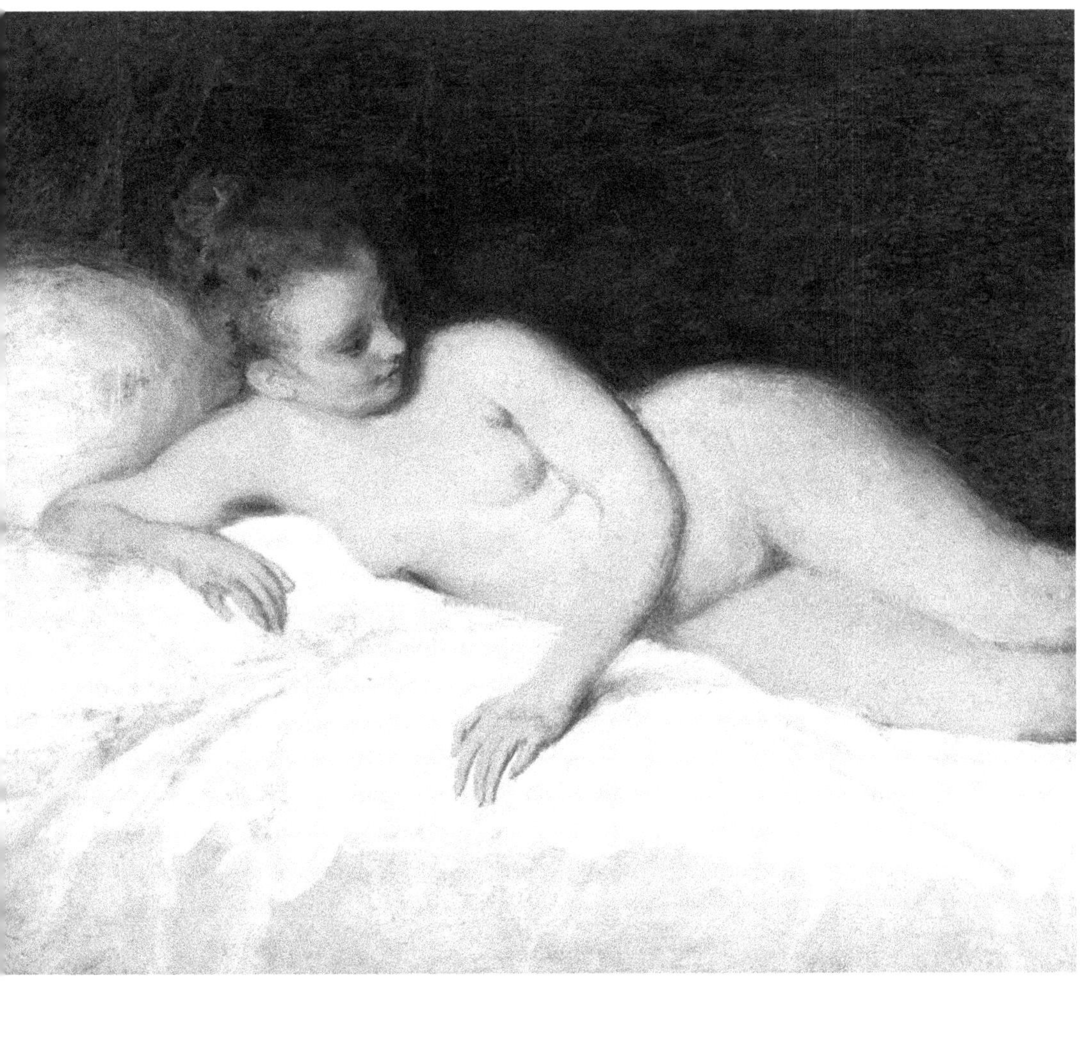

ANTONIO CANOVA

This Renaissance eroticization of the human form finds its apotheosis in the art of Michelangelo Buonarroti, whose *Dawn, David,* early and late *Pietàs,* and of course the most voluptuous of all figurative statues, the *Dying Slave*. The heroic homoeroticism of Michelangelo's sculpture continues throughout post-Renaissance sculpture. In, for instance, the bombast and masculine power of Antonio Canova's *Hercules and Lichas,* or Gianlorenzo Bernini's *David.*[1] Canova's sculpture is marked by a smooth, philosophical idealization of the human form.

1 Canova: *Hercules and Lichas,* 1812-5, marble, 138in high, Gallery of Modern Art, Rome; Bernini: *David*, 1623-4, marble, Galleria Borghese, Rome.

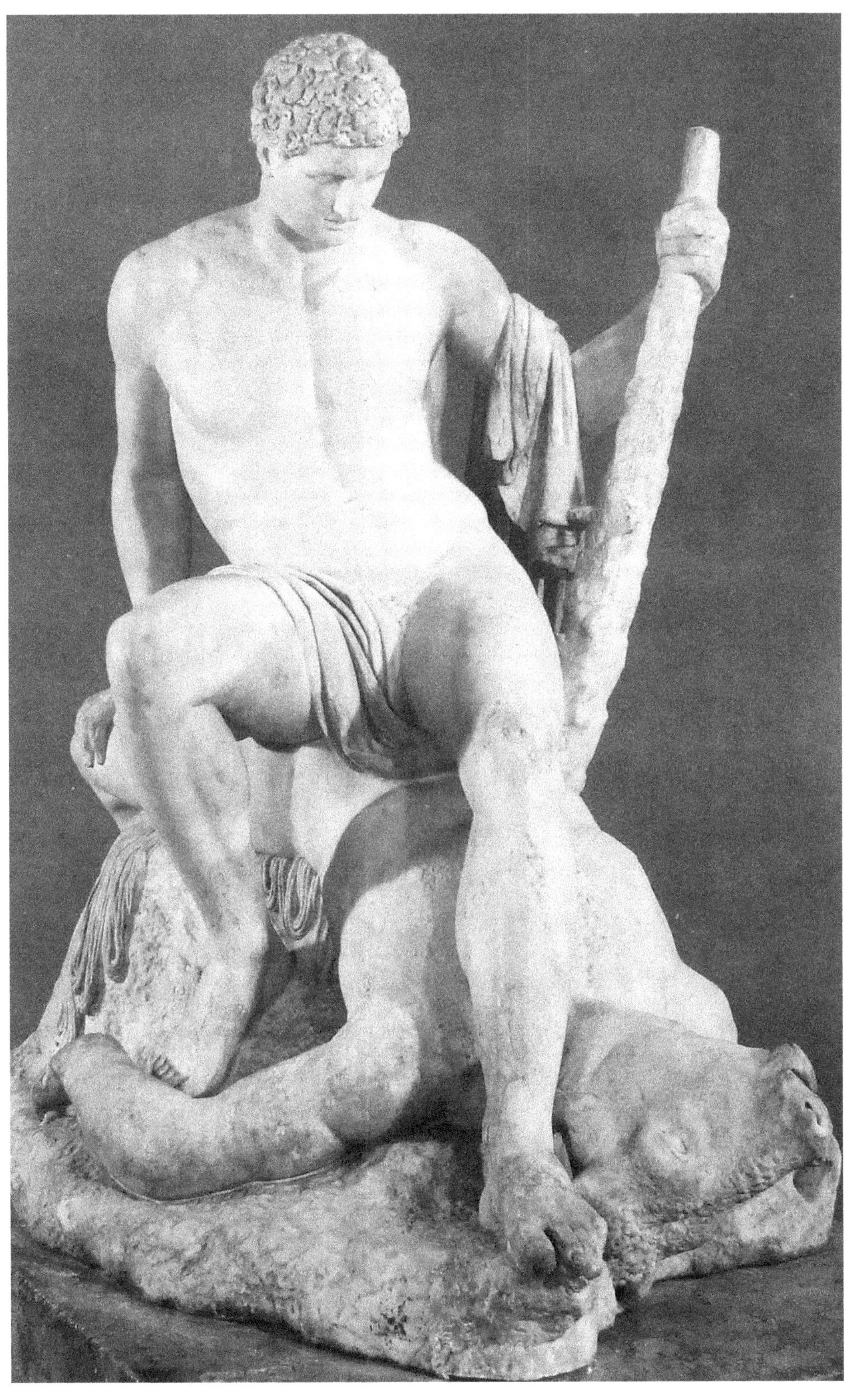

Antonio Canova, Theseus and the Minotaur, 1781-83, London.

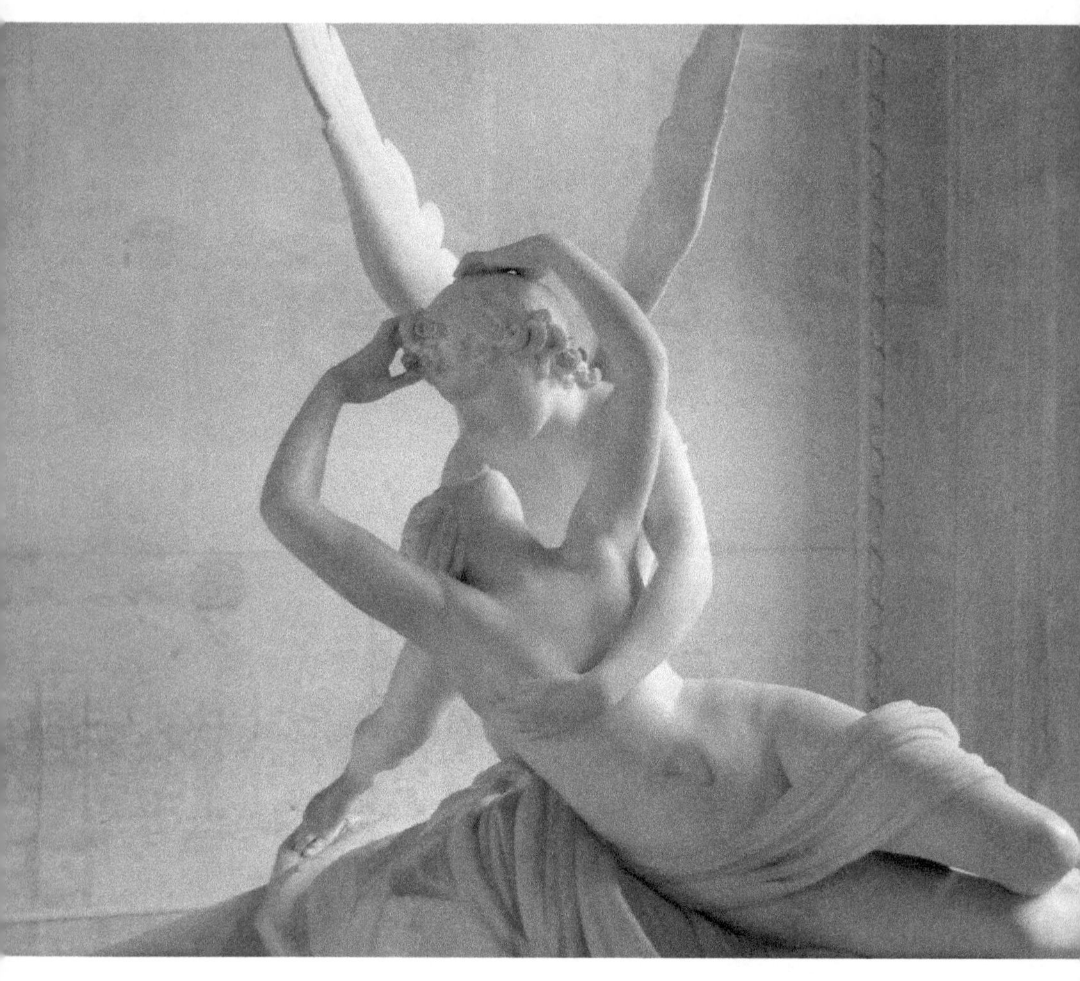

Antonio Canova, Cupid and Psyche, 1793, Louvre, Paris

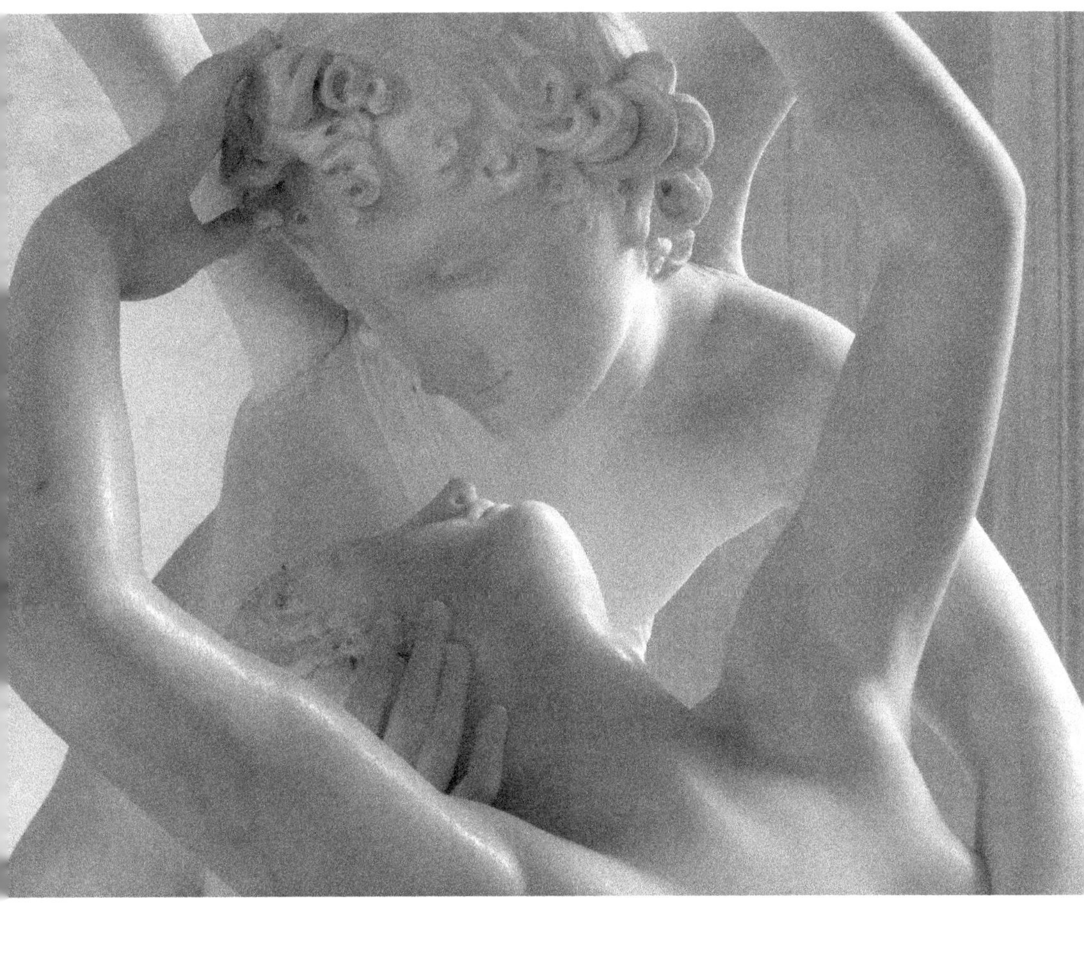

J.A.D. INGRES

Jean Auguste Dominique Ingres (1780-1867) eulogized the female form in some of art's most celebrated nudes (such as in his *A Sleeping Odalisque*). Ingres is the epitome of the cool, Neo-Classical, post-Baroque artist. Ingres follows in the footsteps of artists such as Giorgione in his *Concert Champêtre,* Jacopo Tintoretto in his *Susannah and the Elders,* Pierre Renoir in his *La Nymphe de la Source,* Leon Kroll in his *Nude,* or John Everett Millais in his *The Night Errant.*[1]

1 John Everett Millais: *The Night Errant,* oil on canvas, Tate Gallery, London; Jacopo Tintoretto: *Susannah and the Elders,* 1555-6, oil on canvas, Kunsthisorisches Museum, Vienna; Ingres: *A Sleeping Odalisque,* oil on canvas; Giorgione: *Concert Champêtre,* oil on canvas, Musées Nationaux, Paris; Leon Kroll: *Nude,* 1933-4, oil on canvas, 48 x 36in, Metropolitan Museum of Art, New York

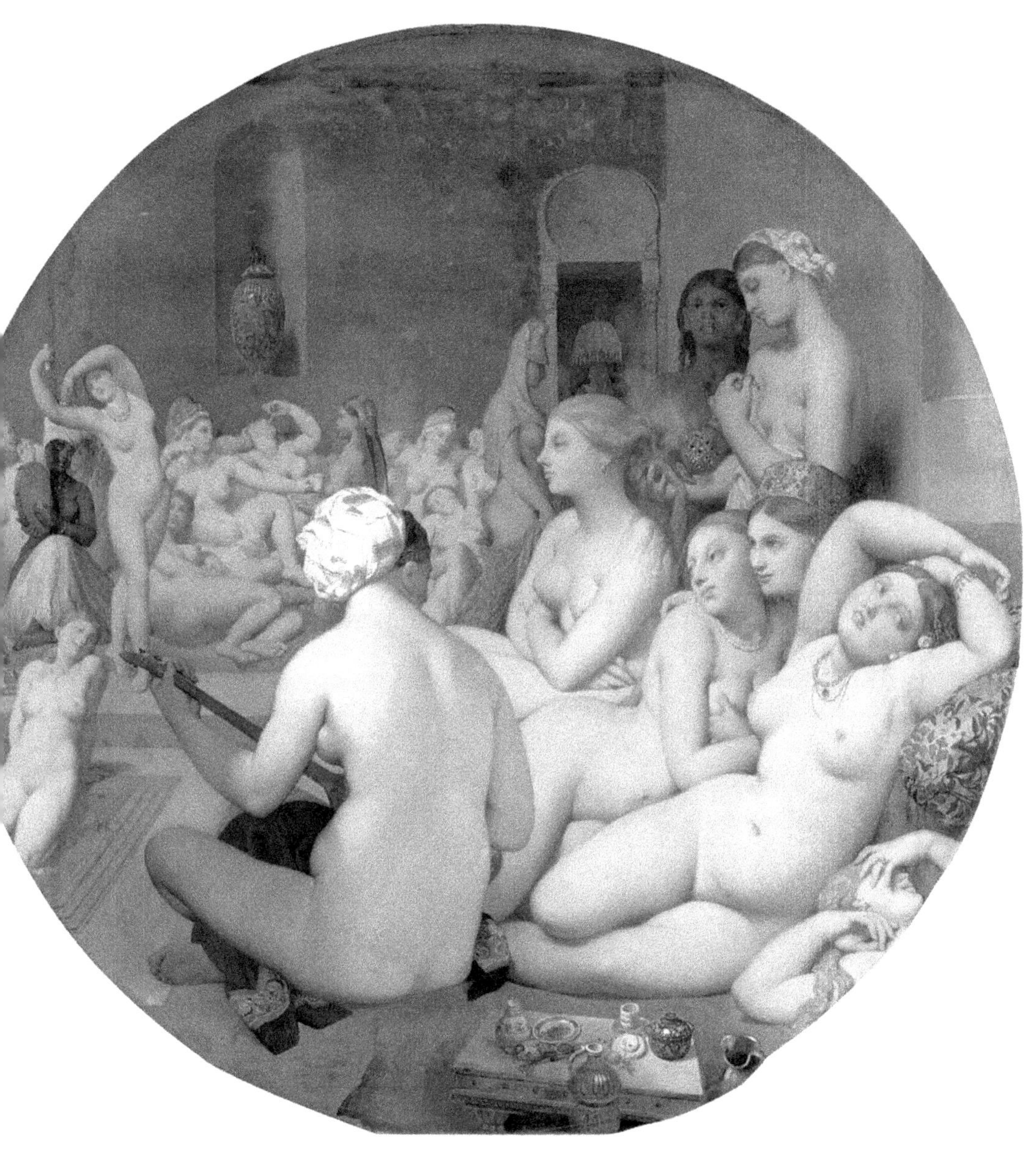

J.A.D. Ingres, Turkish Bath, 1862, Louvre

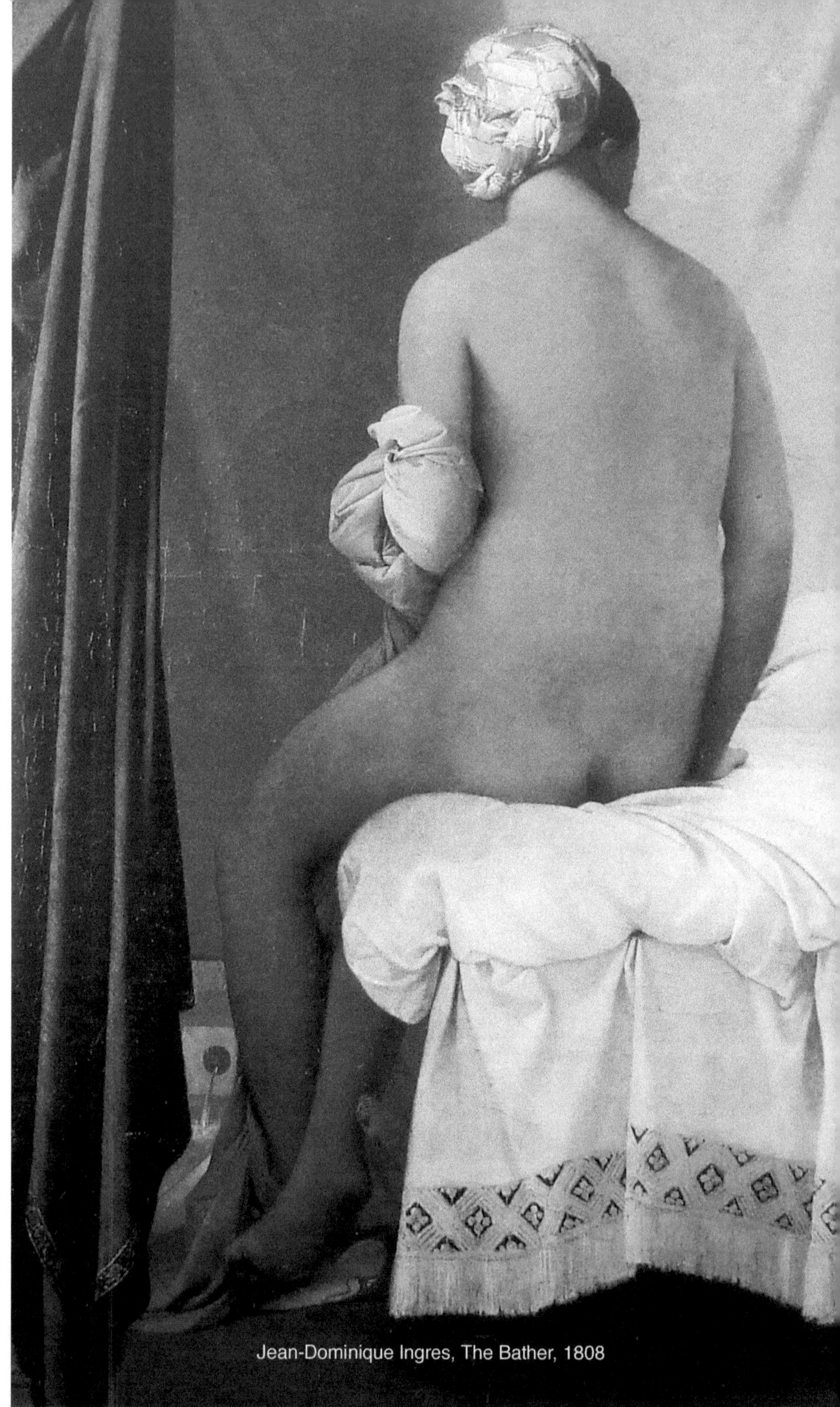

Jean-Dominique Ingres, The Bather, 1808

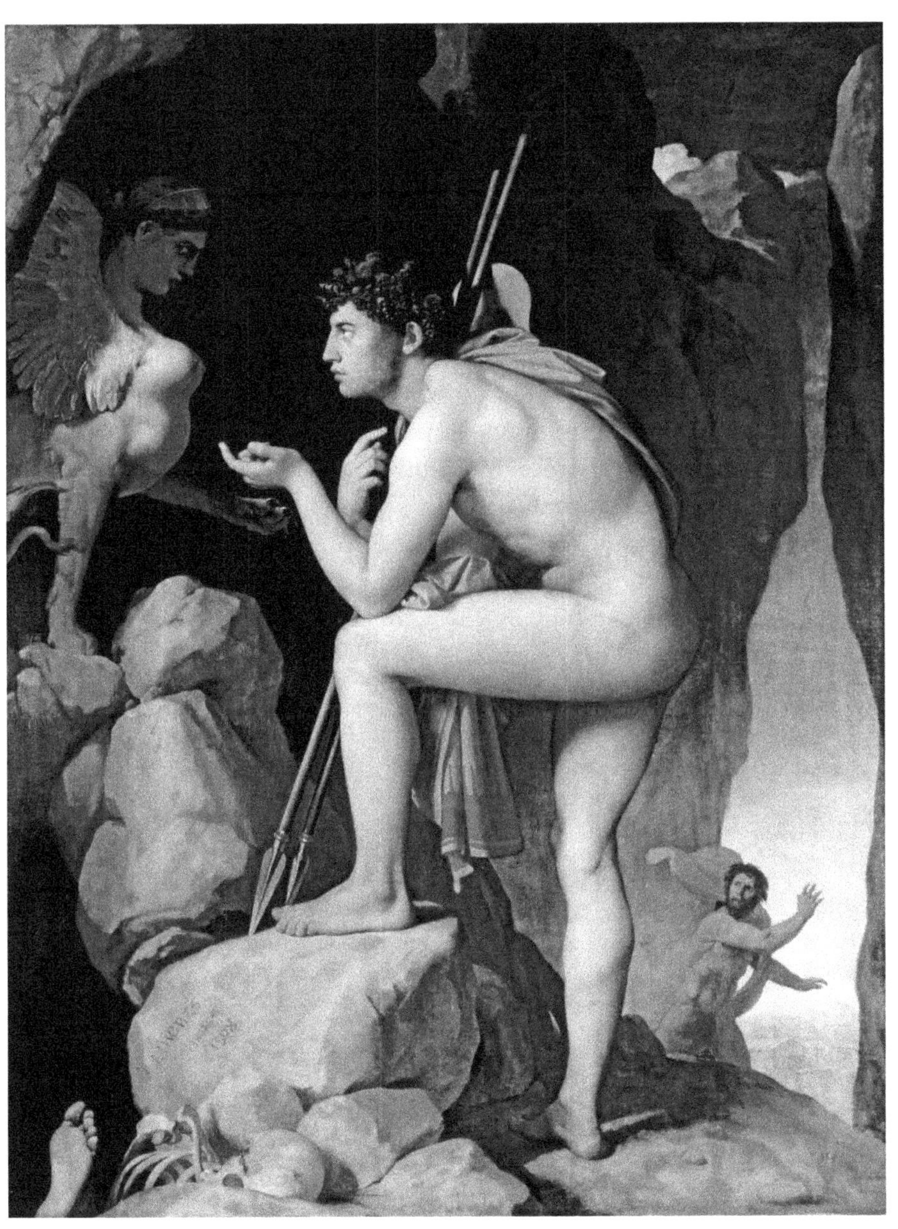

J.A.D.Ingres, Oedipus and the Sphinx, 1807, Louvre, Paris

VELÁSQUEZ AND GOYA

Two of the most famous female nudes in the whole history of art, Diego Velásquez' *Venus* and Francisco de Goya's *Naked Maja*, offer views of women as voluptuous sites of pleasure.[1] These are images of pure desire, pure wish-fulfilment, pure pleasure, which are also pornographic. There is no doubt that the painted 'high art' female nude, as an image, is very like the pornographic image, which offers women as sexualized objects of male lust. They are part of a continuum of representation. What differentiates 'high culture' nudes from the nudes in pornography is largely to do with context, with the sociopolitical environment in which the nudes are consumed. You can put Goya's *Naked Maja* into a soft core pornographic context and it would send only a few conflicting signals with the rest of the photography there. Fashions change - in costume, hair, make-up, pose and props - but it is startling how similar the female nude is in art. The fundamental relation, of sexualized women being offered up to be looked at and lusted over by desirous males is remarkably similar the world over, and through history.

1 Diego Velásquez: *The Rokeby Venus*, 1649-50, oil on canvas, 122.5 x 177cm, National Gallery, London; Francisco de Goya: *Naked Maya*, 1800-5

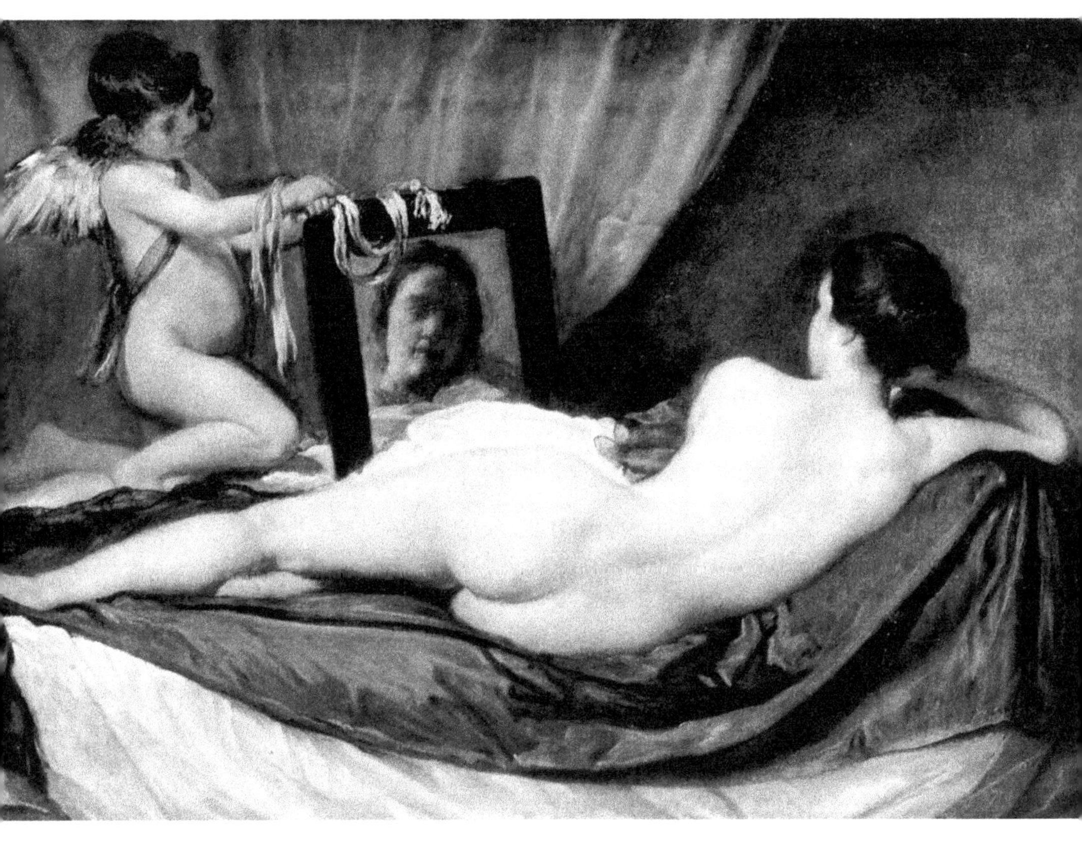

Diego Velásquez, Rockeby Venus, 1649-51,
National Gallery, London

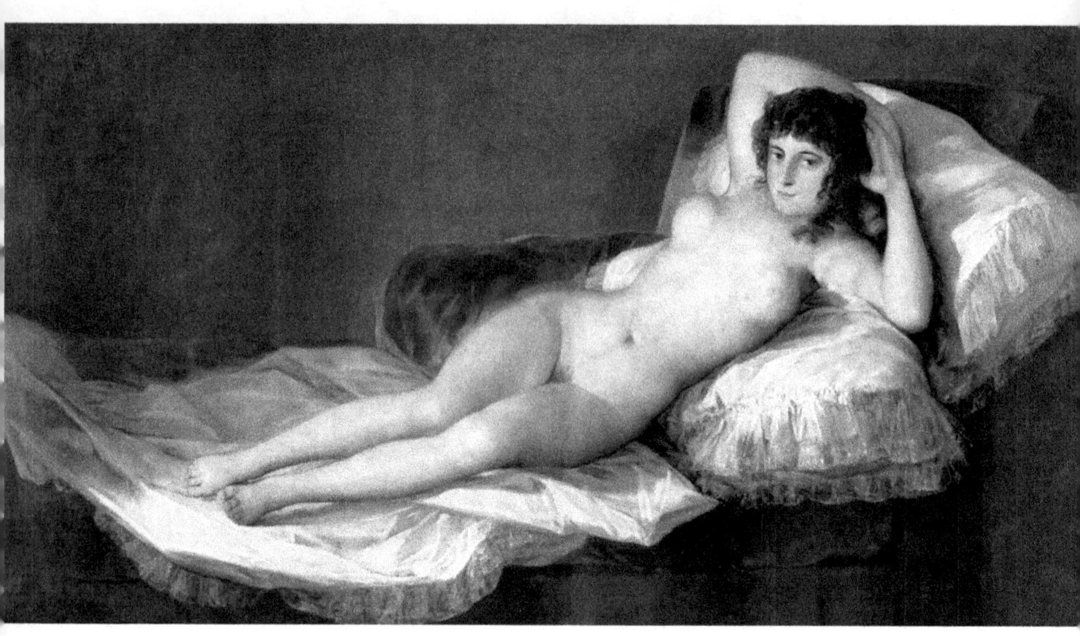

Francisco de Goya, Naked Maja, c. 1801, Prado, Madrid

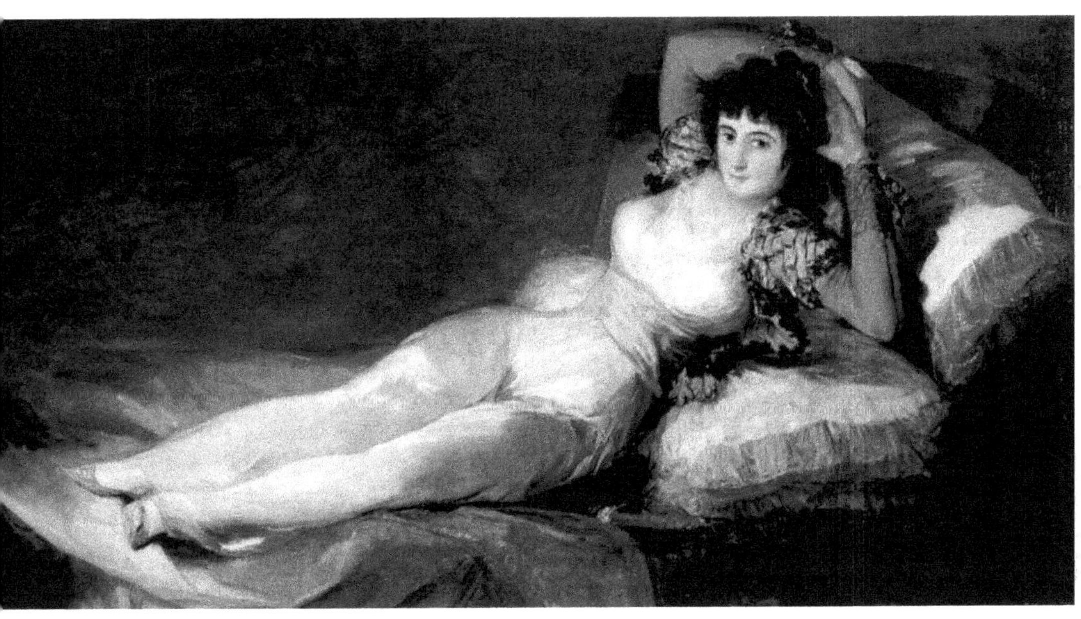

Francisco de Goya, Clothed Maya, 1801

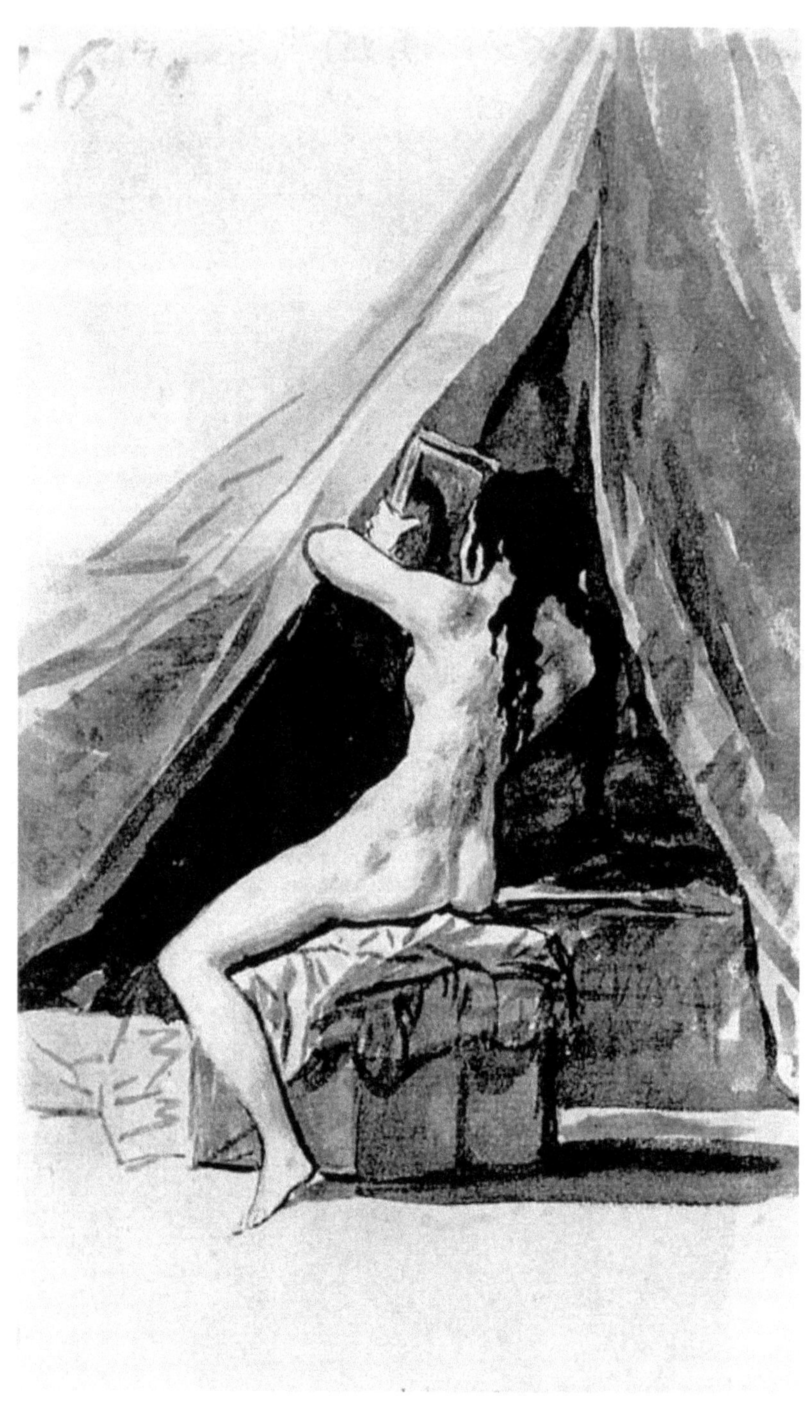

Francisco Goya, Nude, 1796-97

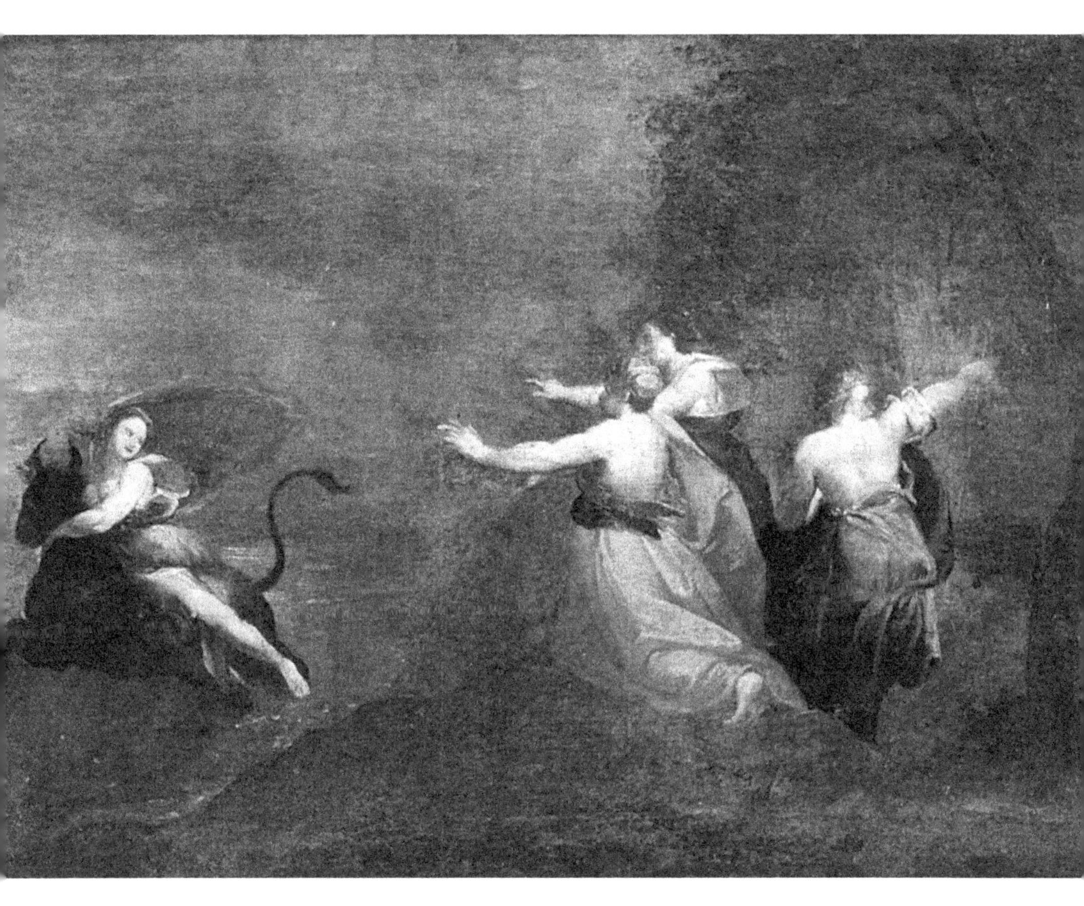

Francisco Goya, The Rape of Europa, 1772

ANNE-LOUIS GIRODET

Anne-Louis Girodet (1767-1824) was one of the early Romantic French artists. Girodet was influenced by, among others, Jacques-Louis David (he joined David's studio in 1783). Girodet's historical and mythological works include *The Sleep of Endymion, Joseph Recognized By His Brothers* and *The Entombment of Atala.*

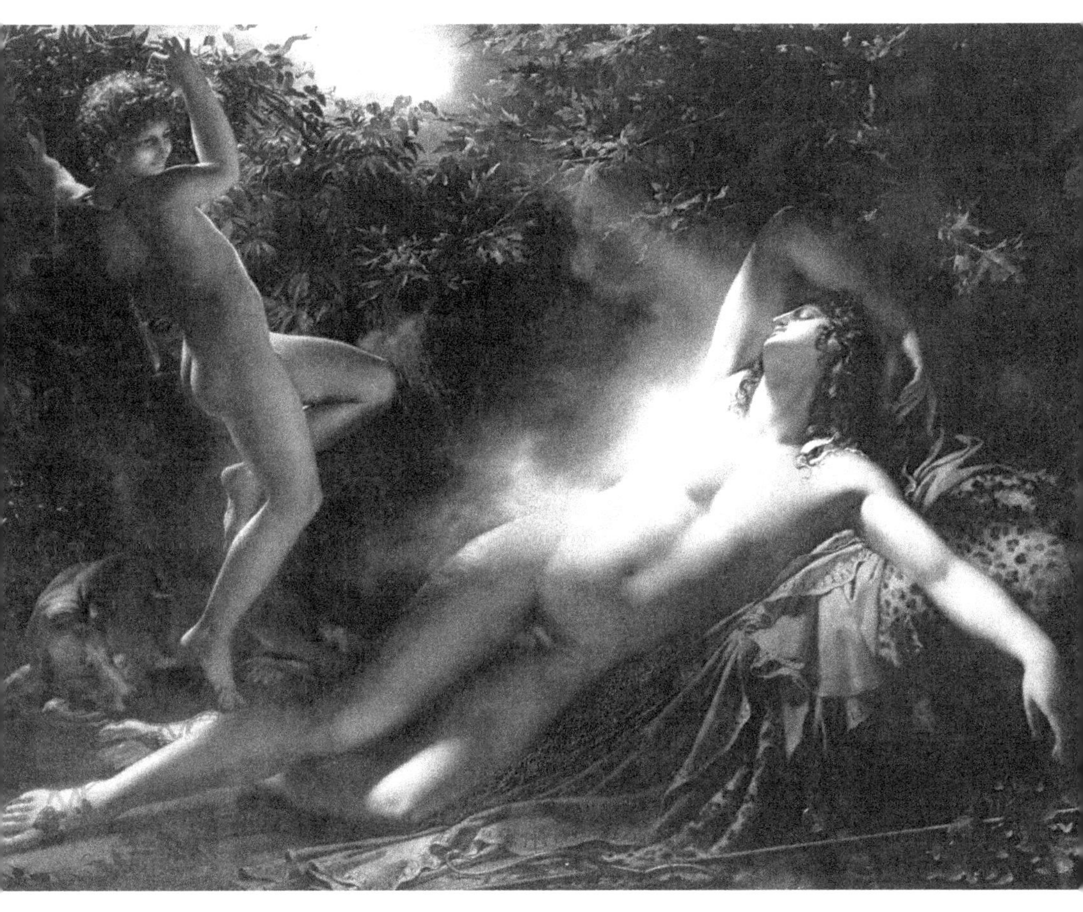

Anne-Louis Girodet-Trioson, Endymion, 1793

JOHN HENRY FUSELI

The Swiss artist John Henry Fuseli is a master of the macabre as well as the erotic. Fuseli's signature works include his *Nightmare* an influential slice of Romantic Gothic imagery. But *Sturm und Drang* art is only element in Fuseli's eccentric and individual work, which includes many erotic subjects, and nudes.

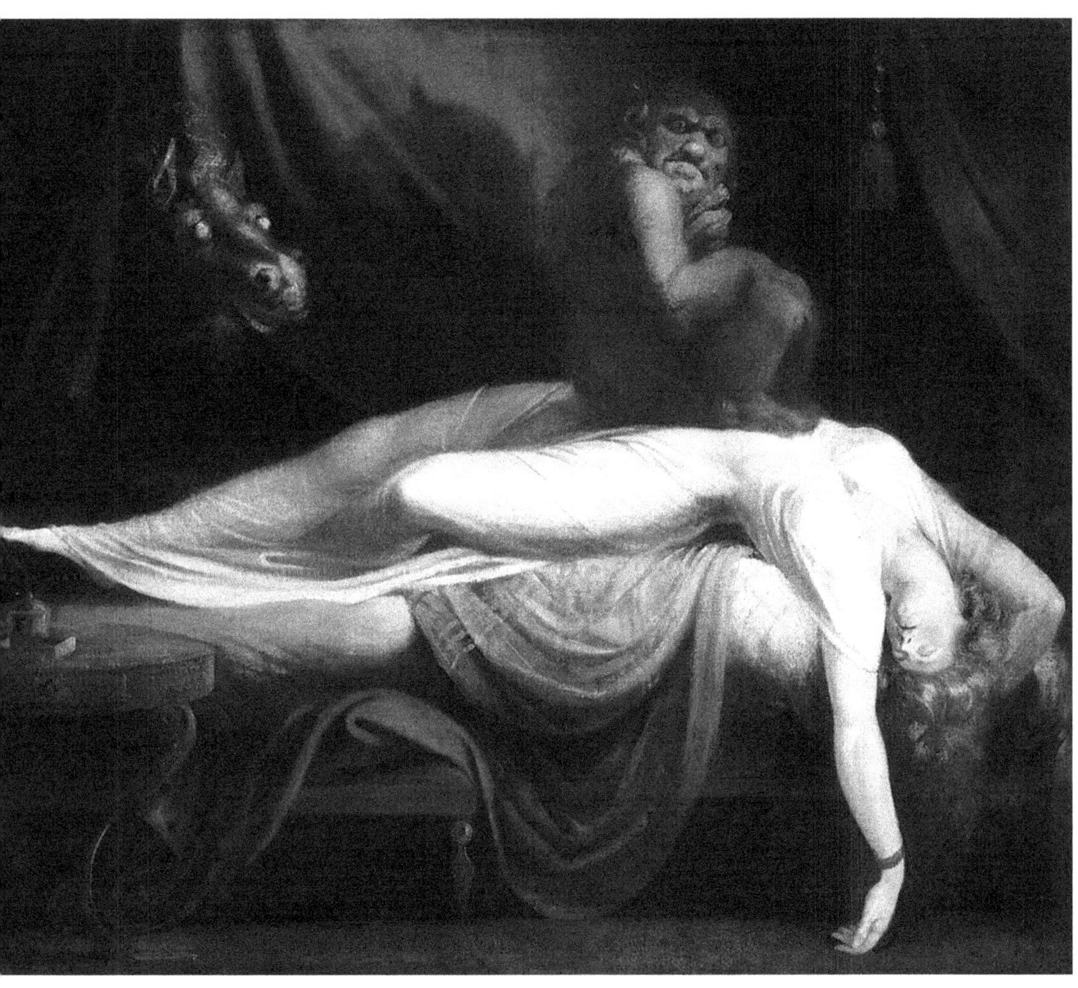

Henry Fuseli, The Nightmare, 1781, Detroit

FRAGONARD, DAVID, INGRES

After the astonishing output of Leonardo and Michelangelo, Renaissance art lost some of its passion, although it became increasingly openly erotic. Images such as Peter Lely's *Nymphs by a Fountain,* anything by Peter Paul Rubens, Jean Honoré Fragonard's *Bathers,* Jacques-Louis David's *Cupid and Psyche,* and Jean Auguste Dominique Ingres' study for *Ruggiero and Angelica* are openly erotic, displaying the body as a sensual object.[1] Myths such as that of the Judgement of Paris and the Three Graces allow ample opportunity for painting acres of quivering female flesh, as in paintings by Raphael, with his Neoplatonically idealized figures, or in the work of Rubens, Lucas Cranach and Hans Baldung Grien.[2] Artists such as Tintoretto, Veronese, Boucher, Tiepolo, Watteau, Reni, Rembrandt, Guercino, Correggio, Gros, Girodet, Géricault, and Delacroix do not hide their depictions of erotic bodies behind mythological narratives. Their images often put eroticism in the foreground: the pretence at mythological or historical painting is not longer upheld, and the nude form becomes primary.

1 Peter Lely: *Nymphs by a Fountain,* c. 1650-5, canvas, 129 x 144.8cm, Dulwich Picture Gallery, London; David: *Cupid and Psyche,* 1817, canvas, 184.1 x 241.6cm, Cleveland Museum of Art; Jean-Honoré Fragonard: *Bathers,* canvas, 64 x 80, Louvre, Paris; Jean-Auguste-Dominique Ingres: *Study for Ruggiero and Angelica,* c. 1819, canvas, 84.5 x 42.5cm, Musée Ingres, Montauban

2 Rubens: *The Judgement of Paris,* c. 1638-9, Prado, Madrid; Lucas Cranach: *The Judgement of Paris,* 1530, Staatliche Kunsthalle, Karlsruhe; Hans Baldung Grien: *The Three Graces,* c. 1540, Prado, Madrid; Raphael: *The Three Graces,* c. 150, panel, 6.6 x 6.6in, Condé Museum, Chantilly

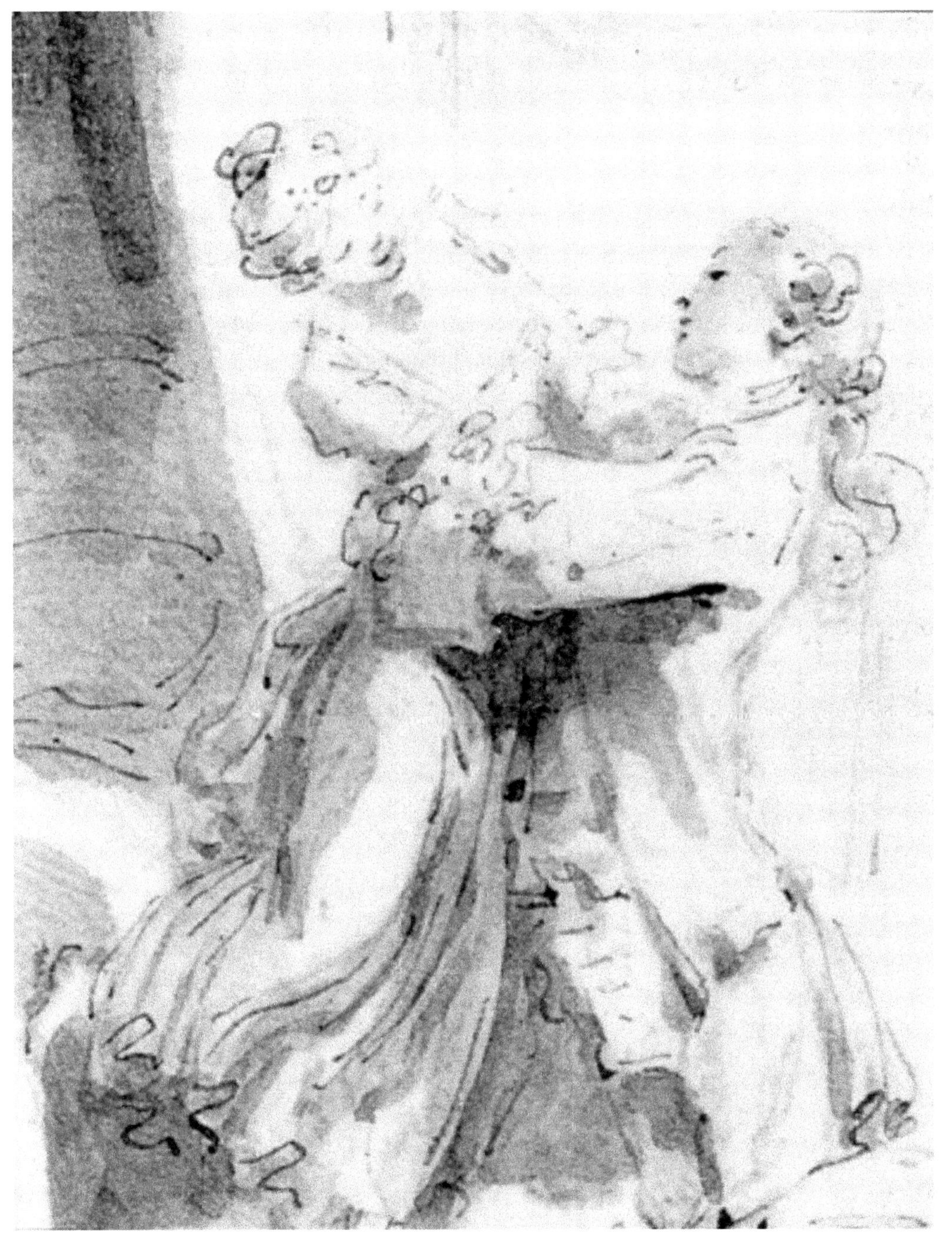

Jean Honoré Fragonard, Libertines, 1770

JEAN-HONORÉ FRAGONARD

Jean-Honoré Fragonard (1732-1806) was an Academy painter who studied with Boucher and Chardin, and enjoyed having Mme. Pompdour and Mme. du Barry among his patrons (and the court of Louis XV). Fragonard's best-known work is *The Swing* (*c.* 1766), housed in the Wallace Collection, London.

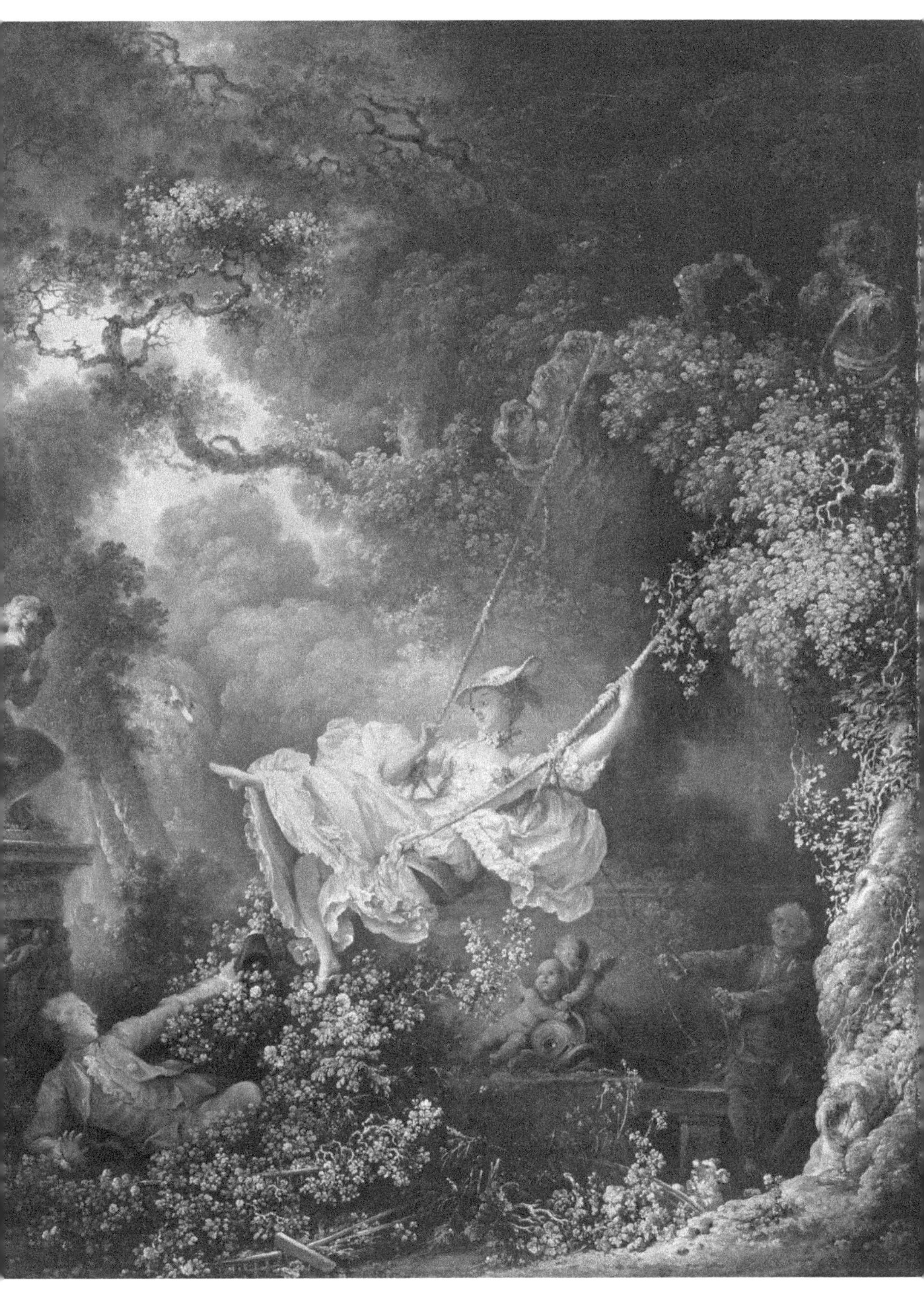

Jean Honoré Fragonard, The Swing, 1767

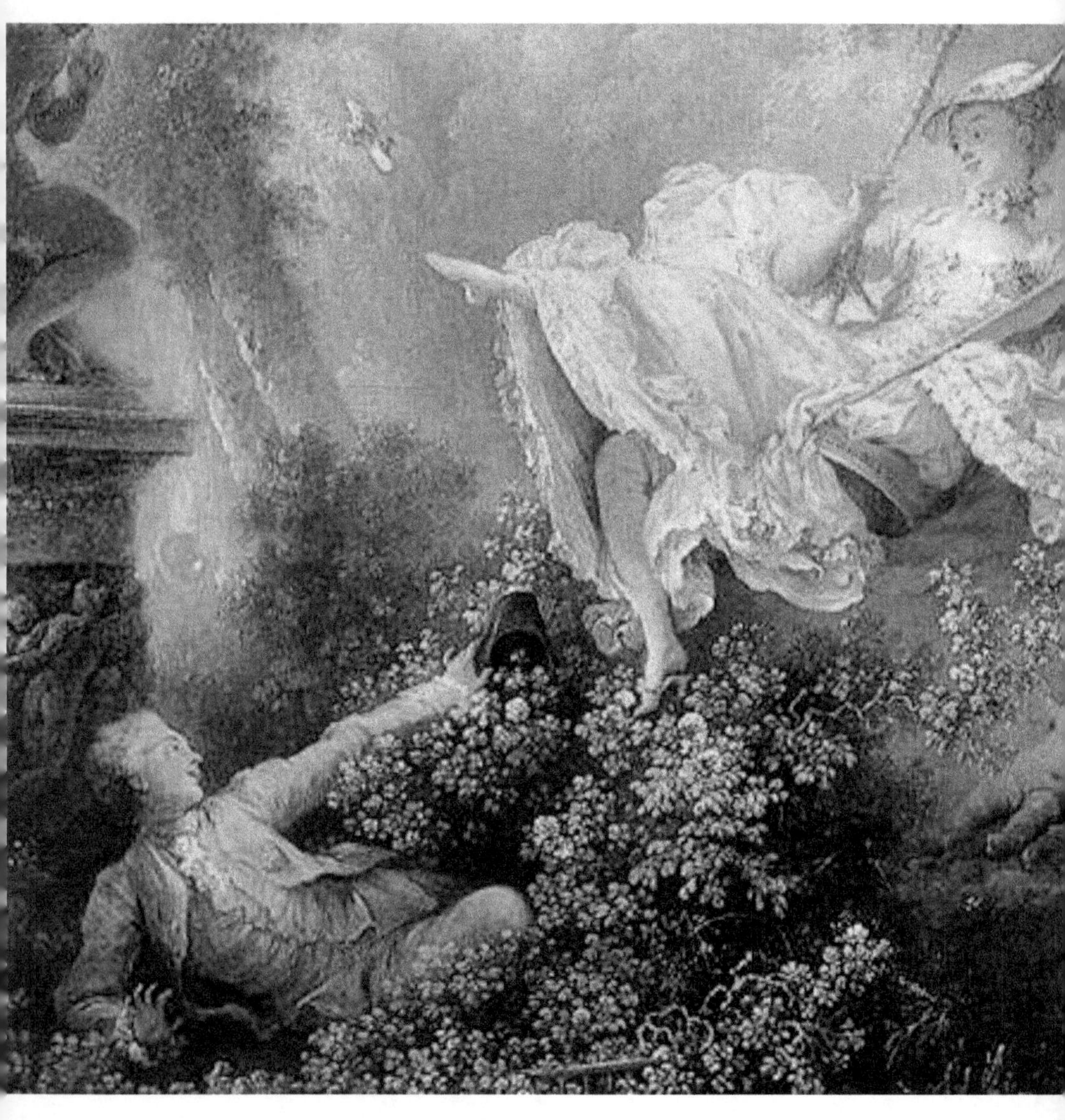

Jean Honoré Fragonard, The Swing, 1767, detail

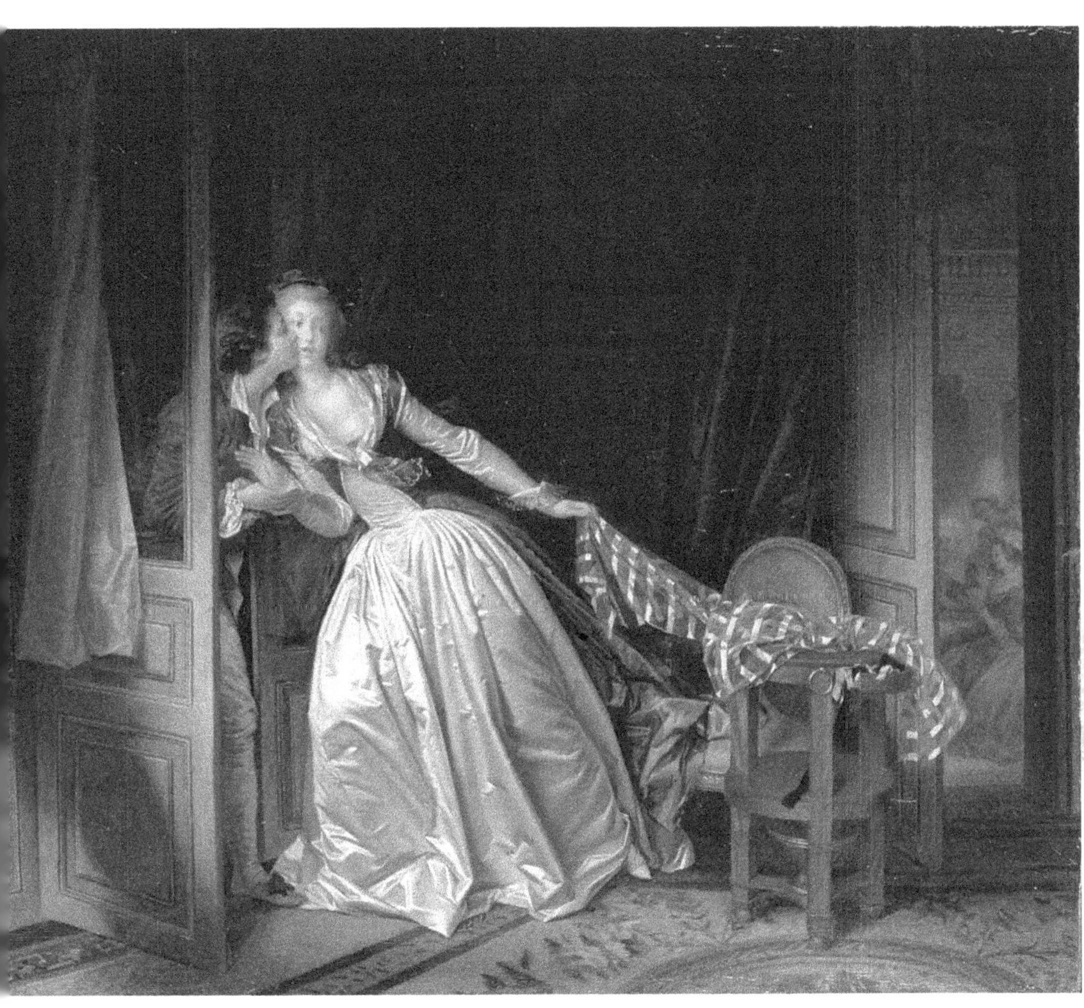

Jean Honoré Fragonard, The Stolen Kiss, late 1780s

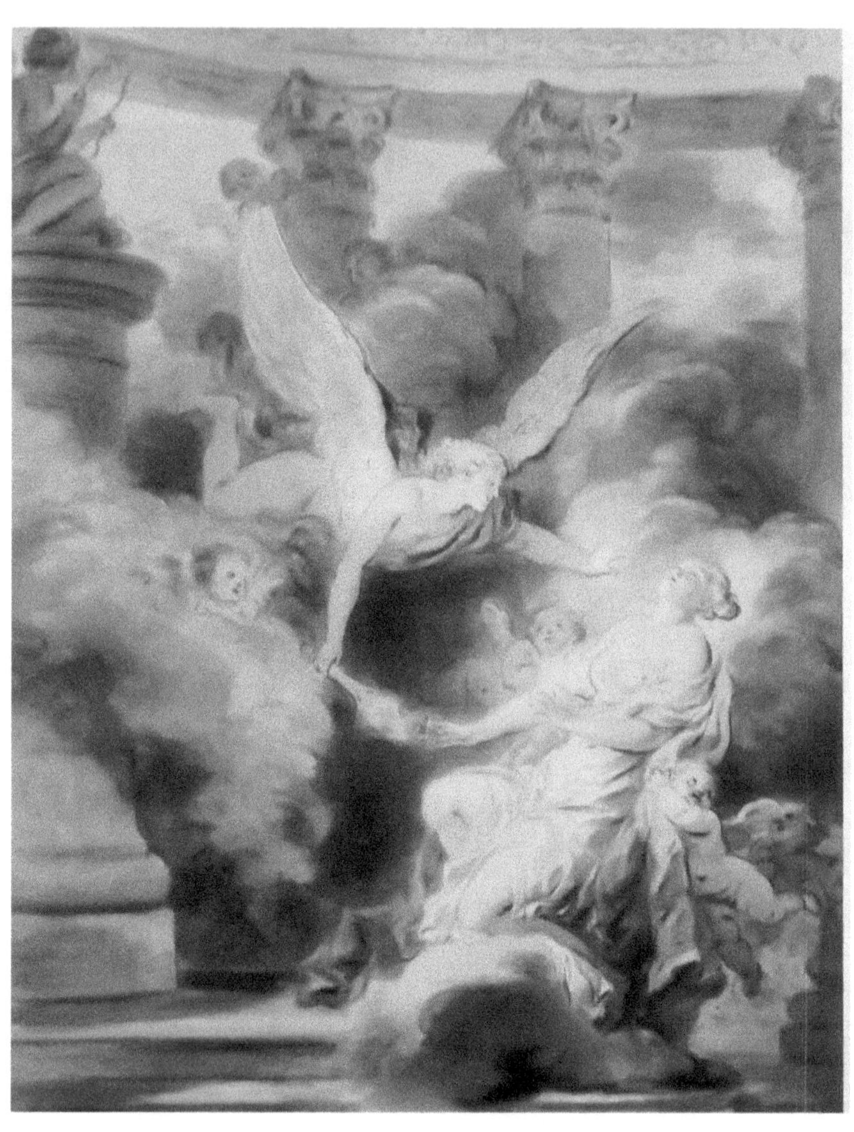

Jean-Honoré Fragonard, The Sacrifice of the Rose, c. 1780,
private collection

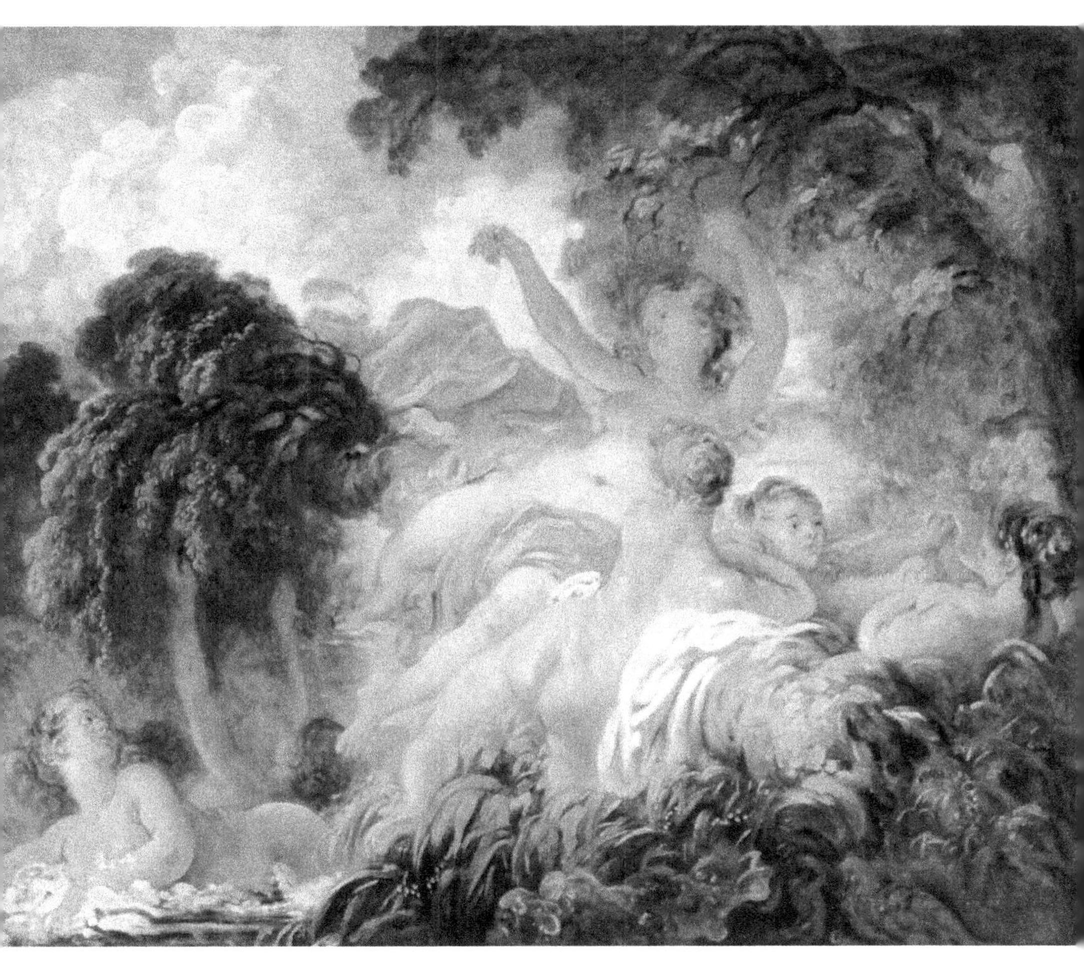

Jean Honoré Fragonard, Bathers, 1756

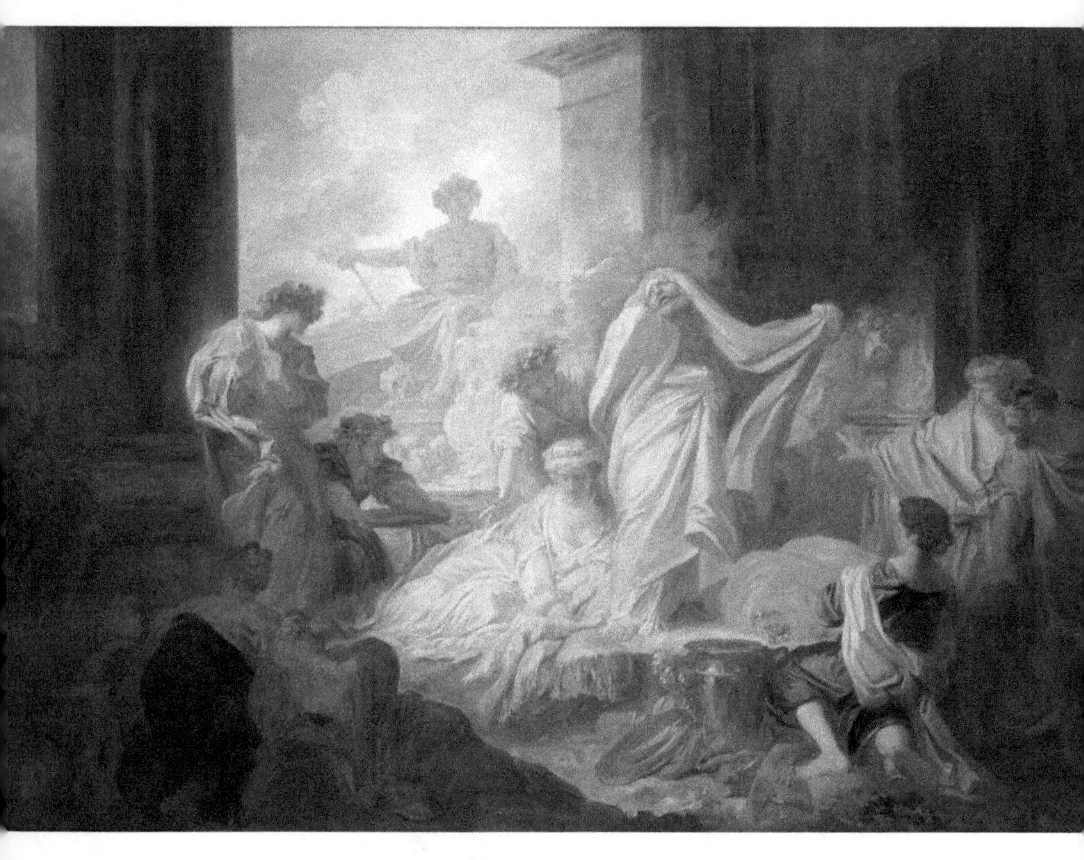

Jean Honoré Fragonard, Coresus Sacrificing Himself, Louvre, Paris

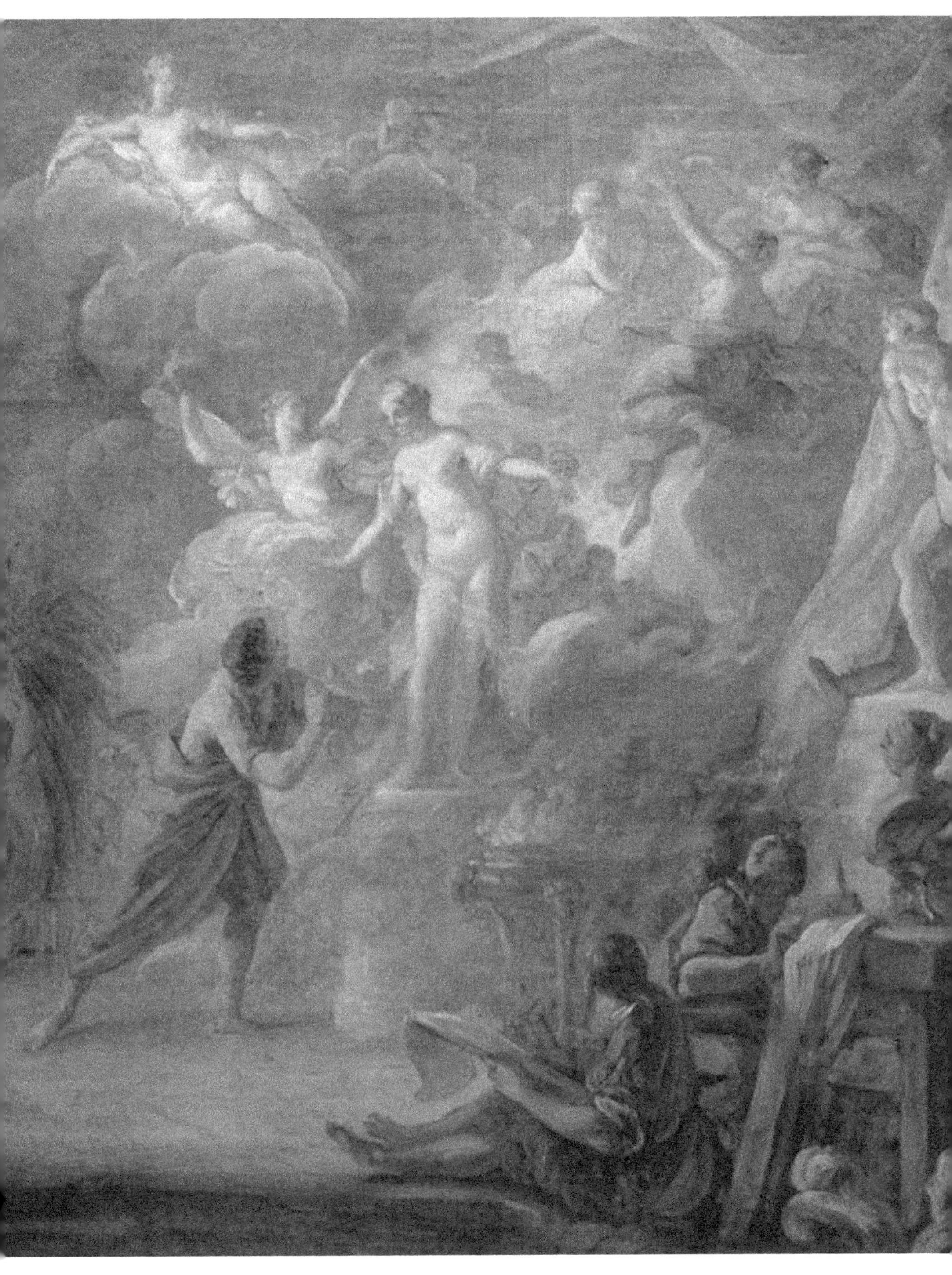

Jean Honoré Fragonard, Pygmalion, Bourges

GIANBATTIASTA TIEPOLO

Gianbattista Tiepolo was one of the superstars of the art world in the 18th century, a genius with a grand vision comprising mainly mythological and religious subjects. A visit to the Tiepolo School in Venice is an overwhelming experience (the Water City also houses numerous Tiepolo works, many of which are frescoes in palaces and churches). Tiepolo knew how to flatter his patrons and his viewers - and his interpretations of Classical mythology enabled him to include the partial nudity that connoisseurs wanted.

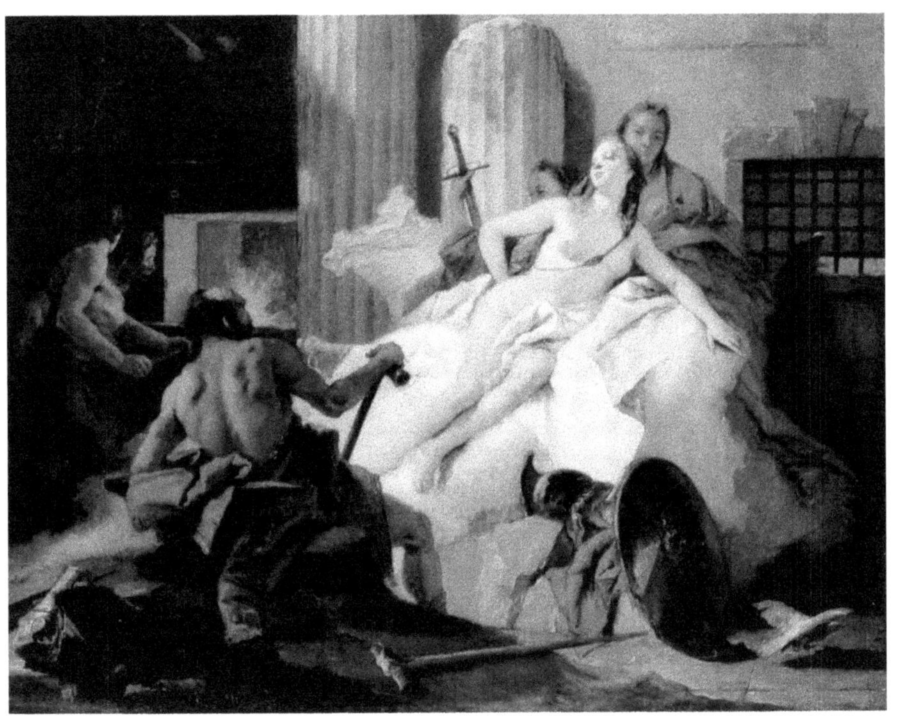

Giambattista Tiepolo, Venus and Vulcan, 1758-60, Philadelphia

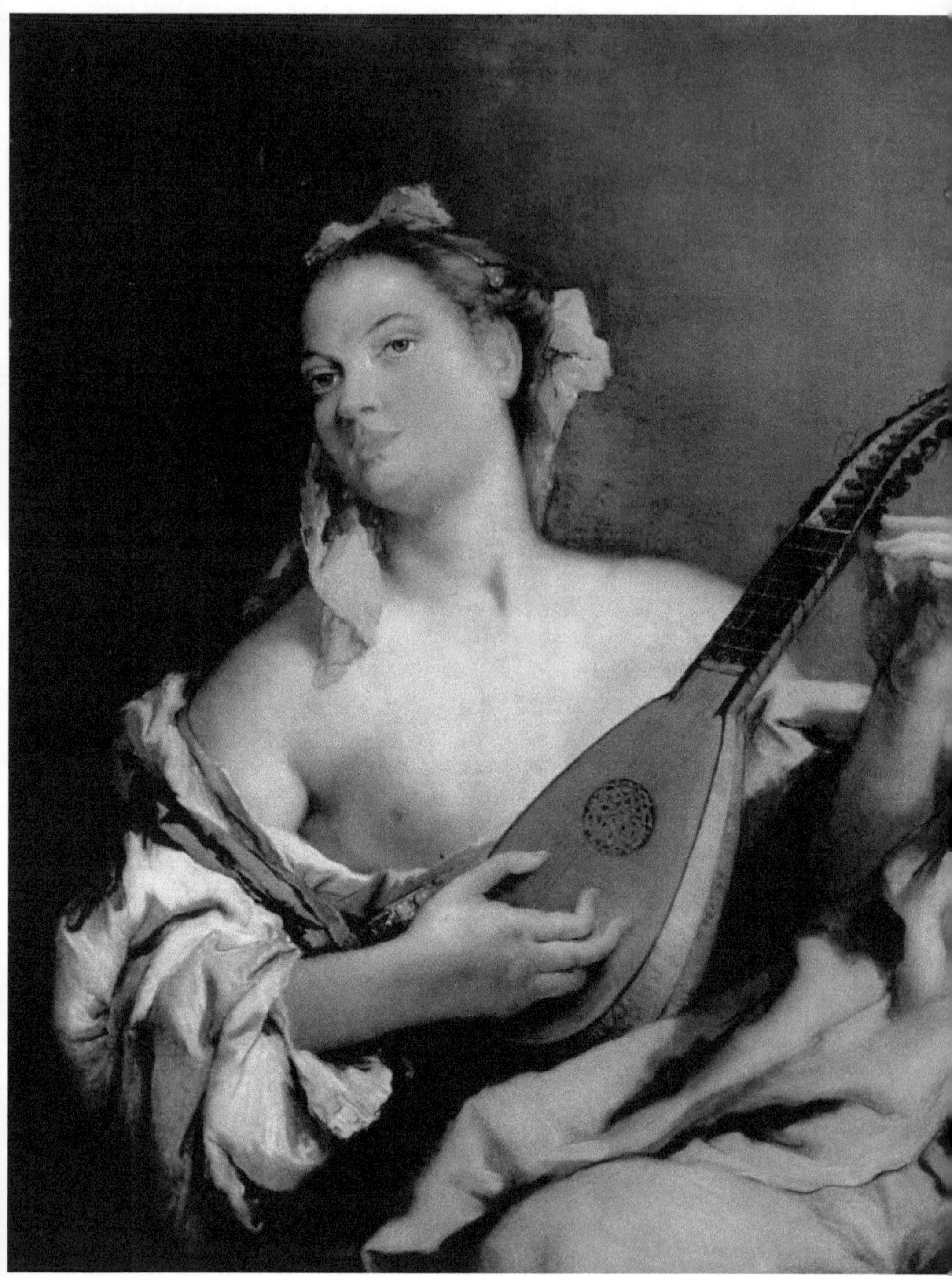

Giambattista Tiepolo, Girl With a Mandolin, 1758-60, Detroit

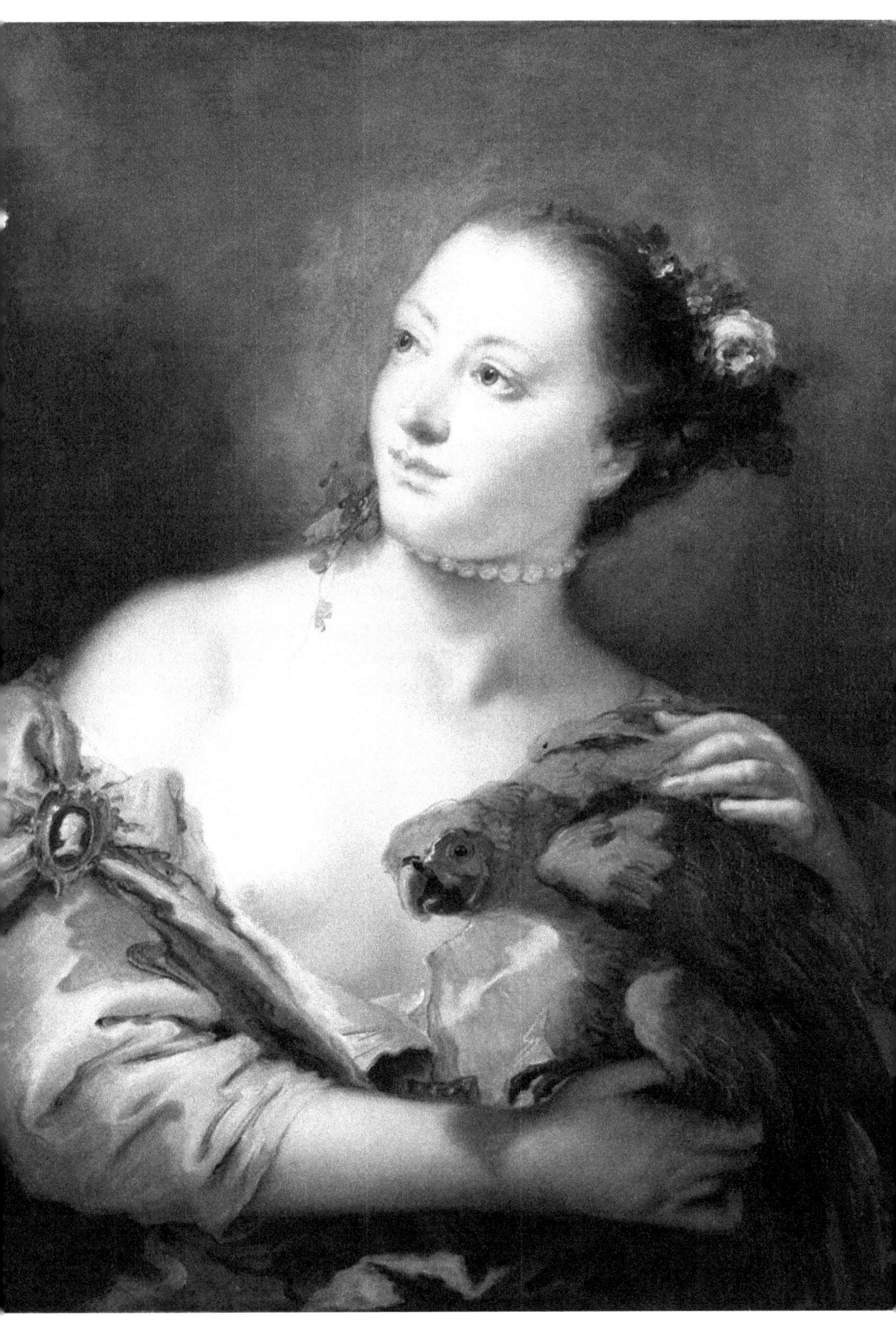

Giambattista Tiepolo, Young Woman With a Parrot,
1758-60, Ashmolean Museum, Oxford.

EROTIC ART IN THE EAST

Hindu, Tantric, Taoist and Chinese erotic art is founded in a religion quite different in some key areas from Western religion. There seems to be less guilt, sin, body-hating and repression in Indian, Japanese and Chinese erotic art (this discussion will focus primarily on erotic art in India, Japan and China). The cosmic energy of life has a sexual dimension which is gloriously celebrated. Indian, Japanese and Chinese erotic art may be just as sexist and misogynist and patriarchal as Western erotic art, but it is also freer, more exuberant, more joyous.

In Oriental erotic art, sexuality is a cosmic energy, an essential part of an authentic religious worldview. Indian, Chinese and Japanese erotica is thoroughly sexist, though. As with witches' covens and Western magic, erotic energy manifests itself in men and women in erotic pairings, in heterosexual components, and the symbols of the *lingam* and *yoni* are, yet again, the penis and vagina.

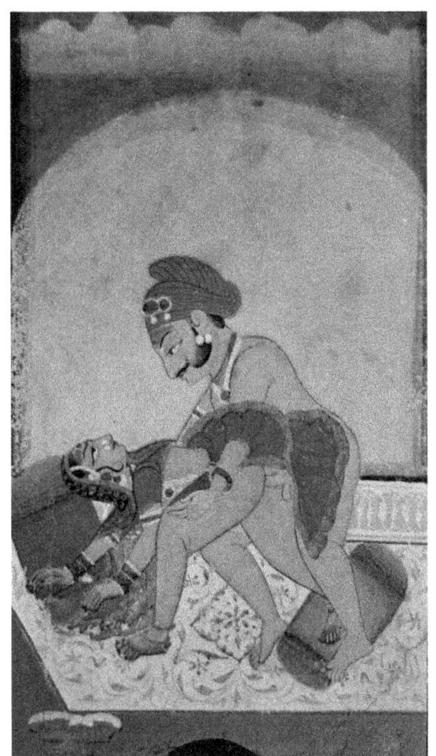

Indian erotic art:
Rajput, late 18th century, above.
Mogul style, 18th century, below.

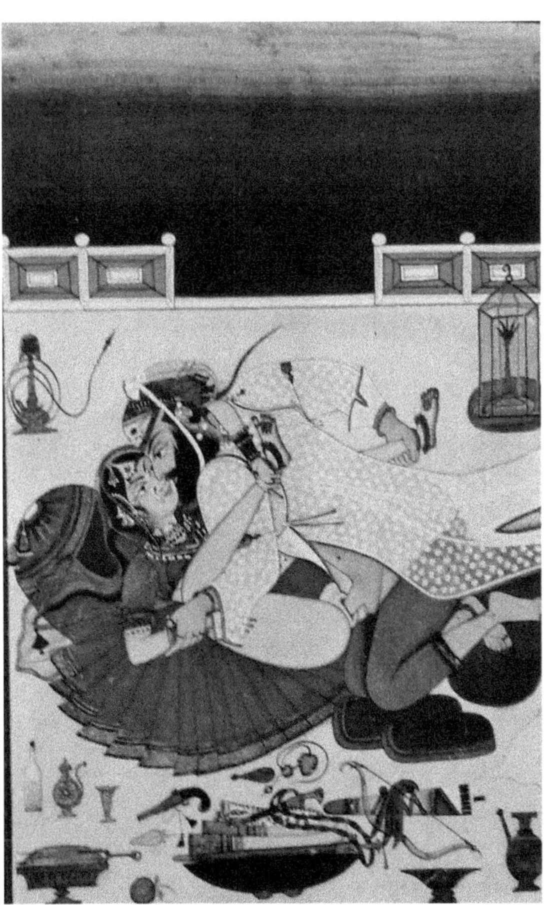

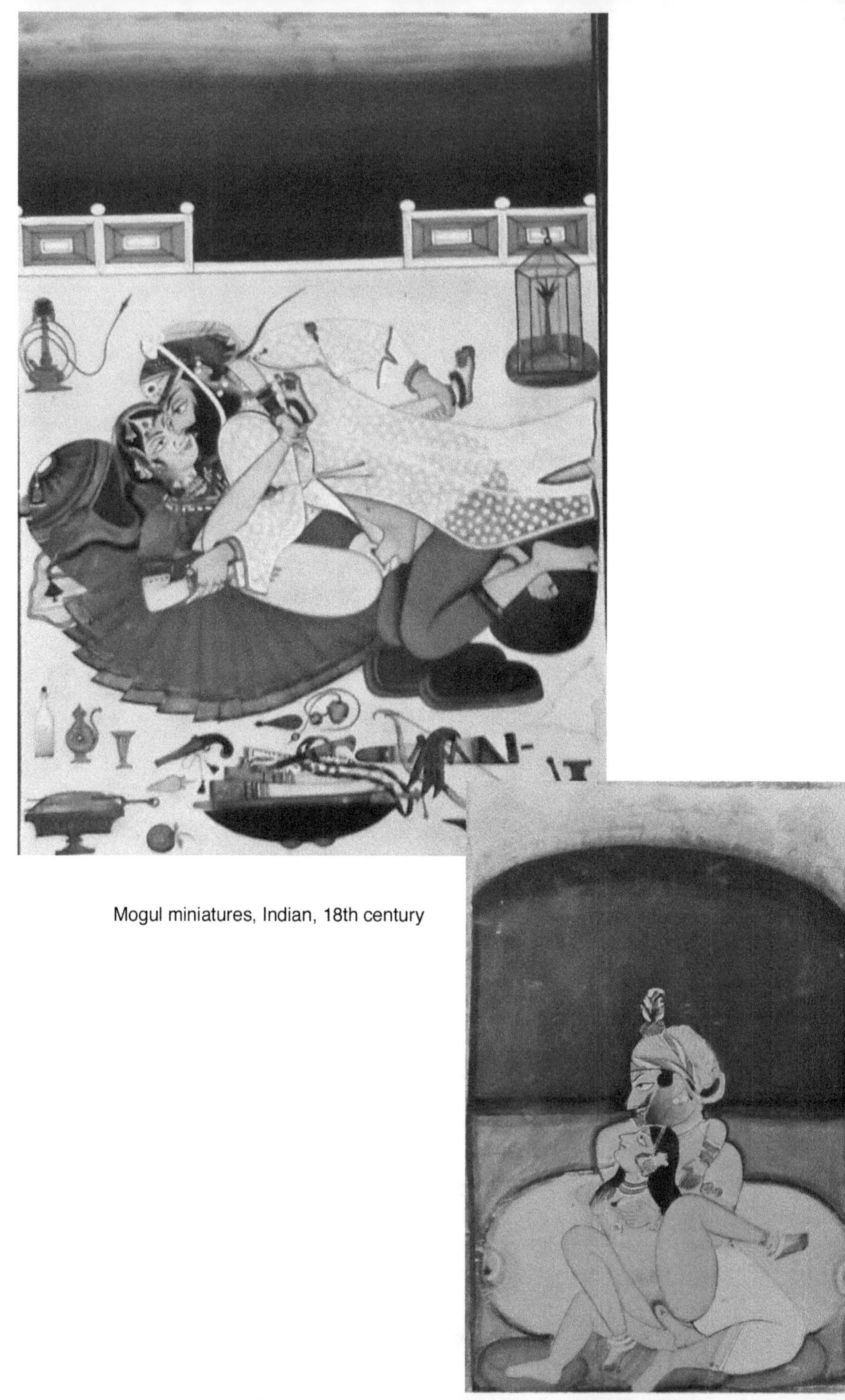

Mogul miniatures, Indian, 18th century

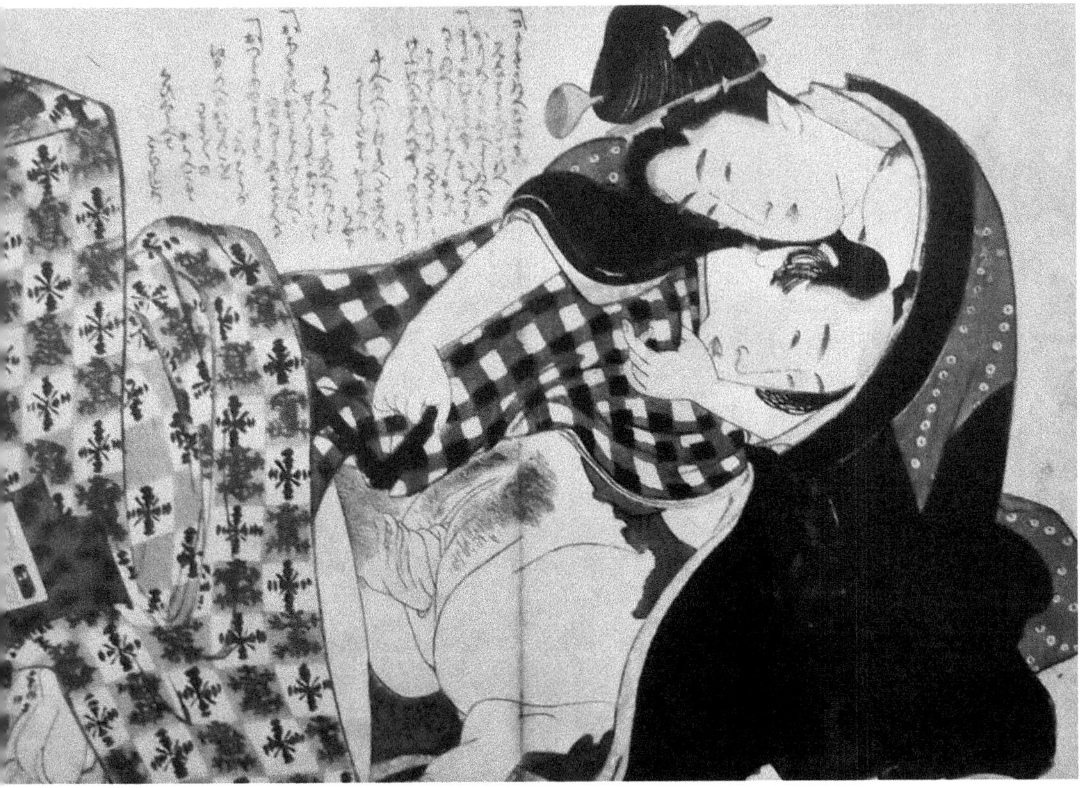

Katsushika Hokusai: Geisha and Lover (above), and Yoshiwara Courtesan and Lover (below).

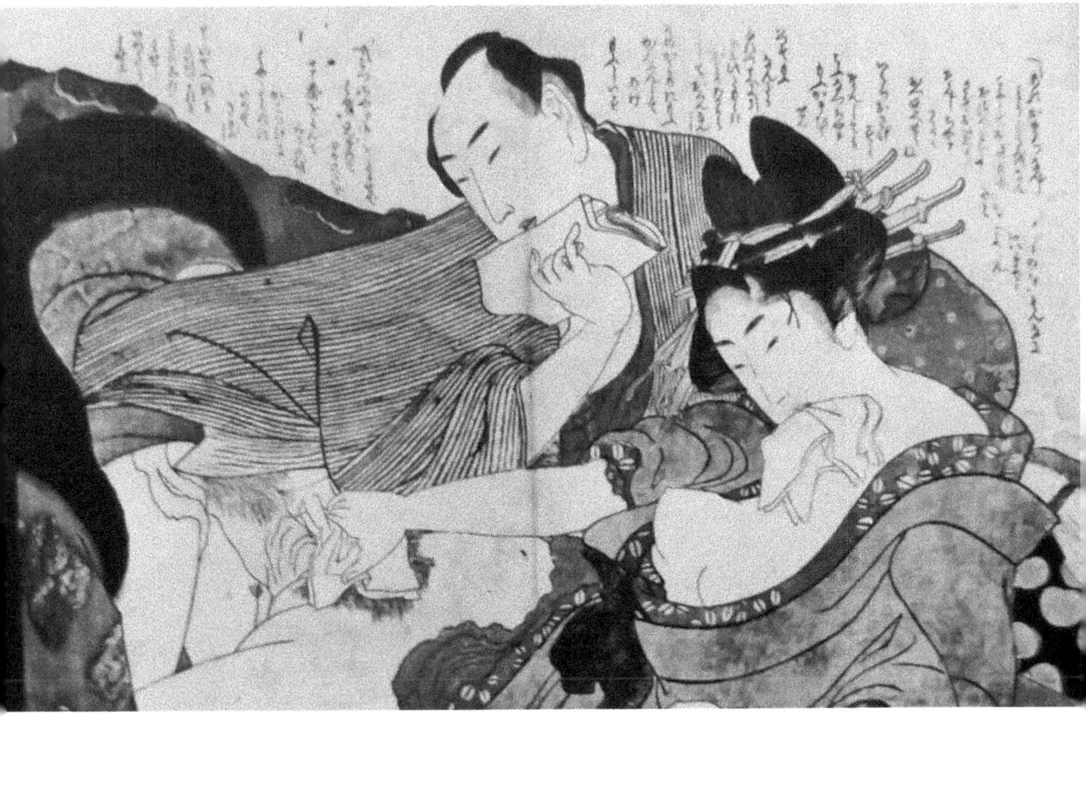

Chinese and Japanese erotic art is distinctive in its portrayal of the human figure, the elegant flowing lines, with the clothes and furnishings and bedding mirroring the curves of the bodies. Genitals are greatly enlarged - penises are hugely engorged, poised at the entrance of swollen, wide-open vulvas, with clitorises aroused and prominent. It's common in this kind of erotic art to see guys walking around with gigantic cocks, sometimes a few feet long, with the men supporting them with their hands. In humorous erotica, men balance fans on their schlongs, or carry buckets, or ride their members on wheels, as cannons. In satirical scrolls, by Jichosai (18th century), men battle with their phalluses like swords.

Exaggerated genitals are a staple of Japanese erotica, and have been since at least the 12th century: the Abbot Toda (1053-1140), for instance, one of the great erotic artists of the period, noted in an anecdote: 'the phallus is always depicted large, far in excess of the actual size. As a matter of fact, if it were drawn only in its natural size, it would hardly be worth looking at'.[1]

The sense of play and fun is readily apparent in amongst the scenes of fucking. But the tupping is only one element in amongst the visual richness on display: just as significant are the patterned clothes, the flowery, printed textiles, and the rich colouring of reds, greens and blues. The bodies in Chinese and Japanese erotic are usually partially naked, and show up as pale cream (the artists use the base, the paper or the scroll itself, as the basis for colouring the bodies).

1 Quoted in P. Kronhausen, 260.

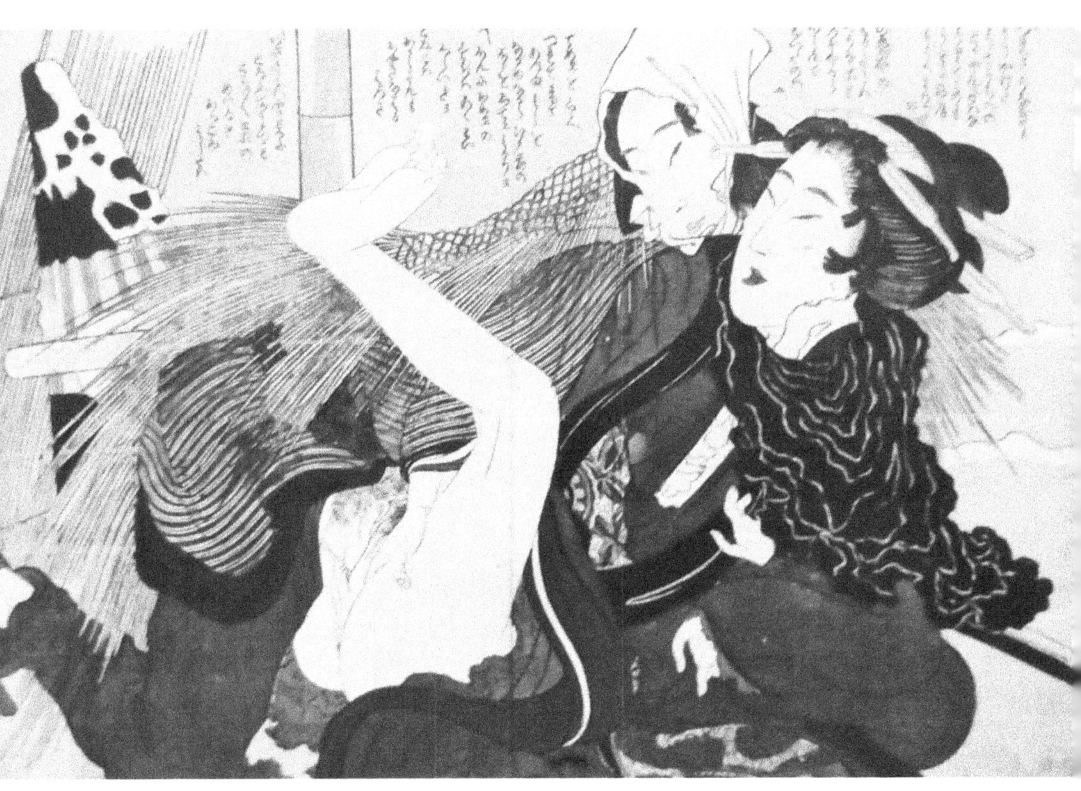

Katsushkia Hokusai, Lover and Geisha

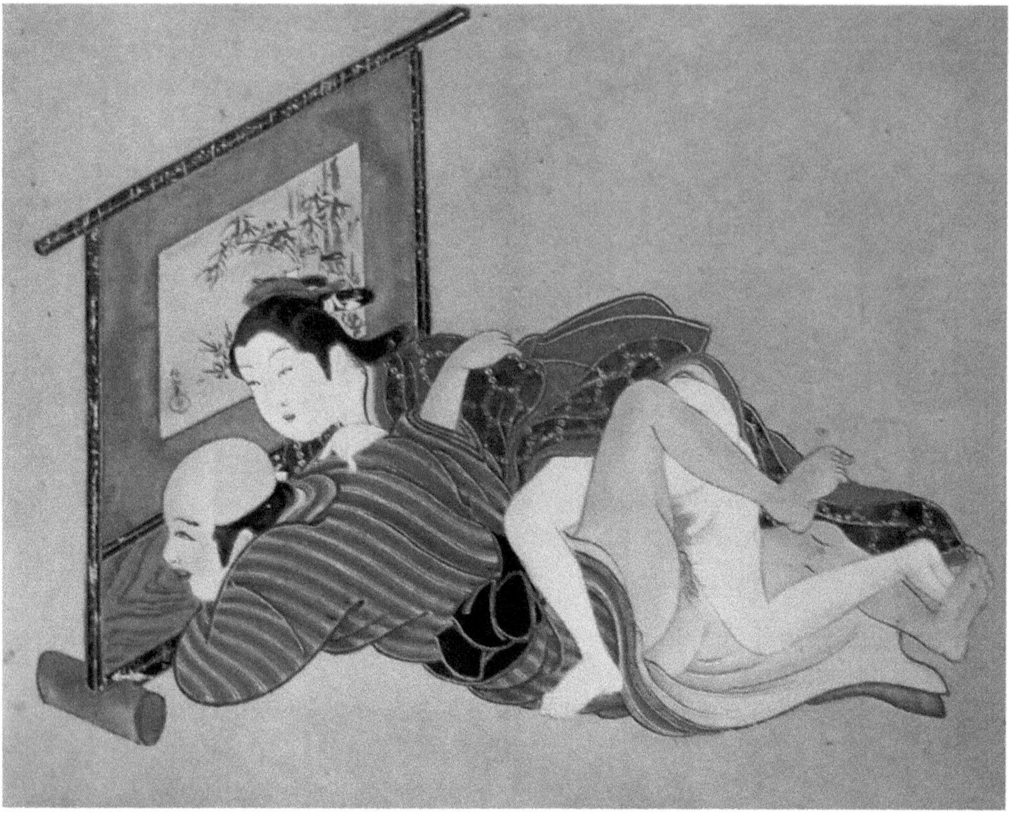

Nikikawa Sukenobu, early 18th century, Japanese

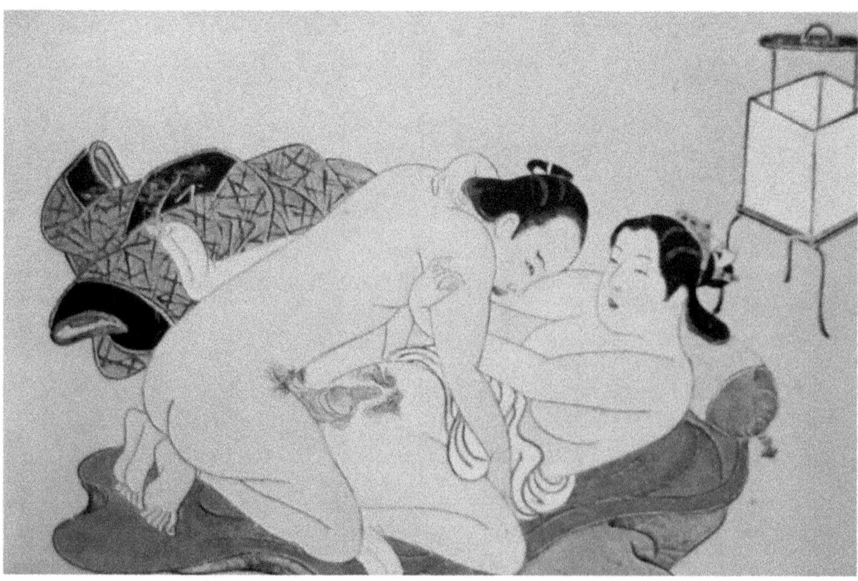

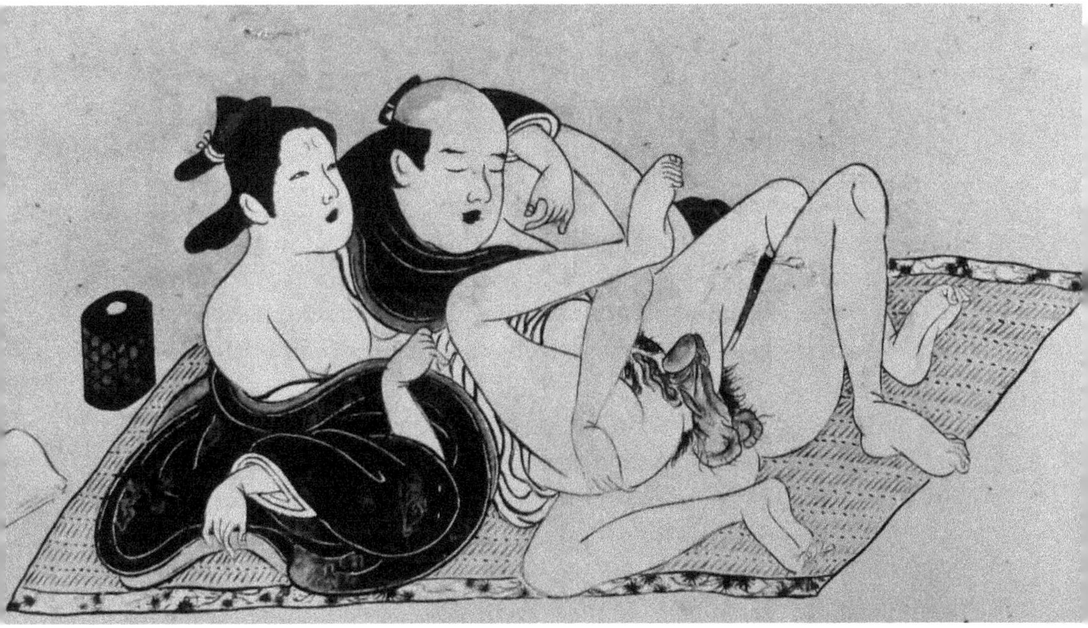

Nishikawa Sukenobu (1671-1751), ukiyo-e scroll, Kyoto, Japan (above).
Settei, Okyo school, 1780s, Japan (below)

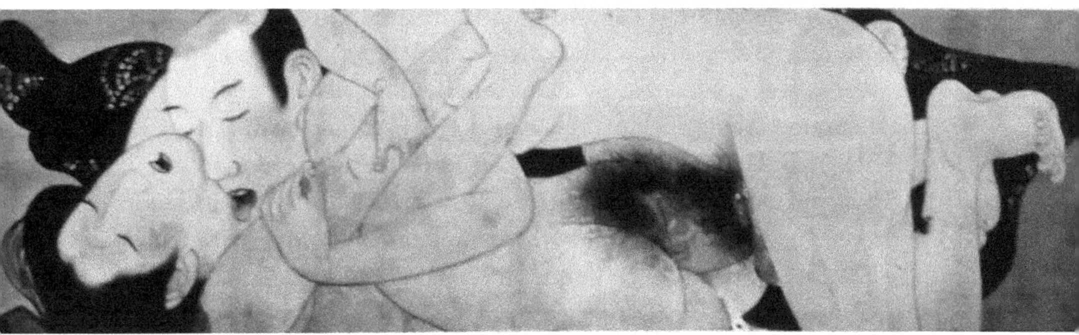

JAPANESE EROTIC ART

Erotic art in Japan goes back way before *hentai manga* and *animé,* to the woodblock print tradition (of the Edo period), and beyond – back to *shunga* ('posture'/ 'reclining postures') of the 7th and 8th centuries.

Japan has a history of erotic art, going back to woodblock prints in the Edo period, the *ukiyo-e* ('floating world pictures'), developed in the 17th century, and pillow books or *makura-e.* The 18th century saw a flowering of Japanese erotic art in print form.

Also it's not only the phallus that gets the royal treatment in Japanese erotic art: albums were also produced of women's genitals – whole erotic albums and sets of woodblock prints of vaginas. Katsushika Hokusai, for instance, created the *Elontsubi no hinagata* (*Models of the Vulva*), a set of twelve colour prints.

In Indian, Japanese and Chinese erotic art, people are shown gleefully and gymnastically contorting and entwining around one another. On hammocks, swinging from trees, on balconies, beds, cushions, tables, beside lakes, they copulate anywhere and everywhere. The depictions, by many anonymous artists, and also by celebrated artists such as Katsushika Hokusai, Utagawa Kunisada, Kitagawa Utamaro, Nishikawa Sukenobu and Torii Kiyonobu, show all manner of sexual activities, including a woman being licked by an octopus (Hokusai's famous image), rape by demons, and a blowjob while waiting in line at Burger King (just kidding).

Japanese *shunga* prints, especially, depict lovemaking as an innocent, pleasurable activity. The couples tup amidst serene Eastern landscapes, with vases filled with flowers, little fences, beautiful gardens, bo trees, lakes and streams. It all seems so pastoral and sublimely tranquil.[1]

1 Harunobu: *A Fantasy*, late 1760s, anonymous: *Trio in a Garden*, 18th century, China; *The Attack from the Rear, or 'The Leaping White Tiger'*, painting on silk from an album of the K'ang-hsi period, 1662-1722, C.T. Loo Collection, Paris; *In the Garden on a Rocky Seat*, painting on silk, K'ang-his period, C.T. Loo Collection, Paris

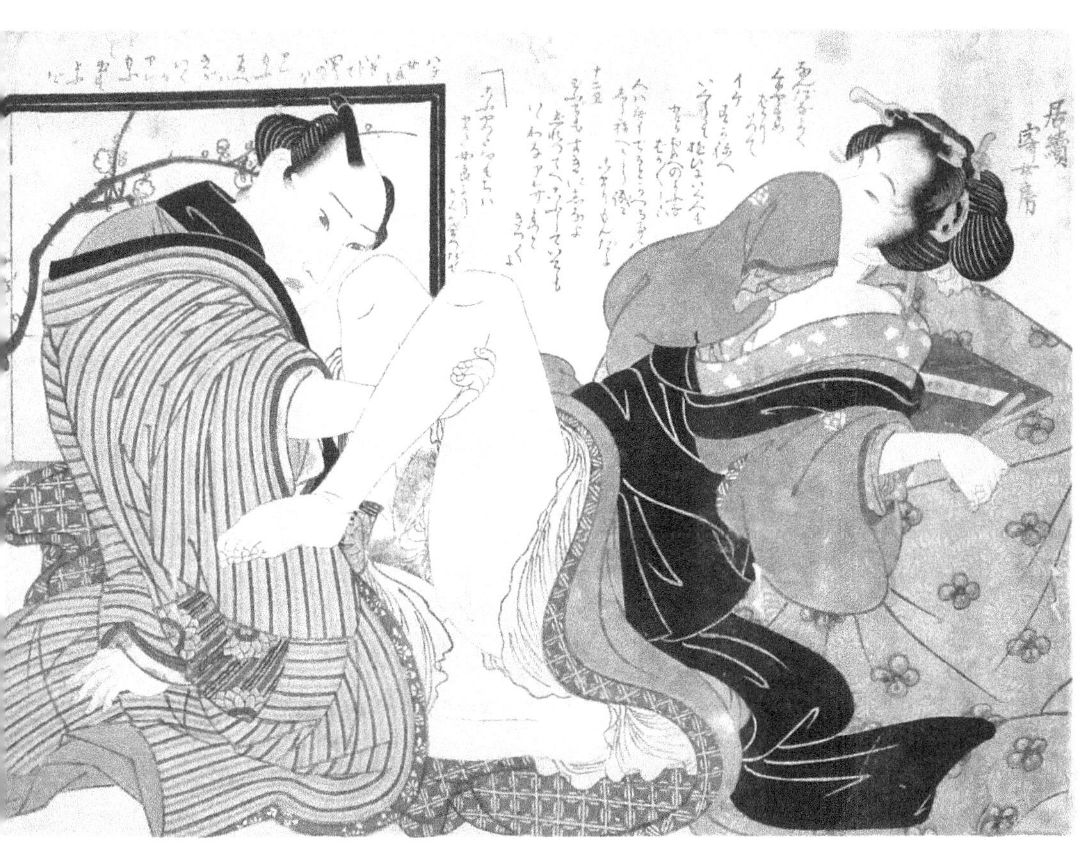

Japanese print, by Eizan

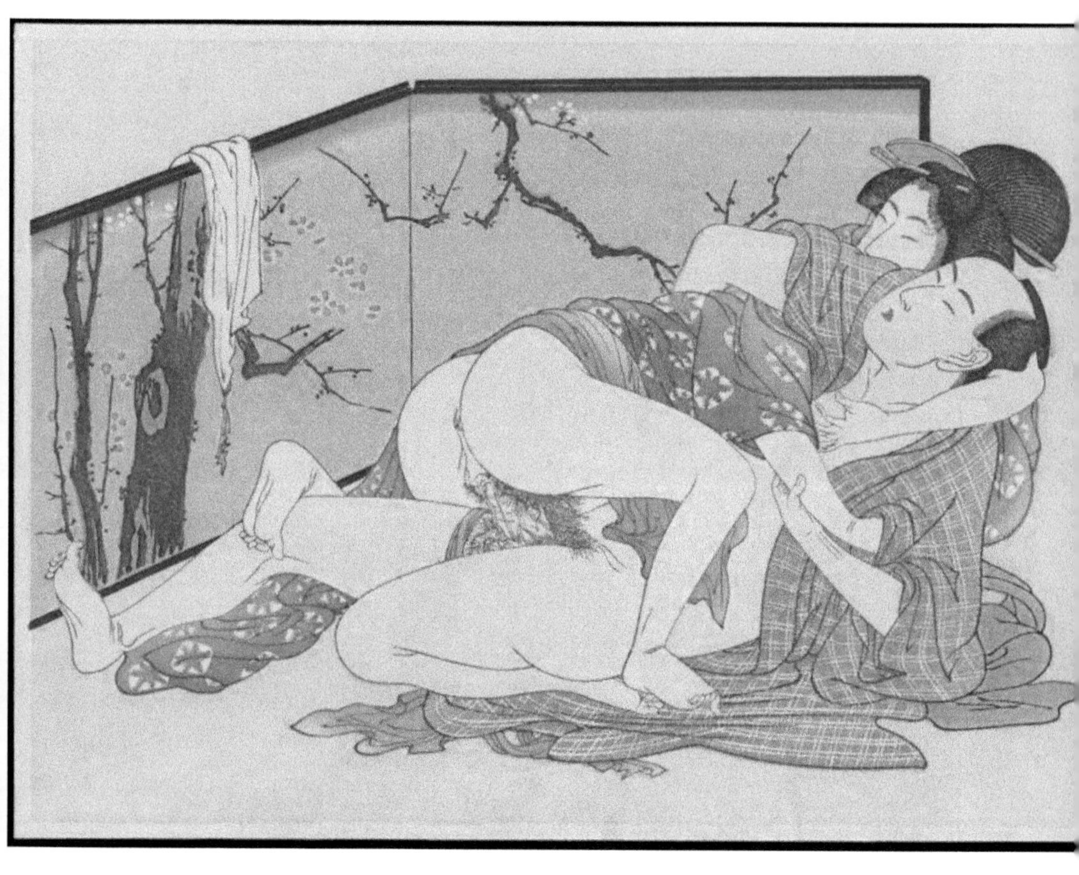

Kitagawa Utamaro (1753-1806), this page and over.
Some images are from Prelude To Desire, 1799

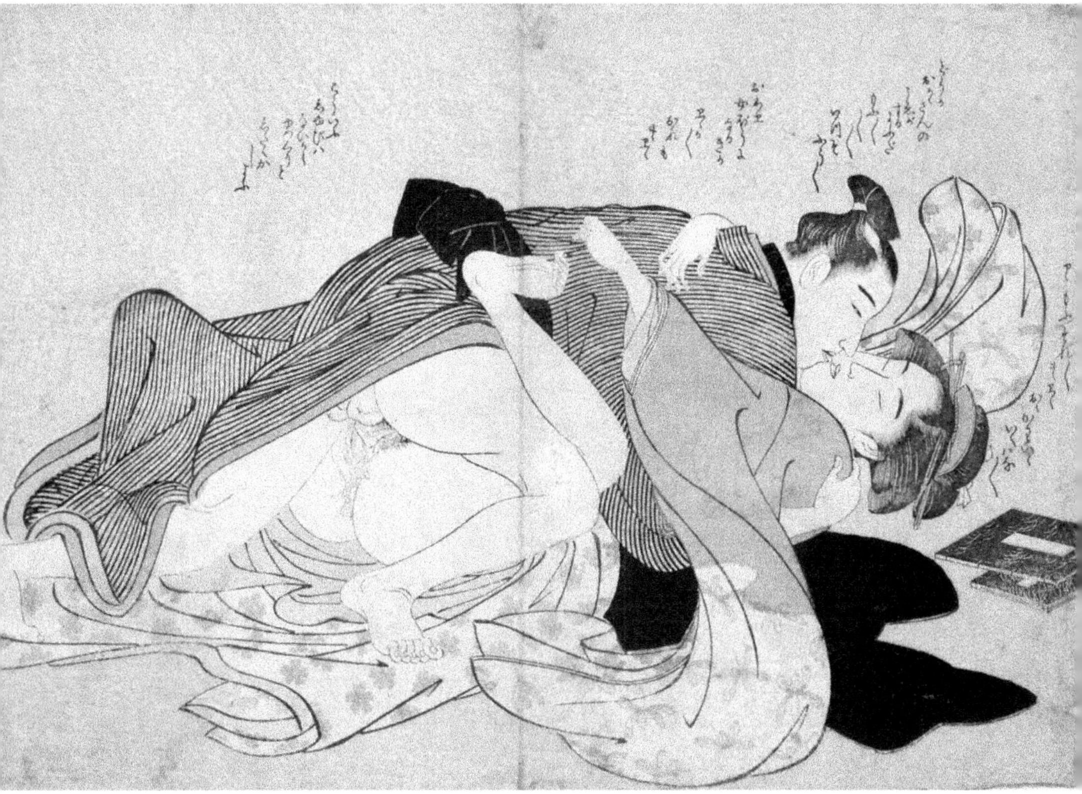

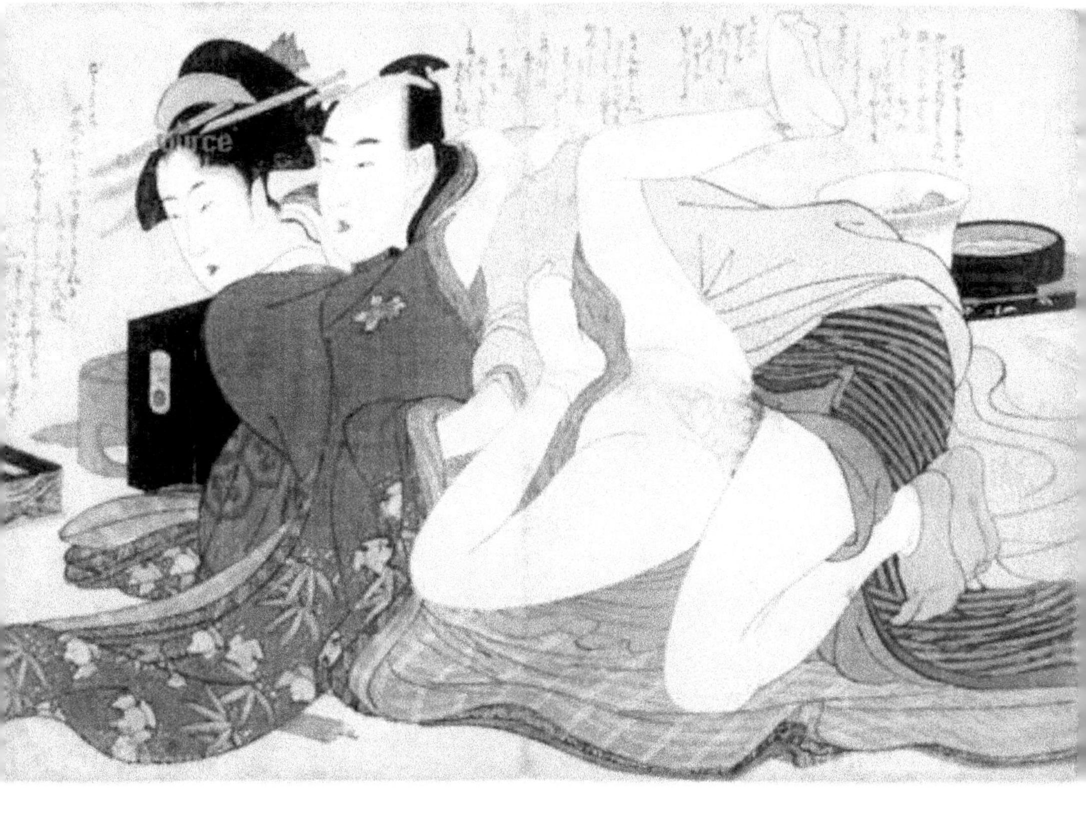

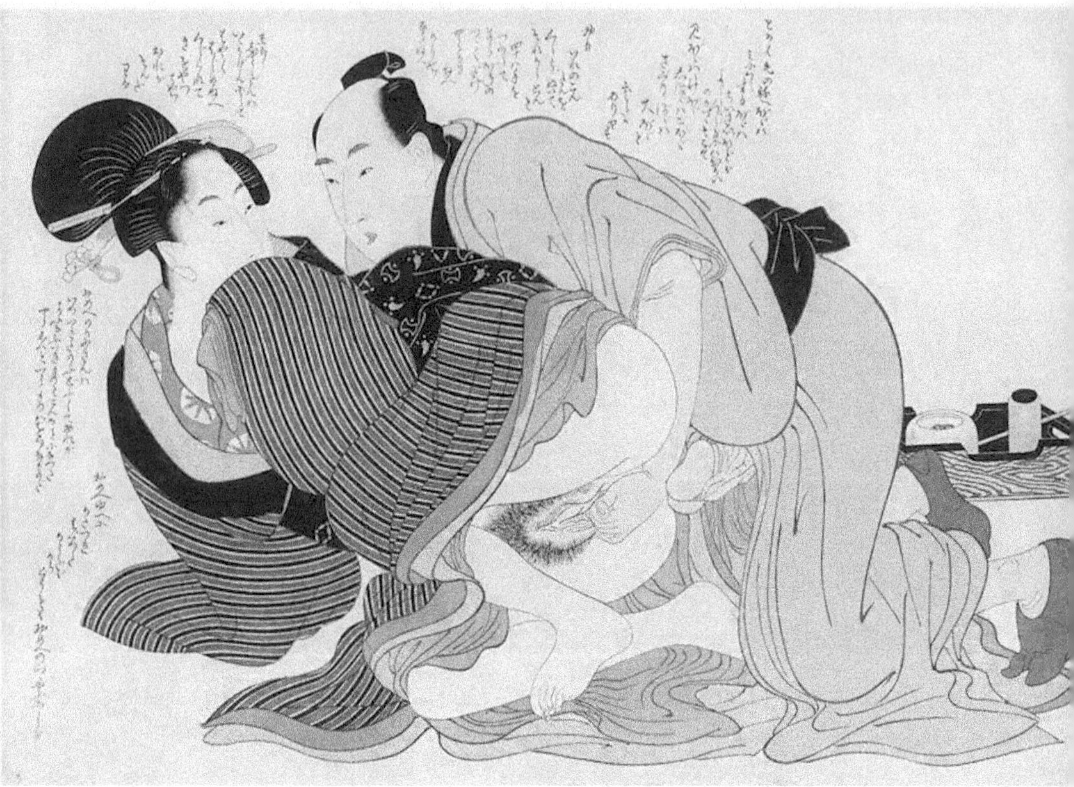

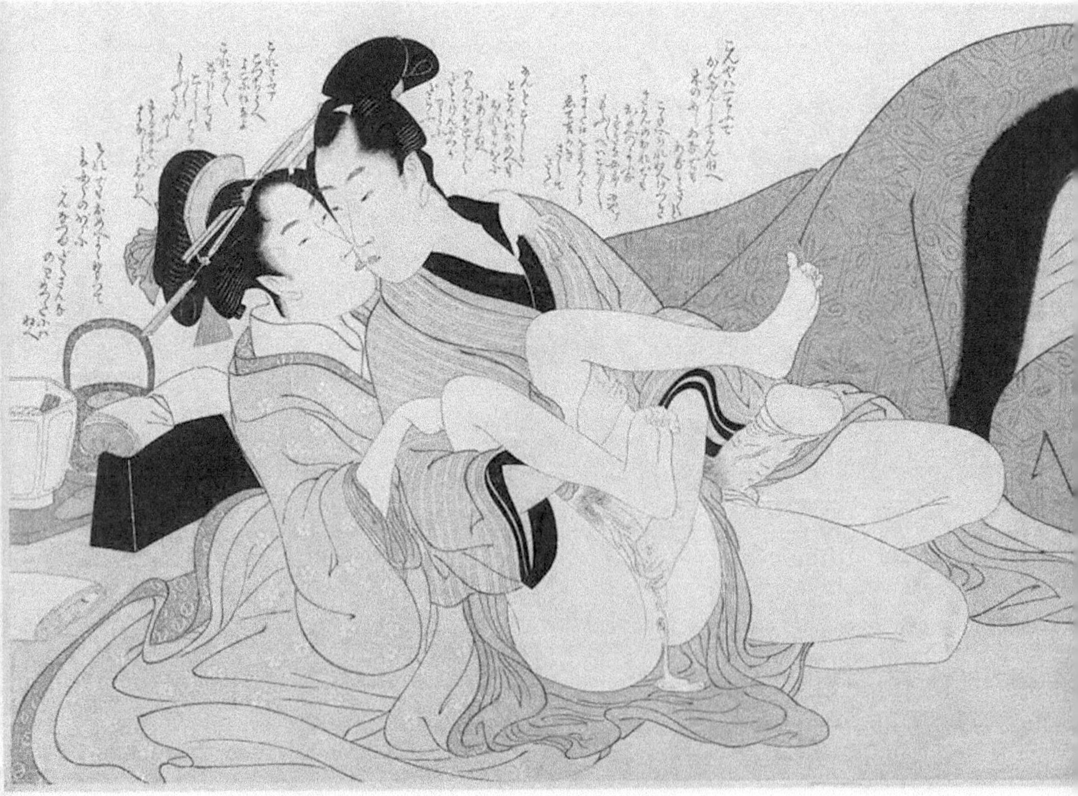

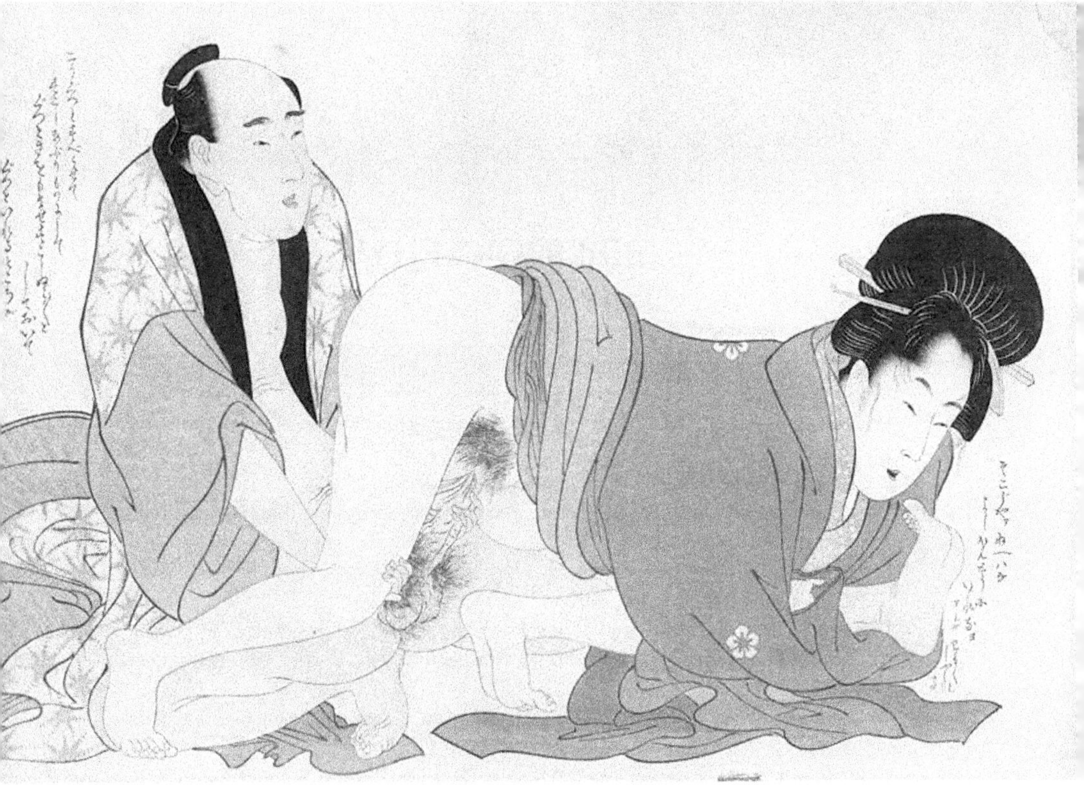

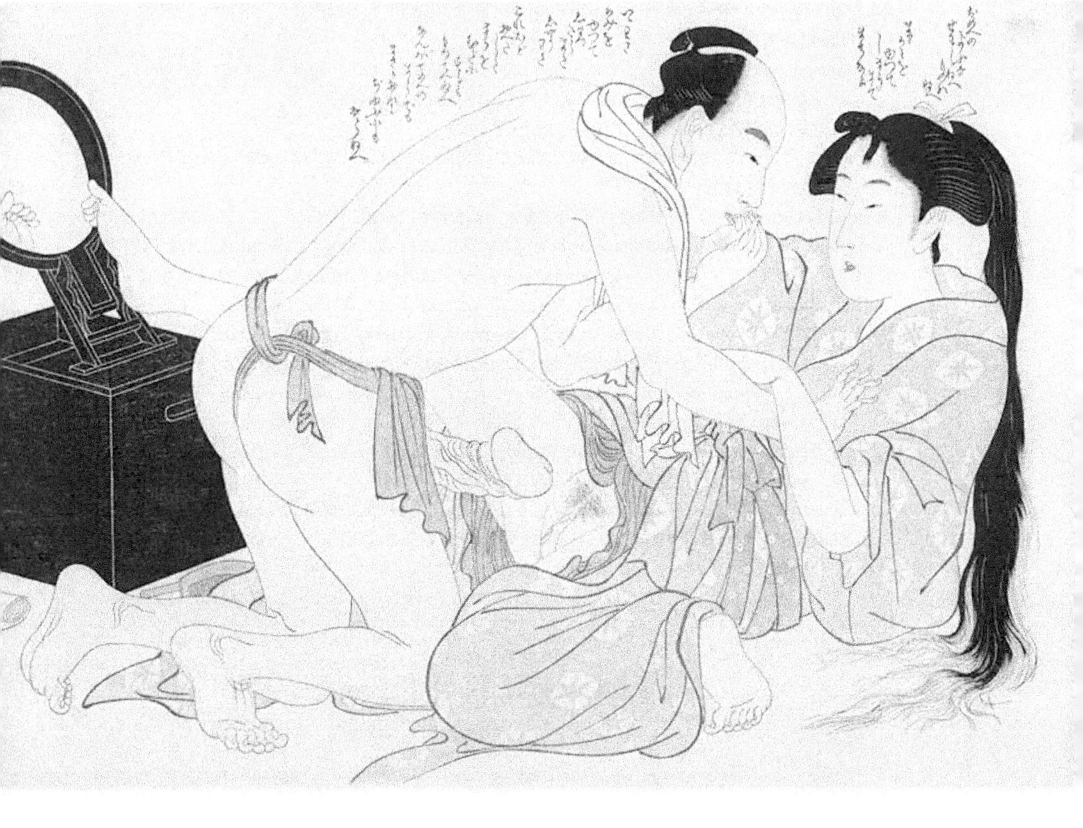

BIBLIOGRAPHY

E. de Antonio & M. Tuchman: *Painters Painting*, Abbeville Press, New York, NY, 1984

C.G. Argan: *The Renaissance*, Thames & Hudson, London, 1969

I. Armstrong, ed. *New Feminist Discourses: Critical Essays on Theories and Texts*, Routledge, London, 1992

J. Atkins: *Sex in Literature*, volume 2: *The Classical Experience of the Sexual Impulse*, Calder & Boyars, London, 1973

P. Bade: *Femme Fatale: Images of evil and fascinating women*, Ash & Grant 1979

M. Baxandall: *Painting and Experience in 15th Century Italy*, Oxford University Press 1988

—. *Patterns of Intention: On the Historical Explanation of Pictures*, Yale University Press 1985

G. Bazin: *A Concise History of World Sculpture*, David & Charles, Newton Abbot 1981

J. Beck: *Italian Renaissance Painting*, Harper & Row, New York, NY, 1981

B. Berenson: *The Italian Painters of the Renaissance*, Phaidon, London, 1952

—. *Looking at Pictures with Bernard Berenson*, selected by Hann Kiel, Abrahams, New York, NY, 1974

B. Bernard: *The Queen of Heaven: A Selection of Painting the Virgin from the Twelfth to the Eighteenth Centuries*, Macdonald/ Orbis, London, 1987

—. *The Bible and Its Painters*, Orbis, London, 1983

F. Bonner *et al*, eds. *Imagining Women Cultural Representations and Gender*, Polity Press, Cambridge 1992

S. Bramly: *Leonardo: The Artist and the Man*, Michael Joseph 1992

A. Brahama: *Italian Renaissance Painters of the Sixteenth Century* National Gallery 1985

J. Burckhardt: *The Altarpiece in Renaissance Italy*, Phaidon, London, 1988

T. Burckhardt: *Sacred Art in East and West*, Perennial Book, Middlesex 1967

W. Chadwick: *Women, Art, and Society*, Thames & Hudson, London, 1990

—. *Women Artists and the Surrealist Movement*, Thames & Hudson, London, 1991

A. Chastel: *Art of the Italian Renaissance*, tr. P. & L. Murray, Alpine Fine Arts Collection, London, 1985

—. *The Studios and Styles of the Renaissance, Italy 1460-1500*, tr. Griffin, Thames & Hudson, London, 1966

G. Chester & J. Dickey, ed. *Feminism and Censorship: The Current Debate*, Prism Press, Bridport, Dorset 1988

H.B. Chipp, ed. *Theories of Modern Art*, University Press of California, Los Angeles, 1968
J.E. Cirlot: *A Dictionary of Symbols*, Routledge, London, 1981
Kenneth Clark. *The Nude*, Pantheon Books, 1957
B. Cole: *The Renaissance Artist at Work*, John Murray, London, 1983
J.C. Cooper: *An Illustrated Dictionary of Traditional Symbols*, Thames & Hudson, London, 1978
L. Dresen-Coenders, ed. *Saints and She-Devils: Images of Women in the 15th and 16th Centuries*, Rubicon Press 1987
W. Dube: *The Expressionists*, Thames & Hudson, London, 1972
S.C. Dubin: *Arresting Images: Impolitic Art and Uncivil Actions*, Routledge, London, 1992
G. Duby & M. Perrot: *Power and Beauty: Images of Women in Art*, Tauris Parke Books,
A. Dworkin. *Intercourse*, Arrow, London, 1988
—. *Pornography: Men Possessing Women*, Women's Press, London, 1984
C. Eisler: *Early Netherlandish Painting: The Thyssen-Bornemisza Collection*, Sotheby's Publications, London, 1989
A. Elsen: *Modern European Sculpture 1918-45*, New York, NY, 1979
J. Evans, ed. *The Flowering of the Middle Ages*, Thames & Hudson, London, 1966
J. Evola: *The Metaphysics of Sex*, East-West Publications, London, 1985
M. Foucault: *The History of Sexuality*, Penguin, London, 1981
—. *The Use of Pleasure: The History of Sexuality*, vol. 2, Penguin, London, 1987
S.J. Freedberg: *Painting of the High Renaissance in Rome and Florence*, Harper & Row, New York, NY, 1972
S. Freud: *Leonardo da Vinci*, tr. A. Tyson, Penguin, London, 1963
E. Gadon: *The Once and Future Goddess*, Aquarian Press 1990
Fred Gettings: *The Hidden Art: A Study of the Occult Symbolism in Art*, Studio Vista, London, 1978
P. Gibson & R. Gibson, ed. *Dirty Looks: Women, Pornography, Power*, British Film Institute, London, 1993
M. Gimbutas: *The Language of the Goddess*, Thames & Hudson, London, 1989
R. Goldwater & M. Treves, eds. *Artists On Art*, John Murray, London, 1975
E.H. Gombrich: *Norm and Form: Studies in the Renaissance I*,Phaidon, London, 1985
—. *Symbolic Images, Renaissance Studies II*,Phaidon, London, 1985
S. Griffin: *Pornography and Silence: Culture's Revenge Against Nature*, Women's Press, London, 1981
J. Hale: *Italian Renaissance Painting*, Phaidon, London, 1977
J. Hall: *A Dictionary of Subjects and Symbols in Art*, John Murray, London, 1984
M. Esther Harding: *Women's Mysteries*, Rider, London, 1989
F. Hartt: *History of Italian Renaissance Art: Painting, Sculpture, Architecture*, Thames & Hudson, London, 1987
N.G. Heller: *Women Artists: An Illustrated History*, Virago, London, 1987
J. Hobhouse: *The Bride Stripped Bare: The Artist and the Nude in the Twentieth Century*, Cape, London, 1988

A. Hollander: *Seeing Through Clothes,* Viking Press, New York, NY, 1980
M. Humm: *Feminisms: A Reader,* Harvester Wheatsheaf, 1992
—. ed. *The Dictionary of Feminist Theory,* Harvester Wheatsheaf 1989
M. Jacobs: *A Guide to European Painting,* David & Charles 1980
—. *Mythological Painting*, Phaidon 1979
P. Julian: *Dreamers of Decadence: Symbolist Painters of the 1890s,* tr. R. Baldick, Pall Mall Press, London, 1971
S. Kappeler: *The Pornography of Representation*, Polity Press, Cambridge 1986
D. Kelder: *Pageant of the Renaissance,* Pall Mall Press, London, 1969
J.A. Kestner: *Mythology and Misogyny: The Social Discourse of Nineteenth-Century British Classical-Subject Painting,* University of Wisconsin Press, Madison 1989
C. Kramarae & P.A. Treichler, eds. *A Feminist Dictionary,* Pandora Press, London, 1987
J. Kristeva: *The Kristeva Reader,* ed. Toril Moi, Blackwell 1986
—. *Desire in Language: A Semiotic Approach to Literature and Art,* ed. L. Roudiez, tr. T. Gora *et al*, Blackwell 1982
J. Lacan and the *Ecole Freudienne: Feminine Sexuality,* eds. J. Mitchell and J. Rose, Macmillan, London, 1982
A. Le Normand-Romain *et al. Sculpture: The Adventure of Modern Sculpture in the Nineteenth and Twentieth Centuries,* Skira, Geneva, 1986
L. da Vinci: *The Drawings of Leonardo da Vinci,* introduction A.E. Popham, Cape, London, 1964
M. Levey: *High Renaissance,* Penguin, London, 1975
—. *Early Renaissance,* Penguin, London, 1967
F. Licht: *Sculpture, 19th and 20th Centuries,* Michael Joseph, London, 1967
L. Lippard: *From the Center: feminist essays on women's art,* Dutton, New York, NY, 1976
—. *Six Years: The Dematerialization of the Art Object from 1966 to 1972,* Praeger, New York, NY, 1973
E. Lucie-Smith: *Symbolist Art,* Thames & Hudson, London, 1972
—. *Sexuality in Western Art,* Thames & Hudson, London, 1991
F. MacCarthy: *Eric Gill,* Faber, London, 1989
E. Marks & I. de Courtivron, eds. *New French Feminisms: an Anthology,* Harvester Wheatsheaf 1981
J.C.J. Metford: *Dictionary of Christian Lore and Legend,* Thames & Hudson, London, 1983
Michelangelo: *The Complete Paintings,* Granada, London, 1980
E. Mitsch: *The Art of Egon Schiele,* Phaidon 1975
T. Moi: *Sexual/ Textual Politics: Feminist LiteraryTheory,* Routledge, London, 1988
E. Mullins: *The Painted Witch: Female Body, Male Art,* Secker & Warburg, London, 1985
L. Mulvey: *Visual and Other Pleasures,* Macmillan, London, 1989
S. Munt, ed. *New Lesbian Criticism: Literary and Cultural Readings,* Harvester Wheatsheaf, London, 1992

P. & L. Murray: *The Penguin Dictionary of Art and Artists*, Penguin, London, 1976
L. Murray: *High Renaissance*, Thames & Hudson, London, 1977
L. Nead: *Female Nude: Art, Obscenity and Sexuality* Routledge, London, 1992
E. Neumann: *The Great Mother*, Princeton University Press, NJ 1972
S. Nicholson, ed. *The Goddess Re-awakening: The Goddess Principle Today*, Theosophical Publishing House, New York, NY, 1989
J. Paladilhe. *Gustave Moreau*, Thames & Hudson, London,1972
E. Panofsky: *Studies in Iconology*, Harper & Row, New York, NY, 1972
—. *Early Netherlandish Painting*, Harvard University Press, Mass., 1953
R. Parker & G. Pollock. *Old Mistresses: Women, Art an Ideology*, Routledge & Kegan Paul, London, 1981
W. Pater: *The Renaissance*, Oxford University Press 1980
R. Payne: *Leonardo da Vinci*, Robert Hale, London, 1979
K. Petersen & J.J. Wilson: *Women Artists: Recognition and Reappraisal from the Early Middle Ages to the Twentieth Century* Women's Press, London, 1978
G. Pollock: *Vision and Difference: femininity, feminism and histories of art*, Routledge, London, 1988
M. Praz: *The Romantic Agony*, tr. Davidson, Oxford University Press 1933
Peter Redgrove. *The Black Goddess and the Sixth Sense, Bloomsbury, London, 1987*
F. Roh: *German Art in the Twentieth Century: Painting, Sculpture, Architecture*, Thames & Hudson, London, 1968
M. Roskill:*What is Art History?*, Thames & Hudson, London, 1976
G. Saunders. *The Nude: a new perspective*, Herbert Press, London, 1989
P. Selz. *German Expressionist Painting*, University of California Press, Berkely, CA, 1974
—. *Art in Our Times: A Pictorial History 1890-1980*, Thames & Hudson, London, 1982
E. Showalter, ed. *The New Feminist Criticism*, Virago, London, 1986
Penelope Shuttle & Peter Redgrove. *The Wise Wound*, Paladin/ Grafton, 1978/86
M. Sjöo & B. Mor: *The Great Cosmic Mother*, Harper & Row, San Francisco 1987
F. Stella. *Working Space*, Harvard University Press, Cambridge, MA, 1986
—. *Frank Stella*, Madrid, 1995
K. Stiles & P. Selz, eds. *Theories & Documents of Contemporary Art: A Sourcebook of Artists' Writings*, University of California Press, Berkeley, CA, 1996
V.I. Stoichita: *Leonardo da Vinci*, Abbey Library, London, 1978
S. Rubin Suleiman, ed. *The Female Body in Western Culture: Contemporary Perspectives*, Harvard University Press, Cambridge, Mass., 1986
William Thompson. *The Time Falling Bodies Take to Light: Mythology, Sexuality and the Origins of Culture*,St Martin's Press, New York, NY, 1981
A. Tilly:*Erotic Drawings*, Phaidon 1986
P. Trevor-Roper: *The world blunted through sight: An inquiry into the influence of defective vision on art and character*, Thames & Hudson, London, 1970
W. Tucker. *The Language of Sculpture*, Thames & Hudson, London, 1974
L. Venturi: *Renaissance Painting, from Leonardo to Dürer*,Skira/ Macmillan 1979
—. *Italian Paintings*, Zwemmer, London, 1950

P. Vergo: *Art in Vienna: 1898-1918: Klimt, Kokoschka, Schiele and Their Contemporaries,* Phaidon 1975
G. de Vries, ed. *On Art: Artists' Writings on the Changed Notion of Art After, 1965,* Cologne, 1974
B. Walker: *Body Magic*, Paladin, London, 1979
—. *Tantrism: Its Secret Principles and Practices*, Aquarian Press, Wellingborough 1982
Marina Warner. *Alone Of All Her Sex: The Myth and Cult of the Virgin Mary,* Picador, London, 1985
—. *Monuments and Maidens,* Weidenfeld & Nicolson, London, 1985
Valerie Wayne, ed. *The Matter of Difference: Materialist Feminist Criticism of Shakespeare,* Harvester Wheatsheaf, Hemel Hempstead, 1991
P. Webb: *The Erotic Arts*, Secker & Warburg, London, 1983
D. Wheeler: *Art Since Mid-Century: 1945 to the Present,* Thames & Hudson, London, 1991
F. Whitford: *Egon Schiele*, Thames & Hudson, London, 1981
L. Williams: *Hard Core*: Power, *Pleasure, and the 'Frenzy of the Visible',* Pandora, London, 1990
C. Wilson: *The Sexual Misfits: A Study of Sexual Outsiders*, Collins, London, 1989
H. Wolfflin: *Classic Art,* Phaidon 1952/80
M. Wudram: *Art of the Renaissance,* Weidenfeld & Nicolson, London, 1985

WEBSITES

eroticbibliophile.com
eroti-cart.com
deltaofvenus.com
erotomane.org

CRESCENT MOON PUBLISHING

web: www.crmoon.com e-mail: cresmopub@yahoo.co.uk

ARTS, PAINTING, SCULPTURE

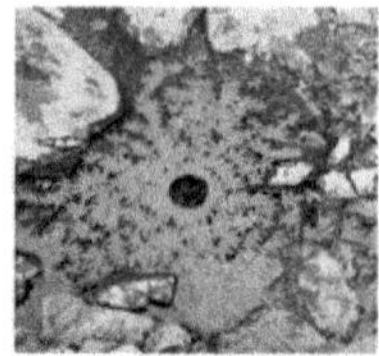

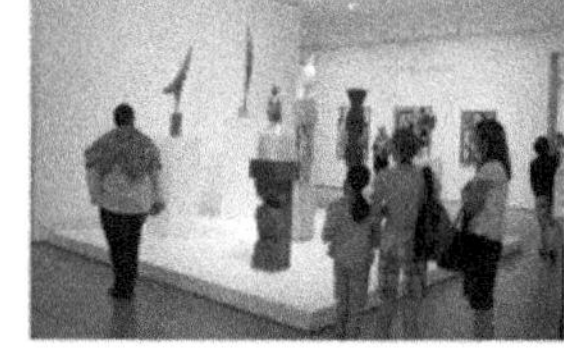

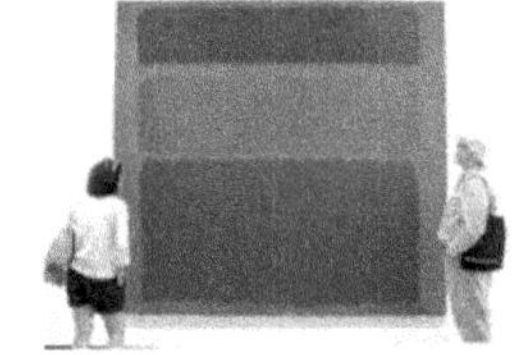

The Art of Andy Goldsworthy
Andy Goldsworthy: Touching Nature
Andy Goldsworthy in Close-Up
Andy Goldsworthy: Pocket Guide
Andy Goldsworthy In America
Land Art: A Complete Guide
The Art of Richard Long
Richard Long: Pocket Guide
Land Art In the UK
Land Art in Close-Up
Land Art In the U.S.A.
Land Art: Pocket Guide
Installation Art in Close-Up
Minimal Art and Artists In the 1960s and After
Colourfield Painting
Land Art DVD, TV documentary
Andy Goldsworthy DVD, TV documentary
The Erotic Object: Sexuality in Sculpture From Prehistory to the Present Day
Sex in Art: Pornography and Pleasure in Painting and Sculpture
Postwar Art
Sacred Gardens: The Garden in Myth, Religion and Art
Glorification: Religious Abstraction in Renaissance and 20th Century Art
Early Netherlandish Painting
Leonardo da Vinci
Piero della Francesca
Giovanni Bellini
Fra Angelico: Art and Religion in the Renaissance
Mark Rothko: The Art of Transcendence
Frank Stella: American Abstract Artist
Jasper Johns
Brice Marden
Alison Wilding: The Embrace of Sculpture
Vincent van Gogh: Visionary Landscapes
Eric Gill: Nuptials of God
Constantin Brancusi: Sculpting the Essence of Things
Max Beckmann
Caravaggio
Gustave Moreau
Egon Schiele: Sex and Death In Purple Stockings
Delizioso Fotografico Fervore: Works In Process 1
Sacro Cuore: Works In Process 2
The Light Eternal: J.M.W. Turner
The Madonna Glorified: Karen Arthurs

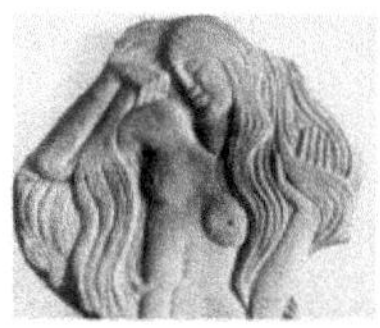

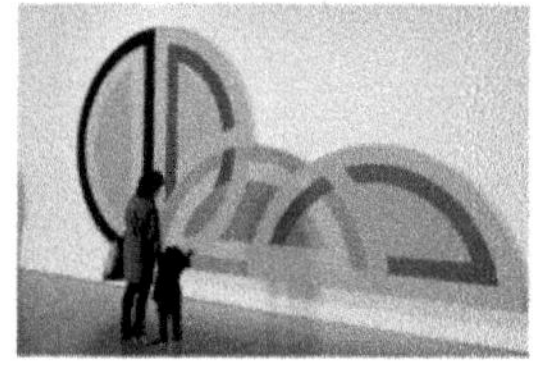

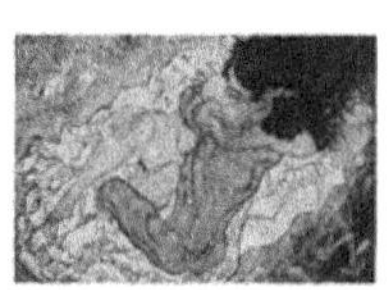

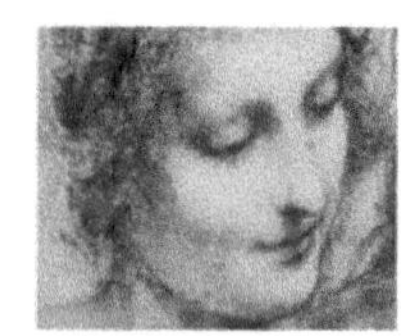

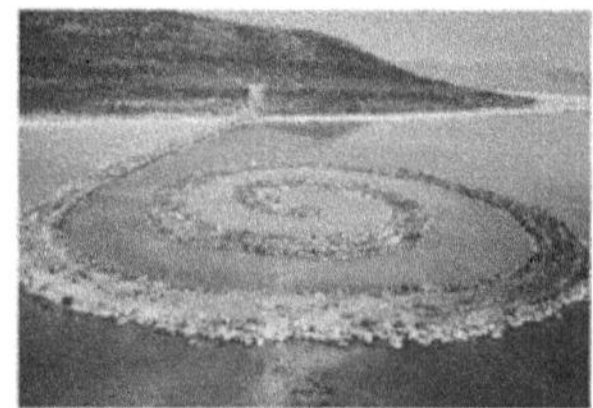

LITERATURE

J.R.R. Tolkien: The Books, The Films, The Whole Cultural Phenomenon
J.R.R. Tolkien: Pocket Guide
Tolkien's Heroic Quest
The *Earthsea* Books of Ursula Le Guin
Beauties, Beasts and Enchantment: Classic French Fairy Tales
German Popular Stories by the Brothers Grimm
Philip Pullman and *His Dark Materials*
Sexing Hardy: Thomas Hardy and Feminism
Thomas Hardy's *Tess of the d'Urbervilles*
Thomas Hardy's *Jude the Obscure*
Thomas Hardy: The Tragic Novels
Love and Tragedy: Thomas Hardy

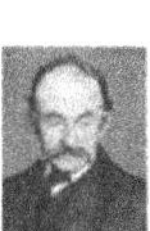

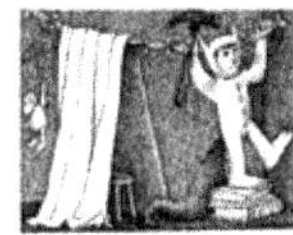

The Poetry of Landscape in Hardy
Wessex Revisited: Thomas Hardy and John Cowper Powys
Wolfgang Iser: Essays and Interviews
Petrarch, Dante and the Troubadours
Maurice Sendak and the Art of Children's Book Illustration
Andrea Dworkin

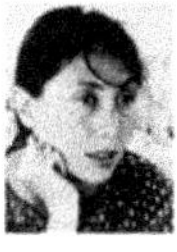

Cixous, Irigaray, Kristeva: The *Jouissance* of French Feminism
Julia Kristeva: Art, Love, Melancholy, Philosophy, Semiotics and Psychoanalysis
Hélene Cixous I Love You: The *Jouissance* of Writing
Luce Irigaray: Lips, Kissing, and the Politics of Sexual Difference
Peter Redgrove: Here Comes the Flood

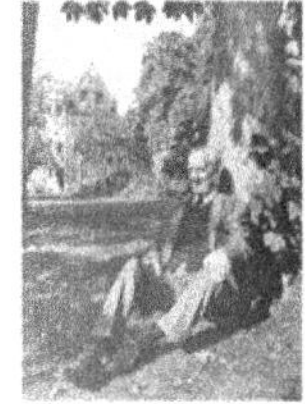

Peter Redgrove: Sex-Magic-Poetry-Cornwall
Lawrence Durrell: Between Love and Death, East and West
Love, Culture & Poetry: Lawrence Durrell
Cavafy: Anatomy of a Soul

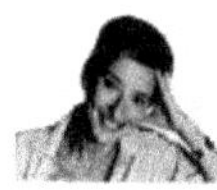

German Romantic Poetry: Goethe, Novalis, Heine, Hölderlin
Feminism and Shakespeare
Shakespeare: Love, Poetry & Magic
The Passion of D.H. Lawrence
D.H. Lawrence: Symbolic Landscapes
D.H. Lawrence: Infinite Sensual Violence
Rimbaud: Arthur Rimbaud and the Magic of Poetry

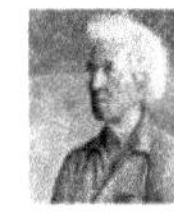

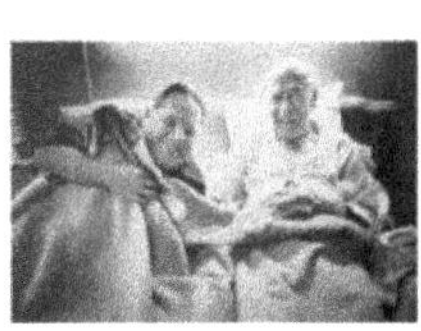

The Ecstasies of John Cowper Powys
Sensualism and Mythology: The Wessex Novels of John Cowper Powys
Amorous Life: John Cowper Powys and the Manifestation of Affectivity (H.W. Fawkner)
Postmodern Powys: New Essays on John Cowper Powys (Joe Boulter)
Rethinking Powys: Critical Essays on John Cowper Powys
Paul Bowles & Bernardo Bertolucci
Rainer Maria Rilke
Joseph Conrad: *Heart of Darkness*
In the Dim Void: Samuel Beckett
Samuel Beckett Goes into the Silence
André Gide: Fiction and Fervour
Jackie Collins and the Blockbuster Novel

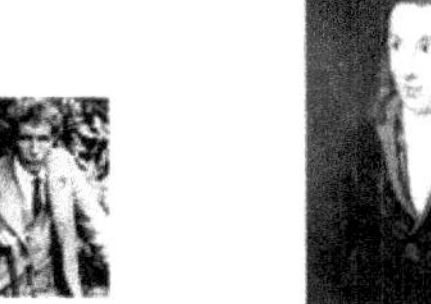

Blinded By Her Light: The Love-Poetry of Robert Graves
The Passion of Colours: Travels In Mediterranean Lands
Poetic Forms

POETRY

Ursula Le Guin: Walking In Cornwall
Peter Redgrove: Here Comes The Flood
Peter Redgrove: Sex-Magic-Poetry-Cornwall
Dante: Selections From the Vita Nuova
Petrarch, Dante and the Troubadours
William Shakespeare: Sonnets
William Shakespeare: Complete Poems
Blinded By Her Light: The Love-Poetry of Robert Graves
Emily Dickinson: Selected Poems
Emily Brontë: Poems
Thomas Hardy: Selected Poems
Percy Bysshe Shelley: Poems
John Keats: Selected Poems
Joh n Keats: Poems of 1820
D.H. Lawrence: Selected Poems
Edmund Spenser: Poems
Edmund Spenser: Amoretti
John Donne: Poems
Henry Vaughan: Poems
Sir Thomas Wyatt: Poems
Robert Herrick: Selected Poems
Rilke: Space, Essence and Angels in the Poetry of Rainer Maria Rilke
Rainer Maria Rilke: Selected Poems
Friedrich Hölderlin: Selected Poems
Arseny Tarkovsky: Selected Poems
Arthur Rimbaud: Selected Poems
Arthur Rimbaud: A Season in Hell
Arthur Rimbaud and the Magic of Poetry
Novalis: Hymns To the Night
German Romantic Poetry
Paul Verlaine: Selected Poems
Elizaethan Sonnet Cycles
D.J. Enright: By-Blows
Jeremy Reed: Brigitte's Blue Heart
Jeremy Reed: Claudia Schiffer's Red Shoes
Gorgeous Little Orpheus
Radiance: New Poems
Crescent Moon Book of Nature Poetry
Crescent Moon Book of Love Poetry
Crescent Moon Book of Mystical Poetry
Crescent Moon Book of Elizabethan Love Poetry
Crescent Moon Book of Metaphysical Poetry
Crescent Moon Book of Romantic Poetry
Pagan America: New American Poetry

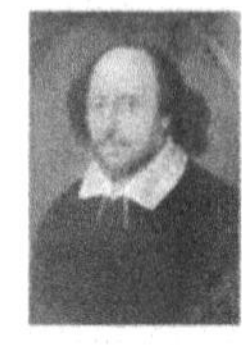
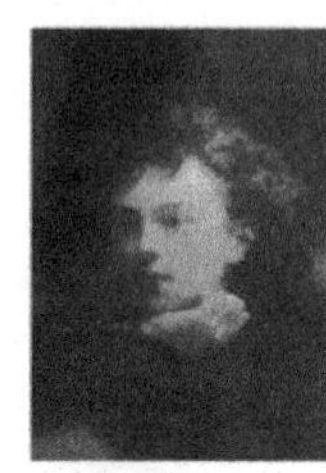
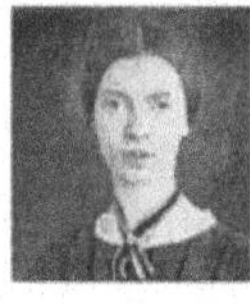
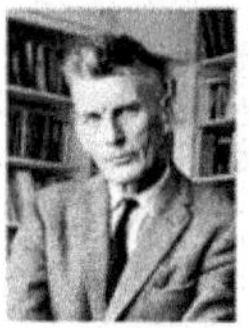
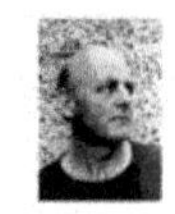
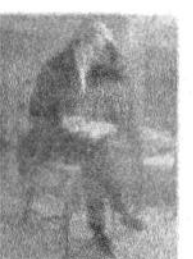
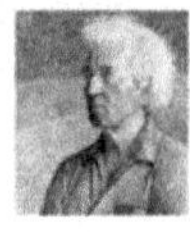
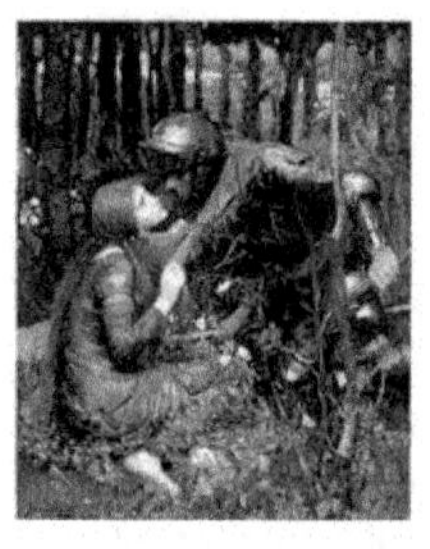
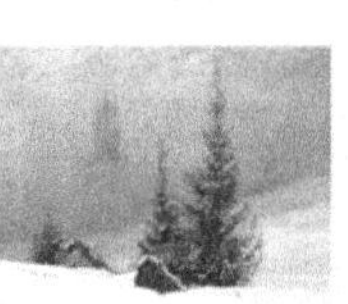
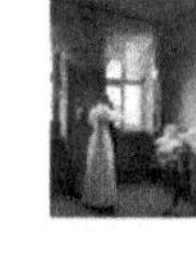
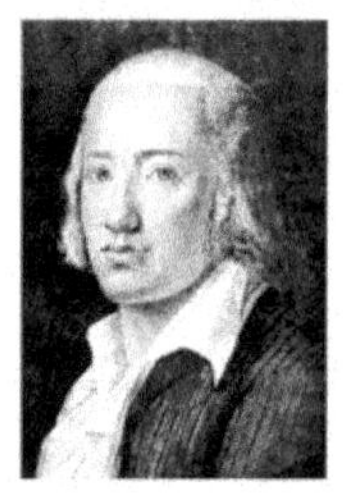
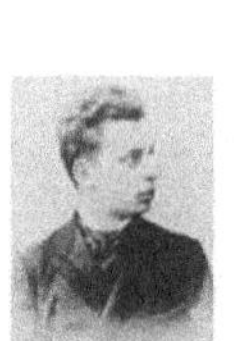
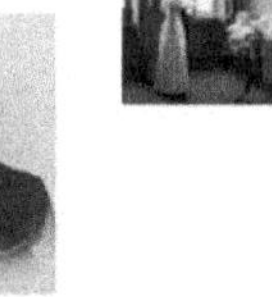
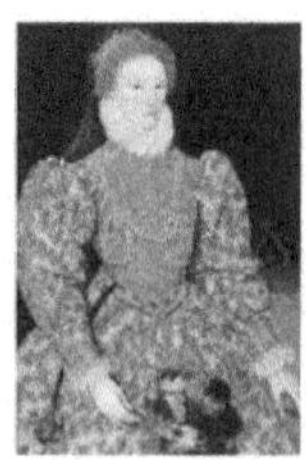

MEDIA, CINEMA, FEMINISM and CULTURAL STUDIES

J.R.R. Tolkien: The Books, The Films, The Whole Cultural Phenomenon
J.R.R. Tolkien: Pocket Guide
The *Lord of the Rings* Movies: Pocket Guide
The Cinema of Hayao Miyazaki
Hayao Miyazaki: *Princess Mononoke*: Pocket Movie Guide
Hayao Miyazaki: *Spirited Away*: Pocket Movie Guide
Tim Burton : Hallowe'en For Hollywood

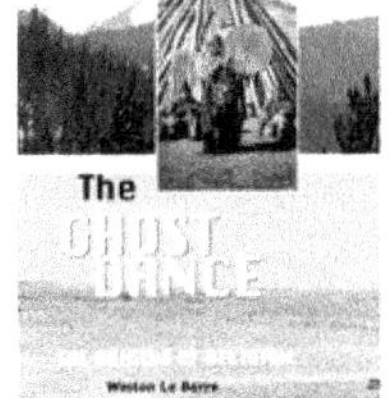

Ken Russell
Ken Russell: *Tommy*: Pocket Movie Guide
The Ghost Dance: The Origins of Religion
The Peyote Cult
Cixous, Irigaray, Kristeva: The *Jouissance* of French Feminism
Julia Kristeva: Art, Love, Melancholy, Philosophy, Semiotics and Psychoanalysis
Luce Irigaray: Lips, Kissing, and the Politics of Sexual Difference
Hélene Cixous I Love You: The *Jouissance* of Writing

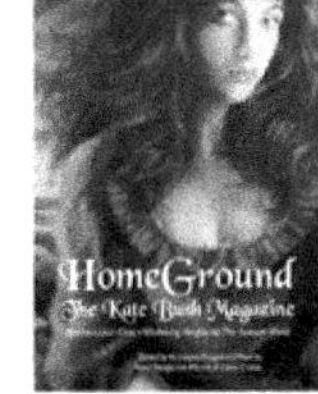

Andrea Dworkin
'Cosmo Woman': The World of Women's Magazines
Women in Pop Music
HomeGround: The Kate Bush Anthology
Discovering the Goddess (Geoffrey Ashe)
The Poetry of Cinema
The Sacred Cinema of Andrei Tarkovsky
Andrei Tarkovsky: Pocket Guide
Andrei Tarkovsky: *Mirror*: Pocket Movie Guide

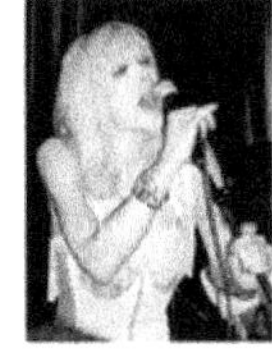

Andrei Tarkovsky: *The Sacrifice*: Pocket Movie Guide
Walerian Borowczyk: Cinema of Erotic Dreams
Jean-Luc Godard: The Passion of Cinema
Jean-Luc Godard: *Hail Mary*: Pocket Movie Guide
Jean-Luc Godard: *Contempt*: Pocket Movie Guide
Jean-Luc Godard: *Pierrot le Fou*: Pocket Movie Guide

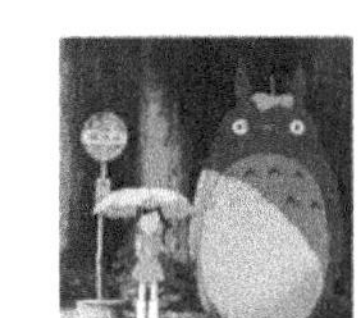

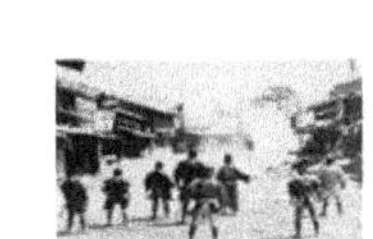

John Hughes and Eighties Cinema
Ferris Bueller's Day Off: Pocket Movie Guide
Jean-Luc Godard: Pocket Guide
The Cinema of Richard Linklater
Liv Tyler: Star In Ascendance
Blade Runner and the Films of Philip K. Dick

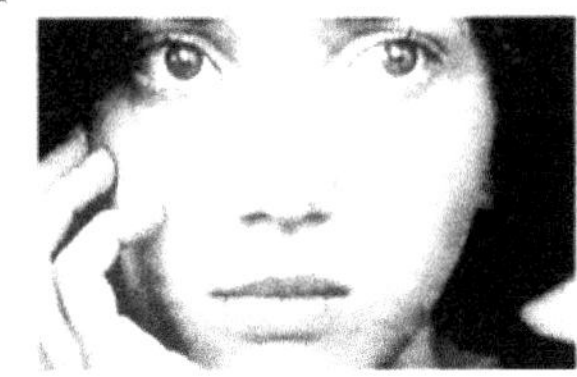

Paul Bowles and Bernardo Bertolucci
Media Hell: Radio, TV and the Press
An Open Letter to the BBC
Detonation Britain: Nuclear War in the UK
Feminism and Shakespeare
Wild Zones: Pornography, Art and Feminism
Sex in Art: Pornography and Pleasure in Painting and Sculpture
Sexing Hardy: Thomas Hardy and Feminism

The Light Eternal is a model monograph, an exemplary job. The subject matter of the book is beautifully organised and dead on beam. (Lawrence Durrell)
It is amazing for me to see my work treated with such passion and respect. (Andrea Dworkin)

CRESCENT MOON PUBLISHING
P.O. Box 1312, Maidstone, Kent, ME14 5XU, Great Britain. www.crmoon.com

cresmopub@yahoo.co.uk www.crescentmoon.org.uk

www.ingramcontent.com/pod-product-compliance
Ingram Content Group UK Ltd.
Pitfield, Milton Keynes, MK11 3LW, UK
UKHW020426250726
13967UKWH00007B/2830